FAMILY THERAPY FOR TREATING TRAUMA

FAMILY THERAPY FOR TREATING TRAUMA

AN INTEGRATIVE FAMILY AND SYSTEMS TREATMENT (I-FAST) APPROACH

David R. Grove
Gilbert J. Greene
Mo Yee Lee

OXFORD
UNIVERSITY PRESS

OXFORD
UNIVERSITY PRESS

Oxford University Press is a department of the University of Oxford. It furthers the University's objective of excellence in research, scholarship, and education by publishing worldwide. Oxford is a registered trade mark of Oxford University Press in the UK and certain other countries.

Published in the United States of America by Oxford University Press
198 Madison Avenue, New York, NY 10016, United States of America.

Library of Congress Cataloging-in-Publication Data
Names: Grove, David R., author. | Greene, Gilbert J., author. |
Lee, Mo Yee, author.
Title: Family therapy for treating trauma : an integrative family and systems treatment (I-FAST) approach / by David R. Grove, IMFT, LISW, Gilbert J. Greene, Ph.D., Mo Yee Lee, Ph.D.
Description: New York, NY : Oxford University Press, [2020] |
Includes bibliographical references and index.
Identifiers: LCCN 2019047227 (print) | LCCN 2019047228 (ebook) |
ISBN 9780190059408 (paperback) | ISBN 9780190059422 (epub)
Subjects: LCSH: Family psychotherapy.
Classification: LCC RC488.5.G765 2020 (print) | LCC RC488.5 (ebook) |
DDC 616.89/156—dc23
LC record available at https://lccn.loc.gov/2019047227
LC ebook record available at https://lccn.loc.gov/2019047228

This book is dedicated to
David Mohler Grove, veteran of and wounded in the Cold War and sufferer of PTSD
and
John Donelson Grove III, former Chief of Social Work, James E Van Zandt VA Medical Center, Altoona, Pennsylvania, who devoted a 30-year career to helping veterans who suffered from PTSD
I (GJG) dedicate this book to my parents Grover Cleveland Greene and Julia Gallagher Greene who experienced and survived trauma in their lives and were models of resilience.
I (MYL) would like to honor my mother, Sho Yean Chan, who has been an inspiration of resilience, strength, and loving kindness in life.

CONTENTS

ACKNOWLEDGMENTS

We would like to thank Jennie Babcock, John Grove, Pam J. Scott, and Lois Stepney who reviewed this manuscript and offered critical and helpful feedback.

CONTRIBUTORS

The following individuals either contributed material for this book or case examples offered throughout the book. All contributors of case examples were either actively receiving training in I-FAST or had completed many years of training in I-FAST with the first author.

Merinda Buoni
Lindsay Davis
Leslie Fehrman-Ridenbaugh
Corrine Fleming
Maria Frank
Chris Gallagher
Ed Gallagher
David R. Grove
d.grove@sbcglobal.net
Lisa Harper
Marilyn Hartline
Michael Kuklica
Rachel Kyle
Penny Maxwell
Leta Planz
Charles Rice
Sarah Scott
Phil Washburn
Tom Wilson

GENERAL ISSUES RELATED TO TRAUMA

I

OVERVIEW OF TRAUMA 1

INTRODUCTION: FREUD AND TRAUMA

In the field of psychotherapy, Sigmund Freud and his theories dominated at least the first half of the 20th century. In the 1950s and 1960s, as other major therapy approaches such as behavior therapy, cognitive therapy, and the various schools of family therapy gained prominence, within psychotherapy, Freud's influence greatly diminished. But has it? The whole idea of going to a stranger and telling what could be described as "family secrets" was made prominent by Freud. It could be argued that all individual therapy owes its existence to Freud. However, it is primarily a Western idea to go to a stranger and tell "family secrets." For collectivistic cultures, cultures in which individual identity and meanings are heavily influenced by group affiliations (Hofstede, 1980), this idea could no doubt be viewed as strange. One is reminded of the line in the film, *The Godfather* (1972), "Never tell anyone outside the family what you are thinking," or "Never take sides with anyone outside the family." With respect to trauma treatment, from a collectivistic point of view, a view that represents much of the world, it is odd to write a special book about including family members in the treatment of a traumatized client as an alternative to having the client go to a stranger individually and tell family secrets.

Regarding trauma specifically, it could easily be argued that Freud began the idea of focusing on past trauma as a therapeutic procedure. In 1897, Freud published *Etiology of Hysteria.* In this paper Freud reported the results of applying free association as a therapy technique with 18 adult clients, 12 women and 6 men. Freud concluded that the symptoms of all 18 clients could be traced back to a childhood sexual assault. The assailant was one of the parents, an older sibling, an adult extended family member, or another caregiver such as a nanny. But Freud states that the assault alone was not enough to produce hysteria. He explains that only after hundreds of hours of analysis did the client "recover" memories of abuse. He was assuming the clients had repressed memories of the event. He further noted that he had interviewed rape victims that could readily recall the assault and they did not suffer from hysteria. He therefore concluded that past trauma plus the repression of that trauma results in hysteria experienced as an adult. Although Freud modified his view 10 months later (Freud, 1898), did his original theory ever really die?

Modern theories of posttraumatic stress disorder (PTSD) posit that not "processing" the trauma can result in memories not properly integrated. Remembering and processing the trauma individually with a professional is a major therapeutic procedure. On a meta-level this is very similar to Freud. One is exposed to a traumatic event, and if it is not dealt with properly on a psychological level, symptoms will result. The idea that mental health problems will result if something bad happens and the person does not "process" what happened could be said to have its origins in Freud's 1897 paper. Avoiding something bad has consequences. And it is primarily the West that has this view. The idea that not processing the memories of traumatic events resonates in Western culture; perhaps Freud is why. With respect to trauma, it could be argued that Freud is even more influential now. It could be further argued that Freud's idea has become part of a Western world view related to trauma and psychopathology; he is in "the cloud." Both the idea that past trauma is a central element of psychopathology and what to do about it (see an expert individually), continue to be dominant.

Because it took many hours of analysis before the client would tell about abuse, Freud assumed the memories were repressed. An alternative explanation could be that because Freud received referrals from his medical colleagues, his clients were reluctant to tell him secrets about family members. They were following the Godfather rule of "Never tell anyone outside the family what you are thinking." The idea that the problem is a secret as opposed to a repressed or unprocessed memory leads to an entirely different type of intervention. A secret is an interactional pattern. Those who have the secrets habitually keep them from those who do not. Telling or not telling family members about a traumatic event could result in the survivor being helped and supported by loved ones or result in greater pain if the survivor is not believed or blamed. Perhaps the rape victims Freud interviewed could receive support from family for an assault committed by a stranger. His hysteria clients, on the other hand, may have been compelled to keep secret an assault by a family member.

Both Freud's theory and current trauma treatments call attention to a past traumatic event or events as the source of the client's afflictions. A family pattern that blocks support for a trauma survivor or exacerbates the effects of trauma, however, is an ongoing occurrence happening in the present. The problem is not a result of a past event or events, but how those events are being handled in the present, particularly by loved ones of the survivor. Telling secrets and/or obtaining family support for the survivor become the main tasks of intervention if a current interactional pattern involves family secrets about trauma or unhelpful family responses to trauma. This idea leads us to family therapy and away from individual therapy. The "processing" happens among family members and therapist, not between client alone and therapist. The support comes from the family not a professional. The key issue is between people, not inside the head of one person.

Interest in trauma as a focus of therapy has exploded in recent years. As we shall report, statistics emphasize the large numbers of individuals who have been exposed to traumatic events. Longitudinal studies are showing the long-term health problems related to exposure to adverse childhood traumatic events. Therapists and organizations are emphasizing "trauma-informed" care. When looking at all traumatized clients, several categories emerge: combat veterans; refugees fleeing dangerous countries and embarking on dangerous journeys to escape; adult sexual assault and domestic violence victims; and children who either witness chronic domestic violence, are the victims of sexual or physical abuse, or live in dangerous neighborhoods in which they may be victimized or witness violence on any given day. This book will focus exclusively on the latter two groups, children who have been traumatized or parents who have been seriously impaired by their own trauma histories. We will show how to approach both these populations by intervening primarily on a family level. We will also show how to integrate numerous intervention procedures from various individually oriented trauma treatments into a family approach.

TRAUMA AND COMPLEX TRAUMA

Trauma can occur when a person finds themselves in a situation in which they fear they may die or experience serious injury or sexual violence. The trauma can result from a person directly having the experience, witnessing the experience, or learning about a person close to them having the experience (Cougle, Kilpatrick, & Resnick 2012; Goldbeck & Jensen, 2017a). The effects of such trauma may manifest themselves in a number of ways, and with a wide range of symptoms. The fifth edition of the *Diagnostic and Statistical Manual of Mental Disorder* (DSM-5; American Psychiatric Association, 2013) now includes multiple diagnoses under the chapter "Trauma and Stressor-Related Disorders." The diagnoses in this chapter include reactive attachment disorder, disinhibited social engagement disorder, PTSD, acute traumatic stress disorder, and adjustment disorders. All these diagnoses result from an acute exposure to an environmental stressor. Taken together, they present a wide range of symptoms that could be thought of as trauma related. Someone who has been exposed to a traumatic event or events could be exhibiting a variety of symptoms and problems such as intrusive thoughts, recurring dreams and nightmares, flashbacks, sleep disturbance, irritability, depression, emotional numbness, derealization, depersonalization, hypervigilance, anxiety, avoidance, and so on (Goldbeck & Jensen, 2017, pp. 8–9). If the symptoms last from 2 days to 4 weeks, it is said the person has acute stress disorder, and if they last longer than 1 month then they have PTSD (Cougle et al., 2012; Pacella & Delahanty, 2012).

Child and adolescent trauma has been defined as "simply feeling afraid, unprotected, unsafe, helpless, and in danger because of one or multiple events including abuse, neglect, witness to violence, medical illness, abandonment/separation, homelessness, or disaster, among other circumstances" (Steele & Malchiodi, 2012, p. 200). Trauma in childhood has also been categorized as being type 1 or type 2 (Terr, 1991). Type 1 trauma has been referred to as *simple trauma* and is a result of a single incident that happens suddenly and unexpectedly such as a "motor vehicle accident; a natural disaster; a terrorist bombing, an episode of abuse, assault, or rape; a sudden death or displacement; or the witnessing of violence or something overwhelming that is highly out of the ordinary" (Courtois & Ford, 2013, p. 11). The cause of a type 1 trauma may be impersonal or interpersonal (Courtois & Ford, 2013). Type 2 trauma has been referred to as *complex trauma* and results from repetitive actions and experiences such as "ongoing physical, sexual, and emotional abuse and neglect and other forms of maltreatment in the nuclear or extended family (or quasi-family; domestic violence; community danger and violence; cultural, gender, political, ethnic, illness and religion-based oppression, violence, and physical and geographic displacement; refugee status; terrorism; torture; war; and genocide" (Courtois & Ford, 2013, p. 11). Complex traumas "are all interpersonal involving intentional acts by, or the failure to act by, other human beings" (Courtois & Ford, 2013, p. 11).

MISDIAGNOSIS

Many clients with trauma histories receive diagnoses unrelated to trauma (Breslau, 2002). In this book are examples of clients with serious trauma backgrounds who were diagnosed with bipolar I disorder, borderline personality disorder, intermittent explosive disorder, conduct disorder, oppositional defiant disorder, and generalized anxiety disorder. These numerous diagnoses are from a sample of only 22 cases all with histories of serious trauma and none having responded to previous treatments aimed at their diagnosis but who did respond well to the treatment described in this book. Clearly, many clients with serious trauma backgrounds are receiving diagnoses other than PTSD. They have a serious trauma history and are struggling with a wide range of symptoms, in addition to or instead of PTSD symptoms. The question here is if suffering from a trauma history can be expressed by a much wider range of symptoms and problems than just those that meet the *DSM-5* criteria for PTSD (Kerig, Vanderee, Becker, & Ward, 2011). The adverse childhood experience (ACE) studies, which are covered in this chapter, reported such findings. If trauma histories can be expressed by a wide range of symptoms, then, for example, diagnoses such as bipolar I, which typically results in the client being medicated, are completely missing the mark.

CROSS-CULTURAL EXPRESSION OF TRAUMA SYMPTOMS

Symptoms related to trauma may vary cross-culturally (Drozdek, Wilson, & Turkovic, 2012; Watters, 2011). Some authors point out that the issue of culture presents challenges in using the diagnosis of PTSD in people from non-Western societies (Bracken, Giller, & Summerfield, 1995; De Silva, 1993; Drozdek et al., 2012). Somatic distress and dissociation are two types of symptoms found to be more prevalent with non-Western individuals exposed to trauma. Turkish women (Sar, Kundakci, Kiziltan, Bakin, & Bozkurt, 2000; Tutkun, Yargic, & Sar, 1995) and Japanese women (Berger et al., 1994; Saito, 1998) who suffered childhood sexual abuse reported a high rate of dissociative symptoms. Trauma survivors from Asian cultures report more somatic symptoms and have a higher association to complaints related to physical health post exposure to trauma (Kleinman, 1982; Stamm & Friedman, 2000; Watters, 2011). Asian sexual abuse survivors can present with eating disorders, particularly bulimia (LaFlair et al., 2008).

There may not be complete agreement that re-experiencing symptoms are a universal response to trauma (Alford, 2016; Watters, 2011). During the One Child policy in China, millions of women were allegedly forced by the government to abort their pregnancies. It is safe to assume this was a very traumatic experience for many of these women. What trauma symptoms do these women express? No studies have been done on this. Anecdotal stories suggest depression and somatic symptoms may be common. Are they re-experiencing symptoms?

Studies documenting PTSD symptoms conducted with survivors of the 2004 Sri Lankan tidal wave were nonconclusive. When Western researchers presented the survivors with symptom lists that included nightmares, the respondents indicated they had them. Criticism of this approach included that the survivors may have been expecting to obtain food by co-operating with who they may have thought were relief workers. When asked more open-ended questions regarding if and, if so, how they were suffering, a great majority of respondents did not mention re-experiencing symptoms. Instead, most respondents mentioned somatic symptoms (Watters, 2011). It does not appear that systematic research has been done regarding how trauma is expressed across cultures. The question of what trauma symptoms are universal may not be settled.

There are a few identified syndromes that are thought to be culturally specific. For example, 150 Cambodian refugees who immigrated to California and who had witnessed and survived atrocities of the Khmer Rouge regime, reported somatic blindness (despite normal eye exam results; Van Boemel & Rozee, 1992). A response to acute stressful experiences, *ataques de nervios* is a well-documented syndrome that people in Latin America often experience, characterized by uncontrollable shouting, trembling, heart palpitations, fainting, seizure-like episodes, and amnesia for the experience (Guarnaccia, 1993).

EPIDEMIOLOGY: CHILDREN AND ADOLESCENTS

The National Comorbidity Survey Replication–Adolescent Supplement (NCS-A; Merkangas, Avenevoli, Costello, Koretz, & Kessler, 2009) lists 12 childhood adversities that include parental loss from death, divorce, or separation, child maltreatment from neglect, physical and sexual abuse, economic adversity, and parental violence and substance abuse. In the NCS-A survey of 6,843 nationally represented adolescent respondents aged 13 to 17, 59.7% experienced multiple adversities. The National Institute of Justice conducted a survey of adolescents aged 12 to 17 and found that 5 million had experienced serious physical assault, 1.8 million had experienced sexual assault, and 8.8 million had witnessed interpersonal violence (Kilpatrick et al., 2000). Finkelhor, Ormrod, and Turner (2009) report that 60% of all children witnessed one potentially traumatic event in the past year, with 15.5 million children exposed to domestic violence, 7 million of those exposed to chronic family violence, and 50% of these children living in urban poor areas. This study underscores the pervasive exposure of children to violence with one in three witnessing violence and with 69% of these children having a chance of revictimization within the next year. In another study (Kilpatrick et al., 2013), one in four children reported witnessing the violent attack of another person with 60.7% of males and 51.2% of females aged 14 to 24 reporting exposure to one or more traumatic events. In a study of urban youth, 60.7% of males and 87.2% of females had been exposed to at least one traumatic event by the age of 23. Rates of exposure to violence are reported to rise after age 15 and peak at 17 for males (Breslau, Wilcox, Storr, Luciea, & Anthony, 2004). Worldwide, in a meta-analysis of 55 studies from 24 countries, Barth, Bermetz, Heim, Trelle, and Tonia (2013) reported that 8% to 31% of girls and 3% to 17% of boys had been sexually assaulted. Barth also reports that 9 girls and 3 boys out of 100 suffer forced intercourse as children.

Children most at risk include those experiencing chronic poverty (Sameroff, 1998) and those in out-of-home placement such as foster care, juvenile justice centers, and residential treatment (W. Harris, Putnam, & Fairbank, 2006). The National Child Traumatic Stress Network (NCTSN), an organization that tracks the prevalence of children exposed to trauma who enter social service systems such as child welfare, juvenile justice, and child mental health, reports a clear relationship between a history of exposure to trauma and involvement with these systems (National Childhood

Traumatic Stress Network Core Concepts and Curriculum Workgroup, 2013). NCTSN is documenting the need for higher levels of care for these children such as out-of-home care and residential treatment (Briggs et al., 2013). Children who are victims of intrafamilial sexual abuse are at greater risk of developing PTSD.

EPIDEMIOLOGY: ADULTS IN THE SOCIAL SERVICE SYSTEM

Numerous studies have identified the epidemiology of trauma-exposed adults in the United States (Breslau, Davis, Peterson, & Schultz, 1997). Almost 60% of the U.S. adult population has been exposed to childhood adversities/trauma (Centers for Disease Control, 2010); this finding echoes the prevalence rate of another study that found that 61% of men and 51% of women reported at least one traumatic event during their lives (Kessler, Sonnega, Bromet, Huges, & Nelson, 1995). Another study reported similar findings from a large sample of Australian adults (Creamer, Burgess, & McFarlane, 2001). A Detroit survey of trauma exposure among adults aged 18 to 45 found that 60% of those surveyed had been exposed to at least one traumatic event in their lives (Breslau et al., 1998).

Regarding adults, trauma survivors are the majority of clients in the human service systems (Najvits, Weiss, & Shaw, 1997). This would also include a large percentage of parents of children who have entered the social service system requesting help for their child. Of women in substance abuse treatment, 60% to 75% reported to have experienced partner abuse. Women with substance abuse histories have experienced more sexual assaults than those who do not (Najavits, Weiss, & Shaw, 1997; Polusny & Follete, 1995).

SUBSTANCE ABUSE AND TRAUMA

PTSD and substance abuse disorders are often co-occurring problems (Heffernan et al., 2000; Najavits, Hyman, Ruglass, Hien, & Read, 2017). Research has found that PTSD creates a vulnerability to substance abuse (Chilcoat & Breslau, 1998; Wolitzky-Taylor, Bobova, Zinbarg, Mineka, & Craske, 2012) and increases the risk of developing substance abuse dependence (Chilcoat & Breslau, 1998). Self-medicating one's uncomfortable emotions is one prominent hypothesis for how PTSD leads to substance abuse (Najavits, Hyman, Ruglass, Hien, & Read, 2017). The relief from PTSD symptoms resulting from using psychoactive substances reinforces the continued use of them resulting in dependence and addiction (Buckner, Heimerg, Ecker, & Vinci, 2013). For example, when anxiety is a major symptom of PTSD, the risk of developing substance abuse to manage anxiety increases fourfold (Crum et al., 2013).

An area of particular interest is the relationship between intrafamilial childhood sexual and physical abuse and future development of substance abuse. Substance abusing adults who have suffered childhood abuse report increased distress and increased use of avoidance as a coping strategy (Hyman, Paliwal, & Sinha, 2007). Rates of childhood abuse are high in adults with substance abuse (Hyman et al., 2007). Adult substance abusers report greater childhood abuse than nonsubstance abusing adults (Enoch, 2011). Hefferman et al. (2000) found that opiate users were 2.7 times more likely to have a history of childhood sexual or physical abuse than nonopiate users. Childhood abuse can set the stage for future substance abuse (Bailey

& Stewart, 2014). Social support is one protective factor that may help prevent childhood sufferers of intrafamilial abuse from developing future substance abuse (Cicchette, 2013; Enoch, 2011). The association of childhood abuse and adult substance abuse is stronger for women than for men (Hyman et al., 2006). Addressing childhood abuse in adult women substance abusers has been identified as a treatment priority (Najavits et al., 2017).

ADVERSE CHILDHOOD EXPERIENCES

There has been an awareness of psychological trauma and its effects on survivors throughout history (Figley, Ellis, Reuther, & Gold, 2017). However, trauma did not become a serious area of study until the work of Sigmund Freud on hysteria followed by the study of the effects of combat on soldiers from World War I and subsequent wars. More recently, there has been an increased interest in the effects of trauma spurred by research examining the long-term impact of ACEs on physical and mental health (Felitti et al., 1998). Kalmakis and Chandler (2013) define ACEs as "childhood events, varying in severity and often chronic, occurring within a child's family or social environment that cause harm or distress, thereby disrupting the child's physical or psychological health and development" (p. 1495).

The initial ACEs study was a collaboration between the Centers for Disease Control and Kaiser Permanente in San Diego, California (Felitti et al., 1998). In this study over 17,000 self-selected outpatients responded to a request to complete the ACEs questionnaire. The questionnaire asked adults to report whether or not they experienced any of the following before the age of 18: emotional/psychological abuse, physical abuse, neglect, sexual abuse, substance abuse in the household, mental illness in the household, witnessing domestic violence, or criminal behavior in the household; this resulted in a questionnaire consisting of 10 questions. The respondents were not asked about frequency of these events, just whether or not they experienced any of them.

The respondents were evenly split by gender; 75% were White, 75% had attended college, and all were employed and had health insurance. Approximately two thirds of the respondents reported at least one ACE; 40%, two or more ACEs; and 12.5%, four or more ACEs. There was a strong association between the number of ACEs and engaging in health-risk behaviors such as alcohol and drug abuse, smoking, sexual promiscuity, and adult obesity. Poorer health outcomes such as heart disease, chronic lung disease, depression, and early death were also documented. The research found a dose–response relationship. The higher someone scored on the ACEs questionnaire (i.e., the more ACEs), the more they engaged in risky behaviors and the more health problems they had (Felitti et al., 1998). One study found that people with an ACE score of 6 or higher, on average, died almost 20 years earlier than those with an ACE score of zero (D. W. Brown et al., 2009). In a systematic review in 2015 of the existing ACEs research that consisted of 42 studies, Kalmakis and Chandler (2015) found that ACEs had adverse effects on physical health, psychological health, health-risk behavior, developmental disruption, and healthcare utilization and cost.

Given that the initial ACEs study was not representative of the general population, efforts have been made to broaden it to include more diverse groups (Cronholm et al., 2015) and types of ACEs (Cronholm et al., 2015; Finkelhor, Shattuck, Turner, & Hamby, 2015; Kalmakis & Chandler, 2013). Recent studies expanded the types of

ACEs to include such experiences as witnessing violence, experiencing discrimination, living in an unsafe neighborhood, exposure to community violence, bullying, peer isolation/rejection, and low socioeconomic status (Cronholm et al, 2015; Finkelhor et al., 2015). Cronholm et al. (2015) made it a point to have a more diverse sample than the original ACEs study, especially in terms of race, education, and age. The respondents in the Cronholm et al. study had a significantly higher number of ACEs compared to the original Felitti et al. (1998) study on nine ACEs common to the two studies.

INTERGENERATIONAL TRAUMA: TRAUMATIZED CHILDREN OF TRAUMATIZED PARENTS

In recent years, there has been an increasing interest in how the ACEs of parents might affect the physical and behavioral health of their children, that is, intergenerational trauma (P. Alexander, 2015; Larkin, Felitti, & Anda, 2014; Le-Scherban, Wang, Boyle-Steed, & Patcher, 2018; Schickedanz, Halfon, Sastry, & Chung, 2018; Sun et al., 2017). Research has consistently found that parents' ACEs adversely affect the physical and behavioral health of their children. Such findings support the need to take an intergenerational approach to working with children and families who present with identified ACEs (Kernsmith, 2006; Kwong, Bartholomew, Henderson, & Trinke, 2003; Larkin et al., 2014; Le-Scherban et al., 2018; Sun et al., 2017).

TRAUMA AND EARLY CHILDHOOD DEVELOPMENT

The trauma of ACEs adversely affects child development (Bick & Nelson, 2016; Larkin et al., 2014; Sun et al., 2017). There does appear to be a dose–response relationship between the amount of stress and trauma in childhood and physical and mental health (Cloitre et al., 2019; Cross, Fani, Powers, & Bradley, 2017). In a review of the research, Cross et al. (2017) state that childhood stress and trauma adversely affect brain development thus negatively affecting child development. The authors suggest that these negative effects include difficulties in executive functioning, emotion dysregulation, and dissociation, and interoceptive avoidance (Cross et al., 2017). Other researchers have reached similar conclusions (Anda et al., 2016; Gaskill & Perry, 2012; Perry, 2005, 2006). Emotion regulation has been found to be a key pathway (mediator) between stress and trauma and physical and mental health (Cloitre et al., 2019). To further understand these dynamics, it is helpful to explore the neurophysiology of trauma.

NEUROPHYSIOLOGY AND TRAUMA

Neurons and Neuro-Networks/Pathways

The basic building blocks of the brain are neurons. Neurons organize into networks, also referred to as pathways. The brain is essentially made up of these neural pathways. As a result of learning, these pathways become integrated with each other making complex actions possible. Learning occurs from trial and error and feedback from the environmental context. Over time, the organization of a neural pathway becomes a stable and predictable ***pattern***. Such patterns then allow humans to perform many tasks without having to think about them. However, the neural pathways of the brain are changeable (Cozolino, 2017). The brain is organized to be responsive to environmental conditions. Learning results in changes of neuropathways (Cozolino, 2017).

Neurotransmitters

Changes in neuropathways are possible because neurons are able to communicate with each other. One of the primary means of communicating is through chemical neurotransmitters. There are numerous neurotransmitters in the brain and body and a few of these play key roles in dealing with stress and trauma (Cozolino, 2017; Hanna, 2014). *Glutamate* excites synapses and facilitates learning and neuroplasticity. *Dopamine* affects voluntary bodily movements, expectation, motivation, and apathy, noting rewards in behavioral reinforcement, learning and memory, mood, and relationship satisfaction. *Norepinephrine/noradrenaline*, which is also referred to simply as *epinephrine* or *adrenalin* (for the sake of brevity and consistency, we will refer to it as *adrenalin*), plays a key role in responding to stress and trauma. It is involved in the fight–flight response and affects the heart rate, blood pressure, lung and muscle capacity, vigilance, and attention. *Cortisol* is a glucocorticoid sometimes referred to as the "stress hormone" (Cozolino, 2017, p. 64). Glucocorticoids are involved in the metabolism of glucose and receptors for glucocorticoids are throughout the body. Cortisol is a frequently used marker for stress. For short-term stress, cortisol is very useful. However, longer periods of stress, and chronic release of cortisol, can interfere with the growth of or even cause the death of neurons. Prolonged cortisol release can also interfere with memory and mood regulation (Cozolino, 2017).

The Brain

The brain consists of three parts with numerous subparts in each of the three areas. The three parts are the *brain stem* also referred to as the *primitive* or *reptilian* brain, the *paleomammalian* brain also referred to as just the *mammalian* brain or the *limbic system*, and the *neomammalian* brain or *neocortex* (Cozolino, 2017; Hanna, 2014). In human evolution, the brain stem was the first to develop and has changed very little over time. Next was the limbic system and finally was the neocerebral cortex. In human development, brains also develop bottom to top. We will provide a brief overview of each part starting at the bottom.

The Brain Stem

The *brain stem* is the inner core of the brain and is fully formed at birth. The brain stem is responsible for controlling messages from the body to the brain and the body's internal operations needed for survival (Cozolino, 2017; G. Hall, 2017). Consequently, the functions of the brain stem "take precedence over other brain activities" (G. Hall, 2017, p. 5). A key system that originates in the brain stem is the *autonomic nervous system* (ANS). The primary purpose of the ANS is survival. The ANS works automatically (unconsciously). The ANS is responsible for the necessary survival operations such as heart rate; breathing rate (respiration); body temperature; digestion; metabolism; elimination (urination and defecation); production of body fluids such as saliva, sweat, and tears; and state of arousal.

Within the ANS is the *sympathetic nervous system* (SNS) and the *parasympathetic nervous system* (PNS). The SNS is on alert for any threats and is responsible for "fight, flight, or freeze" responses. In a perceived threat situation, the SNS mobilizes (accelerates) the body's systems to successfully deal with the threat and thus survive

(Montgomery, 2013). The SNS is responsible for increasing the heart rate, dilating pupils and blood vessels, and so on. The SMS can become overly sensitive and active when a person experiences ongoing or multiple traumatic situations. When this occurs, a person may experience chronic stress and emotional dysregulation.

Polyvagal Theory

The PNS, which develops in the second year of life, slows down and puts the brakes on the SNS and the fight, flight, or freeze response. The PNS helps to restore balance and conserve the body's energy. A major component of the PNS involves the *vagus nerve* (Dana, 2018; Porges, 2011, 2017). The vagus nerve originates in the brain stem. "Vagus" comes from the Latin word *vagary* meaning "wanderer." The vagus nerve affects many organs and parts of the body; thus, it "wanders" throughout a significant part of the body. The vagus nerve branches off into two pathways, the *dorsal vagus* and the *ventral vagus*, which form the basis of *polyvagal theory* (PVT; Porges, 2011, 2017). The dorsal vagus connects with organs of the body below the diaphragm, especially affecting digestion, and the ventral vagus affects organs above the diaphragm (the heart and lungs). The ventral vagus also connects to the muscles of the face, head, middle ear, mouth, larynx, pharynx, and neck. The vagus nerve carries communication between the body's organs and the brain with 80% of communications going to the brain from the organs and 20% from the brain to the organs.

Humans are "wired to connect" with other people (Dana, 2018, p. 7; Fishbane, 2007). As infants, our survival is dependent on other people and their willingness to take care of us. Thus, an important concept in PVT is the *social engagement system* (SES). The SES involves the integrated actions of the ventral vagus connections with the heart and the face and head (Porges, 2018). Our first line of survival is through social relationships and cooperation. In our social relationships, we need to assess for safety and threat from other people and, at the same time, communicate that we are safe to them. We need to feel safe with other people and want them to feel safe with us. Using the SES involves how we read facial expressions and hear and assess someone's tone of voice and assess safety. Feeling safe is essential in maintaining emotional and behavioral regulation and for recovering from dysregulation (Porges, 2018; Tucci, Weller, & Mitchell, 2018). To achieve and maintain feeling safe and a sense of health and wellbeing people *co-regulate* their neurophysiological systems with one another. Such co-regulation and safety are interactional and relational.

Our initial reactions to various situations and other people occurs at a neurological level, referred to as *neuroception* (Porges, 2011, 2017). Neuroception involves using the ANS to look for cues of safety and threat without having to think about it. Porges draws the distinction between neuroception and perception, which involves the cognitive assessment of situations. In a potentially dangerous situation, we do not have time to analyze it. Our very survival may depend on immediate reactions. According to PVT, the ANS reacts to potentially threatening situations in predictable ways. First, we use the *ventral vagus* of the SES; if that does not work, that part of the *SNS* for the fight or flight response is activated, and if that does not work, the *dorsal vagus* is activated to produce a freeze response (Porges, 2011, 2017). The freezing involves responding by immobilization, shutting down, dissociation, or fainting. In some mammals, we see the freeze response when they "play dead." The polyvagal system is therefore a central player regarding fight or flight responses whether the feared stimuli are real or imagined. When a trauma survivor is confused about what is or is not a threat, the vagal system becomes overactive. Because the vagal nerves communicate with the amygdala, the amygdala then also becomes overactive.

The Limbic System

The *limbic system* (paleomammalian complex) is also referred to as the "emotional brain" (G. Hall, 2017, p. 6). The limbic system plays a key role in emotional responsiveness, memory formation, memory integration, and olfaction. Responses to dangerous situations occur in this area of the brain (Cozolino, 2017; G. Hall, 2017). Within the limbic system important areas of interests are the amygdala, hippocampus, and the hypothalamus.

The *amygdala* is responsible for threat detection and the conditioned and unconditioned fear responses to threats. It is fully developed by the eighth month of pregnancy. The amygdala takes in sensory information and evaluates it as to safety or danger. When the amygdala senses any threat, it is primed for an immediate automatic response. To prepare the body for fight or flight, the amygdala releases the stress hormones adrenaline and cortisol.

The *hippocampus* is associated with placing memories in the correct context of space and time and memory recall (Cozolino, 2017; G. Hall, 2017). It plays an important role in encoding and storing explicit memory and learning. The hippocampus also is involved in comparing memoires and using previous knowledge in new situations. The hippocampus sends information to the neocortex to consolidate memory. The hippocampus is also involved in retrieving information and memories storied in the neocortex. With new learning new cells are created (neurogenesis) in the hippocampus. Times of prolonged stress and the release of cortisol can impair the functioning of the hippocampus even damaging cells and resulting in its reduction in size. The hippocampus matures late and the development of its connections to the neocortex continue into early adulthood (Cozolino, 2017). Because of its late maturation, the hippocampus is especially impacted by childhood trauma. This impairment may be the cause of the flashbacks in people with PTSD. It is theorized that when someone with PTSD encounters stimuli similar to the traumatic event, the body perceives the event as occurring again because the memory was never properly recorded or integrated in the person's memory. The hippocampus and amygdala are critical to learning and memory; they work together with parts of the prefrontal cortex in deciding what is important to learn and how to emotionally respond (Cozolino, 2017, p. 183).

The *thalamus*, also referred to as the *sensory thalamus,* is considered the gateway for sensory information to the neocortex, amygdala, and hippocampus (Baranowsky & Gentry, 2015, p. 22; Hanna, 2014, p. 48). The *hypothalamus* connects "the nervous system via the pituitary gland" (G. Hall, 2017, p. 24). When there is a threat, the amygdala is stimulated, which in turns stimulates the *hypothalamic–pituitary–adrenal (HPA) axis*, which sends cortisol to the hippocampus, interrupting learning in the hippocampus and supporting fear-based learning in the amygdala (Cozolino, 2017, p. 183; S. Taylor, 2017, pp. 65–69). It is theorized that some of the brain abnormalities observed on magnetic resonance imaging (MRI) scans of trauma survivors result from chronic flooding of cortisol due to the survivor's habitual perceived threats.

The *neocortex* (neomammalian complex) is the outer part of the brain. In this area of the brain, higher-order conscious activities occur necessary for executive functioning such as abstract thinking, language, and so on (G. Hall, 2017). The neocortex has several subparts that are lobes: occipital lobe, parietal lobes, temporal lobes, and frontal lobes. The part that is mostly involved in PTSD and its treatment is the frontal lobes. It contains the prefrontal cortex, which is "vitally involved in executive functions such as concentration, organization, judgement, reasoning, decision-making, creativity, emotional regulation, social-relational abilities, and abstract thinking" (G. Hall, 2017, p. 31).

The Effect of Trauma on the Brain

Studies using brain imaging technologies, especially functional MRI (fMRI), have found that people with PTSD have abnormalities in the structure and functioning of the brain (Ahmed-Leitao, Spies, van den Heuvel, & Seedat, 2016; Bremner et al., 1995, 2003; Bremner, Elzinga, Schmahl, & Vermetten, 2008; Etkin & Wagner, 2007; Hughes & Shin, 2011; Jatzko et al., 2006; Liberzon & Sripada, 2008; Milani, Hoffman, Fossaluza, Jackowski, & Mello, 2017; Milani, Hoffman, Fossaluza, Jackowki, & Mello, 2016; Shvil, van der Hoorn, Papini, Sullivan, & Neria, 2016; Veer, Oei, van Buchem, Spinhoven, Elzinga, & Rombouts, 2015). People with PTSD appear to have amygdalas that are hyperactive and hippocampi and prefrontal cortexes that are reduced in size and hypoactive when compared to trauma survivors without PTSD and nontrauma exposed individuals (Milani et al., 2017; Shvil et al., 2016). One major effect of PTSD is that survivors become hypersensitive to situations that may remind them of the traumatic event or events (Milad et al., 2009). Also, as a result of damage to the hippocampus and prefrontal cortex, the amygdala becomes insufficiently controlled in particular during extinction. This is consistent with an interpretation of PTSD as a syndrome that impairs extinction ability (Milad et al., 2009; Stein & Paulus, 2009). The underlying mechanism for the effects of trauma on the brain are not very well understood. It is theorized that these frequent fear responses and accompanying release of hormones damage the brain as seen on the MRIs (Cozolino, 2017). For example, damage to the hippocampus may be a direct result of glucocorticoid exposure in response to acute stress (McEwen, 2000).

STATE OR TRAIT

So far, imaging studies of the effects of trauma on the brain have been cross-sectional rather than longitudinal. The methodology and findings raise questions as to whether MRI-observed brain abnormalities in people with PTSD preceded the traumatic experience or experiences (trait), or did the traumatic experience or experiences cause the brain abnormalities (state; Cozolino, 2017; Friedman, Keane, & Resick, 2014). Regardless of the cause of the brain abnormalities detected in people diagnosed with PTSD, it is well-established that the brain possesses neuroplasticity, and thus its structure and functioning are changeable.

NEUROPLASTICITY AND TREATMENT

As previously mentioned in the section on neurophysiology and trauma, the building blocks of the brain are neurons and neuropathways. The more a neuropathway is used, the more it becomes a stable and predictable pattern (Cozolino, 2017). For someone with PTSD, it could be said that they have neuropathway patterns that are biased toward experiencing the symptoms of PTSD. However, the brain has ***neuroplasticity*** and thus is changeable (Bremner, Elzinga, Schmahl, & Vermetten, 2008; Cozolino & Santos, 2014; Fine & Sung, 2014; Goncalves & Perrone-McGovern, 2016; Kolassa & Elbert, 207; Maljeko, Abler, Plener, & Straub, 2017).). According to Cozolino (2017), "plasticity refers to the ability of neurons to change the way they related to one another as we adapt to the changing demands of life" (p. 381). One indicator of the brain's neuroplasticity is our capacity to continue learning and acquiring new knowledge and skills throughout life. Because of neuroplasticity, participating in "enriched environments" will stimulate growing and changing neuropathways (Cozolino, 2017, p. 21). An enriched environment is a challenging one; it includes "the kinds of experiences that encourage us to learn new skills and expand our knowledge" (Cozolino, 2017, p. 21). Cozolino goes on to say that "psychotherapy can be thought of as a specific type of enriched environment that promotes social and emotional development, neural integration, and processing complexity" (p. 22).

There is a growing body of research showing the corrective effects of psychotherapeutic treatments on brain abnormalities associated with PTSD (Barsaglini, Sartori, Benetti, Pettersson-Yeo, & Mechelli, 2014; Butler et al., 2018; Cisler et al., 2016; Felmingham et al., 2007; Fonzo, Goodkind, Gathes et al., 2017; Fonzo, Goodkind, Oathes et al., 2017; Helpman et al., 2016; Laugharne et al., 2016; Lindauer et al., 2005; Malejko, Abler, Plener, & Straub, 2017; Nijdam, Martens, Reitsma, Gersons, & Olff, 2018). These studies used some different scanning technologies, and most had small sample sizes. Consequently, some of the findings were mixed. However, overall, it was more often found that various types of therapeutic approaches to treating PTSD resulted in less active amygdalas and increases in size and activities in the hippocampi and neocortexes of the clients.

Regarding responsiveness to treatment, however, Bradley, Greene, Russ, Dutra, and Weston (2005) report that 30% to 50% of PTSD symptoms persist after completion of exposure treatment. Unresponsive clients had increased amygdala activation (van Rooij et al., 2015; van Rooij, Kennis, Vink, & Geuze, 2016). Greater pretreatment amygdala activity predicted poorer response to exposure therapy (Bryant et al., 2008; van Rooij et al., 2015).

QUESTIONS

Whether the damages to the brain are preconditions to PTSD or a result of PTSD leaves us with several unanswered questions: How much of the damage can be corrected by psychotherapy? Are there differences in corrective capability among different treatment approaches? Do all types of trauma create the same level and type of damage to the brain? These questions require much more systematic research. In addition, all the brain scan studies have been done in the West on Westerners, which raises questions such as, Would brain scans of women from mainland China, forced by the government to have an abortion, look the same as U.S. combat veterans? If re-experiencing symptoms result in steroids flooding the brain, which then produce the damage described by the MRI studies, how would the brains appear of trauma survivors who suffer somatic symptoms but not predominantly from re-experiencing symptoms? Currently, there are not enough brain scan studies or large enough sample sizes in the studies available to answer any of these questions.

Serious methodological limitations in MRI studies have also been noted (Alford, 2016). Brain structures can change for several reasons, not just due to exposure to trauma. Enlarged amygdalae, for example, can result from more complex social relationships and artistic creativity (Asari et al., 2010; Bickart, Wright, Dautoff, Dickerson, & Barrett, 2010). Further, limitations in MRI technology require results to be interpreted as probabilities. This requires sample sizes of 40 or more (Alford, 2016) to reliably interpret the data. A survey of the median number of participants in trauma MRI studies was 12, too small to overcome the uncertainty created by the statistical probability problems (David, 2013). It may be reasonable to only offer tentative and cautious conclusions from MRI studies on the effects of trauma on the brain.

CHARACTERISTICS OF CLIENTS WITH PTSD

Many of the trauma survivors who enter social services are not seeking help for their trauma. They may be substance abusers and sent to treatment or they may be parents seeking help for their child. Saakvitine, Gamble, Perlman, and Sev (2000) report that clients suffering from trauma symptoms related to past violence and sexual abuse create special obstacles for seeking and receiving treatment. Research has found that trauma survivors are likely to be less trusting (Pearlman & Courtois, 2005). Many trauma survivors have been betrayed by family members who have either perpetrated abuse or not supported the survivor when abuse is reported (Classen & Clark, 2017). These survivors then frequently develop coping strategies of avoiding close relationships and withholding trust. Trauma survivors are typically very concerned about safety and staying safe (Classen & Clark, 2017). Fear and anxiety that result from trauma seriously impair the trauma survivor's sense of emotional safety. To stay safe, many trauma survivors may avoid relationships, including with professional treatment providers (Elliot et al., 2005). Another trauma survivor coping strategy for staying safe is attempting to control their environment (Clausen & Clark, 2017; Forsythe & Compas, 1987; Park, Armelz, & Tennen, 2004; Sharkansky et al., 2000). The need for safety and control may also result in trauma survivors who are in therapy trying to control what goes on in therapy. Engaging such clients requires that therapists use special care and procedures.

TRAUMA-INFORMED CARE

Trauma-informed care was first discussed in the literature in 2001 (M. Harris & Fallot, 2001). Since 2001, there has been much discussion of trauma-informed care in the literature (Classen & Clark, 2017; Conners-Burrow et al., 2013; S. F. Hall & Jones, 2018; Hanson & Lang, 2016; Hopper, 2017; Knight, 2015; Palfrey et al., 2019). Trauma-informed care is not a treatment modality, but a set of principals intended to inform clinicians of special procedures and considerations for working with trauma survivors. A major concern in providing trauma-informed care is to not retraumatize someone who has PTSD. To address the treatment engagement challenges of trauma survivors, several trauma-informed care principles focus on building rapport and engaging clients in treatment. These principles include safety, gaining trust, choice, collaboration, and empowerment (Classen & Clark, 2017).

Safety

Comprehensive assessments can be received as intrusive, unwanted, and something to be avoided by trauma survivors. Such clients may be avoiding treatment fearing they will be asked about or will be required to talk about their trauma experiences and histories. One recommendation is for providers to talk openly about safety and seek the client's feedback on what would help them feel safe (Classen & Clark, 2017). Avoiding intrusive comprehensive assessments in which wide ranging questions unrelated to the problems a trauma survivor may be seeking help on can enhance feelings of safety (Elliot, Bjelajac, Fallot, Mrakoff, & Reed, 2005). For clients with PTSD symptoms, it is very important for them to feel safe within the context of a service providing agency and therapeutic relationships. When clients feel safe, they will be more likely to activate their SES, which allows them to access and make more use of their neocortex. The recommendation is to stick to the topic on which the trauma survivor is seeking help.

Trust and Choice

Clinicians must place a special emphasis on winning and maintaining the trust of trauma survivors. One characteristic of a traumatic experience is that the trauma survivor had no choice but to endure the event. Something threatening happened that the survivor could not control or was imposed upon by someone against their will; control was taken away. When survivors do seek treatment, they may not wish the treatment to focus on their trauma history or perhaps not even on themselves. To win their trust, the client's treatment choices must be respected. These client choices include what the treatment will focus on and what treatment procedures will be offered.

In the United States, the Patient Protection and Affordable Care Act of 2010 emphasizes patient-centered care, a concept in complete alignment with the trauma-informed care emphasis on providing choices. Patient-centered care requires the identification of treatment goals that patients care about and an emphasis on patient preference of care as an important factor in the selection of treatment approaches offered. Cloitre (2015) suggests the major task for improving engagement in trauma treatment is to ask the patient what their preferences are such as what treatment goals and intervention procedures appeal to them.

Parents who are trauma survivors may be seeking help for their child. Respecting this choice means focusing treatment on the child and not on the parent's trauma. Understanding and respecting trauma survivor's treatment choices allows them control over what is to happen in treatment and is a key component to engagement of trauma survivors and to winning their trust (Elliot et al., 2005). This means respecting what they want help on, even if it is not help on their trauma, what ideas make sense to them, and what treatment procedures they are willing to participate in. Respecting clients' choices and preferences has been found to be very helpful in preventing premature termination from psychotherapy in general (Swift & Greenberg, 2015).

Collaboration

A central component to trauma-informed care is collaboration. The client must be approached as an expert on their life histories and treatment preferences. Treatment decisions such as what problem to focus on must be made collaboratively with the client's judgment trusted as much as possible.

Empowerment

Clinicians do not empower clients in a direct, linear way but provide a treatment context in which clients develop a sense of personal agency. In such a context, clinicians need to ensure that the client feels safe (Cattaneo & Chapman, 2010), respect clients' treatment goals (Catteneo & Goodman, 2015), and focus on identifying and utilizing clients' strengths (Elliot et al., 2005). In an empowering treatment context, clinicians need to provide and respect clients' treatment preferences and identify problems and goals that are realistic and achievable. When a trauma surviving parent brings in their child for treatment, they can feel a sense of empowerment when they find ways to help their child resolve the presenting problems targeted for treatment. Parents can feel empowered when they are the front-line position in helping their child. Parents are empowered when they discover new and effective ways at addressing and resolving their child's difficulties. If the child is the trauma survivor, the parents can be coached and supported in delivering the trauma-focused interventions.

SUMMARY

Origins

Freud focusing on clients' traumatic histories was the catalyst for the development of the practice of psychotherapy. He oriented us to search in the client's past for traumatic events that have left debilitating effects on clients in the present. Freud set us out to help them identify and process those events. He devised an approach that focuses on the individual trauma survivor and proposed the trauma survivor seek individual therapy from a professional therapist. All these aspects of Freud's original ideas continue to have a powerful influence today. The contemporary field of psychotherapy is very focused on treating client trauma. As will be seen in the following chapter, many approaches emphasize identifying and processing past traumatic events, mostly with a therapist individually; the client's family is left out of treatment.

ACEs Study and Neurobiological Findings

The original ACEs studies are of major historical significance in the examination and treatment of trauma. The ACEs studies called considerable attention to trauma and has been a major contributing factor driving the explosion of mental health professionals focusing on clients' trauma history. Both the ACEs studies and the findings of the scanning studies of the brains of trauma survivors could be interpreted as evidence of damage done by exposure to past traumatic events. Results and images from brain scans from the ACEs studies could represent the scares left behind by exposure to past trauma. This interpretation reinforces the treatment model initially put forth by Freud: Work with the survivor individually, identify the traumatic event(s), and process and change the meaning of those events.

An alternative interpretation of the ACEs and brain scan studies is also possible. The negative health results and the images of the brains of trauma survivors could be the result of continuous and habitual responses of family and social systems to the trauma survivor. The damage caused by exposure to trauma is exacerbated and intensified by ongoing social interaction that does not produce a feeling of safety and security for the survivor. The life lived by the trauma survivor of habitual unhelpful responses from family, friends, and social institutions is reflected in the poor health outcomes and damaged brain images. This interpretation leads to an intervention process that focuses on changing the interactions between trauma survivors and key others in their social networks. This interpretation *requires* family to participate in treatment.

Safety

The neurobiological studies on the effects of chronic and habitual fear responses, the characteristics of many trauma survivors and the emphasis of many of the constructs of trauma-informed care call attention to safety as a fundamental issue. One main motivation of many trauma survivors is to stay safe. Many trauma survivors avoid or prematurely dropout of treatment because they do not feel safe receiving it. They do not feel safe telling their stories or turning over control of treatment to a therapist. To engage trauma survivors in treatment and keep them engaged in treatment, the survivor must feel safe. Trauma-informed care encourages professionals and organizations to create procedures that help trauma survivors feel safe.

Collaboration and Client Choice

To feel safe and trust a professional, trauma survivors must have input and be given control over treatment decisions. Collaboration and respecting client choices are key to engaging trauma survivors in treatment and keeping them engaged. Professionals must devise treatments based on a collaborative process with trauma survivors, offer treatment choices, and respect the choices trauma survivors make. This includes what problems and goals the survivor wishes to focus on, even if those problems and goals are not about trauma. If the client wishes to receive treatment focusing on their trauma, they again must be offered choices on treatment procedures that might help. Perhaps they do not wish to tell their trauma story. Perhaps they do not wish to go through painful exposure procedures. In these instances, if the survivor is to stay engaged in treatment, treatment providers must find a way to be helpful while respecting what treatment procedures the client is willing and not willing to go through.

2 EVIDENCE-BASED TRAUMA TREATMENTS

Most funders of behavioral health services now require providers of those services to use evidence-based treatments. Evidence-based practice is "the integration of the best available research with clinical expertise in the context of patient characteristics, culture, and preferences" (American Psychological Association, Presidential Task Force on Evidence-Based Practice, 2006, p. 273). For treatments to become evidence based, they require the development and use of treatment manuals, measures for monitoring fidelity to the treatment, and valid and reliable instruments for measuring their effectiveness. Such treatment approaches are sought out by referral sources such as child protective services and juvenile court systems for behavioral health treatment for children.

How effective are the manualized evidence-based approaches? Are some more effective than others? We shall explore these questions in the following discussion.

EVIDENCE-BASED TRAUMA-FOCUSED TREATMENTS

There are numerous evidence-based treatments for working with clients with posttraumatic stress syndrome (PTSD) for both adults and children. The majority of these approaches are *trauma-focused*, which "typically include repeated *in vivo* or imaginal exposure to the trauma, reappraisal of the meaning of the trauma and its consequences (cognitive interventions), or some combination of these techniques" (Cloitre, 2015, p. 3). The activity that receives the greatest emphasis is the trauma survivor telling and retelling or writing and/or rewriting their trauma story. This is the primary element of exposure to an anxiety-provoking stimulus that the survivor has been avoiding. In telling or writing the trauma story clients are instructed to do so in the first person as if it is happening in the present. Clients might also expose themselves to stimuli that they associate with the trauma such as places, types of people, food, smells, etc., which are triggers for re-experiencing the fear and anxiety associated with the traumatic experience(s) and thus they have been avoiding. The thinking is that the trauma and the associated symptoms cannot be resolved as long as clients are avoiding triggers. Resolution of the PTSD and its symptoms can be accomplished by the client exposing themselves to the triggers and re-experiencing their fear until the client habituates to the triggers.

For adults, all of these evidence-based approaches place great emphasis on individual therapy. Examples of these approaches include cognitive therapy (Ehlers & Wild, 2015), prolonged exposure therapy (PET; McLean, Asnaani, & Foa, 2015; Najak, Powers, & Foa, 2012), cognitive processing therapy (CPT; Chard, Schuster, & Resick, 2012; Galovski, Wachen, Chard, Monson, & Resick, 2015; Resick, Monson,

& Chard, 2017), eye movement desensitization and reprocessing (EMDR; Shaprio & Laliotis, 2015; Spates & Rubin, 2012), narrative exposure therapy (NET; Elbert, Schauer, & Neuner, 2015), and skills training in affective and interpersonal regulation (STAIR) narrative therapy (Cloitre & Schmidt, 2015).

For children, many evidence-based trauma-focused treatments place an emphasis on individual therapy with the child or therapy with the traumatized child and one caregiver. Examples of these treatments include cognitive therapy for PTSD (Perrin et al., 2017); PET (Capaldi, Zandbeg, & Foa, 2017); NET (e.g., KIDNET; Schauer, Neuner, & Elbert, 2017); narrative therapy (Gudino, Leonard, Stiles, Havens, & Cloitre, 2017); EMDR (Shapiro, Wesselmann, & Mevissen, 2017); trauma-focused cognitive-behavioral therapy (TF-CBT; Kliethermes, Drewry, & Wamser-Nanney, 2017); attachment, self-regulation, and competency (Blaustein & Kinniburgh, 2017); child–parent psychotherapy (CPP; Lieberman, Ippen & Van Horn, 2006; Lieberman & Van Horn, 2008; Reyes, Stone, Dimmler, & Lieberman, 2017); parent–child interaction therapy (Gurwitch, Messer, & Funderburk, 2017); trauma systems therapy (A. Brown, Laitner, & Sax, 2017); and child and family traumatic stress intervention (Epstein, Hahn, Berkowitz, & Marans, 2017).

EVIDENCE-BASED NONTRAUMA-FOCUSED TREATMENTS

Cloitre (2015) reports numerous studies and meta-analyses that show efficacy for approaches that do not focus directly on exposure to the trauma narrative and related triggers (nontrauma-focused treatments) and thus questions the need for trauma-focused treatments. There is now solid evidence-based support for resolving trauma symptoms when treatment does not involve exposure to trauma related triggers (Najavits & Anderson, 2015). These approaches are referred to as present-focused or present-centered treatments (Frost, Laska, & Wampold, 2014; Najavits & Anderson, 2015). Frost et al. (2014) state that present-centered therapy (PCT) for PTSD consists of "altering present maladaptive relational patterns/behaviors, providing psychoeducation regarding the impact of trauma on the client's current life, and teaching the use of problem-solving skills" (p. 2). In their review of efficacious treatments for PTSD, Najavits and Anderson (2015) include more nontrauma-focused (present-centered) treatments than Frost et al., including cognitive therapy for PTSD; seeking safety, stress inoculation training (SIT); and Trauma Affect Regulation: Guide for Education and Therapy (TARGET). These nontrauma-focused approaches include all the elements delineated by Frost et al. but some also included developing coping skills and cognitive restructuring while excluding exposure interventions. According to Najavits and Anderson (2015), studies and meta-analyses have now found that the nontrauma-focused approaches are just as effective as the trauma-focused ones. However, the trauma-focused and nontrauma-focused treatments did differ in one important area—client dropout. In one meta-analysis (Imel, Laska, Jakupcak, & Simpson, 2013) the trauma-focused treatment had a dropout rate of 36% whereas the nontrauma-focused treatment had a dropout rate of 22%, and in another meta-analysis (Frost, Laska, & Wampold, 2014), the dropout rates were 31.3% and 14.3%, respectively. One possible explanation for the differences in these dropout rates is that many people find that they cannot tolerate the exposure interventions.

In addition, there is a growing body of literature supporting interpersonal therapy, which also takes a nontrauma-focused approach, as an effective treatment for PTSD (Bleiberg & Markowitz, 2019; Markowitz, 2017; Markowitz et al., 2015; Markowitz, Choo, & Neria, 2018).

The important implication from these findings is that many different types of trauma treatments are effective, and no one type of treatment is necessary for the recovery from PTSD. Treatment providers need to be flexible, work collaboratively with clients, and find the best treatment fit for them (Cloitre, 2015; Najavits & Anderson, 2015).

EFFICACY OF EVIDENCE-BASED TRAUMA TREATMENTS FOR ADULTS

There are numerous meta-analyses comparing the efficacy of many of the EBTs for adults (Benish, Imel, & Wampold, 2008; Cusack et al., 2016; Ehring et al., 2014; Imel, Laska, Jakupcak, & Simpson, 2013; Tran & Gregor, 2016; Institute of Medicine of the National Academies, 2007). In 2007 the Department of Veteran's Affairs asked the U.S. Institute of Medicine (2007) to review evidence-based trauma treatments. The U.S. Department of Medicine reviewed the efficacy of cognitive behavioral therapy (CBT) for PTSD, PET, EMDR, and critical incident stress debriefing and found that all approaches were effective and no approach was more effective than the others. Benish et al. (2008) compared the relative effectiveness for trauma desensitization hypnotherapy, EMDR, PET, CBT for PTSD, PCT, and exposure CBT therapies in a meta-analysis. This study also found all the treatments to be effective and no one approach was more effective than the others. Although the primary focus of Imel et al.'s (2013) meta-analysis concerned dropout rates of evidence-based trauma treatments, their analysis supported Benish et al.'s findings of similar efficacy for EMDR, PET, and CBT for PTSD. Tran and Gregor's (2016) meta-analysis comparing efficacy of EMDR, PET, and CBT for PTSD and found all the treatment approaches to be equally effective. Cusak et al. (2016) conducted a meta-analysis examining the efficacy of PET, EMDR, CPT, and CBT mixed therapies for treating PTSD and also found all the approaches equally efficacious.

One often-cited meta-analysis reveals that over 40% of clients who completed evidenced-based approaches continued to meet criteria for PTSD or, if not, continued to suffer from significant residual symptoms (Bradley, Greene, Russ, Dutra, & Weston, 2005). This analysis reviewed 26 studies that included 13 exposure-based therapies, 9 combined exposure based and cognitive reprocessing therapies, and 10 EMDR studies. Twenty-three studies had control conditions. The total number of patients reported in all studies combined was 1,535, with 966 in trauma-focused treatment, 317 assigned to a wait list, and 252 receiving placebo treatment. Forty-four percent of those who entered the study and 54% of those who completed treatment were substantially improved at the end of the study. In 30% to 60% of patients who met prescreening criteria for controlled clinical trials, symptoms were reduced but continued to be clinically significant. Persistence of PTSD symptoms after completion of treatment for such a large number of clients has become an increasing concern (Fonzo et al., 2017; van Rooij et al., 2016).

EFFICACY OF EVIDENCE-BASED TRAUMA TREATMENTS FOR CHILDREN AND ADOLESCENTS

In a meta-analysis of evidence-based treatments for children with PTSD, Dorsey et al. (2017) reviewed studies comparing efficacy of TF-CBT that includes parent involvement, individual CBT (no parent component), group CBT, group CBT with parent involvement, individual EMDR, individual integrated therapy for complex trauma, group mind–body skills, individual client-centered play therapy, and CPP. In reporting their findings, they divided treatment efficacy into the following categories: well-established treatments, probably efficacious treatments, and possibly efficacious treatments and experimental treatments. TF-CBT was listed as the only approach in the well-established category; this was largely due to TF-CBT having been researched far more than any of the other child treatments for trauma. Although other approaches such as CPP and EMDR showed efficacy, they did not have the volume of research required by the authors to be classified as "well established." Interestingly, this study found that explicit exposure to trauma, such as repeated telling of the trauma story and imaginal or in vivo exposure to trauma, may not be necessary to resolve trauma symptoms.

COMMON CHARACTERISTICS OF EVIDENCE-BASED TRAUMA TREATMENTS

Several authors have identified a number of common characteristics of evidence-based trauma treatments (Benish, Imel, & Wampold, 2008; Schnyder et al., 2015; Wampold et al., 2010). For treating adults with PTSD, Benish et al. (2008) identified these characteristics as a direct focus on specific trauma symptoms such as nightmares or intrusive thoughts, a treatment rationale that offers an explanation of the problem and organizes the treatment, and a set of procedures consistent with the treatment rationale. Schnyder et al. (2015) listed common elements of trauma-focused approaches as psychoeducation, teaching emotional regulation and coping skills, imaginal exposure, cognitive processing and restructuring, and meaning-making. Wampold et al. (2010) published an article as a follow up to the Benish et al. (2008) article. In this article Wampold et al. listed the following as "possible factors important to successful treatments of PTSD" (p. 931):

- cogent psychological rationale that is acceptable to client
- systematic set of treatment actions consistent with the rationale
- development and monitoring of a safe, respectful, and trusting therapeutic relationship
- collaborative agreement about tasks and goals of therapy
- nurturing hope and creating a sense of self-efficacy
- psychoeducation about PTSD
- opportunity to talk about trauma (i.e., tell stories)
- ensuring the client's safety, especially if the client has been victimized as in the case of domestic violence, neighborhood violence, or abuse
- helping clients learn how to avoid revictimization
- identifying client resources, strengths, survival skills and intrapersonal and interpersonal resources and building resilience

- teaching coping skills
- examination of behavioral chain events
- exposure (covert in session and in-vivo outside of session
- making sense of traumatic event and client's reaction to event
- client attribution of change to his or her own efforts
- encouragement to generate and use social supports
- relapse prevention

Remember that Wampold et al. (2010) said that this list is of "possible factors important to successful treatments of PTSD" (p. 931). They did not say that all of the factors are required for treatment of PTSD to be successful.

The identified common elements of efficacious treatment for children are psychoeducation about the impact of trauma and intervention, training in emotion regulation strategies, imaginal exposure, in vivo exposure, and cognitive processing. Although parent involvement was not common to all approaches, there is empirical support for involving a caregiver in treatment (Dorsey et al., 2017). Those approaches that do emphasize parent or caregiver involvement focus on how one or each parent or caregiver is interacting with the traumatized child. None involve the larger family system nor focus on how adults in the family system are interacting with each other and how this, in turn, may affect how adults are interacting with the traumatized child.

While some of the approaches for both adults and children treat the individual client and others include the client and one parent in the case of children, they all emphasize using exposure interventions. Interestingly what all these approaches also have in common is they do not treat the family. One last common characteristic of all the listed manualized evidence-based approaches is they are all very prescriptive. These approaches lay out sequential therapy steps that the clinician and client should follow. They all focus on using exposure interventions, decide who should participate in the treatment, give treatment rationales (frames) that are specific to their approach, and dictate what therapeutic procedures to offer to which the client must buy into and accept.

DROPOUTS

Clients either dropping out of trauma treatment or not engaging in trauma treatment at all has been a serious concern of both treatment providers and researchers of manualized trauma approaches. That many trauma survivors avoid treatment is well documented (Armbruster & Kazdin, 1994; Olfson et al., 2009). Dropout rates for clients who have started trauma treatment have been the subject of several meta-analyses. Benish et al. (2008) compared the relative effectiveness and dropout rates for trauma desensitization hypnotherapy, EMDR, PET, CBT for PTSD, PCT, exposure CBT therapies in a meta-analysis. This study found that all the treatments focusing directly on trauma symptoms and exposure had between 25% and 50% dropout rates.

Imel et al. (2013) reviewed 42 studies, 17 of which were direct comparison studies of PET, CPT, EMDR, and PCT. This meta-analysis found dropout rates in clinical trials ranging from 0% to 48% with an average dropout rate of 18% for controlled clinical trials. Controlled clinical trials typically have inclusion and exclusion criteria that dictate who will be selected to participate in the study. By excluding clients from participating in studies for various reasons, dropout rates may be drastically reduced in these trials; this is not the case in the real world. In real-world studies, where there are no exclusion categories, dropout rates averaged 44% (Imel et al., 2013).

Attrition for children receiving trauma-focused treatment is also problematic. Most children who need mental health treatment are not in treatment to begin with and, of those who are, 30% to 75% drop out (Armbruster & Kazdin, 1994; Olfson et al., 2009; Wierzbicki & Pekarik, 1993). Supporting the difficulty of keeping clients engaged in treatment in real-world settings, Saxe, Ellis, Fogler, and Navalta (2012) report a dropout rate among minority, urban youth being as high as 90%. In their meta-analysis of child and adolescent treatments for trauma, Dorsey et al. (2017) report that in the TF-CBT studies reviewed, attrition rates were not reported. We know from our own clinical experience, however, that there are children who do not wish to talk about their trauma. Thus, these children cannot participate in TF-CBT. In a study focusing on dropouts for trauma-focused treatment of children, of 466 children who began treatment, 69% prematurely terminated treatment (Wamser-Nanney & Steinzor, 2016).

FLEXIBILITY

Benish et al. (2008) take the position that flexibility is the key to avoiding dropouts. The flexibility to adjust treatment to accommodate to client choices is thought to be key to maintaining engagement. Kerig and Alexander (2012) go so far as to say that flexibility is the current "gold standard" regarding trauma treatment. This finding supports the principals laid out by trauma-informed care and the emphasis on patient preference stipulated by the Affordable Care Act. To truly provide client choices, collaboration, and empowerment, treatment approaches should be flexible and able to adjust and adapt to choices clients are requesting.

SUMMARY

Flexibility

Considering the difficulties of engaging trauma clients and the emphasis on giving clients choices as a method of engaging them, there is a great need for approaches that can both adequately resolve trauma symptoms and simultaneously give clients choices. These choices could include what problem to focus on, who should attend treatment, what treatment rationale to offer, and what treatment procedures to offer. The very nature of all the prescriptive approaches, however, render them inflexible on all these therapy choices.

Many clients have a trauma history but not all are customers for trauma treatment. Some clients are not willing to talk about their trauma narratives. Other clients are not willing to carry out treatment procedures such as exposure to traumatic reminders while other clients are not willing to focus on trauma as a problem at all. We observe that often clients with trauma histories who do not want to focus on trauma in therapy are being labeled by their therapist as "not ready for treatment." In cases like this, the therapist is not flexible enough to shift out of the trauma-focused approach they know and find another way to help. Unfortunately for these therapists, there are few or no options of treatment models for them to choose from that allow both the flexibility to adapt to client choices while simultaneously helping with trauma.

Trauma-Based Treatment Procedures

Although manualized evidence-based treatment approaches have limited flexibility, taken together, there is considerable wisdom in their intervention procedures. Helping a client learn to regulate their emotions, the benefit of telling the trauma story and processing its meaning, exposure to symptoms or situations a client is avoiding, and improving the attachment between a traumatized child and a caregiver can all be very helpful interventions on any given case. What is needed is an overarching framework for the flexible and individualized application of any of these intervention procedures.

SUMMARY OF META-ANALYSIS FINDINGS

We would like to conclude this chapter with a summary of major points supported by meta-analysis and research on trauma.

- For adults, the various evidence-based approaches are all essentially equal.
- For children and adolescents, TF-CBT has the strongest support partly because it has been studied much more than other child-focused trauma treatments.
- For evidence-based treatments that focus directly on trauma symptoms, engaging and keeping clients engaged in treatment is a serious problem.
- There is evidence that focusing directly on exposure is not necessary to help resolve trauma symptoms.
- There is considerable efficacy for improving PTSD symptoms by using therapies that are nontrauma-focused.
- These findings allow for options. Clients that do not wish to focus on trauma in treatment can still be helped by using approaches that do not focus on trauma directly.
- Identifying and respecting client preferences are important to engaging clients in treatments that focus directly or indirectly on trauma as a problem.
- Flexibility in what to offer is the key to promoting treatment that emphasizes patient preferences and maximizes engagement in and completion of treatment.
- None of the existing evidence-based trauma treatments focus on or involve the whole family.

TRAUMA AND THE FAMILY

3

EFFECTS OF TRAUMA ON A FAMILY LEVEL

Experienced family therapists have learned to respect both the hurtful and healing capabilities of family. Both great psychological harm and great psychological benefit can result from the nature of intimate family relationships. In this chapter, we will explore how the detriments and benefits of family relationships effect trauma survivors.

PTSD AND RESILIENCY: RISK AND PROTECTIVE FACTORS

Despite widespread exposure to traumatic events, studies have consistently shown that only a fraction of trauma-exposed individuals develop posttraumatic stress disorder (PTSD). For trauma-exposed adults, the National Comorbidity Survey found that 20% of adult women exposed to trauma and 8% of adult men exposed to trauma develop PTSD. Among children exposed to trauma at or before age 15, 35% of females and 10% of males developed PTSD (Breslau, Davis, Andreski, Peterson, & Schultz, 1997; Breslau, Wilcox, Storr, Luciea, & Anthony, 2004). Cohen, Mannarino, and Deblinger (2017) note the resiliency of children, which protects them from developing PTSD and highlights external sources of support as a key protective factor.

The presence of various risk and protective factors at the time of trauma exposure have been identified to explain why an individual may or may not develop PTSD (Freidman, Keane & Resick, 2014). These risk factors and corresponding effect sizes include gender (female), 0.13; younger age, 0.01; low socioeconomic status, 0.15; low intelligence, 0.04; race (minority status), 0.11; psychiatric history, 0.13; previous trauma, 0.13; family psychiatric history, 0.18; trauma severity, 0.30; and lack of social support, 0.36. Thus, there are several identified factors that play a major role in risk protection from experiencing trauma (Freidman et al., 2014). Of all the protective factors, social support—family support in particular—appear to be the greatest risk and protective factors (Gaudin, Polansky, Kilpatrick, & Shilton, 1993).

FAMILY SUPPORT AS A PROTECTIVE FACTOR FOR PTSD

To what extent can family relationships alleviate negative effects of trauma? Can secure attachments between a caregiver and trauma survivor, a loving relationship between adults in the home and family, and a secure stable living environment moderate or ameliorate PTSD? Can a harmonious environment that promotes safety and security prevent PTSD? These questions are of fundamental importance both for the issue of whom to include in child trauma treatment and regarding to what degree trauma symptoms can be alleviated by solely focusing on improving family relationships.

Several researchers have found that family support outweighs other protective factors in preventing or minimizing PTSD (Afifi & MacMilan, 2011; Jaffee, Caspi, Moffitt, Polo-Toma, & Taylor, 2007; Lesham, Haj-Yahia, & Guterman, 2016; Hitchcock, Ellis, Williamson, & Nixon, 2015; Ozer, Best, & Lipsey, 2003; Marshall, English, & Stewart, 2001; M. Price, Pallito, & Legrand, 2018; Thabet, Shivram, Winter, & Vostanis, 2009; Williamson et al., 2017). In a meta-analysis of protective factors, Berwin (2000) found social support to have the highest impact on preventing PTSD.

Numerous studies have shown the moderating effects of family support on development of PTSD (Belsky, Jaffee, Sligo, Woodward, & Silva, 2005; Caliso & Milner, 1992; Chan, 1994; Coohey, 1996; Egeland, Jacobvitz, & Sroufe, 1988; Guadin, Polansky, Kilpatrick, & Shilton, 1993; Hashima & Amato, 1994; Matsakis, 2007; Rak & Patterson, 1996; Travis & Combs-Orme, 2007). Social support was listed as the key factor in recovery for trauma (Lauth-Lebens & Lauth, 2016). Ludy-Dobson and Perry (2010) note: "[h]ealthy relational interactions with safe and familiar individuals can buffer and heal trauma-related problems (p. 28)." Jones (2007) found that family support for African American children aged 9 to 11, living in high-crime, high-poverty neighborhoods had a moderate effect size on preventing the development of PTSD.

Neurobiological Effects of Family Support

A nurturing family environment can have healing and positive effects on the brain and on brain development of children exposed to trauma. Positive family interactions regulate the brain's stress response and help create positive and healing neuroendocrine and neurophysiological conditions that promote healing and healthy development for children exposed to trauma (Ludy-Dobson & Perry, 2010).

Family Support and Sexual Abuse

For intrafamilial sexual abuse, receiving or not receiving family support appears to be the most important moderator for developing PTSD. Family support is a main factor for child sexual abuse victims not developing PTSD (Marriot, Hamilton-Giachritsis, & Harrop, 2014). Perception that family members value the survivors (self-esteem support) and that advice can be obtained when coping with symptoms and issues (appraisal support) were found to be the largest moderators to developing PTSD (Hyman, Gold, & Cott, 2003). Self-esteem support is essentially defined as the survivor being believed and not blamed for the abuse. Self-esteem support resulted in the victim feeling valued and counteracted victim self-blame, which is associated with poor long-term adjustment (Hyman et al., 2003).

Expanded View of Family Support

Family support can be viewed as not just how various family members interact with the trauma survivor but also more expansively to include the overall family environment. This expanded view also includes how the adults in the home are getting along with each other and how household family members get along with extended family. Numerous studies point to both how adults interact with the child survivor and how adults get along with each other as both protective and risk factors.

A meta-review of findings list several aspects of family support that moderate PTSD symptoms (Marriot, 2004). The list includes a stable, connected, supportive family environment; one or more caregivers present throughout the child's life; stable caregiving by at least one adult, particularly the mother; the survivor feeling supported and understood by their parents; and living in a family where other stressful events such as hostility between caregivers, divorce, death, illness, and financial difficulties are minimized.

Family Support From a Cross Cultural Perspective

All the discussed studies listed focus on Western trauma survivors and represent a Western perspective on what constitutes family support. In many non-Western cultures it is even more taboo to report sexual abuse, and the survivor is more likely to be blamed. Is it necessary for families from non-Western cultures to respond in the previously defined ways to be helpful and supportive of trauma survivors in general and sexual assault survivors specifically? It appears this question has not been researched. The first author (DG) has experience consulting on sexual assault survivor cases in Hong Kong, China. The author is aware of several instances of sexual assault survivors recovering and receiving family support in different forms than what has been defined in the West.

A 38-year-old married woman with two pre-teenaged daughters lived with her husband and her father-in-law in Hong Kong. She immigrated to Hong Kong from mainland China with a history of childhood intrafamilial sexual abuse. Her husband worked in mainland China during the week and was home on the weekend. When home, he was very connected to his father and was neglectful of his wife. The wife was suffering from severe anxiety. She was concerned her father-in-law would sexually assault her daughters. When home from school, the wife kept her two daughters sequestered in their room to protect them from the abuse she feared might occur. Her daughters did not understand why they had to stay in their room. They were not afraid of their grandfather. The wife did not report anything the father-in-law had done or said that would explain her anxiety.

The husband was invited into treatment. He was aware of his wife's sexual abuse background. He was told his wife did not feel safe, and it was necessary for him to be more connected to her. He responded by spending more time with her when home on the weekend. The wife felt very supported by her husband as a result. Consequently, her anxiety disappeared, and she no longer sequestered her daughters in their rooms.

The author has learned of several Hong Kong cases in which a husband or father becomes more connected to a wife or daughter who is a trauma survivor and the trauma survivor's fears and symptoms are resolved. When the husband or father became more connected to them, they felt supported and validated. The trauma was not necessarily discussed. Although these examples are anecdotal, they call into question the universality of how family support is defined and whether it is necessary for families to respond to trauma in the way Western trauma literature suggests is most helpful.

LACK OF FAMILY SUPPORT AS A RISK FACTOR FOR PTSD

Of all the risk factors associated with developing PTSD, lack of social support has by far the greatest impact. Ludy-Dobsen and Perry (2010) note that children in a relationally impoverished setting will likely be unable to recover or heal from the effects of trauma without a change in their family setting. Berwin, Andrews, and Valentine (2000) listed effect size of numerous risk factors and reported an effect size of 0.4 for lack of family support. Dinkzwager, Bramsen, Ader, and Van der Ploeg (2005) states that low social support is a precursor for PTSD. It is well established that lack of social support is a major risk factor for developing PTSD (Vogt, King, & King, 2014).

Interactional Patterns That Interfere With Family Support

THE "NO TALK RULE"

For a traumatized family member, lack of family support can come in the form of avoidance of talking about trauma on a family level. Numerous authors have pointed out the "no talk" rule (Figley & Figley, 2009). Regarding intrafamilial sexual abuse, disclosure of abuse by the survivor is less likely than when abuse is perpetrated by a nonfamily member, with male survivors less likely than female survivors to disclose abuse (Ullman, 2003). In these instances, the trauma itself is a secret that is not discussed.

Secondary trauma is often cited as an inhibiter to family discussions regarding trauma. Secondary trauma to parents can create intolerable emotions, which, in turn, can impair family members ability to empathize with the trauma victim (Kerig & Alexander, 2012). The same authors also report that traumatized youth often can view their parents as fragile and thus are reluctant to share trauma histories with them. The trauma survivor fears sharing the trauma with family will be too emotionally upsetting for them. They are essentially being protective of family by keeping the trauma a secret.

INTRAFAMILIAL CHILDHOOD SEXUAL ABUSE

Childhood sexual abuse represents a major category of trauma survivors. The most recent estimates of childhood sexual abuse survivors in the United States is between 8% and 33% of women and 1% and 16% of men (Barth et al., 2013; Briere & Elliott, 2003). Worldwide a meta-analysis of studies found 20% of women and 8% of men were adult survivors of childhood sexual abuse (Pereda, Guilera, Forns, & Gomez-Benito, 2009). Survivors of childhood sexual abuse are at substantially higher risk of developing PTSD than trauma survivors in general. Rodriguez, Kemp, and Foy (1998) found that two thirds of a sample of adult sexual abuse survivors met the criteria for PTSD. Adult sexual abuse survivors display more avoidant, intrusive, and arousal symptoms of PTSD than nonabuse trauma survivors. Sexual abuse victims of family members or close family friends manifest higher degrees of PTSD symptoms (Ullman, 2007). Ullman theorized that the greater severity may be a result of the betrayal that occurs when a family member is the abuse perpetrator.

When sexual abuse is disclosed, how family members respond can seriously affect future development of PTSD. Delayed disclosure and negative family reactions are associated with poorer adjustment. Female survivors and survivors abused by fathers are more symptomatic (Ullman, 2003). Unsupportive family responses to disclosure of intrafamily sexual abuse are both common and associated with negative effects including psychological symptoms, somatic and health symptoms, incomplete memories, and problems in adult relationships (Ullman, 2003). Betrayal that accompanies intrafamilial sexual abuse and negative family responses seriously impacts survivor responses and future symptomology (Freyd, 1996). Unsupportive family reactions and family disbelief can be viewed as a betrayal (Ullman, 2003).

Family not validating, not believing, and/or blaming the survivor for abuse are the most common family reactions to abuse that seriously increase risk of the survivor developing PTSD. Several factors are associated with these types of responses. Disclosure in childhood is more likely to be met with negative reactions than disclosures in adulthood. Parents' reactions to female incest survivors' abuse disclosures are worse than those of other sexual assault survivors. Those abused by relatives reported more negative family reactions to disclosure than those abused by strangers. More PTSD symptoms are exhibited by survivors who blame themselves and were abused by relatives than survivors who blame themselves but were not abused by relatives. More PTSD symptoms are exhibited for those blaming themselves than for those who do not blame themselves (Ullman, 2007). Clearly, the family blaming or not blaming the survivor heavily influences whether the survivor blames themselves for abuse, with self-blame being a major moderator in developing PTSD (Marriott, Hamilton-Giachritsis, & Harrop, 2014).

DISTORTED FAMILY NARRATIVES AND DIVIDED FAMILY CAMPS

When trauma is not discussed openly within the family, distorted narratives about the traumatic event(s) that involve invalidating, not believing, or blaming the survivor can be maintained that then contribute to ongoing trauma symptoms for the survivor (Grove, 2002). This phenomenon has also been referred to as "consensual distortion" (Catherall, 1998).

When intrafamilial sexual abuse is disclosed, the family can be divided into camps of those who believe the survivor and those who do not believe or blame the survivor (Grove, 2002). If unaddressed, these divisions can last years. Who attends and who does not attend family events such as graduations, holidays etc. is then driven by the division among family members over beliefs about the abuse. These family events then become a message to the survivor that the family continues to be divided over the consequences of their disclosure of abuse. For trauma-focused child therapies that include only one parent, larger family narratives and/or family divisions are not directly addressed and can easily remain unchanged.

Family Patterns That Predate Trauma

It has been noted by several authors (P. Alexander, 2015; Coulter, 2011; Kerig & Alexander, 2012) that family interactional patterns that predate a trauma episode can end up reinforcing or exacerbating trauma symptoms. As has been discussed, secure attachments between the trauma survivor and at least one caregiver can moderate the effects of trauma. Family structure and patterns regulate the quality of attachments between trauma survivors and caregivers (P. Alexander, 2015). Secure attachments can be compromised by several classic family patterns such as disengaged or enmeshed relationships between caregivers and trauma survivors, triangulation of trauma survivors between two adults in the family, cross-generational coalitions involving an adult and the trauma survivor, and role reversal in which the trauma survivor is in a care-taking position with a parent (P. Alexander, 2015).

DISENGAGED RELATIONSHIPS

This is a type of relationship in which the client and caregiver are not emotionally close to begin with and can reinforce the "no talk" rule if trauma occurs. The trauma survivor and the caregiver already do not share emotionally important aspects of their life (Haley, 1987; Minuchin, 1974). When a trauma occurs, simply following this pre-existing pattern results in not discussing the trauma.

ENMESHED RELATIONSHIPS

In this type of relationship, the parent and child are very close and the parent may already be overprotective, which can reinforce patterns of avoidance symptoms (Minuchin, 1974). Intrusive parenting has been associated with insecure attachments, impairing feelings of safety in trauma survivors (Green & Werner, 1996; Kretchmar & Jacobvitz, 2002). Intrusive and enmeshed primary caregiver–child relationships are most often paired with withdrawn or disengaged relationships between the primary caregiver and a second adult in the home or the other parent (P. Alexander, 2015).

CHRONIC OPEN CONFLICT

Unresolved and open conflict between parents and children and/or two or more adults in the home can also interfere with talking about trauma and feeling safe and secure in the home (P. Alexander, 2015). Chronic hostility between a caregiver and trauma survivor is a common pattern that seriously interferes with the survivor receiving support from the caregiver. This pattern can occur when the caregiver views the survivors as defiant.

CHRONIC CONFLICT BETWEEN ADULTS

Parental conflict has major impact on family support (Finger, Hans, Bernstein, & Cox, 2009) and on both the mother's and the father's parenting (P. Alexander, 2015). Couple conflict leads to family instability, parenting problems, and emotional insecurity in a child (Davies & Cummings, 1994; Davies, Harold, Goeke-Morey, & Cummings, 2002). Overt parental conflict is often associated with external child symptoms. Covert parental conflict is often associated with internal child symptoms. (Benson, Buehler, & Gerard, 2008; Buehler & Gerard, 2002; Bradford & Barber, 2005; Gerrard, Krishnakumar, & Buehler, 2006). Spousal conflict can increase a father's intrusiveness and insensitivity to a child's distress (Davies, Sturge-Apple, Woitach, & Cummings, 2009; Katz & Gottman, 1996). Spousal conflict can also decrease father involvement with children (Coiro & Emery, 1998; Katz & Gottman, 1996; Stroud, Durbin, Wilson, & Mendelshoh, 2011). Chronic partner conflict by itself can lead to a child experiencing parents as frightened or frightening (Finger et al., 2009; Owen & Cox, 1997).

DETOURING, TRIANGULATION, AND CROSS-GENERATIONAL COALITIONS

When two caregivers are unable to resolve chronic conflict, a child can be enlisted by one or both. When that child is a trauma survivor, family support is seriously impaired. Managing adult conflict becomes the priority, not addressing support needs of the trauma survivor. Detouring occurs when hostilities between parents are aimed at the child. The child's disruptive behavior functions to divert attention from parent conflict (Fivaz-Depeursinge, 2009; Fosco & Grych, 2008).

In triangulation, both caregivers pressure the child to side with them against the other adult. There is no consistent alliance. Each parent competes for the child's alliance. Triangulation is observed when parental conflict is more frequent and poorly resolved (Fosco & Grych, 2008). Triangulation takes a heavy toll on the child resulting in both internalizing and externalizing problems and increased self-blame (Buehler & Welsh, 2009; Fosco & Grych, 2008, 2010; B. Schwarz, 2009). As with detouring, the goal is managing conflict between adults, not providing family support to a trauma survivor.

Cross-generational coalitions are stable coalitions between one caregiver and a child against another caregiver or family adult. In this pattern, a trauma survivor's relationship with the adult they are aligned against is damaged rendering support from that adult seriously impaired.

PARENTIFICATION/ROLE REVERSAL

In this pattern, the parent relies on a child for nurturance. The child's attention and energy are diverted from age-appropriate developmental tasks and deprives the child of necessary support in coping with developmental challenges (Shaffer & Sroufe, 2005). For a trauma survivor in this role, feeling safe and secure is seriously compromised when the child, not the adult, is in the role of caretaker. Mothers with a history of childhood sexual abuse and current dissatisfaction in their marriage engaged in parentification of their child (P. Alexander, Teti, & Anderson, 2000).

All the previously mentioned family patterns interfere with attachments and can diminish a feeling of safety and security for trauma survivors.

Intergenerational Trauma: Impaired Parents

Intergenerational trauma has become a serious barrier facing treatment providers for traumatized children. One serious issue concerns the effects of trauma on parenting (Christie et al., 2019; Cohn, Silver, Cowan, Cowan, & Pearson, 1992; Cowan & Cowan, 2005). Parents who are themselves trauma survivors may be unable to provide family support to child survivors. Galvski, Wachen, Chard, Monson, and Resick (2004) highlight the difficulties for traumatized parents in raising emotionally healthy children. Traumatized parents can avoid discussion of their child's trauma, reinforcing the "no talk" rule, cutting them off from family support and empathy. Traumatized parents can become very overprotective, intensifying their child's PTSD related avoidance symptoms. The parents own trauma symptoms reinforce the child's trauma symptoms (Lang & Gartstein, 2018; Pynoos, 1993).

Guilt and shame can interfere with traumatized parents' ability to be emotionally available for and empathic to their traumatized children (Sevel-Brooks & Fitgeraldd-Rice, 1997). Traumatized children can end up viewing their traumatized parents as fragile, reinforcing the problem of the child receiving support from their parent (Kerig & Alexander, 2012).

Family Involvement in the Treatment of Trauma

Family involvement in treatment was found to activate or reactivate healing processes and family support was found to help ameliorate PTSD symptoms (Coulter, 2011). Family support can reduce intensity of PTSD symptoms (Matasakis, 2004). Systemic approaches have been found to strengthen key interactional processes that foster healing (Walsh, 2007, 2016). Promotion of recovery requires family participation, and family intervention promotes mutual support, problem-solving, and the impact of trauma symptoms on a family level (Bernardon, 2010). If parents cope well and are supportive, many younger children will not develop PTSD (Cohen et al., 2017). The quality of parental support was a significant predictor of children developing PTSD in three outcome studies (Cohen & Mannarino, 1996, 1998, 2000).

For traumatized children, therapists involving parents in treatment has been found to be a key element promoting recovery (Cohen et al., 2017; Coulter, 2011; Deblinger, Lippman, & Steer, 1996). When involving caregivers in treatment of traumatized children, E. Brown (2005) found parents must be coached to respond with empathy and to promote coping skills.

A child trauma survivor's emotionally supportive relationship with a caregiver was found to moderate effects of trauma (Egeland et al., 1988). If one adult family member is supportive of the victim, the supportive adult can serve as a modifier of the effects of family of origin abuse (P. Alexander, 2015; Fishbane, 2007). Emotional support between intimate partners was also found to moderate effects of trauma for the survivor (DuMont, Wisdom, & Czaja, 2007; Egeland et al., 1988; Lackey & Williams, 1995; Langeland & Dijkstra, 1995).

INTERGENERATIONAL TRAUMA: INCLUDING TRAUMATIZED PARENTS IN TREATMENT WITH THEIR CHILD

Intergenerational trauma and the effects of trauma on parenting can render the parents incapable of responding to their children in the ways treatments aimed at including them require. On one hand, there are clear advantages to including parents in the treatment of traumatized children. On the other hand, traumatized parents may be unable to help their children in the ways that a treatment approach recommends (Newcomb & Locke, 2001).

What is to be done when a traumatized child is brought to treatment by a traumatized parent? For parents who are seriously impaired by their own trauma histories and unwilling or unable to carry out treatment procedures in therapies that include a caregiver, the standard approach is to refer the traumatized parent to their own treatment and then work with the child individually. In TF-CBT, for example, parents who are too traumatized to carry out the tasks of the treatment are referred for their own treatment (Cohen et al., 2017). This is a problem if the parent does not accept treatment for themselves. These parents did not initially request treatment for themselves and are often unlikely to follow through on such referrals.

Neurobiological Effects of Trauma and Family Environment of Trauma Survivors

In this chapter, we reported substantial literature support for both the harmful and healing effects of relational environments on the neurobiological consequences of trauma. Living in a day-to-day family environment that is unstable, unpredictable, and/or hostile can exacerbate the neurobiological impact of trauma and impair the possibility of neurobiological healing. Conversely, living in a stable, predictable, harmonious, and loving family environment can actually begin to heal neurobiological damage from trauma. The treatment implications of these findings clearly favor a family approach.

Call for More Family Treatment

Given that how family reacts to trauma can have either positive or negative impact on trauma symptoms, numerous authors have called for more family treatment for trauma (Coulter, 2011; Figley & Figley, 2009). Despite calls for more family treatment for trauma, there continues to be a lack of family treatment offered. Coulter (2011) reviewed the family literature and found PTSD was not a central focus. Coulter also found family approaches for PTSD vary considerably on consistency with established family therapy models. Riggs, Monson, Glynn, and Canterino (2009) reports that many authors recommend family therapy for PTSD, but few provide details of the focus or stages of such approaches.

4 FAMILY APPROACHES FOR TRAUMA

HOW TO DEFINE A FAMILY THERAPY APPROACH

What are the requirements of a family approach that can address the multiple ways family patterns can reinforce or exacerbate trauma symptoms? We would like to offer a three-level definition of a family approach capable of addressing the issues raised in the first three chapters: theoretical level, assessment level, and intervention level.

THEORETICAL LEVEL

On the theoretical level, we define family approaches as those that are organized around systems theory and/or constructivism. Examples would include structural family therapy (Minuchin, 1974; Minuchin & Fishman, 1981), Bowen's family systems therapy (Bowen, 1978), strategic family therapy (Haley, 1973, 1987; Madanes, 1981), strategic therapy of the Mental Research Institute (Watzlawick, Weakland, & Fisch, 1974; Fisch, Weakland, & Segal, 1981), solution-focused therapy (de Shazier, 1985, 1988, 1991), and narrative therapy (White & Epston, 1990).

Systems Theory

A family is an organization and organizations are systems. A system contains parts that interact with each other over time, and in the case of families, the members are the interacting parts. The interactions with each other over time become routine interactional (interpersonal) patterns. A system has a boundary that separates it from its environment. The boundary is inferred by the intensity and frequency of interactions of system members with their environment. Family members typically interact with each other more frequently and intensively than with people in the environment depending on the stage of the family life cycle. A system continually interacts with its environment so it must be both flexible while maintaining its organization and wholeness; it must both change and maintain stability. This stability is referred to as homeostasis. As a family system interacts with its environment, it maintains homeostasis by exchanging feedback with the environment. Feedback is when output from the family system becomes input. Feedback is either positive, deviation amplifying, or negative, deviation reducing; the deviation is from the current homeostasis. Feedback processes can also become interactional patterns.

Two tenets of systems theory of great importance to family treatment of trauma are circular causality and interaction across boundaries.

CIRCULAR CAUSALITY

Circular causality calls attention to repetitive patterns that perpetuate the status quo. Identifying past "causes" of current symptoms is not emphasized in systems theory (Watzlawick, Bavelas, & Jackson, 1967). Looking for past causes of present problems assumes the notion of linear causality. Applied to trauma, a person may have a history of trauma and meet the diagnostic criteria for posttraumatic stress disorder (PTSD), but their symptoms are occurring in their current life within the context of their relationships. Repeating interactional patterns between the client and family members may be reinforcing or perpetuating trauma symptoms, or it could be the other way around. For example, in the case of an acting-out child and a stressed parent, it is helpful to ask if the child is acting out because the parent is stressed or if the parent is stressed because the child is acting out. For positive change to occur in the situation, one could focus on changing their here-and-now interactions without having to address their pasts.

WHOLENESS AND INTERACTION ACROSS BOUNDARIES

Wholeness suggests there are no boundaries between individuals, problems, relationships, or levels of treatment focus. A term relevant to systems including family systems is "nonsummativity," that is, the whole is greater than the sum of its parts.

> The analysis of a family is not the sum of the analyses of its individual members. There are characteristics of the system, that is, interactional patterns, that transcend the qualities of individual members . . . Many of the "individual qualities" of members, especially symptomatic behavior, are in fact particular to the system (Watzlawick et al., 1967, pp. 135–136)

In a family, everyone is connected to and affected by everyone else. Systems theory allows for the possibility of solving one problem by solving another. Given the wholeness, or interconnectedness, of family systems, if one person changes how they respond to another person and maintains that change, it will create a ripple effect that can result in changes in all the relationships in that family.

Systems theory allows for the possibility of solving one problem by solving another. Resolving one symptom can lead to spontaneous resolution of other interrelated symptoms. Changing one relationship can change another. For example, changing how a mother and father interact can also spontaneously change how either parent interacts with their child. This allows for treatment options.

Systems theory also posits that there are no boundaries between levels of experience and human processes. There is no boundary between biological, psychological, experiential, spiritual, or social levels of experience because they are all interconnected; that is, a change in one leads to changes in the others. We noted in Chapter 1 of this volume that repetitive behavior patterns create neuropathways. Communications theory equates behavior to interaction. All behavior sends a message.

> [b]ehavior has no opposite. In other words, there is no such thing as non-behavior, to put it even more simply: one cannot *not* behave. Now, if it is accepted that all behavior in an interactional situation has message value, i.e., is communication, it follows that no matter how one may try, on cannot *not* communicate. Activity or inactivity, words or silence all have message value: they influence others and these

> others, in turn, cannot *not* respond to these communications and are thus themselves communicating. (Watzlawick et al. 1967, pp. 48–49)

A pattern of behavior is the same as a pattern of interaction. There is, therefore, no boundary between behavior, interaction, and neuropathways. Change at one of these levels can potentially change all levels.

Changing how one person frames something can also lead to changes in how that person interacts with other family members. Changing how two individuals get along can improve the immune system of both. Changing how two people interact can change how both frame the other. Systems theory allows for the possibility that interventions at one level can potentially change all other levels.

Change Is Always Happening

One basic assumption of a systems theory is that change is constant. Although family systems create a homeostasis that defines their structure, all systems are constantly in flux. Regardless of how rigid the family structure may be, there are deviations, or "ups and downs," in the patterns. These "ups" become exceptions to the multiple deficiencies and/or problems clients/families may perceive that they have and represent the unnoticed strengths, resources, and potential (de Shazer, 1988). While these small changes are always occurring, they may be too small or inconsistent to create a change in the system's homeostasis. Consequently, one option for the therapist can be to assist clients/families in noticing, amplifying, sustaining, and reinforcing these small interactional exceptions at a larger systems level (De Jong & Berg, 2013; Fraser, Grove, Lee, Greene, & Solovey, 2014), to make the ordinary "extraordinary" so that these exceptions are no longer exceptions but become part of the behavioral repertoire of the family (M. Y. Lee, Sebold, & Uken, 2003).

Systems Theory and Trauma

Related to trauma, systems theory provides theoretical support for the possibility that a treatment not focused on trauma symptoms can still resolve trauma symptoms. If a client desires help on a nontrauma related symptom, their trauma symptoms may still be resolved due to the interconnection between the two. A parent may have a serious trauma history and suffer from trauma-related symptoms. She or he may not be interested in focusing on their own trauma but may be very motivated to help their child. Systems theory lends theoretical support for respecting the parent's preference and still resolving problems not targeted by the parent. They can be enlisted to help their child. What they then do to help their child may also help resolve their own trauma symptoms. Systems theory allows for client preferences to guide treatment and resolve trauma symptoms even if focusing on these symptoms is not a client's choice. Systems theory supports the trauma-informed care concept of respecting client treatment choices.

Constructivism

Constructivism posits that our taken-for-granted assumptions of reality are socially constructed. Greene and Lee (2011) list the essential elements of constructivism:

- Language and dialogue are integral to the social construction of reality.
- Reality is co-constructed through social interaction.

- People are active participants in developing their knowledge of the world rather than passive recipients of stimulus-response interaction with their environment.
- There is not an objective reality standing outside individuals; thus, reality is not discovered but created by human observers.
- There is no such thing as an objective observer because the very act of observing changes that which is being observed.
- The cultural context affects how people interpret and co-construct reality. (pp. 14–15)

Our socially constructed taken-for-granted assumptions are categories for making sense of our lives. In our waking hours, our senses experience more input than we can consciously attend to and make sense of. Thus, our assumptive categories guide us in knowing what to pay attention to and what to ignore, which helps us from getting overwhelmed with trying to make sense of all the sensory input. However, when people develop problems, they often get stuck in vicious cycles of trying to resolve a new situation by using information and skills they already have but are not working for them. What they may need for resolving their problematic situation may be getting filtered out because they are not paying attention to it.

Therapy of any kind involves the therapist facilitating a conversation with the client that is different from any others the client has had or is having in his or her life. In family therapy, the therapist also helps the family members co-construct desired changes in their reality by facilitating conversations with each other that they are not having at home. For this to successfully happen, the therapist must help the family members *feel safe* with her or him and especially with the other family members involved in therapy. Two concepts from constructivism are central to family treatment of trauma: narrative and the nonobjectivity of knowledge.

NARRATIVES

Humans are storytelling creatures. We make meaning by telling and retelling stories. A narrative is a story that is accepted and perpetuated within a group. Ideas do not just exist and are reinforced inside one person's mind. They are shared and reinforced among groups. Narratives are a social phenomenon, not an intrapsychic phenomenon. Related to trauma, a sexual assault survivor's view that the assault was his or her fault is not just a distorted belief maintained by the victim but a narrative most likely shared by family members of the survivor as well as members of the larger community. The view must change within the group, not just inside the victim's mind.

NO OBJECTIVE KNOWLEDGE

We can only have subjective knowledge about any given phenomenon. We can only know a given phenomenon's characteristics as they relate to the observer. Regarding trauma and especially theories related to trauma, we only have theories, not objective truths. The frames governing trauma treatments are just frames, not objective realities. If a clinician believes, for example, that "fear networks" are an objective reality, then that clinician must follow the treatment procedures to correct the "fear network." This is not a problem if the client receiving the treatment accepts both the idea of "fear networks" and the corresponding treatment procedures. This is a serious problem, however, if the client does not accept either the idea or the procedures. The clinician who believes fear networks are real will have a difficult time adjusting and providing an alternative to the clients who do not accept the idea. However, if trauma treatment theories are just theories, we can keep them or change them to match what any given client believes and is willing to cooperate with.

Concepts in systems theory and constructivism provide a theoretical foundation for allowing maximum flexibility in devising treatments. Constructivism allows for treatment rationales to vary from one therapy case to another. Treatment rationales can be co-constructed between the therapist and client and thus avoid dropouts due to the client not accepting the treatment rationale.

Summary

In systems theory, the concepts of circular causality and interconnectivity allow for maximum flexibility on a procedural level. Utilizing systems theory, one problem can be solved by solving another, or one person can be changed by changing another. A therapy can focus on changing social interactive processes but simultaneously change cognitive and/or biological processes. For clients with trauma histories, this allows therapists to offer clients and families choices on goals and procedures that the clients will cooperate with. The trauma-informed care concept of collaborating with trauma survivors is supported by systems theory and constructivism.

ASSESSMENT LEVEL

Observational Field

Assessment of factors influencing trauma symptoms is highly influenced by the observational field of the treatment approach being offered. Who is included in the unit of analysis of a given trauma treatment approach? Trauma approaches that stress exposure or processing trauma between a client and a therapist are typically monadic: cognitive therapy for PTSD (Perrin et al., 2017), prolonged exposure therapy (Capaldi, Zandbeg, & Foa, 2017), and eye movement desensitization and reprocessing (EMDR, Shapiro, Wesselmann, & Mevissen, 2017) all focus on how the individual client is processing trauma. In these approaches, the individual client's behavioral and cognitive responses to trauma constitutes the observational field of the treatment provider.

The National Child Traumatic Stress Network Core Concepts and Curriculum Workgroup (2013) lists the inclusion of parents or other important caregivers in treatment of children suffering from PTSD as the number one criteria of effective trauma treatments for children. Numerous child trauma treatments include one caregiver in treatment and emphasize improving the attachment between the caregiver and trauma survivor and/or coaching the caregiver on how to respond to trauma symptoms. Examples include trauma-focused cognitive behavioral therapy (Kliethermes, Drewry, & Wamser-Nanney, 2017); attachment, self-regulation, and competency (Blaustein & Kinniburgh, 2017); child–parent psychotherapy (Reyes, Stone, Dimmler, & Lieberman, 2017); parent–child interaction therapy (Gurwitch, Messer, & Funderburk, 2017); and child and family traumatic stress intervention (Epstein, Hahn, Berkowitz, & Marans, 2017). Although there may be treatments that coach several caregivers on how to treat the trauma survivor, these are dyadic models that look at one or more sets of two-person patterns and focus on how a caregiver or caregivers interact with the child survivor.

Neither the monadic or dyadic models are equipped to assess or intervene in several types of family patterns that moderate family support for trauma survivors. Conflict between adults in the family, larger family patterns that influence family trauma narratives, and triangulation (i.e., three-person coalitions that include a trauma survivor and two adults) are not in the observational field of monadic or dyadic approaches (Cox, Paley, Payne, & Burchinal, 1999).

To assess families and intervene in family patterns that influence trauma symptoms and survivor feelings of attachment and security, at a minimum, a three-person unit of analysis is required. Understanding how the relationship between two adults affects the symptoms of a traumatized child or recognizing triangulation or coalitions between the trauma survivor and two adults in the family requires a three-person observational field. For treatment approaches to address these triadic issues, the assessment must be based on a triadic unit of analysis. Dyadic approaches that are labeled "family" approaches do not fit this criterion.

Three-Person Interactional Assessment

On the assessment level, we define "family approaches" as those that focus on assessing interactional patterns or interactional exceptions on a triadic level. Triadic understanding of symptoms is a major component of several of the traditional family models such as structural family therapy, strategic family therapy, and Bowen family systems therapy. A triadic unit of analysis allows for assessment that includes not just how caregivers are interacting with a traumatized child, but also how adults in the family are interacting with each other and if they are enlisting the child survivor in their struggles with each other. An analysis on this level can address how family patterns interfere with a traumatized child receiving family support. For traumatized clients, this means obtaining an interactional understanding of their symptoms on a larger system level, whether those symptoms are having nightmares, avoidance behaviors, or emotional dysregulation symptoms.

INTERVENTION LEVEL

On the intervention level, we define family approach as the utilization of intervention procedures to either interrupt the interactional patterns that support symptoms or the identification and enlargement of interactional exceptions that occur when symptoms are not active. Interactions of focus are not limited just to how one or more caregivers are interacting with the trauma survivor. Also included are how adults in the family are interacting with each other, if a trauma survivor is triangulated between two adults, and the impact of trauma on interactions between the nuclear and extended family systems. This definition allows for interventions on a broader family level. Integration of intervention procedures from any treatment model, including any of the evidence-based trauma treatment approaches, can be utilized in a family approach if these procedures have the aim of interrupting interactional patterns that reinforce or exacerbate trauma symptoms or the quality of attachments between family members and the trauma survivor.

Direct Focus on Trauma

For clients and families that define the problem as trauma, a family treatment that focuses directly on trauma symptoms can be organized. Trauma symptoms and the family patterns supporting them can be a direct focus of intervention. For these cases, intervention procedures from the various trauma treatment manuals can be integrated into family treatment. For example, changing family patterns associated with trauma can include a family discussion and processing of the trauma or a parent or parents put in charge of helping a trauma survivor overcome avoidance symptoms. The trauma intervention procedures from the various manuals can be employed to both help ameliorate trauma symptoms and change the family interactional patterns that support them.

Indirect Focus on Trauma

Research reported in Chapter 2 of this volume strongly suggests that treatments that do not focus on trauma directly can still result in improvement of trauma symptoms. Family treatment in general offers advantages for indirectly improving trauma symptoms. Family support for trauma survivors can be improved whether or not a given treatment uses exposure interventions and directly focuses on trauma symptoms. For clients and families that are not willing to use exposure interventions, producing harmonious, supportive family relationships can still be a focus of treatment. A trauma survivor may not be willing to talk about their nightmares or tell their trauma narrative. A family may not accept the idea that a child they bring to therapy is suffering from a trauma history. In either case, changing family patterns associated with whatever problem the client and family is willing to focus on can be a goal of treatment. When changing these patterns results in feelings of safety and improved attachments between a trauma survivor and caregivers, improved relationships among key adults in the family, and breaking up coalitions or triangulation involving the trauma survivor and two adults, family support for the trauma survivor can be substantially improved and, along with it, the amelioration of trauma symptoms improved.

Changing family patterns that interfere with family support for trauma survivors can be achieved whether treatment is directly focusing on trauma symptoms or not. A family treatment model that operates on a triadic level can address family patterns that moderate family support and feelings of safety no matter what problem the treatment focuses on.

FAMILY TREATMENT MODELS FOR PTSD

An up-to-date review of family approaches does indeed find a wide range of approaches that vary considerably. One major focus of many family approaches for trauma is to facilitate a family discussion of the trauma. The "no talk" rule is broken, and not only a discussion of the trauma is undertaken but also the meaning of the event is changed and a family narrative is created. Numerous approaches fall into this category (Bernardon & Pernicie-Duca, 2010; Figley & Figley, 2009). Bernardon and Perncie-Duca (2010) utilized narrative therapy concepts when working with families of trauma victims. They emphasized assessing the family belief system, fostering family communication, and telling and retelling trauma stories as a way of addressing trauma. These approaches address the problem of family narratives regarding trauma but do not assess or focus on changing family patterns that influence family support for trauma survivors such as enmeshed or disengaged relationships, serious conflict between care givers, triangulation, or detouring or cross-generational coalitions involving a trauma survivor.

A second common approach for utilizing family treatment appears to be combining a family model, such as structural family therapy or narrative therapy, with one of the procedures barrowed from an individual model, such as cognitive processing therapy or EMDR. Krerig and Alexander (2012) and J. Alexander, Waldron, Robbins, and Neeb (2013) paired functional family therapy concepts and procedures with concepts and procedures from trauma-focused cognitive behavioral therapy such as affect regulation and cognitive processing. K. James and MacKinnon (2012), combined the use of genograms and trauma timelines as assessment tools for working with traumatized clients and their families. Bardin (2004) combines structural family therapy techniques to address family issues related to trauma with EMDR to focus on symptoms experienced by the traumatized family member. Coulter (2011) outlines how Walsh's (2007) key family processes, such as resilience and collaboration, and a strengths-based approach can be used to organize family therapy for traumatized clients.

By limiting the approach to a combination of one family therapy school with a few intervention procedures borrowed from one of the individual trauma approaches, none of the previously listed family approaches offer the flexibility required to engage and keep engaged a wide range of trauma clients and their families.

What is missing is a coherent family systems model that utilizes key theories and elements of the major family therapy approaches and fully integrates these elements with the numerous treatment procedures employed by the various individual trauma treatments. There is nothing offered that integrates under one theoretical umbrella individual and family treatment for trauma. In short, there is no trauma treatment that is strictly a family therapy–only approach.

CROSS-CULTURAL COMPETENCE AND TRAUMA

Most trauma treatment models are based on Western concepts (Alford, 2016; Summerfield, 1999). Western mental health introduces core concepts of Western culture including a theory of human nature, a definition of personhood, a concept of time and memory and a religious source of moral authority. None of these concepts are universal (Alford, 2016; Summerfield, 2005). The cross-cultural challenge is to find an appropriate balance between Western and non-Western conceptualizations of trauma and its consequences. Cross-cultural perspectives on trauma provide a richness and complexity that must be respected and understood (Stamm & Friedman, 2000).

Numerous authors have pointed out the importance of culturally competent trauma treatment (De Silva, 2006; Schnyder, 2016; Shah, 2007; Stamm, & Friedman, 2000). Some argue that cultural sensitivity is *required* to successfully treat trauma survivors (Schnyder et al., 2015). Key concepts of various trauma treatments, however, may not be culturally universal. Trauma-related disorders, treatments, and meanings of traumatic events may vary cross-culturally (Shah, 2006). Empirically supported Western treatments may need to be modified or abandoned to fit with the client's cultural background. To address cross cultural competence, Western traumatologists have suggested that clients may need to write, paint, dance or sing, or use other ways of accessing traumatic memories (Schnyder et al., 2015).

Cultural competence in the United States has focused on adjusting practitioner behavior and attitudes to engage diverse groups in treatment. Practitioners are given skills to enhance their ability to persuade clients from diverse ethnic backgrounds to cooperate in Western treatments. Literature addressing cultural competence make the ethnocentric mistake of believing that trauma survivors must understand their Western treatment options (Shah, 2007). The previously noted approach to cultural competence from Schnyder et al. (2015) is an example. The treatment approach assumes traumatic memories must be "accessed," a Western trauma treatment concept. The treatments themselves are based on Western views of trauma. According to Shah (2007), "cultural competency involves a translation of knowledge, attitudes, and behaviors that allow Western trauma practitioners to deliver Western treatments" (p. 58). Ethnically indigenous beliefs and treatments are not explored or utilized (Shah, 2007).

Western responses to international disasters have been criticized for offering Western trauma treatments without regard to healing practices of the cultures in which they are intervening (De Silva, 2006; Shah, 2007). The balance between Western trauma treatments and cross-cultural healing practices for trauma is uneven (Stamm & Friedman, 2000). Despite their demonstrated efficacy, Western trauma treatments rarely utilize indigenous treatments when responding cross-culturally to trauma (Shah, 2007). In the South Pacific, for example, community drumming and dancing are one response to disasters, which, although effective, were ignored by Western responses to disaster relief (A. J. W. Taylor, 2000). Other treatments indigenous to Southeast Asia such as therapeutic yoga, meditation, pranayama (breath work), spiritualism, and shamanism were largely ignored in the Western effort to respond to trauma after the Sri Lanka tidal wave (DeSilva, 2006; Shah, 2006).

Resistance and protests result when indigenous healing practices are ignored, and native beliefs are not taken seriously (Shah, 2006). On a broader scale, this idea can be applied to all families seeking help on trauma. The family belief system must be identified, respected, and engaged in the healing process. If family beliefs are ignored, engagement in treatment can be seriously compromised. The meta-analyses of western trauma treatments cited in Chapter 2 of this volume note that clients not accepting the treatment rationales of these approaches partially accounts for the high dropout rates reported in the studies.

Ethnomedicine is the study of culturally embedded beliefs and practices for health care (R. Lee, 2001; Nichter, 1991). Ethnomedical competence requires a capacity to discern, utilize, and preserve culturally embedded healing practices. Ethnomedically competent treatment modalities mix Western and non-Western treatments into best practice models for any given ethnic group.

An example of a family utilizing ethnic healing practices and not accessing mental health trauma treatment can be found in Chapter 11 of this volume. A teenage boy who lived in a very violent neighborhood witnessed a killing at a neighborhood basketball court. One boy stabbed and killed another over a dispute in a basketball game. The boy who witnessed the killing had nightmares, unwanted thoughts, and anxiety after the event. After he had grown up, his mother asked him if he continued to have nightmares concerning the traumatic event. He said he did not. He told his mother that family prayer helped him over the nightmares. The family was African

American and very devoutly Christian. They practiced what the mother described as daily "meditative prayer" as a family. This was a family activity that accessed the healing practices and beliefs of this boy's ethnic group. He attributes the nightmares going away to this specific activity. No professional mental health services or trauma treatment were ever sought.

How much of what we think we know about trauma only applies to the West?

- What is considered to be a traumatic event?
- What meaning is attached to these events?
- What symptoms are expressed?
- What are the neurobiological consequences of untreated or unresolved symptoms?
- What is defined as a supportive family response?
- What treatment options should be offered?

We believe none of the listed items may be culturally universal. In 2006, DeSilva reported that none of the previously cited questions had been systematically researched among multiple ethnic groups and cultures. We believe that continues to be the case.

Culturally competent trauma treatment, first and foremost, requires clinicians to be willing to understand, respect, and integrate different beliefs and values into an appropriate, ethnosensitive treatment regardless of their connection to Western trauma theories and interventions (Stamm & Friedman, 2000).

To be mindful of Western biases and flexibly adapt treatments to culturally diverse clients, trauma treatment providers must first let go of rigid adherences to Western trauma concepts and theories. Trauma treatments must be respectful of client goals. Treatment providers must be skilled at tracking and utilizing client belief systems and integrating these with indigenous healing practices. Yet, be truly integrative, structured, ethnomedically competent treatments must offer a larger organizing treatment framework that can accommodate diverse beliefs and healing practices into a well-defined treatment model.

SUMMARY

The following list represents a summary of what is missing and what is needed in the current array of trauma treatments to provide a clearly defined integrative, organized family systems approach for trauma:

- Able to assess on a larger family systems level (minimum of three persons) the impact of trauma on the family and the impact of family on trauma
- Equipped to intervene on a larger family level
- Flexible enough to offer a wide range of treatment choices to easily accommodate a wide range of requests from difficult-to-engage clients
- Able to simultaneously address both child and intergenerationally traumatized adult symptoms
- Can integrate the full range of trauma intervention procedures into an organized family systems framework
- Is culturally sensitive and can integrate a wide range of cultural beliefs and culturally diverse healing practices into an organized treatment framework

I-FAST TREATMENT FOR TRAUMA

II

5 OVERVIEW OF INTEGRATIVE FAMILY AND SYSTEMS TREATMENT (I-FAST)

Integrated family and systems treatment (I-FAST) is an evidence-supported family treatment model that can be applied to outpatient, case management, and intensive in-home services (Fraser, Grove, Lee, Greene, & Solovey, 2013; Fraser, Solovey, Grove, Lee & Greene, 2012). As a treatment model, I-FAST is organized around common factors that are present in all the evidence-based family treatment models. The efficacy of I-FAST has been researched in three different studies involving eight different clinical sites in both rural and urban areas (M. Y. Lee et al., 2009, 2012, 2016; M. Y. Lee, Greene, Fraser, Edwards et al., 2013). Data are being gathered from three additional sites representing a fourth and a fifth major study. I-FAST can also be applied to adults with mental health symptoms. A current study using I-FAST with adults is being conducted in Hong Kong, China. This study may be able to establish the cross-cultural efficacy of I-FAST for addressing adult mental health problems.

The purpose of I-FAST is to provide integrated family treatment to children and adolescents who exhibit a wide range of symptoms and diagnoses as defined by the *Diagnostic and Statistical Manual of Mental Disorders* (American Psychiatric Association, 2013). As an integrative model, I-FAST allows for the incorporation of treatment procedures from any treatment model into the overall I-FAST framework. The integrative aspect of I-FAST allows for maximum flexibility and a treatment that can match and adapt to a wide range of client beliefs and types of symptoms. A unique treatment is organized for each case while adhering to the I-FAST treatment protocols. I-FAST is an episode of care model. Treatment focuses on specific symptoms and problems that families identify as their main concerns. Treatment is administered in episodes, which end when goals are met and can be resumed if problems reoccur.

THEORETICAL AND RESEARCH FOUNDATION

Common Factors Research

I-FAST is organized around common factors research that seeks to identify trends in successful therapy as well as identify what treatment activities have the largest impact on successful outcomes (Frank, 1961; M. J. Lambert, 1992; Wampold, 2010, 2019; Wampold & Imel, 2015). Common factor research has also identified factors relating to and remedies for reducing high drop-out rates associated with specific factor manualized treatments (Benish, Imel, & Wampold, 2008). Common factors utilized in I-FAST include the following:

- **Alliances and common goals.** Establishment and maintenance of therapeutic alliances has the greatest impact on the effectiveness of treatment. A therapeutic alliance is defined by the establishment of positive therapeutic bonds plus an agreement on therapy goals and tasks for achieving the goals. To maintain an alliance, the treatment must focus on what the client is motivated to focus on.
- **Overarching treatment frames.** An overarching treatment frame is offered that explains the client's problem and associated treatment procedures for remedying the problem.
- **Dropouts.** To avoid high drop-out rates, clients must accept the treatment approach's overarching frame and accompanying treatment procedures. When clients do not accept the treatment approach's overarching frame and/or treatment procedures, clinicians are advised to be flexible and adapt a new frames and procedures that the client will accept.
- **Common factors and flexibility.** Common factor research identifies treatment flexibility as the key to engaging and keeping clients engaged until the end of treatment. For maximum engagement, the treatment should adapt to the client, not the client adapt to the treatment. This is especially important related to trauma treatment. I-FAST is a coherent metamodel designed to offer maximum flexibility. In I-FAST, a unique treatment approach is designed for each family, while staying within treatment parameters that define a clear approach. In this way, a treatment can be devised specially to match a given client's and family's beliefs and motivations.
- **Client feedback–informed treatment**. Common factor researchers are reporting that treatment outcomes are enhanced when feedback is sought from clients on their progress and what they find helpful. Treatment is then adjusted to accommodate this feedback (Wampold & Imel, 2015, 2019).

THEORY BASE

Systems Theory, Constructivism, and Flexibility

I-FAST is based on systems theory and constructivism. As noted in Chapter 4 of this volume, systems theory and constructivism provide theoretical support for maximum flexibility in devising a treatment approach. Regarding trauma treatment, client preferences can be respected. Even if trauma symptoms are not selected as a focus, they can still be resolved by resolving the problems the client is motivated to focus on. Constructivism allows for the overarching treatment frames that organize treatment to be adjusted to fit any given client. Procedures can be selected based on what any given client is willing to cooperate with. Systems theory and constructivism allow for a treatment approach that can match what each client and family are motivated to work on, what treatment ideas make sense to them, and what procedures they are willing to undergo.

Strength-Based Philosophy

One last organizing principle of I-FAST is use of a strengths-based philosophy. A strengths-based approach not only views clients and family as capable of change but also offers major principals that inform and organize treatment. First is the notion that the client's judgment can be trusted. In I-FAST, what the client thinks the focus of treatment should be, what ideas make sense to the client, and what treatment procedures the client thinks might help are respected and incorporated into treatment. Collaboration between the client and the I-FAST practitioner is maximized by trusting the client's judgment as much as possible.

Utilization

In strengths-based approaches, treatment is organized around the utilization of what the client *can* do. I-FAST treatment decisions are informed as much as possible by utilizing what the client brings to treatment. Utilization is also applied to client responses to interventions. In I-FAST, practitioners track, adjust to and utilize how clients are responding to interventions such as reframing or use of tasks. Adapting to how clients are responding to treatment interventions results in a therapy that is constantly matching the client. The principal of tracking and utilizing how clients respond to interventions intensifies the flexibility of I-FAST practitioners.

OVERVIEW OF TREATMENT PROCESS

I-FAST Treatment Stages

Although I-FAST is not strongly prescriptive, a given I-FAST case can be expected to unfold in a manner that may approximate the following stages:

1. Beginning Treatment: Family Assessment
   - Collaborate with colleagues
   - Form alliances
   - Track client frames (ideas and beliefs)
   - Identify specific problems and goals
   - Track interactional patterns and exceptions
   - Decide who to include in treatment
2. Middle Treatment: Devise and Implement Interventions
   - Devise and offer frames that make sense to the family
   - Offer questions, frames, and tasks to change patterns and resolve problems
3. End Treatment: Following Up/Consolidating/Terminating
   - Follow-up on interventions/track changes
   - Help family take credit for changes
   - Help family adjust to changes
   - Terminate

ASSESSMENT

General Considerations: Assessment is Ongoing

There is no boundary between assessment and intervention. In I-FAST, assessment informs intervention and intervention informs assessment. Both are continuous.

Keep Questions Focused on the Clients' Primary Concerns

How information is obtained is perhaps as important as the information itself. In a collaborative assessment process, clinicians are invited to ask any question that is obviously related to the problem the family wants help on. Asking questions outside of this category can invite suspicion and runs the risk of appearing to be more like an investigation than a therapy interview.

How Families Respond to Interventions Intensifies Assessment

A principle skill in I-FAST is tracking and utilizing how clients and families respond to interventions. How a family responds to any intervention further informs the I-FAST clinician about family patterns, exceptions, and frames. In I-FAST, these family responses are utilized and incorporated into treatment. In this way, every I-FAST therapy is organically adjusting to and adapting to the family. Tracking, utilizing, and adapting treatment to how clients respond to ideas and interventions offered is one major way that I-FAST utilizes feedback from clients.

Frames Versus Facts

When receiving information, I-FAST clinicians must distinguish between frames and facts. A divorced mother may say their children's father is not involved. If taken as a fact, deeper inquiry into the father's role may not occur and the father's participation in patterns may not be understood. Deeper inquiry may reveal that the father communicates with one of the children in the family via social media. The information that he is "not involved" is the mother's frame, not what is actually happening. Understanding the mother's frame is important. We are not suggesting that her view be challenged. However, the clinician must recognize they are being given a frame; they are not tracking an interactional pattern.

Treatment Decisions

To achieve maximum flexibility, in I-FAST major treatment decisions are not prescribed but are made for each case:

- Whom to include in treatment
- What frame to use to organize treatment
- What goals to work on
- What intervention procedures to offer

What to Assess

When designing a treatment for each case, I-FAST clinicians assess and track the following information to adapt treatment to a particular client and family:

- Family motivations: What they are upset about and motivated to focus on
- Interactional patterns that perpetuate the problem
- Life cycle (developmental) stages
- Family frames (beliefs) about the problem and about treatment
- Exceptions: What is done if or when the problem is successfully dealt with
- Family strengths and coping strategies

I-FAST TREATMENT PROCESS

Collaborate With Professionals

In I-FAST, other professionals on a case are part of the unit of analysis and part of the intervention process. This is especially important regarding professionals who have power such as probation officers or child protective case workers. These professionals have power to place children out of a home or reunify children with their families. Medical doctors are also professionals who can have major influence on a case. Medical doctors can medicate or withdraw medications. Medical doctors can also have a major impact on how problems are being framed, and on what to do about a given problem. In I-FAST, working alliances must be established with any or all of these professionals. Most important, agreements must be reached in the following areas:

Goals and Methods

Agreements on treatment goals and the larger treatment method must be reached. Regarding goals, a consensus must be reached that accommodates what goals both the family and powerful professionals want. Treatment methods must also be agreed to. "Treatment method" is defined in a broad sense. Will treatment be delivered with the client in their natural environment or in foster care? Will the client be seen individually or with their family?

All professionals that have power to remove children from their family or have influence on how problems are defined must reach the previously noted agreements. Ideally, these agreements can be obtained at the beginning of a given case. Often, however, for one reason or another, these agreements are not obtained until later. Whether these agreements can be obtained at the beginning, middle, or end of a case, they often must be obtained for the case to end successfully.

Additional Services and Placement Decisions

Agreements also must be obtained regarding additional mental health services and placement of children. Will an individual trauma focused therapist for a child client be added to a case when the I-FAST clinician is working primarily with the family? Will a marriage therapist be added when it becomes clear that marital problems are seriously affecting parenting of a traumatized child? Will a parent who is seriously impaired by their own trauma history be referred to their own therapist? In I-FAST, these decisions must be made collaboratively, not unilaterally. Other professionals on a given case must agree to not unilaterally refer any family member for additional services without collaborating with the I-FAST clinician. Decisions regarding placing a child out of the family or reunifying a child with the family must also be made collaboratively.

ALLIANCES

For children and adolescents in treatment, evidence shows engagement in treatment and treatment outcomes are most dependent on forming an alliance with the client's parents or caregivers. This does not mean alliances with the client are not also important. It also does not necessarily mean parents participate in all therapy sessions. At a minimum, the key adults must agree with the treatment goals, the treatment rationales and the treatment procedures. In I-FAST, alliances with parents are enhanced in a number of ways, which we discuss next.

Focus on Goals the Caregiver Is Motivated to Work On

Treatment goals will be addressed separately; however, it is important to note that engagement in treatment is greatly enhanced by selecting treatment goals that make sense to the parents. Clinicians can propose treatment goals that differ from what a parent initially wants help on, but ultimately the parent must be truly persuaded to focus on whatever goals are selected for treatment. Without such an agreement, parent and client engagement can be seriously compromised.

Track and Utilize Client Frames

Frames organize our perceptions of reality. Gregory Bateson first introduced the use of frames to the social sciences in 1955 (Bateson, 1955/1972). In 1974, Irving Goffman provided a major expansion of Bateson work on frames. From an I-FAST perspective, client and family beliefs about traumatic experiences and the associated meanings involve how the event is ***framed***. Frames represent the client's and the family's assumptions and their frames of reference for how they define, relate to, and negotiate specifics in their lives. Framing is a process for how focus is narrowed. A frame tells us what to pay attention to and what to ignore and the meaning of what we do pay attention to.

From a constructivist perspective, frames come from social narratives. Frames are constructed *socially*, not independently from the survivor's social field. Understanding and assessing frames regarding trauma, therefore, must attend to the survivor's social field. That would primarily consist of the larger culture and ethnic group the survivor identifies with, their community, the family they belong to, and, if professionals or authorities become involved, how this group frames the survivor, their behavior, and their family members.

Two types of frames central to treatment are *overarching treatment frames* and *task frames*. Overarching treatment frames offer an explanation of the problem and organize treatment procedures for addressing the problem. Task frames are frames that therapists can offered to set up and provide rationales for the tasks given to the family. The task frame is meant to help the task make sense to the family. I-FAST practitioners track client and family frames and utilize them with both types of frames as one way to engage client and family. How the family views the client (e.g., traumatized, defiant, damaged), how the family frames the problem (e.g., involuntary behavior, learned behavior), how the family frames the solution of the problem (e.g., the client must be punished, the client must be seen alone and psychoanalyzed, the client must be sent away) are all tracked and utilized if possible.

In I-FAST, overarching treatment frames and task frames are constructed for each case utilizing existing family beliefs. Treatment is organized around ideas that make sense to the parents. This is a powerful tool for enhancing alliances. Our own belief and overarching frame is that healing is more likely to occur if the family belief system is engaged and utilized in treatment.

Organizing treatment around family frames is one way I-FAST is culturally sensitive. Diversity of beliefs regarding why symptoms occur and what should be done to help are incorporated and utilized in I-FAST. This offers major advantages in engaging and maintaining engagement of clients from a wide range of ethnic backgrounds. Any family is most likely to cooperate with what makes sense to them. Identifying and utilizing what this is for each family is a major skill and treatment technique in I-FAST.

Use of Compliments

The skillful use of compliments is a technique embraced in I-FAST to enhance alliances and engagement. I-FAST clinicians must learn about the family background, values, what they are proud of, and efforts to help so that sincere and genuine compliments can be offered to the family. This is especially important for families that have had chronic involvement in social service systems. Typically, families, especially parents, have often felt mistreated by social service agencies. For these families, it is out of the box to be sincerely complimented by a social service professional. In this context, compliments stand out and can greatly enhance alliances.

Emphasize Collaboration

Trusting the client's judgment and truly collaborating with the family may also be out of the typical experience for many families involved with social service agencies. For I-FAST, collaboration means trusting the families' judgment as much as possible on issues such as what problem should be focused on, what ideas make the most sense to organize treatment, around and what treatment procedures might best help.

Impaired and/or Traumatized Parents

By emphasizing collaboration and respecting parent treatment preferences, therapists can motivate parents who suffer from trauma histories or other mental health problems and are not seeking help for themselves to be engaged in I-FAST treatment for their child. As will be seen in cases presented in this book, this has resulted in gaining the trust of these parents, who then may also allow for help with their own problems. Sometimes parents are helped to overcome their own symptoms in the process of helping their child. In other cases, when parents permit, the treatment can end up focusing more directly on the parent's problems. In either case, in I-FAST, parents are generally not referred out to services for themselves, especially after trust and rapport has been established.

TREATMENT GOALS

In I-FAST, specific goals are identified that represent what the caregivers are motivated to focus on. I-FAST treatment goals aim to

- **Frame problems and goals in an interactional context.** Problems and goals must be framed and understood as part of an interactional context and that improvements will most likely occur by producing change on an interactional level.
- **Establish a clear focus, maintained across sessions.** Whatever problems and goals are selected the treatment must have a clear focus. This means defining problems and goals behaviorally and keeping the family focused on identified goals across sessions. Treatment cannot focus on one goal one session and another goal the next session, with no resolution of the first goal.

When several family members are in treatment simultaneously with multiple providers, even if each treatment is focused on a clear goal, the family as a whole is simultaneously pursuing multiple goals. This is not a clear focus.

- **Goals are defined as something family members can do something about themselves.** Problems and goals must be defined as something the family can change themselves. A family cannot help a "bipolar" child. On the other hand, a family can help a child regulate their emotions and learn to control temper tantrums.
- **Whenever possible, accomplish goals with the client remaining in their natural environment.** A client may learn to regulate their emotions in residential treatment, but this does not mean they can do so once placed back with their family. A child may change outside of their home, and the family may or may not change their patterns related to their child. Ultimately, family patterns associated with the problems must change. The most expedient way of accomplishing this is for treatment to occur with the child and family in their natural environment. When safety issues preclude this, including family in the treatment wherever the child is, is the preferred option.
- **Obtain goal consensus among family members and professionals sharing the case.** All parties must reach agreements on goals. This may require negotiating, making deals and asking other professionals to trust the judgment of the treatment provider.

INTERACTIONAL UNDERSTANDING

In I-FAST, problems and solutions are understood within an interactional context. Bateson (1979) defined context as "patterns through time" (p. 14). An individual's problems and solutions are embedded within the larger context of relational patterns in the family and often with the larger community as well. In I-FAST we focus on working with families to make changes in interactional patterns—the focus is on ***pattern change***. Symptoms are viewed as the client's side of repeating interactional patterns between and among the client and family members and often community systems involved with them such as schools, courts, children's services, and so on. Individuals and families can become stuck in interactional patterns that represent their attempts to solve problems. They try making changes by doing more of the same of what did not work previously. They are trying to make changes according to their existing assumptions, so it seems logical to them to do more of the same; this is referred to as ***first-order change*** (Watzlawick, Weakland, & Fisch, 1974).

However, what is required is something novel, outside the box of their assumptive categories. They must change how they are classifying the problem and/or its solution. Because the solution requires something novel, it may seem illogical to the family. To make changes, the therapist and family must co-construct an intervention that will disrupt the interactional patterns supporting the problems or identify interactional exceptions to those patterns that have worked in the past. Watzlawick et al. (1974) refer to this as ***second-order change***. When symptoms are resolved, the solution is viewed as the client and key family members exhibiting exceptions from the interactional patterns that support the symptoms. In I-FAST, clinicians must learn to track both interactional patterns and interactional exceptions.

Larger Family Patterns

I-FAST recommends a triadic unit of analysis. A three-person unit allows for an organization with a hierarchy and coalitions among members. This model allows for a family assessment that includes all the aspects of family patterns noted in Chapter 3 of this volume that regulate secure attachments. A triadic analysis of families has been used by several traditional family therapy approaches to describe numerous aspects of how families are organized (Bowen, 1985; Haley, 1978; McGoldrick, Gerson, & Petry, 2008; Minuchin, 1974; Zuk, 1981). Habitual strong or weak boundaries between family members, coalitions, hierarchy, and how conflict is managed define how a given family functions. These larger family patterns have a profound influence on how a given family will respond to a traumatized family member and the interactional patterns that can develop that support the trauma symptoms. Changing these interactional patterns, therefore, can simultaneously change how the whole family is organized. A full understanding and appreciation of interactional patterns that support symptoms is enhanced by having an understanding of larger family patterns, not just of how one family member is interacting with the identified client.

Terms

When describing family patterns in our case presentations we may use terms such as "enmeshed," "weak boundary," "disengaged," "strong boundary," and so on. We view these terms as descriptors of patterns with no positive or negative connotation. An enmeshed relationship can be a positive relational attribute at times when support is needed. A disengaged relationship can be a positive relational attribute at times when autonomy is needed. From our view, these types of relationships are not inherently bad or unhealthy. They only can become a problem if they interfere with the resolution of or exacerbate a problem.

Interactional Patterns that Reinforce the Problems

A detailed understanding of how each participant habitually interacts with each other regarding symptoms targeted for treatment must be obtained. This has been referred to as sequence of interaction (Haley, 1987), attempted solutions, or problem-maintaining behavior (Watzlawick et al., 1974; Fisch et al., 1981). When tracking interactions, I-FAST clinicians must understand that all behavior sends a message. All behavior is interactional. One cannot not interact (Watzlawick et al., 1967). Family members who appear to be nonparticipants are sending a message by not participating.

In many families, when one family member is exhibiting a problem, there will typically be three important participants: The *client,* a *frontline person* who is chronically and intensively involved with the client, and a *background person(s)* who is much less involved with the client, but more involved with the frontline person. When assessing interactional patterns that reinforce problems, we encourage clinicians to identify all three.

Interactional Exceptions

Several family therapy approaches emphasize assessing what is being done differently when problems are absent or decreased in severity (de Shazier, 1985, 1988, 1991; White & Epston, 1990). When change occurs, interactional exceptions have contributed to them. When families deviate from either their habitual interactional patterns or their beliefs about what the problem is or how to deal with it, often they will "spontaneously" produce new behaviors and new beliefs; exceptions are produced. I-FAST clinicians are encouraged to track to a three-person level what those exceptions are. What did the client do differently, what did the frontline person do differently, and what did the background person do differently? A clear understanding of the interactional patterns that support the symptoms can greatly enhance the I-FAST clinician's ability to identify and offer exceptions to the client and family.

Exceptions are tracked

- at all stages of treatment, including the first session;
- when the clinician observes improvement or pattern change;
- when a client reports improvement; and
- as a follow-up to interventions offered in a previous session.

Exceptions are tracked to reinforce and enlarge improvements and to facilitate the client and family acknowledging and taking *ownership* of those improvements.

Family Life Cycle and Family Transition Informed Treatment

I-FAST clinicians are encouraged to understand how to use family life cycle transitions to define problems interactionally, identify goals that are congruent with developmental stages and to promote pattern change (Carter & McGoldrick, 1989; Haley, 1973). The life cycle defines what is normative. For any ethnic group, the family life cycle defines what is normal for that family at the given stage of the life cycle. Families can become organized around symptoms in ways that interfere with what should be happening within the families' current life cycle stages. Understanding what should be happening instead can help define goals that make sense to the family.

Problems can occur at transition stages of the life cycle. The theory that symptoms can begin or be exacerbated at transition stages of the life cycle has been noted (Carter & McGoldrick, 1989; Haley, 1973). Families may have difficulty adjusting to the changes required by a given life cycle stage. Difficulty adjusting to a change, such as divorce, remarriage, or an older sibling emancipating, can be offered as a potential contributor of a given problem. This places the problem in an interactional frame. Goals can then be identified that resolve the adjustment difficulties associated with the life cycle transition.

For example, consider a depressed girl who lived with her mother and stepfather. She was very close to her father who had recently moved far away. When both parents lived close to each other, the mother acted as the disciplinarian and the father as the girl's emotional support. The family framed the father as more like a mother than a father. When he moved, the girl lost this support. In her home, both stepfather and mother were very structured and strict. The family frame that the biological father was like a mother, was utilized, and the problem was framed as the girl struggling to adjust to her father's move. She no longer had a "mother," only two "fathers." This frame defined the problem as difficulty adjusting to a family transition and placed it in an interactional context, as opposed to a medical frame such as "depression." It also defined the problem as something the family could do something about. It suggested the goal should be for the mother to change her role as disciplinarian to one offering more emotional support. The mother accepted the frames and the goal and became more supportive to the daughter; her depressed symptoms greatly improved.

DECIDING WHOM TO INCLUDE IN TREATMENT

In I-FAST, which family members participate in treatment is decided on each case. The decision regarding who should attend treatment is viewed as an intervention in and of itself. I-FAST practitioners are expected to be skilled at working with individuals, couples, one parent and one child, and whole families and have a rationale for when to do which. I-FAST practitioners are also expected to be skilled at recruiting family members who do not initially participate.

Guidelines are offered within I-FAST to aid the decision process for who to include. These guidelines include the following:

- What pattern is targeted for change, and whose participation will promote pattern change? Who is invited to participate in treatment can either change or reinforce a pattern. In a case of a daughter who was sexually assaulted and reluctant to speak to her mother about the assault, this pattern is reinforced if she is seen individually. On the other hand, including the mother in treatment is a first step at changing this pattern.
- Who is most upset about the problem and most motivated to change? Whoever this is, is already in the action stage of change and will most likely cooperate with changing their side of the patterns targeted for change.
- Who should be added/removed when a treatment is at an impasse? Family members can be added to interviews or subtracted from interviews. When a treatment is stuck, changing who is coming can often break the impasse.

INTERVENTION PROCEDURES AND GENERAL CONSIDERATIONS

All Interaction Is Intervention

Clients and families can change at any point of the treatment process, including while on a waiting list. Clients can change as a result of developing an alliance with a clinician, when a clinician is offering psychoeducation, or when a clinician is offering intervention procedures. Change can happen and go unnoticed by a clinician who is following prescribed treatment steps. When this happens, the clinician losses opportunities to reinforce and amplify changes that have already occurred. A strict adherence to treatment steps can render a clinician inflexible and unable to adjust when clients change before treatment steps intended to promote change are offered. In I-FAST, change is tracked throughout the treatment process and reinforced when it occurs. When improvement does occur, treatment stages and steps are adjusted to accommodate and promote change.

Intervene in the Least Restrictive Way

I-FAST promotes least restrictive intervention methods. If symptoms can be brought under control without medications, then the use of medications is not encouraged. If clients can change in their natural environment, out-of-home placement is not encouraged. If a client is in foster care, preventing residential placement is a priority. When more restrictive interventions have already been applied, helping families step down to a less restrictive setting or function with less restrictive interventions becomes a goal. For example, if a child is already heavily medicated to help them regulate their emotions, the parents are encouraged to learn behavioral methods to help their child regulate emotions so medications can be reduced or discontinued.

Match Client Readiness for Change

When clients are not overtly requesting help on a problem, advice regarding what to do about that problem is not offered. On the other hand, when clients are desperate for help on a problem, advice on what to do is not withheld. I-FAST treatment is sensitive to and adjusted to where families are in the change process. We want to keep the focus on the clients' goals or, in other words, what the clients are customers for.

Interventions as Experiments Versus Assignments

Interventions are not offered as assignments in I-FAST. A family may be given a between session task, for example, but they are not expected to do it. In I-FAST, what is important is how the family responds to being given the task. Do they try it, does it inspire them to try something new instead, or do they reject it altogether? In I-FAST, however, a family might respond to an intervention is just information that further informs the clinician how to work with the family. It is feedback from the client to the I-FAST clinician on how to help. Interventions are experiments, not assignments. This keeps the family in a respected position in which their responses are what is most important, not the clinician's intervention.

I-FAST TREATMENT PROCEDURES: FRAMES, TASKS, AND QUESTIONS

Entire classes of interventions from any treatment approach or any ethnic healing practice can be integrated and offered in I-FAST when

- the intervention has an obvious connection to what the family desires help on (what are they customers for).
- the intervention promotes change in the interactional patterns that support the symptoms targeted for treatment.
- the parent(s) or caregiver(s) are put in a central position to delivering the intervention.
- the interventions result in changes that empower parents or caregivers and put them in a position to help their child.

In this way, I-FAST can integrate intervention procedures from any and all approaches specific to trauma. Exposure therapy procedures can be offered in I-FAST, for example, if avoidant symptoms of the child are identified as a treatment focus, the parent is put in charge of exposing the child to the avoided stimuli and asking the parent to do so changes interactional patterns. Healing practices from diverse ethnic backgrounds can also be integrated into I-FAST in the same manner.

Framing and Reframing

Treatment frames from trauma approaches such as fear networks can be offered within I-FAST when the client and family buy into (i.e., accept) them. However, I-FAST clinicians are encouraged to utilize family frames in the construction of rationales that organize and guide treatment. Any given I-FAST treatment can have unique frames co-constructed with the family. Tracking and utilizing family frames and beliefs allows I-FAST to be culturally sensitive. Beliefs from diverse ethnic backgrounds can be utilized to organize treatment in I-FAST.

In I-FAST, family frames are tracked, with some *accepted and utilized,* some *ignored,* and some *reframed.* Once family frames are understood, some are preserved and utilized to promote collaboration and family engagement in treatment and to construct overarching treatment frames. As treatment progresses, reframing may be used as an intervention procedure to change

- how a family classifies why the problem is happening;
- how family members view the client; and/or
- what must be done to help resolve the problem.

A family may view a traumatized client as defiant, for example. Perhaps they are unaware of the trauma the child experienced. Helping the family reframe the child from being defiant to being traumatized is a major intervention that requires the family to also change how they are trying to help their child. Successful reframing can simultaneously promote interactional pattern change.

I-FAST treatment promotes family frames or clinician reframes that

- define clients and family members in a positive way;
- define clients and family as capable and changeable;
- promote harmony among family;
- stress areas of agreement;
- define problems as solvable and goals as achievable;
- promote goals that produce a clear focus of treatment;
- define problems and goals interactionally;
- promote interactional pattern change;
- promote normal activities; and
- define problems and goals as something the client and family can do something about themselves

I-FAST treatment ignores or reframes family frames that

- define clients and family negatively;
- define clients and family as fixed and incapable of changing;
- define problems as unsolvable;
- are blaming;
- promote disharmony;
- promote disagreement;
- define problems and goals as something that requires long-term professional involvement; and
- require the client to be defined as abnormal

Use of Tasks

Directly requesting families to deviate from their patterns can be used in multiple ways as *between-session* or *in-session tasks* in I-FAST. Tasks can be offered to families to be done between sessions and borrowed from any approach that uses *between-session tasks*, when the purpose of the task is to change interactions. Between-session tasks have been referred to as "directives," or "homework" in other treatment approaches. *In-session tasks* may also be utilized in I-FAST. These include enactments (Minuchin & Fishman, 1981), coaching parents how to interact with children (Cohen et al., 2017; Epstein et al., 2017; McNeil, Hembree-Kigin, & Anhalt, 2011), play therapy that directs a parent and child to play together in the session (Gil, 2016; Lieberman, 2008), and so on to change interactional patterns in the session.

Tasks can be direct, paradoxical (Haley, 1987), or solution-focused (de Shazier, 1985, 1988, 1991). The main purpose of tasks in I-FAST is to promote deviations from the patterns supporting the problems families are requesting help on. When offering tasks in I-FAST, it is not important if the family does the task. Tasks are meant to inspire families to change their patterns. Whatever they do in response to a task is tracked and supported if it results in pattern change.

All in- or between-session tasks given must be preceded by a *frame* that provides a rationale for the task that makes sense to the family. In-session tasks typically reveal patterns and/or create discussions that further reveal family frames. I-FAST therapists must adjust to any new information regarding either patterns or frames. In-session tasks can be asked to be repeated as a between-session task. All between-session tasks must be followed up on in the next session. Whether the family did the task or not, details regarding whatever they did do must be tracked. If positive change occurs, whether due to the task given or due to a deviation the family initiated on their own, the changes must be consolidated using the questions outlined in the "consolidating change" section to follow.

Use of Questions

The use of questions as an intervention procedure is utilized in several major treatment approaches. In CBT, solution-focused therapy, and narrative therapy, questions are not just used to obtain information. They are used as interventions intended to promote change. Questions as interventions can be used in I-FAST in two major ways: as constructive interventions and as directive interventions.

QUESTIONS AS CONSTRUCTIVE

Questions as an interventions can be used as a tool to construct new frames. The presupposition of any question can challenge a family frame. If the family accepts the presupposition of the question, they have accepted the new frame imbedded in that question. For example, "Are you a good witch or a bad witch?" If the family picks either choice, they are accepting the frame of being a witch.

QUESTIONS AS DIRECTIVE

Questions can also be offered as an indirect way to promote pattern change by the family. Questions that identify or reinforce exceptions are indirectly suggesting that families continue to do the exceptions. Implied in the question is the directive to continue the behavior.

CONSOLIDATING CHANGE

Tracking, Consolidating, and Reinforcing Change

As previously stated, change can occur at any point in a treatment process. In I-FAST change is tracked and amplified whenever it occurs. A given treatment is then adjusted to accommodate changes whenever they occur.

Family, Client, and Professionals Notice Change

When change does occur, the first step is for it to be noticed. Does the clinician notice? Does the client notice? Do family members notice? Do other important professionals involved in the case notice? When change happens, the first task is to make sure important parties notice and agree change is happening. A client may improve, but the parents may not think so. A family may improve, but a probation officer may not think so. When changes begin, a major task is to make sure important parties notice and agree change is happening.

Family Takes Ownership of Change

Change can occur, but a client or a family or another professional may not give credit to the family or client. The ultimate outcome for I-FAST treatment is for change to occur and for the client and family to understand what they each did that produced change. The client and family must take ownership of change. Other professionals must see that the client and family did something themselves that produced the improvements. When this happens, cases can be terminated. When change happens but the client or family does not take ownership or other professionals are not giving credit to the family, negative outcomes such as relapses or out-of-home placements can still occur.

Exception Questions

When I-FAST clinicians notice change, the following types of solution-focused and narrative therapy questions are used to promote and amplify change and to encourage families to take ownership of change.

- What did you do differently?
- How did you do that?
- How did you decide to do that?
- Do others agree change has occurred?

The use of these questions promotes discussions that result in noticing and reinforcing change and in helping a family take ownership of change. For example, asking how a family member decided to change how they were dealing with their child implies ownership. When they answer this question, they are taking ownership of doing something different. When used for this purpose we refer to these questions as *personal agency questions*.

When to Track Exceptions

The previously listed series of questions should be asked whenever a family reports change, as a standard follow-up to previous session interventions or if the clinician notices improvements or changes in the family's interactional patterns even if the family does not notice. One argument for clinicians tracking both interactional patterns and interaction exceptions is if the therapist knows the family patterns, they will more likely notice pattern changes even if the family does not notice or report them.

TWO-STEP TREATMENT PROCESS

Many case examples in this book follow two major steps. In *Step 1*, I-FAST clinicians offer interventions that help the family and client deviate from their *interactional patterns*. The clinician's primary task in Step 1 is to initiate or support a change process. Clinicians may do this by offering reframes, asking questions, directing families to notice something new, directing them to notice what they do when the problem is not happening, or by giving tasks that direct them to deviate from their patterns. Sometimes when families begin treatment, they have already begun a substantive change process on their own. They have already noticed or produced *interactional exceptions*. When this happens, the therapist must become aware that a change process has already began and reinforce and support it. When families succeed at deviating from their patterns, they will then often produce new changes on their own between sessions, producing additional interactional exceptions. These are family-initiated changes and are not asked for by the clinician. Helping the family get unstuck from their habitual patterns can create a domino effect of changes. This now is *Step 2*. In Step 2, further new suggestions for change by the clinician may not be needed. Instead, the clinician's primary task in Step 2 is to track, validate, and amplify the changes the family is initiating on their own. Often the family-initiated changes are the most profound. In many of the most dramatic cases in this book, the treatment follows these two steps. The families are able to make profound changes, and those changes are the ones initiated by the clients and their families, not the therapist.

Note on IFAST: The cases reported in this book represent the work of the first author, either as the therapist or supervisor. These cases represent the way the first author employs IFAST. IFAST as an approach is not limited to these illustrations. Other IFAST therapists or supervisors might emphasize other aspects of IFAST such as the amplification of exceptions as a major intervention strategy.

I-FAST SUMMARY

In the first three chapters of this volume, several issues and concepts were identified as crucial for working with traumatized clients and their families and in some instances missing from the current trauma literature. We would now like to show how I-FAST addresses and incorporates these concepts.

Trauma-Informed Care

Collaborating with trauma survivors and respecting their treatment choices regarding treatment goals, treatment frames, and treatment procedures has been identified as crucial for engaging trauma survivors in treatment. I-FAST is completely consistent with this principle. In I-FAST, treatment goals reflect what the client and family wish to focus on. Frames and procedures are offered that make sense to the client and family and represent what the client and family are willing to carry out.

Treatment Flexibility

Treatment must be flexible to accommodate client and family choices, integrate treatment procedures from diverse approaches, and adjust to client feedback. I-FAST is organized around flexibility. I-FAST offers an organized overarching metatheoretical framework that allows a wide range of choices within each treatment category. Treatment procedures from a wide range of approaches and healing practices from diverse ethnic groups can be integrated into the I-FAST treatment framework.

Client Feedback–Informed Care

I-FAST utilizes client feedback in three major ways. First, I-FAST is very collaborative. Treatment decisions are all made eliciting feedback from clients. Second, tracking and utilizing how clients respond to interventions provides feedback for identifying and adjusting treatment to fit what clients are responding positively to. Third, tracking exceptions provides information on what is helping and why. All these procedures produce client feedback–informed treatment within I-FAST.

Culturally Competent Care

I-FAST is not married to a specific trauma theory or a set of trauma interventions. Instead, I-FAST treatment is organized around the family's and the survivor's belief systems. This allows I-FAST to be truly culturally competent. I-FAST provides an overarching framework that allows diverse ethnic beliefs and healing practices to be integrated into any given treatment.

I-FAST and PTSD

A large portion of children who are exposed to traumatic events are children who witness chronic domestic violence. For these children, it is not only the terror of the violence itself, but also the fear that violence could erupt at any moment, which intensifies the trauma. In earlier chapters, we reported research that identified nurturing parent–child relationships and harmonious and loving relationships among adults in the home as protective factors for developing posttraumatic stress disorder (PTSD). These relationships contribute to secure attachments, which, in turn, can help deter PTSD. By contrast, we reported research that identified chronic hostile arguments among adults, chronic hostile arguments between the trauma survivor and caregivers and threats of divorce as risk factors for developing PTSD. We also reported research that identified cross-generational coalitions that pit one adult and the trauma survivor against another adult as risk factors that interfered with secure attachments and therefore also increase risk for PTSD.

We reported that allowing trauma survivors to choose treatment goals, even if these goals do not focus on trauma, was a trauma-informed principal that enhances treatment engagement. We identified meta-analyses that reported strong evidence for efficacy of treatments that keep trauma survivors engaged but do not focus directly on trauma symptoms. Trauma symptoms can be resolved even if they are not focused on directly, provided the client remains engaged in a structured treatment approach.

I-FAST provides a flexible, structured treatment framework that can easily adapt to clients who do not want to focus on trauma symptoms. I-FAST treatment can both respect what clients want help on and help resolve trauma symptoms. If the goals the client wishes to focus on can include producing more harmonious and loving relationships within the home, the improved atmosphere can then help improve trauma symptoms. The following case is offered in detail to exemplify I-FAST concepts and how an I-FAST treatment process can unfold.

A MEAN GRANDFATHER

Anne, age 14 and Jane, age 12, lived with their maternal grandparents. They had lived with them for one year after being placed there by the authorities. While living with her mother and stepfather, Anne's stepfather had beaten her repeatedly, and her mother did not protect her. Both girls had also witnessed their stepfather beat their mother on numerous occasions. Anna was a girl who had witnessed chronic domestic violence and was herself a target of domestic violence, a major category of traumatized youth.

Soon after being sent to her grandparents, Anne developed serious behavior problems at school. The school placed her in a special classroom setting for disruptive children. Despite this classroom placement, she continued to have serious behavior problems at school. At one point, she became violent with a teacher, and charges were filed against her. She was placed on probation with Juvenile Court and had to report weekly to a probation officer. The probation officer suggested that the grandparents take the girl for mental health therapy. Although Anna had been repeatedly exposed to traumatic events, the court framed her as a defiant child. This only increased Anna's anger.

The grandmother accompanied Anne to her mental health therapy. Anne was referred for therapy and medication. She was diagnosed with as having bipolar disorder and put on mood stabilizer medications. Only she and the grandmother would participate in her therapy. Both the grandmother and Anna complained to the therapist about the grandfather. They described him as mean and verbally abusive.

After six months of therapy, Anna was getting worse. She began to cut herself and threaten suicide. After the first incident, she was hospitalized and diagnosed with borderline personality disorder. While in the hospital, both Anna and the grandmother blamed the grandfather for Anna's problems. He was verbally and emotionally abusive, both Anna and grandmother continued to assert. She was put on several additional medications and released home. She then began cutting again. She was also very uncooperative in therapy. Her therapist thought she could no longer help Anna. Anna was given a new therapist and case management services. Anna also alienated her new case manager who also concluded she could not help Anna. Anna was then assigned yet another case manager.

During this period of transferring to new therapists and case managers, Anna was hospitalized three more times. She had now been hospitalized four times in three months. Anna and the grandmother continued to blame the grandfather, accusing him of verbally and emotionally abusing Anna. All the therapists, case managers, and hospital staff encouraged the grandmother to leave the grandfather. During her fourth hospitalization, the hospital staff suspected the grandfather of sexually abusing Anna and called the authorities. The authorities interviewed both Anna and the grandfather. Both denied any abuse had happened. The investigation, however, increased the tension at home. Anna was exhibiting classic trauma symptoms of emotional dysregulation, self-harm, and threats of suicide.

Interactional Patterns and Family Frames

Anna reported that her grandparents fought continuously over her. Her grandfather felt she was irresponsible and not being held accountable for her behavior. The grandmother had sympathy for Anna due to the abuse she had suffered from her stepfather and did not want to be hard on her. The grandparents fought bitterly over how to deal with Anna's problems. Just prior to Anna's first hospitalization, the grandmother began threatening her husband with divorce if he did not leave Anna alone abut household chores and her school behavior.

The professionals were also stuck in a pattern. They only worked with Anna and the grandmother. They never included the grandfather. This may be fine in cases in which improvements are forthcoming, but on this case, Anna was deteriorating. Not only did the family need to change their patterns, so did the professionals.

The professionals framed Anna as mentally ill. She was now diagnosed with borderline personality disorder, took several medications, and placed in a special class for behavior problem children at school and on probation with Juvenile Court. She had been hospitalized four times in three months and had gone through two therapists and three case managers during that period. No one was able to help so far.

I-FAST Intervention

Mike, an intensive in-home program worker was assigned to the case. After reading Anna's file, Mike noted her trauma background. The reports of the physical abuse she had suffered and the witnessing of chronic domestic violence was in her file. Despite this, all the previous professionals framed her either as defiant or mentally ill. One of the previous therapists had attempted to focus on Anna's trauma history, but Anna refused to talk about what had happened and did not want treatment to focus on her past. The therapist concluded Anna was not ready for trauma treatment and decided she could not help Anna.

DECIDE WHOM TO INCLUDE IN TREATMENT

In I-FAST, the decision on whom to include in treatment is flexible and strategically decided on for each case. One guideline for determining whom to include in treatment is when a therapy is stuck, add family members. Since the grandfather had not been participating in any of the treatment, Mike's immediate goal was to engage him. To do so, he made sure he set an in-home appointment for when the grandfather could participate. Of all the treatment Anna had received over the past year, Mike was the first professional to reach out to and meet the grandfather. When meeting him for the first time, instead of accusing him of mistreating Anna as previous providers had done, Mike sought out the grandfather's views on what he thought Anna's problems were and what he thought might help. Mike treated the grandfather with respect. Knowing he had been accused of sexually abusing Anna by past providers, the grandfather was very appreciative of Mike respecting and eliciting his views. As a result, Mike developed a very strong and rapid rapport with the grandfather.

SETTING GOALS THE FAMILY IS MOTIVATED TO FOCUS ON

Regarding treatment goals, I-FAST is consistent with respecting patient preferences and choices. This is especially true for trauma clients. Emphasis is placed on goals the trauma client wants help on, even if that is not on trauma. In the first meeting, with the entire household, Mike asked everyone what problem they each wanted help on. All, including Anna, said they wanted help for the arguing and fighting. Everyone argued with everyone. Anne and her sister Jane argued with each other. Anne and the grandfather argued with each other. And the grandfather and the grandmother argued with each other and even threatened divorce. Anna was very upset about the chronic hostility in the home. That is what Anna wanted help on. She explicitly stated she did not want help on her "past."

TRACKING INTERACTIONAL PATTERNS

The pattern was the grandfather and Anne would begin to fight over Anne being disrespectful or her not doing chores. The grandmother would then come to Anne's defense, and soon the couple would fight with each other. When the couple fought, the whole household joined in with Anna and grandmother squaring off on one side against Jane and grandfather on the other. At times the fights would escalate to grandmother threatening divorce. It was later learned that when grandmother threatened divorce, Anne would cut herself and sometimes end up in the hospital. When this happened, the grandmother would drop her threat to divorce, and the grandparents would fight less. When Anne would return from the hospital or stop cutting, the cycle would start over.

Anna and her grandmother were in a cross-generational coalition against the grandfather. The grandparents had chronic conflict, which they either habitually avoided by one going to treatment and one staying home or had escalating fights. Neither way of dealing with conflict resulted in an organized, reasonable discussion needed to actually reach agreements.

TRACKING FAMILY FRAMES

The fight between the grandparents occurred over a disagreement about how each were framing Anne. The grandfather framed her as disrespectful, and the grandmother framed her as fragile. To the degree that Anne might be suffering from PTSD, it was the pervasively hostile and intense atmosphere in the home that made her feel unsafe and perhaps reminded her of her parents' fighting. The threats of divorce and resulting instability were no doubt also pushing her over the edge. It was assumed that if the family's request to help stop the fighting could be achieved and everyone could get along, this alone might resolve all Anne's trauma symptoms.

Mike honored the family's request to focus on stopping the fighting. He included the grandfather in every session. The initial focus was on helping the grandparents agree on rules and consequences for both girls. This helped but the divide between the grandparents over how each framed Anne had to be addressed.

TRACKING THE GRANDFATHER'S FRAMES AND REFRAMING ANNA

The grandfather framed himself as "old school": Children should have rules and be held accountable. According to the grandfather, Anna was "getting away with murder." Mike had reached out to the grandfather, heard out and respected his views, and made sure he was included in every session. He had established a very good rapport with the grandfather. He was now about to call in those chips. Mike learned that the grandfather was a Vietnam War veteran. In an attempt to get the grandfather to change how he was framing Anne, he asked the grandfather about being a war veteran. The grandfather said he was. Mike asked, "You must know about PTSD." The grandfather said he did, telling Mike about a veteran friend of his. Every Fourth of July, when fireworks were shot off, his friend became very afraid and did not come out of his house. Mike then made the comment, "Anne witnessed a lot of serious violence and was beaten herself. Did you ever consider that she might have PTSD?" The grandfather became very quiet. Mike ended the conversation just asking him to consider the possibility.

TRACKING INTERACTIONAL EXCEPTIONS

The next time Mike went to the home, everything had change. The mood was very different. The grandparents reported that they had made a new agreement. Everything was changing. After Mike's suggestion to the grandfather that Anne might have PTSD, the grandfather decided his wife might be the better person to be in charge of how to deal with Anne. The grandfather turned Anne over to his wife. He no longer fought with Anne and no longer viewed her as disrespectful. Since grandfather and Anne were no longer fighting, grandfather and grandmother stopped fighting also. The hostile atmosphere and threats of divorce were gone. As predicted, Anne was already beginning to settle down behaviorally.

Mike was not expecting such a drastic change. He was just trying to lay down a foundation for helping the grandfather reframe how he viewed Anne. Unexpectedly, grandfather changed his frame for Anne. This led to a change in how grandfather and grandmother were interacting with each other and how the family itself was organized. The grandfather and grandmother changed their respective roles with Anne. Instead of competing for who should be in charge of Anne, they both agreed the grandmother should assume that role. Mike expressed how impressed he was with the grandparents' new agreements and how this was helping Anna.

REINFORCING EXCEPTIONS

Mike expressed how impressed he was with the grandfather's decision to turn Anna over to his wife. He asked the grandfather how he decided to do that. The grandfather said he knew Anna had been abused and had seen a lot of very bad things but never made the connection that she may have PTSD. He realized that an "old school" grandfather might not be the best person to help her. Mike complimented him saying not many "old school" grandfathers would be able to take a step back like that and see that what they think is best might not actually be best. The grandmother was also very complimentary of her husband saying she knew it was not easy for him to do what he did and that she was very proud of him.

CONSOLIDATING CHANGE

One month later, Anne was completely free of behavior problems both at home and at school. The grandparents not only reported Anne's improvement, but they also told Mike how they were getting along much better and that their marriage was "back to normal." A nurturing environment between both adults and between the adults and Anne had been established and maintained. With Anna, there was no more cutting and no further hospitalizations. Her school behavior problems eventually went totally away. Her anger outbursts completely stopped. Three months later, Anna was off all her medications. Four months later, she was off probation. At the beginning of her next school year, she was back in regular classes at school. She was now a normal teenage girl—no medications, no special classes, and no probation officers.

Summary

This example illustrates several concepts outlined in the previous four chapters of this volume. The client had a serious trauma history but did not wish to focus on this in treatment. I-FAST provided a flexible treatment framework that allowed this client choice to be respected. The client's self-injurious symptoms and her emotional dysregulation symptoms were not a direct focus of the treatment. Nor was her trauma history a direct focus of treatment. There was no identification or processing of Anna's "trauma narrative." Anna, who had suffered from a serious trauma history, did not want to focus on her trauma history. Instead, the treatment focused on what the family wanted, a stop to all the fighting. These treatment choices were respected. The goal selected by the family allowed the treatment to help produce a nurturing home environment free of fighting and threats of divorce. Anna's trauma symptoms were focused on indirectly, by helping to provide her with a safe, secure, and stable family environment. The resolution of Anna's trauma symptoms could be attributed to the changes in her family environment. Threats of divorce were eliminated, Anna was no longer enlisted in a struggle by one of the adults in the home against the other, the two adults in the home were able to improve their relationship, and both adults in the home were able to obtain secure attachments with Anna.

6 TRAUMA AND INTERACTIONAL PATTERNS

One goal of involving family in treatment is to enlist the healing power of intimate relationships for therapeutic ends. For trauma this entails two areas. The first relates to how the family responds to trauma. Are they supportive, empathic, and compassionate? Does the victim feel understood? Can the family have discussions that help the trauma survivor make sense of what happened? Second, the trauma survivor must feel safe and secure. Safety is paramount. The family can either be a source of safety and security or one more thing the trauma survivor must be anxious about. To bring the potential healing power of the family to bear, therefore, both how family react to trauma and how the family is structured and organized must be attended to in family treatment of trauma. Secure attachments between trauma survivors and individual caregivers are regulated by the larger family system in which those relationships are imbedded in. To promote secure attachments, the family system must accommodate them.

When assessing patterns related to trauma symptoms, attention focuses on both *how family members are responding to trauma* and *family patterns that predate trauma*. The first concerns understanding trauma symptoms in relation to family members' habitual ways of responding to them. If a child has nightmares, what are the habitual ways the nightmares are dealt with? Does the child tell a family member? Do they tell the details of the nightmare? How does the family member respond? Who else is told? Who is not told? We assume if trauma symptoms are not resolved, the family's way of responding to them may be perpetuating them.

Family patterns that predate trauma refer to how the family is structured and organized. Who is close to whom? Who is distant from whom? How is conflict habitually dealt with? Who is habitually on whose side? These patterns can have a major effect both on how trauma symptoms will be addressed by the family and if family responses to trauma will be helpful or not.

When trauma symptoms are a direct focus of treatment, patterns that perpetuate them can be a direct target for change. Treatment can focus on eliciting a family discussion of what happened and facilitating compassionate responses from family members. A therapeutic family trauma narrative can be constructed. In many cases, however, trauma is not a direct focus of treatment. The trauma survivor or caregiver(s) may be unwilling to discuss trauma, or family members may not accept the frame that trauma is a driving contributor to what the family is requesting help on. In these cases, healing from trauma is still possible by focusing on changing family patterns that result in the trauma survivor feeling unsafe and insecure.

FAMILY INTERACTIONAL PATTERNS THAT EXACERBATE AND/OR PERPETUATE TRAUMA SYMPTOMS: THE "NO TALK" RULE

It has been suggested that those exposed to trauma who do not end up with posttraumatic stress disorder (PTSD) "spontaneously recover" through a process of discussion within their intimate group, namely, their family (Figley & Figley, 2008). When family can talk and process trauma, many exposed to trauma do not develop PTSD. A problem response to trauma that blocks the family's natural healing power is the "no talk" rule (Figley & Figley, 2008). Something terrible happens to someone, and family members do not talk about what happened. The trauma survivor is deprived of the reflection and meaning-making that can occur naturally through family discussions.

The "no talk" pattern can occur in two forms. First, the trauma survivor may not disclose to family that they were exposed to a traumatic event. This is common with intrafamily sexual abuse. As noted in Chapter 2 of this volume, intrafamily child sexual abuse victims are less likely to disclose as children or adolescents, and males are less likely to disclose than females. Cross-culturally, Asians are less likely to disclose sexual assault (Rao, DiClemente, & Ponton, 1992, J. Lee, Pomero, Yoo, & Rheinboldt, 2005). The victim essentially is keeping what happened a secret. This is often due to feared or real consequences that can ensue if the secret is told. For intrafamilial sexual abuse, the perpetrator could be expelled from the family or go to jail. In many cultures, the family may react with shame. In either case, the victim is essentially protecting the perpetrator from facing consequences or is protecting the family from experiencing shame. In cultures in which family honor is viewed to be injured due to sexual assault, the sexual assault victim may be physically assaulted or even killed by their own family if the sexual assault is revealed.

The family either not believing the victim or blaming the victim is another potential consequence of disclosure that results in the victim keeping trauma secret. This can be true for both intrafamily sexual abuse and sexual assault by a nonfamily perpetrator. Sexual assault victims are at higher risk of being blamed in cultures that place a high value on chastity and family honor and avoid open discussions about sexuality. Within some of these groups, victims are expected to suffer in silence (La Flair, Franko, & Herzog, 2008).

A second form of the "no talk" pattern can occur after the family has become aware of trauma. The trauma can be intrafamilial sexual abuse, sexual assault, exposure to serious violence, or other types of trauma. Despite awareness of the trauma, a pattern of not discussing it develops among family members. This pattern can occur for a multitude of reasons, based on how family members and the victim frame the trauma and each other. The trauma survivor may frame family members as fragile. They may be concerned that telling about their trauma will be too painful for the family to hear. The "no talk" rule is then followed. Frames in relation to trauma will be discussed in detail in Chapter 5 of this volume. One main consequence of the family not discussing the trauma is that the meaning of the trauma among the group remains unchanged. If, for example, the family never discusses the details of sexual abuse or sexual assault, the family may blame or not believe the victim. Not discussing the facts of what happened allows distorted views to be maintained by the family with serious psychological consequences for the victim (Grove, 2002).

In this chapter, we will introduce five case examples and identify both family responses to trauma and family structure that predates trauma. In subsequent chapters, we will reintroduce these cases to show how they proceed through the integrative family and systems treatment (I-FAST) treatment process.

THE EVIL STEPMOTHER

Danny, aged 6, lived with Melissa, his single biological mother, 30; his brother, aged 3; and his maternal grandmother in the grandmother's house. Danny was referred for in-home therapy due to extreme fits. Melissa explained when he had one of these episodes, he was in another world. His eyes would roll to the back of his head, and he would become arbitrarily violent—biting, hitting, and kicking. He would become enraged for unknown reasons. He had fits at school as well and had to sit separately from the other children. He was diagnosed with intermittent explosive disorder and put on Adderall®. He had also been diagnosed bipolar. Melissa was uncertain how to help him. She was confused and uncertain how to deal with his fits.

Danny also had anxiety and soiled his pants. He was afraid he might see his biological father. Melissa told the in-home therapist a story of Danny being abused at his father's home. She became very emotional when telling the story, crying and being visibly upset. The parents divorced when Danny was one. After the divorce, both parents moved back with their respective mothers. Danny visited his father regularly after the divorce, but Melissa explained that the paternal grandmother did most of the child care. The couple did not fight after the divorce. They were able to talk and collaborate as parents when needed. Things changed after Danny's father got remarried. Danny's father became more demanding regarding visitation dates and less compromising. He became inconsistent with sending child support. Not wanting to make problems, Melissa went along with Danny's father's demands. An additional change after Danny's father remarried was that Danny did not want to visit him.

The boys had standard visitation with their father, his new wife, and her three sons, 15, 11, and 1. After a visit with his father, Danny's younger brother told Melissa that when visiting at the father's, the stepmother would discipline Danny by duck-taping his mouth shut and his arms and legs together and putting him in a closet for several hours. After these incidents, Danny began sleeping with his mother and was afraid of the dark. Danny did not want to go anywhere in public. When told this story, Melissa reported it to the police. The visits were stopped. The father minimized what had happened but did not press for visits. There was no court order to stop the visits; Melissa was just advised to stop them by Children's Services. Melissa then lived in fear that Danny's father could insist that visits begin again. The two parents had not discussed the abuse allegations. After the visits were stopped, Melissa stopped all communication with Danny's father. She had no idea what his response was to his son not visiting anymore.

The in-home therapist proposed that Danny had PTSD and referred him to an outpatient therapist who would work with the in-home worker. In the first outpatient session, when asked about the abuse, Melissa began to cry. It was painful for her to discuss the trauma. She avoided the topic. When Danny threw his fits, Melissa would try feebly to redirect him or give him time-outs. She was reluctant to punish him due to the abuse. She viewed him as traumatized and fragile. Melissa's mother, however, viewed Danny as out of control and needing punished. After one of Danny's episodes, Melissa's mother would scold her for not being firm with Danny.

Danny had intrusive thoughts every day. He startled very easily. Melissa reported Danny flew into physical rages without provocation approximately once a week. Danny was afraid of going to the store and other local places fearing he would see his father. He said he was afraid "they would do what they did before." While in public, Danny and Melissa did encounter his father and stepmother at a store. Melissa was unsure how to deal with the situation and became paralyzed; on seeing his father, Danny clung to his mother. It was after encountering his father and stepmother in public that his rages began.

Interactional Patterns

FAMILY RESPONSES TO TRAUMA

There are several key aspects to how the adults in the family habitually responded to Danny's trauma. First, Melissa was also traumatized by what had happened to her son. This rendered her too upset to be able to talk to Danny about what happened to him. Melissa would cry at the mere mention of what had happened. Danny was not going to talk to his mother about any aspect of his fears if she became so upset. Second, Melissa was uncertain how to respond to Danny's anger fits. She viewed him as fragile and did not want to punish him. However, she had no idea what to do instead. To compound matters, her mother, with whom she lived, was critical of how she dealt with Danny. Thus, the background adult was not supporting her.

PATTERNS PREDATING TRAUMA

After Danny's father remarried, there were two significant interactional patterns between the parents. First, Danny's father became more demanding, and Melissa just acquiesced. She did not stand up to him if he insisted on something she was opposed to. She could not protect Danny from his father if she could not stand up to him. Second, after the visits stopped, Melissa stopped all communication with Danny's father. By capitulating to his demands, Melissa gave Danny's father too much power, and by cutting off all communication with him, he became too mysterious. Melissa now feared him. When Melissa and Danny encountered the father publicly, Melissa was just as afraid as Danny; this intensified his anxiety and trauma symptoms.

SECRETS

Mark, aged 41, lived with his second wife, Cathy, aged 39; his 10-year-old son, Todd; and Cathy's 14-year-old daughter, Melinda. Mark also had an 18-year-old son, John, who was court-ordered out of the house and lived with Mark's mother. Mark came to treatment by himself asking for help to reintegrate his son into his family. Mark explained that one year earlier, Melinda told her mother that she had woken up at night and discovered that John was sexually abusing her orally. Cathy immediately reported the abuse to the authorities. Interviews of both children were conducted. John revealed that he had gone into Melinda's room on four occasions over a one-month period and orally abused her while she was sleeping. John was ordered to live with his grandmother and into juvenile sex offender group treatment. Cathy was livid. She took the position that John was no longer a family member. He would never again live with or visit their home. No one in the family was to interact with him.

Despite Cathy's rule, Mark had been secretly meeting with his son for some time. After one year, John had successfully completed his juvenile sex offender treatment. The authorities no longer had a rule that he could not be at his home. Mark said his son had taken responsibility for what he had done and was remorseful. While in sex offender treatment, John disclosed that at age 10, while visiting at his mother's, he was sexually abused by his mother's live-in boyfriend. On one of their secret visits, John told his father about this. Mark could not tell Cathy any of this or he would have to admit he was having secret visits. Cathy was adamant and unbending.

Mark either avoided the topic of reintegrating John into the family or would bring it up with Cathy if the two were fighting. Cathy and Mark had had several tumultuous fights about the idea of John associating with the family. Cathy was threatening divorce if John was ever allowed to associate with the family again. These intense fights had a serious effect on the two children left in the home. Melinda, who was seeing her own trauma therapist, was upset with herself for ever telling. She blamed herself for the conflict between the parents. She assumed her stepfather was very angry with her for telling what John had done because now John was never allowed back. Although she and her mother were close, she did not want to share any of this with her mother, fearing it would cause a terrible fight between her mother and stepfather.

Todd also had secrets. He had observed his brother coming out of Melinda's room on one of the abuse occasions. He knew something wrong was happening, but he did not tell anyone. Now Todd was especially afraid to admit he knew something, fearing he also would be banned from the family by Cathy. He felt very guilty, thinking if he had told someone, he might have helped to prevent all the conflict that ensued but could not tell anyone this.

Interactional Patterns

PATTERNS PREDATING ABUSE DISCLOSURE

Both parents had been divorced for years before marrying each other. The time between marriages resulted in Cathy and Melinda becoming very close. Cathy's first husband had an affair and left her. He abandoned both his wife and daughter. Cathy was devastated. Melinda was confused about why her father left her. They were both lonely and sometimes ended up sleeping together. Boundaries were blurred. Cathy's bedroom and bathroom also became Melinda's.

Mark also became close to his son after his divorce. He obtained custody of both boys due to his ex-wife abusing drugs. He felt bad for the boys and was inclined to indulge them. John took advantage of this. After remarrying, both Mark and Cathy had a difficult time carving out emotional space for each other from the close relationships they had with their respective children. Melinda had to give up her mother's bedroom. When she complained to her mother that the bedroom was now off limits, Cathy blamed Mark, saying it was his rule Melinda could not go in there anymore. Regarding John, Cathy viewed him as very manipulative and in charge of his father. She accused Mark of allowing John to manipulate him. The couple fought bitterly about this. They were already having marital problems when John's abuse of Melinda came to light.

This families' struggles began with the couples' mutual difficulty adjusting to a life cycle transition of remarriage. They both had difficulties changing their respective patterns with their children. The remarriage required both to make new boundaries with their children that each was reluctant to do. Cathy's bedroom was symbolic of her dilemma. She could not tell her daughter herself that now that she was remarried, they could no longer share a room. Mark also could not set new boundaries on his son. Both parents were in cross-generational coalitions with their respective child against each other. This resulted in the couple being in constant and serious conflict. They were unable to compromise and negotiate. Then the abuse happened.

FAMILY RESPONSES TO ABUSE DISCLOSURE

With the threat of divorce, Cathy unilaterally ordered John out of the family. Although the authorities ordered him out of the home, Cathy ordered him out of the family. Before the abuse, the couple could not negotiate less serious issues. After the abuse disclosure, however, they were unable to negotiate the issue of John's role in the family. They either avoided this topic or had tumultuous fights about it. The pattern precluded their reaching a negotiated compromise. Their intense fighting and complete disagreement regarding John resulted in many secrets and strong boundaries between several sets of family members. Cathy unilaterally ordered John out of the family, and Mark unilaterally visited him in secret, emphasizing his coalition with his son against his wife. Because he had to keep the visits secret, he could not report key information to Cathy such as John's remorseful attitude regarding the abuse or that John himself had been sexually abused. The couple could not talk about these issues without fighting.

The terrible fights between John and Cathy had serious effects on Melinda and Todd. Melinda withdrew from her mother. Not wanting to make things worse between her mother and Mark, Melinda kept it a secret from her mother that she blamed herself for the couple's fights and that she thought her stepfather was angry with her. She could not get support from her own mother fearing it would cause a divorce. Fearing Cathy's response, Todd also had to keep the secret that he knew his brother had done something wrong but did not tell about it. He felt terrible guilt about this secret but could not get the support he needed either. These secrets represented strong boundaries on communication and blocked healing for all involved.

In the two previous examples, both how the family responded when learning about trauma and the patterns the family was following before the trauma exacerbated the trauma symptoms and interfered with their resolution. The "no talk" rule was in effect in both families for different reasons.

CHRONIC HOSTILITY AND PUNITIVE RESPONSES TOWARD THE SURVIVOR

When trauma is not disclosed by the survivor, or when family respond to trauma by blaming or not believing the survivor, the survivor can develop behavior problems. The relationship between trauma and delinquency has been strongly established (Kerig, 2012; Kerig & Alexander, 2012). One study found that 90% of youth in the juvenile justice system had been exposed to traumatic experiences and that exposure to trauma is a predictor of antisocial behavior (Kerig & Becker, 2010). PTSD among delinquent youth has been found to be two to eight times higher than in the community, (Wolpaw & Ford, 2004). Female juvenile offenders experience more interpersonal trauma than males, experiencing more sexual or physical abuse (Chesney-Lind, 1989). Further, the number of females entering the juvenile justice system has been increasing (Snyder & Sickmund, 2006). Females in detention have higher rates of PTSD than males (Kerig & Becker, 2010; Solomon, Davis, & Luckham, 2012).

Traumatized girls entering the juvenile justice system can be classified as "incorrigible" (Acoca, 1999). Anger and irritability are often a major trauma symptom for juvenile girls who have experienced interpersonal trauma (Kerig, Vanderzee, Becker, & Ward, 2012). When the family and/or community responds to the behavior problems with punishments, a vicious cycle can result in which the more the victim is treated as a behavior problem, the more behavior problems they exhibit. Within the family, parents or caregivers can respond with harsh, hostile, or critical statements. Traumatized girls exhibiting anger and irritability were found to be subject to harsh parenting (Schwartz & Steffensmeier, 2012).

The survivor, who knows something bad happened to them, is misunderstood and may feel unfairly treated. They may fight back verbally, creating a home environment of hostile and hurtful exchanges between caregiver and survivor. Often in this pattern, threats of expelling the survivor from the home accompany these exchanges. The hostile home atmosphere, especially if threats of expulsion are made, creates an unsafe environment for the trauma survivor.

A DEFIANT GIRL

Kristen, aged 15, lived with her younger sister Ellen, aged 14, her mother Barbara, and her stepfather, Albert. Albert also had an 18-year-old daughter, Stephany, from a previous marriage. The couple had been married for 13 years. The girls' biological father left the family when they were young. They did not know him. Albert was the only father the girls knew, and they both called and considered him "Dad."

Kristen and her older stepsister were very close. When Kristen was 12, Stephany took Kristen to a sleepover birthday party at one of Stephany's girlfriend's home. During the party, an older boy (aged 18) had shown interest in Kristen. He and Stephany were close friends. During the party, he made sexual statements to Kristen that made her feel uncomfortable. She did not report this to anyone at the party. Although Kristen felt flattered that the boy might like her, she did not show any interest in him or send mixed signals to him. Kristen eventually fell asleep on the couch. She woke up when the boy was taking off her clothes. She did not know what to do. There was no one else in the room. He touched her breasts under her shirt and penetrated her vagina with his hand and penis. She asked him to stop. He said, "No." Kristen was scared and did not know what to do or whom to tell. He told her that he would kill her family if she ever told. She believed the boy would indeed harm her family and so she told no one.

After this sexual assault, Kristen began to have serious behavior problems, which would last for three years. She frequently lied, stole, and snuck out of the house. She began smoking marijuana and spending time with older boys. Not knowing about the sexual assault, both parents viewed her as defiant. They took her to counseling where she was diagnosed as oppositional defiant disorder. Her problem behaviors escalated. She was put on probation and sent to residential treatment where she stayed for six months and was put on lithium. After she was released from residential treatment, she improved temporarily, but then her behavior problems returned. She was then placed in a second residential treatment center, where she finally disclosed the sexual assault.

The therapist at the residential center reported the abuse to the authorities. She told Kristen's parents that she was molested but did not tell them the details. The authorities investigated the abuse. They interviewed Kristen and the boy, but the boy denied the allegations. Children's Services classified the abuse as "indicated." They did not disclose the details of Kristen's story to Albert or Barbara, nor did they explain what "indicated" meant. Since no charges were filed against the boy, Albert concluded the authorities did not think the abuse happened. He was never told the details of his daughter's story. The parents did not talk with each other about the assault, nor did either of them ever talk to Kristen about what happened.

There was one interactional exception to the "no talking" rule. Barbara asked Kristen one time about the assault. Barbara was upset and crying when she brought up the abuse with Kristen. Seeing her mother crying, Kristen also cried and did not want to talk about what happened. Not wanting to upset her further, Barbara did not ask again.

Kristen had given the family fits for over one year. The family lived in a small town where Kristen developed a bad reputation. Albert's family viewed her as a serious problem. Although Kristen's mother believed her allegations, Albert's family did not, citing she had been a chronic liar. Albert was now caught between his stepdaughter and his family of origin. He did not know what to believe. Kristen was crushed. She viewed Albert as her father, and he did not believe her. When she encountered his relatives, they shunned her. The family was divided into camps with Kristen and her mother on one side, Albert's family on the other, and Albert caught in between.

In the hope of finding better paying work, Albert moved his family to Ohio. Kristen's problems became worse. She continued to sneak out of the house. She met an 18-year-old known drug dealer. She and the boyfriend planned to run away together. Kristen stole a hand gun and $1,000 from her parents. The money was to be used to pay rent. Before the teens could get away, the money was discovered missing, and the parents confronted Kristen. She told them her boyfriend's mother was ill and needed money to go to urgent care. None of this was true. The parents filed charges in juvenile court, thinking the court would teach her a lesson. Instead, the court placed her in foster care. The parents were confused and very upset and felt blamed.

Interactional Patterns

PATTERNS PREDATING TRAUMA

Not much is known about the family's interactional patterns prior to Kristen's sexual assault. What is known is that Kristen felt very close to both her mother and stepfather Albert and that the family had a weekend tradition of going camping together. It does not appear that the couple had serious marital issues. The most important family interactional patterns were those in response to the sexual assault.

FAMILY RESPONSES TO TRAUMA

The "no talk" rule was very prominent. Kristen lived in a small town and would encounter the assailant periodically. She feared him and believed he would harm her or her family if she disclosed the abuse. She kept the assault a secret. Her acting out was a result of her silence. Her parents, not knowing she had been assaulted, framed her as defiant. Her behaviors escalated. She and her parents became stuck in a pattern of them treating her as defiant, of her responding with more defiance, and of them then punishing her more. Once Kristen and her parents were at war, Kristen was certainly not going to tell them about the assault.

Finally, she disclosed the assault to professionals who also followed the "no talk" rule. The residential therapist and the children's services investigator knew the details of Kristen's story, but neither told the parents. One exception was when Barbara asked Kristen about the abuse. Both mother and daughter were crying and framed each other as fragile. Not wanting to upset each other further, the subject was dropped. After this, neither parent talked to Kristen about what happened. In the absence of knowing the full story, negative frames were free to continue.

Albert's family did not believe Kristen, and Albert was caught in the middle. Not knowing the full story, Albert was not sure he could believe his daughter. This resulted in two serious problems for Kristen. First, she did not feel supported by her father. Second, the extended family, who lived in close proximity, were divided into camps with some who believed her and some who did not. The ones who did not made their disapproval known, and this resulted in numerous painful encounters for Kristen. Even though her mother believed her, the "no talk" rule resulted in Kristen not getting the family support she needed, and her problem behaviors continued to escalate.

FAMILY INTERACTIONAL PATTERNS THAT PREDATE EXPOSURE TO TRAUMA

Family interactional patterns (also labeled family structure) that predate exposure to trauma can interfere with secure attachments for the trauma survivor and intensify their feeling insecure and unsafe (Lyons-Ruth, Melnick, Bronfman, Sherry, & Llanas, 2004). In family treatment, whether the family wishes treatment to focus on trauma or another problem, family interactional patterns that promote safety, security, and improved attachments can be promoted. Whether trauma is brought to treatment as a problem or if it is in the background, treatment can focus on creating a safe and secure family environment in which the trauma survivor feels attached to key caregivers and the adult relationships in the family are stable. Family support for the trauma survivor can be obtained by improving attachments between the survivor and family members.

Habitual family responses to trauma symptoms are largely determined by family patterns that predate the trauma. Suppose, for example, a mother and child are very close. The father and child are not close. The mother and father are not close and in conflict. In this instance, the child will most likely turn to their mother for help, not their father. The mother may also leave the father out of the process. The trauma survivor is then deprived of support from their father. If the mother and trauma survivor have been in coalition against the father, the mother may even feel betrayed if the child opens up to the father.

The trauma-surviving child's feeling of safety and security and the quality of their attachments to various family members will often be substantially influenced by habitual family patterns that predate exposure to trauma. As noted in Chapter 3 of this volume, intrusive parenting, disengaged parenting, serious conflict between adults in the family, and adults triangulating a child or enlisting them in a coalition against another adult can all impair secure attachments and a feeling of safety for the survivor. Adults in serious conflict with each other, especially if there are threats of actual separations, can create an insecure environment for a trauma survivor. Finally, caregivers who are struggling with serious problems of their own can also impair the trauma survivor feeling safe and secure. A depressed parent, a parent with serious substance abuse problems, or a parent with serious medical problems may not be able to help their trauma-surviving child feel safe. For a traumatized child, any of these patterns can contribute to their feeling unsafe.

BROTHER–SISTER SEXUAL ABUSE

Aaron, aged 15, had been sexually abusing his 11-year-old sister, Carla, for three years. He lived with his sister and both biological parents, Brenda and Steven. He and his mother had been in serious and chronic conflict over Aaron's poor school performance. They had intense and hostile arguments every night. After months of this fighting, Aaron ran away. He went to a shelter for run-away teens. While he was out of the house, Carla was afraid he left because he was upset with himself over what he had done to her. She then told her mother about the abuse.

Brenda believed her and did not blame her. The authorities became involved and substantiated sexual abuse. Much of the abuse involved Aaron fondling Carla's genitals above and underneath her clothes. Sometimes Carla resisted, and sometimes she did not. Aaron framed the encounters as consensual. On three occasions, they had intercourse. On one of those occasions, Aaron physically forced Carla to have intercourse. Most of the abuse happened at night in Carla's bedroom. While his parents were asleep or downstairs watching TV, Aaron went into Carla's bedroom and abused her.

Aaron was found and sent home. Steven and Brenda were informed of the details that Carla had disclosed, but they were not told what their son said to the investigators. They only knew that he admitted to fondling but was denying intercourse and he viewed the abuse as consensual. The authorities ruled he had to cooperate with sex offender therapy, and if he did not, he would be removed from the home.

After returning home and awaiting his first therapy appointment, Aaron was very agitated. Three times he became violent, breaking furniture. To help Carla protect herself once Aaron was back in the home, Steven installed a lock on Carla's bedroom door, so she could lock her brother out of her room at night. This was an interactional exception for the father, who was otherwise very disengaged and unassertive.

Even though this terrible secret was now in the open, the "no talk" rule was in effect. The parents did not talk with each other about the abuse, and they did not talk with Aaron about it. Because Aaron was so volatile after returning home, they were afraid to talk to him about the abuse. The parents did not talk to each other about the abuse either. Their pattern, which predated the trauma disclosure, was to avoid conflict and not talk to each other about anything. The consequence of them not talking was that it allowed Aaron to maintain his distorted belief that his sister was equally responsible for the abuse. With her brother not taking responsibility for abuse, Carla did not feel safe. She was having regular nightmares of Aaron coming into her room with a washcloth. When abusing his sister, Aaron used a wash cloth to clean up after ejaculating.

The family interactional patterns prior to the disclosure of the abuse was a major contributing factor. The couple had an empty marriage. They were a blue-collar family. Steven had had a very good-paying job and had high status in the family. After years of work, he injured his back and could no longer work. He went on disability. He lost his job and then his wife. She did not respect him after he went on disability. His response to his wife's rejection was to withdraw. He was totally disengaged. His spirit and presence in the home was minimal. This contributed to Aaron thinking he could do what he wanted at home. In fact, Aaron was open about not having respect for his father. A view he shared with his mother. It appeared that Brenda and Aaron were in a coalition against the father.

Brenda and Aaron had very weak boundaries and could be characterized as enmeshed. Their intense fighting was one indicator. But they also play-wrestled and rolled around on the floor together. Aaron was 15, and he and his mother were still wrestling. Once, while in public, they were observed standing face to face, very close, laughing and giggling. It looked like an older woman with a younger boyfriend. Aaron may have viewed these encounters as sexual. On one occasion, while she was sleeping, Aaron fondled his mother's breasts. Brenda was also overprotective of Aaron. She was reluctant to allow him to leave the house and have friends. As a result, Aaron and his sister were best friends. They spent much time playing together at home.

Family therapy was scheduled for Aaron, with all his family invited, starting with the two parents. Scheduling family treatment produced interactional exceptions by the parents. Knowing they would have to talk about what happened in therapy, they began to talk to each other about the abuse. They had several talks, which were major exceptions for them. They never talked with each other about anything important. Their habitual way of managing conflict was to avoid it.

Interactional Patterns

FAMILY RESPONSES TO ABUSE

To summarize, the interactional patterns following the disclosure of abuse were dominated by the family not talking with each other about what happened. The parents did not talk to each other about the abuse, they did not talk to their son about it, and the son's probation officer did not inform the parents about what the son had told her about the abuse. One exception of the parents talking resulted from the therapy intervention of inviting them both to therapy.

PATTERNS PREDATING DISCLOSURE OF ABUSE

Prior to the abuse disclosure, the family interactional patterns were dominated by a poor marital relationship in which conflict was avoided, weak boundaries between mother and son, a coalition between mother and son, a disengaged father, and a son with no friends outside the house, setting up a situation in which his sister was his only friend. These patterns no doubt contributed to the sexual abuse. The mother–son relationship had a sexual overtone with numerous boundary violations, which may have confused Aaron and paralleled his boundary violations with his sister. The distant spousal relationship resulted in the wife having no respect for her husband. He had no function in the family. He was withdrawn and disengaged. This may have given Aaron the idea he did not have to fear his father's reaction to abusing his sister.

SUICIDAL MOTHER

Eight-year-old Carl, lived with his father, Robert; Robert's live-in girlfriend, Jenny; and her three children. Carl's parents were divorced when he was very young. After the divorce, he lived with his mother, Rebecca, and visited his father on weekends. On his first overnight visit with his father for a Christmas holiday, while at his father's, Rebecca made a serious suicide attempt. She shot herself. To avoid making a mess in the house which her son would see when he came home, she went outside and laid down on the ground to shoot herself. The gun recoiled so she did not kill herself. After shooting herself, she was still conscious. She decided not to shoot herself again but to go into her house and clean up. She then discovered how injured she was. When her boyfriend came home and found her, he called an ambulance. Rebecca explained that she tried to kill herself because she thought Carl's father was going to steal him from her.

Rebecca had an extended recovery in the hospital, and over the next year had several reconstructive surgeries. Carl went to live with his father and now visited his mother every other weekend. At his father's house, Carl was not talking at all about what happened. He just cried and said nothing. Carl also was becoming angry and aggressive. He was biting his father and father's girlfriend. Prior to his mother's suicide attempt he had no history of aggression or behavior problems. He had also been a straight-A student in school. Now he was failing most of his classes. Carl was having nightmares and anxiety at night and waking up very frightened. He reported having nightmares and unwanted thoughts five times per week, including after he visited his mother. Carl had self-injurious symptoms. Several times in school he cut his arms with a paper clip. The school would panic and called Robert to come and get him.

Robert described Carl's mother as "crazy." Their relationship was full of conflict and blame. Robert blamed all of Carl's symptoms on his "crazy" mom. Rebecca suspected Robert was trying to "steal" Carl from her. Robert was, in fact, attempting to win custody of Carl and did not believe it was in Carl's best interest to see his mother at all. Robert pointed out that Carl had his nightmares and night anxiety after every one of his visits with his mother. Robert was, in fact, attempting to exclude Rebecca from Carl's life.

The parents had a very messy divorce and were in chronic conflict with each other ever since the divorce. Carl was caught in the middle. Robert continuously threatened to take custody of Carl, even before Rebecca's suicide attempt. They fought with each other at pick-up and drop-off for visits with Carl. This happened while Carl lived with his mother and continued after he went to live with his father. Before his mother's suicide attempt, the conflict between his parents upset him and made him anxious. He dreaded the car ride to the pick-up or drop-off point. After his mother's suicide attempt, the conflict exacerbated his trauma symptoms. Carl was in a loyalty bind, triangulated between waring parents. After visiting either his father or his mother, each parent would interrogate Carl regarding his just-completed time with the other parent. Carl did not want to take sides with either parent so he would just say nothing. The parents would openly fight in front of Carl, and these fights added to his anxiety.

Carl blamed himself for his mother's suicide attempt. His mother had multiple sclerosis and serious physical impairments. She also had a trauma background and was cut off from her family of origin. Carl was all she had. While living with his mother, Carl took care of and looked out for her. She fell very easily. Carl would help her up or help her get around the house, so she would not fall. He waited on her, bringing her water and food so she would not have to try to walk. Eventually, Rebecca moved her boyfriend Steven into the house. But, by then, Carl was established in his role of caretaker for Rebecca. After moving to his father's house, Carl was afraid no one was taking care of his mother. This became a major source of his anxiety.

Carl and Rebecca had a very enmeshed relationship. Weak boundaries in multiple areas characterized their relationship. This pattern continued after Rebecca's suicide attempt and exacerbated Carl's trauma symptoms. He continued in his caretaker role even after moving to his father's. If Rebecca became upset about anything while her boyfriend was at work, she would call Carl, and Carl would have to calm her down. She told Carl everything. On his visits with Rebecca, she told Carl of all her surgeries resulting from her suicide attempt. She would show Carl her scars and tell him of her upcoming surgeries. On one of Carl's visits, she showed him the actual gun casing of the bullet with which she shot herself. Rebecca viewed it as normal to tell Carl everything. Rebecca would also interrogate Carl about what would happen at his father's house. Rebecca was on a campaign to convince Carl that Robert was trying to steal him from her. She would cry about how much she missed him. This reinforced Carl's idea that his mother was fragile and needed his protection.

Interactional Patterns

RESPONSES TO TRAUMA

Weak boundaries between Carl and Rebecca fueled Carl's anxiety and nightmares. But he could not talk to his father about this because his parents were at war with each other. Telling his father about his fears for his mother would give his father ammunition in his war with Carl's mother. If he expressed his fears to his father, Carl would be betraying his mother. The parents conflict resulted in Carl not being able to obtain support from the parent he lived with.

PATTERNS PREDATING TRAUMA

The family interactional patterns both before and after Rebecca's suicide attempt played a profound role in exacerbating Carl's extensive trauma symptoms. Carl and his mother had very weak boundaries. Carl knew too much and what he knew only served to make him more anxious about his mother's well-being. He was also in a role reversal with his mother, having to be her caretaker. This role continued even after he lived with his father. His parents were in constant conflict with each other, and Carl was triangulated by each of them. All these patterns continued after Rebecca's suicide attempt and seriously exacerbated Carl's symptoms. Carl was afraid for his mother's safety. He viewed her as fragile and capable of harming herself again. The enmeshed pattern with his mother reinforced this belief. But he could not share his fears with his father, who would use the information against Carl's mother in the war over Carl's custody. The parents' conflict put the "no talk" rule in effect for Carl.

SUMMARY

In all of the families discussed in this chapter, family patterns exacerbated trauma symptoms. In I-FAST, changing these patterns becomes a therapeutic priority. To demonstrate how I-FAST can be applied to trauma, in the following chapters we will revisit these cases and follow them through the I-FAST treatment process.

I-FAST TRAUMA AND FRAMES 7

Emotional reactions to trauma are about meaning. What meaning does the trauma survivor attach to what happened to them? The experiencing of trauma can evoke strong emotional reactions in people. They may struggle to make sense of what happened to them. The traumatic experience may not fit within their beliefs about themselves or the world. When this occurs, the traumatic experience can "shatter" the survivor's previous taken-for-granted assumptions (Chu, 2011; Janoff-Bulman, 1992; Kauffman, 2002; Neimeyer, 2001). Trauma can challenge fundamental beliefs of the survivor: The belief that the world is safe and meaningful, the belief that the self is worthy and invulnerable. Major trauma can result in serious disruptions of these beliefs (Janoff-Bulman, 1992; Kauffman, 2002; Schuler & Boals, 2016). One consequence of trauma is that the client's beliefs about the world are changed: The world is now believed to be unsafe, not benevolent. The self is now believed to be unworthy and vulnerable. Experiencing a traumatic event can result in the survivor struggling with major questions such as, Why did this happen to me? Is this my fault? What could I have done to prevent this? (Figley & Figley, 2008).

From an integrative family and systems treatment (I-FAST) perspective, the beliefs about what happened and the associated meanings involve how the event is *framed*. From a constructivist perspective, frames come from social narratives. Frames are constructed *socially*, not independent from the survivor's social field. Understanding and assessing frames regarding trauma, therefore, must attend to the survivor's social field. That would primarily consist of

- the larger culture and ethnic group the survivor identifies with;
- the family they belong; to/and
- if professionals or authorities become involved, how this group frames the survivor, their behavior and their family members.

CULTURE AND FRAMES

Culture has a major impact on the meaning of a traumatic event. Family narratives regarding trauma are heavily influenced by the belief systems inherent in the family's ethnic group. It cannot be assumed that similar traumatic events occurring across cultures carry the same meaning (Summerfield, 1999). Reaction to the individual's traumatic event by a given culture contributes to the meaning. Is the survivor framed as a martyr, a victim, a mercenary? In cultures where self-determination is valued, victims may struggle with blaming themselves (Alford, 2016; De Silva, 1993). One's culture provides an overarching meaning to all events experienced by members of that culture. Family support has been identified as a moderator for posttraumatic stress disorder (PTSD). What is framed as family support in one culture may be different than how it is framed in another culture.

Individualistic Versus Collective

It is argued that Janoff-Bulman's (1992) description of how trauma shatters beliefs is relevant to Western, industrialized cultures only (Alford, 2016; De Silva, 2006). We might add to that description, White. Important issues are implicit in this argument. First, De Silva is raising the issue of how the world view and overarching beliefs within a given culture effects the meanings of traumatic events. Janoff-Bulman is describing issues that reflect beliefs in what has been described as *individualistic cultures*. Individualistic cultures place emphasis on the individual as central. Individualistic cultural frames emphasize individual personal autonomy and self-fulfillment (Hofstede, 1980; Kagitcibasi, 1994; S. Schwarz, 1990). *Collectivistic cultures* represent a second category. In these cultures, group identity heavily influences one's identity and meanings. Collectivistic cultural frames emphasize mutual social obligations and fulfilment of in-group expectations (Hofstede, 1980; Kagitcibasi, 1994; S. Schwarz, 1990). Religion and economic development also play a heavy role in influencing cultural belief systems. Can cultural belief systems moderate or exacerbate reactions to traumatic events?

The beliefs that the world is safe and benevolent and the self as invulnerable and worthy go with an individualistic, First-World culture that may also emphasize beliefs about individual responsibility and choices. Do the cultural beliefs that place heavy emphasis on individual choice and individual responsibility create greater vulnerability for the survivor? Within this belief system, is the survivor more likely to blame themselves for choices they made regarding traumatic events? Does membership in a society that has the belief that one can control one's own destiny contribute to anguish trauma victims may experience when processing why trauma happened to them? Does living in a wealthy, safe community or being a member of a privileged ethnic group contribute to the belief of invulnerability? In cultures where self-determination is valued, victims may have greater difficulty preserving self-worth (De Silva, 1993). Alford also theorizes that Western cultural beliefs make Westerners particularly vulnerable to trauma and goes even further to argue that PTSD itself is a Western-only phenomenon (Alford, 2016).

In collectivistic cultures, none of these beliefs may be predominant. The beliefs that one is invulnerable, or the world is safe, or that individuals can control their own destinies are absent in many cultures. An ethnographic study of the Sri Lankan population's response to the 2004 tidal wave and its destruction provides an example of how members of a collectivistic culture respond to trauma (Watters, 2011). The Sri Lankan population is primarily Buddhist and collectivistic. The prevailing religious philosophy and world view helped survivors of the Sri Lanka tsunami overcome their personal losses (Fallot & Heckman, 2005). Buddhism provides several beliefs that helped moderate the effects of the disaster. The Buddhist belief of impermanence and the belief that suffering is a part of life helped moderate the effects of the trauma (De Silva, 2006). No one had the belief that the world is safe and that individuals are invulnerable. The collectivistic aspect of the Sri Lankan people also impacted their reaction. Individuals were traumatized by being separated from loved ones and not being able to perform their family duties. Trauma survivors also experienced distress over the idea that they could have done more to help save victims. They were not as traumatized by what did or could have happened to them personally. Their beliefs may have protected them from the types of crises Janoff-Bulman (1992) described. But their collectivistic perspective may have created anguish regarding their responsibilities to their family and fellow villagers.

Protecting family honor is also a powerful belief in many cultures that impacts trauma survivors. Within this belief system, family honor and family reputation supersedes individual emotional needs. Loyalty to the family is paramount. Sexual assault survivors in many Asian and Middle Eastern cultures are expected to protect family honor. Their individual needs are secondary and must be sacrificed. This can result in not reporting the abuse. The survivor is expected to suffer in silence (La Flair et al., 2008).

In urban America, do the beliefs of oppressed ethnic minorities moderate or exacerbate responses to trauma? Urban ethnic minorities are perhaps exposed to trauma more than any other group in the United States. Witnessing gang violence and having to make life-and-death decisions just to get to school safely can be common. There is no sense of invulnerability. Society has already erased the sense of self as worthy. The existential crisis that Janoff-Bulman (1992) describes may be unlikely with this group as well. Jones researched the impact of spiritual beliefs in the African American culture as a protective factor in developing PTSD for urban, African American youth living in high-crime areas (Jones, 2007). She found that youth were less likely to develop PTSD if their family was spiritual and practiced their spiritual beliefs.

Understanding cultural beliefs is therefore one crucial element to understanding a trauma survivor's reactions to traumatic events and to trauma in general. Is the vulnerability to traumatic events the same across cultural belief systems? To what degree do cultural beliefs moderate or exacerbate traumatic reactions? It appears that systematic and empirical study of this question are still lacking (De Silva, 2006).

In I-FAST, frames organizing treatment and setting up interventions should fit with the belief system of the client and family and their culture. Reframes are more easily accepted when they fit with cultural frames and the client's belief system (Uskul & Oyserman, 2010). Health instructions that focus on personal self are accepted by Westerners and families from individualistic cultures. Frames focusing on relational obligations are accepted by Asian Americans and families from collectivistic cultures (Uskul & Oyserman, 2010; Yu & Shen, 2013). In I-FAST, ethnomedical competence is enhanced by identifying and utilizing family belief systems.

HOW FAMILY MEMBERS FRAME EACH OTHER

Recovery for children is enhanced by the development of a family narrative related to the meaning of trauma (Bernardon & Pernice-Duca, 2010). What do family members believe about the meaning of the traumatic event(s)? Do all family members believe the same story? Family narratives, as social constructions, are heavily influenced by interactional patterns among family members. Who talks to whom about what influences family frames. Likewise, frames influence interactional patterns.

Interactional patterns associated with trauma and the beliefs, meanings, narratives, and frames associated with trauma have dual directional influence. Although we are presenting interactions and frames as separate phenomenon, they are intertwined and reinforce each other (De Silva, 2006).

As noted in Chapter 3 of this volume, family support is a major moderator regarding trauma survivors developing or not developing PTSD. How family members frame each other and the traumatic event itself play a major role in whether a trauma survivor receives family support. Parents may be supportive but reluctant to talk with the survivor about what happened, framing the survivor as fragile. Parents may avoid discussions with the survivor out of a desire to protect them, fearing that talking about what happened would be too upsetting. But, by not talking, support is not forthcoming.

A misunderstanding of the trauma survivor's behavior can also result in frames that interfere with receiving family support. The trauma survivor may be exhibiting destructive, unsafe, or self-injurious behavior or emotional lability. The family may then frame the survivor as bipolar, defiant, or some other mental illness diagnosis. When family frames the survivor as mentally ill or defiant, family support for the trauma is absent. Feeling misunderstood, the trauma survivor may also be more reluctant to seek support regarding trauma.

As noted, when trauma involves sexual assault, the victim may be blamed for the assault or held equally responsible. Cultures that place an emphasis on chastity commonly blame the victim for sexual assault (Lee et al., 2005). If a younger victim is abused by an older sibling or an adult in the family, the victim may be blamed or held equally responsible. In these instances, the family is protecting the perpetrator or the family honor. They are framing the perpetrator or family honor as the victim. Understanding their frame as protective offers a potential avenue to engage and perhaps ultimately change family members who are blaming the victim.

The phenomenon of secondary trauma also can result in lack of family support (Figley & Figley, 2008). Secondary trauma occurs when others such as family members are traumatized by the trauma suffered by the survivor. In these instances, the victim may frame family as fragile (Kerig & Alexander, 2012). When a loved one is harmed, everyone who loves that person is also harmed. The trauma survivor may be protective of loved ones and spare them the emotional pain associated with what happened. The trauma is not discussed because the survivor fears it is too upsetting for loved ones to hear about. Absent any talking, family support may also absent.

HOW PROFESSIONALS FRAME FAMILY MEMBERS

When they become involved with trauma survivors and their families, professionals may use frames that can either promote healing or exacerbate problems. Professionals who miss that trauma may be a driver of a child's symptoms can diagnose the survivor with a mental illness such as bipolar disorder for emotionally volatile clients or borderline personality disorder for self-injurious clients. As noted, a large percentage of juveniles in the juvenile justice system are trauma survivors. It is common for these youths to be framed as defiant or having serious conduct problems (Kerig & Alexander, 2012). Traumatized girls entering the juvenile justice system can be framed as "incorrigible" (Acoca, 1999). Urban youth may be framed as "criminals" and incarcerated. Besides promoting further misunderstanding of the trauma survivor, these frames interfere with empathy for the client. It is difficult to have empathy for someone framed as defiant, as having personality disorders, or as a criminal.

Parents impaired by their own trauma can also be framed negatively by professionals. Overprotective, controlling, and mentally ill can be common frames used by professionals to describe some of these parents. The parent may be framed as "enjoying chaos" or "thriving on crises." These frames also do not promote empathy. Instead, these frames may contribute to avoidance of social services by parents with trauma histories and grossly interfere with establishing trusting alliances when they do enter social service systems.

Regarding intrafamily sexual abuse, professionals often frame the offenders very negatively. They may be framed as "incurable," only interested in "power and control," or unable to control their sexual impulses. These frames discourage professionals from viewing intrafamilial sexual offenders as a possible source of help for survivors. Instead, survivors are protected from interacting with offenders and joint interviews can be discouraged. While there are certainly circumstances where it is correct to protect the survivor from contact with family perpetrators, therapeutic opportunities are lost by summarily dismissing all family perpetrators as being only harmful. There is tremendous potential therapeutic benefit for trauma survivors in cases where the perpetrator is willing to accept responsibility for the abuse and express their sorrow for the pain they caused (Grove, 2002; Madanes, 1990, 1995; Trepper & Barrett, 1989).

HOW I-FAST FRAMES FAMILY MEMBERS: STRENGTH-BASED

I-FAST operates from a strengths-based collaborative perspective. In I-FAST, the family is framed as the experts on their lives. They are approached from a collaborative position in which their knowledge and beliefs about the issues they bring for treatment are respected and utilized. This collaborative stance is totally consistent with trauma-informed care recommendations, which place emphasis on client choices. When there is a significant trauma history, the client or parent is not viewed as mentally ill or defiant. In I-FAST, resiliency is emphasized. Positive frames are sought to explain negative behaviors and family reactions. The behaviors of trauma survivors can be framed as their way of trying to survive. Trauma survivors can be framed as resilient and adaptive to extreme circumstances.

I-FAST emphasizes using positive frames such as framing family members as being motivated to protect each other or of doing the best they can, framing trauma survivors as protecting family members from the emotional pain resulting from the disclosure of abuse, framing family members as protecting either survivor or perpetrator or the whole family, and so on. A mother with a trauma history may be extremely overprotective or controlling with her child. In I-FAST, we view this as adaptive behavior given what she has suffered. Unfortunate behaviors may be motivated by adaptive or protective aspirations. While we may not approve of behaviors, such as blaming victims or defiant actions or minimal conduct, in I-FAST we can approve of the motivations to survive and protect and frame survivors and family in a positive light.

FAMILY FRAMES AND TREATMENT FRAMES: FRAMES UTILIZED AND FRAMES DELETED

Western psychotherapies reflect a particular world view. Compliance is enhanced if the treatment is consistent with the survivor's belief system (De Silva, 1993). In I-FAST, how family and professionals are framing the problem and each other and how to intervene are tracked. Some frames are utilized, some are ignored, and some are reframed. In any case, we are trying to co-create with the families a shared treatment framework that incorporates and utilizes family beliefs and frames that promote key concepts and drivers of I-FAST treatment. In this way, I-FAST is culturally sensitive and can be adapted to a wide range of family beliefs and frames.

Review: Frames We Promote

We promote frames that define clients and family members in a positive light and as capable and changeable; frames that promote harmony among family and stress areas of agreement; frames that define problems as solvable and goals as achievable and as something the client and family can do something about themselves; frames that see goals as interactional and produced by a clear focus of treatment; and frames that promote interactional pattern change and normal activities.

Family frames that already promote the previously listed concepts are utilized in treatment. In this way ideas that already make sense to the family are incorporated into a given treatment. This has the advantage of strengthening family engagement and facilitating a change process the family will cooperate with.

Family Frames That Are Ignored or Reframed

Frames are ignored that define clients and family negatively or as fixed and incapable of changing; frames that define problems as unsolvable and goals unachievable and as requiring long-term professional involvement and define the client as abnormal; frames that are blaming or promote disharmony or disagreement.

We will now revisit the cases introduced in Chapter 4 of this volume. In the previous chapter, we identified the interactional patterns and exceptions associated with how family were responding to trauma. In this chapter, we will examine the frames associated with those patterns. With each case, we will identify how family and survivor are framing each other and/or what happened and how professionals are framing both family and survivor. We will show what family frames we utilized and what frames were offered by the I-FAST practitioner on the case.

THE EVIL STEPMOTHER

Family and Professional Frames

Danny was locked in the closet by his stepmother. He did not want to share the details of what happened with his mother. She cried at the first mention of the incident. Although he did not say it, Danny framed her as fragile. When his mother sought services for him, despite knowing the trauma history, he was first diagnosed (framed) with intermittent explosive disorder and placed on medication and then later diagnosed bipolar. he diagnoses emphasized mental illness, not trauma. Prescribing medication reinforced the mental illness frame. These diagnoses and the medication rendered his mother paralyzed in the face of his symptoms. She was uncertain how to respond to a "bipolar" boy. Danny's maternal grandmother, with whom he also lived, was also not framing him as traumatized. She criticized his mother for not being stern in the face of his fits. This suggested she framed him as defiant and under voluntary control of his temper. His mother's and teacher's description of his fits, however, suggested he was dissociating and did not have voluntary control over his reactions. These opposing frames of mother and grandmother put them in conflict over how to respond to Danny's trauma symptoms.

It is unclear how his stepmother framed Danny. The fact she put him in a closet and duck taped his mouth shut for hours suggests he was framed very negatively. When visiting his father's, his father would not spend time with him but would leave him under the care of his new wife. Perhaps some of her anger was at Danny's father for leaving her alone with Danny. Danny's father changed after his new marriage, becoming more demanding, less agreeable, and less available to discuss Danny and his brother. He became mysterious to Danny's mother. She framed him as unpredictable. She also framed him as powerful, having the ability to force her to resume Danny's visits. This resulted in her fearing Danny's father and believing that she could not keep Danny safe from his father and stepmother. Danny was affected by this frame of his father as frightening and no doubt contributed to his anxiety and other trauma symptoms. A six-year-old trauma survivor boy cannot feel safe if he lives with a scared mother.

I-FAST Frames and Reframes

When an I-FAST team of Phil Washburn, outpatient therapist, and Mike Kuklica, intensive in-home case manager, became involved, new frames were offered. Mike was aware of Danny's trauma history. Mike suggested Danny might be suffering from PTSD. He was the first professional to frame Danny this way. Mike referred Danny to Phil. After hearing all of Danny's symptoms, Phil reinforced the diagnosis of PTSD and framed Danny's reactions and symptoms as a normal response to severe treatment. Phil explained that it could be worse if Danny were having no reaction. Phil was much older than Danny's mother. She framed him as an expert and was very relieved at Phil's suggestion that, given what happened to Danny, his reactions were expected.

After observing Melissa become upset at just mentioning what happened to Danny, Phil excused Danny from the session and met with Melissa individually. Phil asked Melissa if she were Danny's therapist, how would she respond to him telling her about what happened. Phil was asking Melissa to reframe herself. What if she were his therapist? I-FAST seeks to put parents in a lead role at helping their children with whatever symptoms are brought to therapy. This reframing was a step in that direction. I-FAST is also strength-based. In I-FAST, we would not assume that Melissa was incapable of responding more functionally. Instead, we would assume she is capable of producing a more helpful response if she feels supported by a therapist. She told Phil that if she were Danny's therapist, she would not cry when he tried to talk to her about his fears but would stay calm. Phil affirmed that is how she would react. Phil suggested Danny be brought into the session and for Melissa to practice responding to him as if she were his therapist. The stage was now set for Danny's mother to help him with his trauma symptoms.

A DEFIANT GIRL

Family and Professional Frames

Kristen, aged 15, had been sexually assaulted at an overnight party. Her mother and stepfather were never told the details of what happened to her. This greatly influenced their frames of both her and of what happened. Although he was her stepfather, Kristen framed Albert as her father. Prior to the assault, she looked up to him, loved him, and felt loved by him. Her perpetrator threatened to kill her parents if Kristen told what happened. She was only 12 at the time of the assault. She believed the threat. To protect her family, she kept the secret. When she began to have behavior problems, her parents framed her as defiant and treated her as such. This just exacerbated her behaviors.

When professionals became involved, she was initially framed as bipolar and placed on medications. This introduced the idea to the parents that their daughter had a mental illness that was biologically induced. Although this helped initially, after her release, her behavior problems returned and escalated. Finally, in her second residential placement, she told of the assault. Although the professionals believed her, they did not tell the details of the story to her parents, only that she had been assaulted. When an investigation was done, the assault was framed by the investigators as "indicated." This was an ambiguous frame, which left the family confused. The only time Barbara attempted to ask Kristen what happened, both Barbara and Kristen cried. They both framed the other as fragile, and the conversation was stopped. Each was protecting the other from further upset by stopping the discussion and not bringing it up again.

The family lived in a small town among Albert's relatives. Kristen's behavior problems resulted in her having a very bad reputation among Albert's relatives. They all framed her as a "chronic liar" and "out of control." When no charges were filed on the perpetrator and the investigators labeled the assault as "indicated," Albert's relatives' negative frames of Kristen were validated. In the absence of the family being told details of what happened, Albert's relatives could maintain the view that she was a delinquent child. Some of Albert's family framed the assault as Kristen's fault, saying she must have been "flirtatious." Albert was caught between his family and his daughter. He took a noncommittal position of "did not know what to believe." Kristen was crushed. She framed Albert as not believing her. She then got worse.

Albert continued to respond to Kristen's behavior problems with punishments, sending the message that he framed her as delinquent. The parents turned to the juvenile court for help, but the court placed Kristen in foster care. This act framed the parents as the problem. Both parents felt blamed and unsupported. The caseworker framed the family as very uncooperative. She viewed them as "unworkable." The caseworker observed that Kristen had been in residential care twice in the family's home state. She wondered if this was the real reason that the family had "fled," noting there had been legal issues for the girl there. The caseworker was sure Kristen would eventually become a permanent ward of the state.

While in foster care, Kristen was put on additional medications. The foster mother reported that Kristen had often thrown her medication away after insisting she had taken them. Kristen had difficulty sleeping. The foster mother assumed Kristen was trying to stay awake, so she could sneak out. The foster mother framed Kristen as the most difficult child she had ever had. She was "unruly," "sneaky," not to be trusted. One night, thinking Kristen was trying to sneak out, she entered Kristen's room without knocking. When she opened the door, Kristen screamed hysterically and started crying. She thought Kristen was asleep but was not sure. Kristen said something about "being raped." After only two months in this home, the foster mother wanted her out. She suspected that there was a lot the girl was keeping secret.

How Kristen's parents framed her, how Albert's family framed her, and how professionals framed both Kristen and Kristen's parents all perpetuated and reinforced the patterns of Kristen misbehaving, with both parents and professionals responding punitively. The frames also reinforced the pattern of Kristen not talking about the sexual assault and her not receiving support.

I-FAST Frames and Reframes

After her failed foster placement Children's Services referred Kristen to an I-FAST team consisting of an outpatient therapist and an in-home intensive case manager, Ed Gallagher. Ed was hired to stabilize the second placement and prevent another foster home disruption. Ed visited Kristen in her new foster home and found her to be very guarded. The second foster mother was very positive toward Kristen, had an adult daughter living with her, and did not need much help with Kristen. Ed decided to aim his efforts at helping Kristen and her family.

Engaging and Aligning With the Parents

Ed made a home visit with Albert and Barbara. He approached them from a strengths-based perspective. In the first session, Barbara was doing most of the talking. Ed made a special effort to connect with Albert. The couple were from the Deep South. Ed asked them if they felt like they were in a foreign country. They both gave a heavy sigh and told how out of place they both felt in the North. Ed noticed Albert collected comic books. He asked Albert about his collection, and Albert talked for 30 minutes about his comic book collection. Albert then spoke more about Kristen and his family situation. He said they had no family support in Ohio and felt blamed by all the professionals involved. Both parents said that before Kristen became so defiant they both had a very close relationship with her but that was now damaged. Barbara said Kristen had been very close to Albert, who was the only dad she knew. Albert said he was concerned that he would lose his daughter. He felt like Children's Services was misjudging him and his family. He was worried that his daughter would be placed in permanent foster care or residential treatment again.

Tracking Family Frames

To understand more about the parents' frames, Ed asked if they had a theory about why their daughter became so defiant. Asking family what their theory is of why their child has problems is a question that can be used to uncover family frames. Barbara cried and told about the sexual assault. Ed asked if the parents were told exactly what happened or if Kristen was able to tell them. They said no one had ever told them what happened and that Kristen refused to talk about it. Barbara also said the allegations had caused problems in the family. Barbara explained that some of Albert's family either did not believe Kristen or thought she brought the assault on herself by being flirtatious. Albert's oldest daughter, Kristen's stepsister, was upset that her friend, the accused perpetrator, could get in serious trouble. Albert himself said he did not know what to believe. Kristen had a history of lying and stealing. He was not sure what happened regarding the sexual assault. Ed asked Albert if he wanted to know exactly what happened. "No," Albert said emphatically. It was assumed Albert was suffering from secondary trauma. Knowing exactly what happened would be too painful for him.

It was clear Albert cared deeply about his daughter and was distressed at her being placed out of the home. Ed utilized these beliefs and asked if Albert was willing to do anything to get his daughter back. "Yes," Albert replied. Ed framed it as a bad idea for there to be secrets about sexual abuse. He framed it as more important for Albert and Barbara to know than anyone else. They were Kristen's parents, and if anyone on earth should know what did or did not happen to their daughter, they should. If Kristen was sexually abused, she would expect Albert to protect her. Albert responded by saying he was going to trust Ed. If Ed said he had to know what happened, then he would go along. Kristen represented one of many traumatized clients who do not want to talk about their trauma and so cannot participate in treatments that require them to do so. Ed said since Kristen was refusing to talk, perhaps the residential treatment records contained Kristen's story. He would need their permission to obtain this. They agreed.

Ed was now in position to focus the family directly on the sexual assault of Kristen. He had formed an alliance with both parents. He made a special effort to join with Albert, a key participant who would have to be persuaded to both face the details of the assault story and become supportive of his daughter. Since Kristen did not want to talk about the sexual assault, Ed was hoping the report from the residential center where she first disclosed the abuse would contain the details of what happened. If so, he was in a position to help change the family narrative regarding the assault and obtain support for Kristen from her father.

BROTHER–SISTER SEXUAL ABUSE

Family and Professional Frames

Both Carla's parents framed the sexual abuse of their daughter as her older brother Aaron's responsibility. They both believed Carla and were supportive of her. Aaron, however, was framing the abuse as "consensual." Although she was believed by both parents, she still did not feel safe because Aaron was not taking responsibility for the abuse.

In this family, the frames that were operating prior to the disclosure of the sexual abuse were very influential. Brenda, the children's mother, was the dominant figure in the family. She was protective of both her children and discouraged them from doing much outside the family. As a result, the two children were each other's playmates. The parents explained since Carla was around four, the two children played "tent." They made a tent out of the covers on their beds and pretended to be camping. After the abuse began, Steven went upstairs one evening and discovered the two children under the covers. Carla looked disheveled, and Aaron was "all sweaty." Steven told Brenda but they both framed the incident as the two children playing tent.

During the abuse, Aaron told Carla that if she told their parents, both would be in trouble. Because Brenda was such a disciplinarian, the frame that both children would get in trouble was believable. Steven's peripheral position in the family contributed to how he was framed. Brenda lost respect for him when he became disabled. She framed him as "useless." This frame was shared by Aaron who admitted to "looking down" on his father. Steven was framed as inconsequential. Aaron did not fear his father's potential response sexually abusing his sister.

Perhaps because of their closeness and intense relationship, Aaron was framing his mother in a sexual manner. An indication of this frame was the fact that on one occasion he fondled her breasts while she was sleeping. Often mother and son wrestled and played on the floor even though Aaron was 15. In public, they made the impression they were an older woman and a younger boyfriend. Aaron was confused by his relationship with his mother which at one minute was volatile and hostile and another minute seductive.

When Aaron ran away from home, Carla assumed it was because he felt bad about the abuse. She thought what he had done to her was weighing on his conscience. Despite all he had done to her, she was protective of him and worried about his emotional state. She was framing him as having a human response to inflicting pain on a loved one. Aaron was very upset about "letting his parents down." He was having nightmares about angels falling from grace.

When the abuse was uncovered, Steven was torn about how to frame it. He told a story of how he grew up in the country and had many cousins. They all "played doctor" and "checked each other out." He was baffled about why his son would "go all the way." Steven thought that because his son was not allowed out of the house, he gave in to his sexual urges. He said, "Boys have their urges," and when imprisoned at home he directed them at his sister. This was his theory of why the abuse happened. He was criticizing his wife for keeping the children inside.

I-FAST Frames and Reframes

Karen Grider was assigned to work with the family. After the investigation was completed, the family was referred for therapy with the agreement that if the family and Aaron cooperated with treatment, Aaron could remain in the home. If they did not cooperate, Karen would have to tell Children's Services, and Aaron would most likely be removed from the home. Because Aaron was so volatile prior to the session and because he was not taking responsibility for the abuse, a special effort was made to engage him in treatment.

Joining the Parents

In the initial family meeting, Karen started with the parents together. The act of meeting with the parents first framed them as the heads of the family. Their permission was sought for the children to tell about what happened. Karen treated both parents with great respect. She framed the goal of the family session as one in which the family needed to talk about what happened. She told the parents she would need their help to get the children to talk. They would have to talk first and role model talking about what they knew. She framed them as her co-therapists. This was done partly because it was true—Karen did need their help. It was also done to put them at ease and reassure them they were not invited to be blamed for the abuse. They were invited to participate in helping their children.

When meeting with the entire family, Karen used positive frames, explaining that the goal was to help the entire family feel better. She told Aaron that she hoped that included him. Karen was framing herself as caring not just about Carla but about Aaron as well. Karen framed the abuse as not just something that caused physical pain but also as something that caused emotional pain. She explained that when someone in a family is emotionally harmed, everyone who loves that person is also emotionally harmed. Again, she included Aaron in this frame. The idea was that when you hurt someone you love, you hurt yourself. Karen asked Aaron if he understood. He said, "It made everyone feel bad." "You included," Karen asked. "Me included," Aaron responded. Aaron was being framed as a human being, not a monster. As a human being, he had a conscience, and he severely damaged that conscience. His nightmares of falling angels confirmed this. It was hoped that if Aaron was approached as a human being who was also in pain, he would cooperate and perhaps give up the idea that the abuse was consensual.

Karen had now established a framework that would allow for a family discussion of what happened in which the narrative could emphasize Aaron taking responsibility for what he did and as someone who was also in pain. How the discussion was structured could also provide steps at helping the parents work as a team and restore the father's position in the family as more consequential. All these steps had the potential to helping Carla feel safe.

SUICIDAL MOTHER

Family and Professional Frames

The central frames driving Carl's anxiety and nightmares were his belief that his mother was fragile and that he was her caretaker and protector. Once at his father's, he was cut off from his mother. He could not judge her condition or need for care. This was intensely upsetting to him and the main source of his anxiety. He framed his mother's suicide attempt as his fault because he was not there to care for her. His parents, on the other hand, framed each other as enemies. Rebecca believed Robert was trying to "steal" Carl from her. Despite having a live-in boyfriend, she viewed Carl as all she had. She had been abused as a child and had nothing to do with her family of origin. From her perspective, she was seriously ill, and Carl was the only one who would care for her properly. The idea that she could lose Carl drove her to attempt suicide.

Rebecca and Carl's relationship was characterized by very weak boundaries. Rebecca told Carl everything. Once he became afraid for her safety, the things Rebecca told Carl made him more concerned and anxious. Rebecca, however, framed it as normal for her to tell everything to her son. She had been doing so for years. She did not believe it was upsetting to him.

Robert framed Rebecca as the source of Carl's problems. He was, in fact, determined to gain full custody of Carl. This put him and Rebecca in a competing posture and intensified the belief that they were enemies. Robert was very reluctant to allow Carl to have extra contact with his mother and for much of the therapy was adamant about her not participating. Robert framed Carl as traumatized and fragile. He believed Carl needed to be protected from his mother. Letta, the therapist, also framed Rebecca as someone Carl needed protected from.

Strengths-Based Perspective on Family Frames Utilized

Despite Carl's misbehavior, aggression at school and at home, and his terrible academic decline, Robert did not view Carl as defiant. He fully recognized Carl as traumatized. He stood up for Carl at school when the school wanted him punished. Although Rebecca did not understand how her weak boundaries with Carl were exacerbating his anxiety, she did view him as resilient, a strengths-based frame. The main strength of Carl, which was also fueling his anxiety, was that he was so protective of his mother. Framing Carl as protective of Rebecca, and not as afraid of her, was a key to understanding what interventions might help him settle down. Viewing Carl as afraid of his mother or in danger of being further harmed by her implied he should be protected from her. Viewing him as protective of his mother, however, implied he needed more contact with her, not less.

I-FAST Reframes and Potential Treatment Directions

The first reframe had to be between supervisor and therapist. Letta Platt had been assigned as Carl's therapist. Letta was trained in trauma-focused cognitive-behavioral therapy but could not employ this model with Carl because Carl refused to talk about what was upsetting him. Letta was also trained in play therapy. She used a sand box and play to help Carl express himself. From her play therapy sessions, Letta learned that Carl felt very anxious at his mother's house but felt obligated to visit her. Letta administered the Child PTSD Symptom Scale with Carl. Carl rated having unwanted thoughts or nightmares five times per week, feeling as if he were reliving what was upsetting him several times per week, and feeling upset in his body five times per week.

Letta had to be convinced that Carl's mother was a potential source of healing for Carl, not someone to be avoided. Several sessions of getting nowhere helped convince Letta. Carl himself helped Letta to understand he was protective of his mother. He told her he felt obligated to be with her. Letta began to understand that Carl thought he needed to take care of his mother. When Letta discovered this, she realized he needed more contact with her to reassure him that she was safe. Carl himself felt safe; the problem was he feared his mother was not safe.

Letta then had to convince Robert that Carl needed his mother, that he should not excommunicate her from Carl's life. Again, Carl's lack of progress in treatment was called upon to help convince him. This was done in stages and eventually resulted in Robert granting permission to include Rebecca in Carl's treatment. The deciding factor came after another crisis in school in which Carl cut himself severely. Letta used the crisis to convince Robert that Carl's mother had to be included in the treatment. This whole process took months.

There were two issues: the intense conflict between the parents in which Carl was triangulated and the weak boundaries between Carl and his mother. The conflict between the parents was intense and very upsetting to Carl. He was interrogated by each parent about the other, was being pressured by both to take sides, and could not discuss his fears about his mother with his father because his father would use the information against her. However, this competition was also a major motivator for both parents. They both were on a campaign to discredit the other, especially in court. Could this motivation be used in a positive way?

Once Rebecca was enlisted in the treatment, Letta could not convince her that too much information about her health, her suicide attempt, and other aspects of her life was upsetting to Carl. Carl's anxiety and nightmares were fueled by these weak boundaries. The dilemma was, if his contact with his mother was restricted, he had worse anxiety. On the other hand, having contact with her resulted in him knowing too many details about her daily life, which then also fueled his anxiety. One potential latent family resource was Rebecca's boyfriend. How did he frame the weak boundaries between Carl and Rebecca? Could he be enlisted as a co-therapist?

SECRETS

Family Frames

Before it was discovered that John was sexually abusing Melinda, negative frames were already taking a toll on this newly blended family. Cathy believed John was manipulating his father Mark and that Mark was completely fooled by his son. She and Mark were already in conflict over parenting of John. Then Melinda disclosed John was sexually abusing her. Melinda now framed John as an "incurable pervert" and banned him from the family. Mark did not frame his son negatively. He continued to see him secretly. Mark framed his wife as uncompromising and avoided conflict with her. When the topic of John did come up, the couple fought bitterly. Several times Cathy threatened divorce. These terrible fights took a toll on the children left in the home. Melinda framed the conflict between her mother and stepfather as her fault, regretting that she ever revealed to anyone what John did to her. She also believed Mark was angry with her because her telling about the abuse meant John had to leave the home. Todd also felt guilty and was blaming himself for the family problems. He had witnessed John leaving Melinda's bedroom one night and knew something wrong was happening. He did not tell his parents, and now he believed if he had, perhaps all the problems would not be happening. All the children viewed the family as unstable due to the intense fights between the parents. They kept all their secrets fearing the family could break up if they told. All the children were suffering in silence.

Family Strengths and Frames Utilized

As adamant as Cathy was, she was trying to protect her daughter. She was concerned about Melinda's safety and emotional well-being and was motivated to help her daughter. This motivation to protect and help Melinda could be embraced and utilized in the treatment.

John had completed juvenile sex offender treatment. He was taking full responsibility for the abuse, was not blaming Melinda at all, and was very sorry for all the pain he had caused. These were obvious strengths that could be utilized in the treatment. Mark loved his son and believed he had truly improved. He stayed by him even after he had done such terrible things to Melinda. Both the parents did love each other and wanted the marriage to work and the family to stay together. They were all motivated to find a solution.

The frames and motivations of all family members were now understood. It was now possible to construct an overarching treatment frame for how to organize the therapy so all members' respective agendas could be included, a frame they would all likely cooperate with and one that pointed the way for what interventions to offer.

DECIDING WHOM TO INCLUDE IN TREATMENT

8

DECIDING WHOM TO INCLUDE IN TREATMENT AS AN INTERVENTION

Who attends treatment in integrative family and systems treatment (I-FAST) is not prescribed but rather is decided upon for each case. We view this as a major treatment decision and an intervention in and of itself. We have provided guidelines for making this decision elsewhere (Fraser, Grove, Lee, Greene, & Solovey, 2012). Regarding trauma treatment, this flexibility on whom to include in treatment is a defining feature of I-FAST. Many evidence-based trauma treatments either work with the individual trauma survivor or, if a child is the survivor, only the child client individually or the child survivor and one caregiver. I-FAST offers many more options. For child survivors, we may include one or both of their parents or caregivers, siblings, or extended family members. We may conduct entire family interviews or individual interviews. In some circumstances, when the trauma involves intrafamily sexual abuse, we may include the perpetrator in a family interview together with the survivor. For adult survivors, we may include a spouse or intimate partner. As any given treatment unfolds, depending on the treatment goals, who attends treatment may vary from session to session. Regarding trauma, there are two special circumstances involving whom to work with that will be covered in detail: whole-family interviews and bringing intrafamily sexual abuse survivors and family perpetrators together.

DECIDING WHOM TO INCLUDE IN TREATMENT TO CHANGE INTERACTIONAL PATTERNS

The decision on whom to include in treatment can be partly based on a strategy to promote changing interactional patterns. For example, when attempting to shift an intrusive parent to a less involved position and a disengaged parent to a more involved position, an agreement can be reached that the disengaged parent will attend treatment with the child without the intrusive parent attending.

The following case illustrates how the decision on whom to include in treatment can be one way to change interactional patterns. A seven-year old boy was placed by his mother with an older husband and wife, while the mother attended inpatient drug treatment. After completing treatment, she was living alone. Her son, however, remained with the caregivers. Although both the caregivers and the boy's mother agreed he should return to his mother, both sides were reluctant to do so. The caregivers were concerned about the mother's parenting, and the mother herself felt guilty about her drug history and lacked confidence in her parenting.

The boy was having serious emotional dysregulation and impulsive symptoms at the caregivers' home. Of the two caregivers, the "auntie" was very much involved in his day-to-day care and was seeking help on his behaviors. Because the boy lived with the caregivers, the initial recommendation was for parenting classes for the auntie. However, if the ultimate goal of both caregivers and mother was for the boy to return to his mother, parenting classes for the auntie would reinforce the current arrangement. Instead, it was decided to give parenting classes to the mother, whom the boy did not live with. This strategy could strengthen the attachment between the two, increase the mother's confidence in parenting her son, and alleviate the auntie's concern about returning the boy to her. The decision of whom to give the parenting classes to was, in fact, a major intervention designed to change the patterns among all the participants. It is an example of how deciding whom to include in treatment is an intervention in and of itself.

DECIDING WHOM TO INCLUDE IN TREATMENT WHEN TREATMENT IS AT AN IMPASSE

An informal rule in family therapy has long been, "When stuck, add people." When therapy is at an impasse, changing who is participating in treatment can be a powerful tool for moving the therapy forward. This requires I-FAST practitioners to be skilled at recruiting family members who have not been participating in sessions. Family who have been participating must be persuaded to add someone else. The new person must be persuaded to participate. Once additional family have joined the treatment, I-FAST treatment practitioners must be skilled at how to add them to a process that has been proceeding without them.

When recruited, new family participants can provide information regarding interactional patterns, exceptions, and new frames that are useful for treatment. The same intervention ideas offered to the family previously can be offered again with new participants. What was not working with one set of family members may now work with new participants added to the process. Throughout this book, there are numerous case examples of adding new family members to a therapy that is stuck and how adding the new participants changed the outcome.

TWO SISTERS

Background and Trauma History

Marleen, aged 13, and Wendy, aged 16, had lived with their maternal grandmother for two years. Prior to living with their grandmother, both girls lived with their mother and stepfather. The stepfather was both verbally and physically abusive toward the girls' mother. Beginning when Marleen was 10 years old, her stepfather began sexually abusing her. The abuse went on for two years, was frequent, and involved rape.

After the first incident of sexual abuse, Wendy told her mother. Her mother confronted the stepfather, and the stepfather then beat her badly. The mother responded by taking both daughters to a battered women's shelter. She was unable to break away from her husband, however. She and the two girls went back to him. He then resumed the sexual abuse of Wendy, and Wendy again told her mother. Her mother again confronted her husband, and the husband again beat her. She again took both girls to the shelter. But, as before, she was unable to break away from her husband and went back. As before, after returning home, the sexual abuse resumed. This time, however, Wendy did not say anything. She did not want her mother to be beaten again.

During this period, the police began investigating the stepfather for other sexual crimes. He had befriended the mothers of several of his daughters' friends and began sexual affairs with them. He used his relationships with these women to gain access to their daughters and sexually abuse them as well. When alerted to this, Wendy's mother pleaded with the other mothers not to turn her husband in. However, the father was charged with several counts of child molestation, and the mother, with attempting to interfere with an investigation. Both were found guilty and went to jail. When the parents went to jail, both sisters went to live with the maternal grandmother.

Re-Experiencing and Self-Harm Symptoms

One year after moving with their grandmother, their mother was released from jail. Both girls visited their mother but were afraid to talk to her about all that had happened. Wendy then began having nightmares. She had two repeating nightmares. One nightmare was of her stepfather raping her. Her other nightmare was of she and her sister hiding in a closet while their stepfather was beating their mother. She had these nightmares several times per week. She would awake shaken and afraid. She would then cut herself to try to forget the bad dreams. When the grandmother discovered Wendy was cutting herself, she took her to counseling.

In counseling, it was discovered that Wendy was very close to her sister. The counselor suggested that when she woke up at night after having a nightmare, she could tell her sister instead of cutting herself. She liked this idea. She did begin telling her sister about the nightmares, and this did stop the cutting. The nightmares, however, persisted at their previous frequency. In one session, both sisters told the therapist that they needed their mother's help and asked if the mother could be recruited into the therapy.

The therapist was torn. Both girls were saying they needed their mother's help. On the other hand, the therapist felt the mother was a serious problem because she tried to protect the abusive husband from the police. The therapist decided to consult with the I-FAST consultant.

Strengths-Based Perspective

After hearing the story, the I-FAST consultant was impressed with the mother's attempts to protect the daughter. The consultant was viewing the mother from a strengths-based perspective. Many women have a difficult time escaping an abusive relationship. It was unknown what pressure the husband put on the mother to protect him from legal consequences. It was suggested that the mother be invited in for an individual session for a discussion on how she could help. The therapist could make her own judgments about the mother based on a face-to-face meeting.

Adding the Mother to Break an Impasse

The mother agreed to attend an individual session. Both sisters were told their mother had agreed to come. The therapist enlisted the help of a clinic supervisor who decided to tape the session. This was an unfortunate decision because it made the mother suspicious. She was very cautious during the interview. Nonetheless, the therapist explained that her daughter was having nightmares and described the nightmares to her. She was told that her girls had requested that she come to therapy because they needed her help. She was asked to join her daughters for a session in which she would be asked to listen to the daughter's nightmares and express her apologies for all the painful events the daughters had to endure. The mother agreed to this plan. The girls were seen one week later and told their mother had attended her individual session.

Tracking Exceptions

Before a session with mother and daughters could be arranged, the girls had a visit with their mother. At one point during the visit, Wendy asked her mother if she remembered the times the stepfather had beaten her after Wendy had reported the abuse. The mother said she did remember and spontaneously told both girls how sorry she was. Both girls and their mother broke into tears and sobbed.

Wendy reported all this at her next therapy session. She said her talk with her mother was very helpful. Before the talk she thought her mother might be angry with her. She did not know how sorry her mother felt and how badly her mother felt about what had happened. She was in a much better frame of mind and reported that her nightmares had stopped. One helpful encounter between Wendy and her mother resulted in her nightmares completely going away. The therapist continued to see Wendy for four more months on a periodic basis. In every session, Wendy reported that her nightmares were over and she, her sister, and her mother were having very good visits.

WHOLE-FAMILY INTERVIEWS: CHANGING FAMILY TRAUMA NARRATIVES

The impact of trauma on a family level is well documented (Figley & Figley, 2009; Walsh, 2007). When a loved one is traumatized, all those who love that person are also harmed. Children rely on their family for appraisal of traumatic events (Pynoos, 1993). For trauma treatment of children, it is vital to develop a helpful and supportive family consensus regarding the meaning of traumatic events (Bernardon & Pernice-Duca, 2010). Secondary trauma can block discussions on a family level, interfering with the ability of a family to process the trauma in a helpful and meaningful way. Family members may be framed as fragile by the trauma survivor, resulting in a reluctance to talk to family members about what happened (Kerig & Alexander, 2012).

In earlier chapters, we defined distortions regarding the meaning of traumatic events as occurring on a family level. Blaming the survivor for sexual assault is one example. Numerous narrative treatment approaches for trauma emphasize telling the trauma story in family interviews (Bernardon & Perinice, 2010; Ralph, 2005; Walsh, 2007). A family may be divided into camps regarding what narrative to believe about traumatic events. One way to change unsupportive family narratives is to conduct a family interview in which the trauma is processed among the entire group. The goal of such a session is to change unhelpful or blaming narratives into something more supportive. A second goal of such a session is to obtain an agreement among the whole family on how to view the traumatic events. Family sessions regarding trauma aim to result in the survivor obtaining family support, especially if it is absent beforehand. Conducting whole-family sessions focusing on the story of what happened and constructing supportive narratives on a family level can be a powerful tool for I-FAST treatment of trauma.

SUICIDAL FAMILY

Thirteen-year-old Kevin lived with his 35-year-old single mother, Lucy; 15-year-old sister, Teresa; and 17-year-old sister, René in a small trailer. The biological father had committed suicide one year prior to the family getting treatment after a long struggle with cirrhosis of the liver due to severe alcoholism. He had been suffering with chronic pain for one year. He shot himself in the head at night in his room. Lucy went and found him still alive. He died at the hospital. Extended family lived in California except for Lucy's brother who lived close by.

Presenting Problem

One year after the father's death, none of the three teenagers were attending school. The school filed truancy on the children, and juvenile court became involved. An intensive in-home case manager and an outpatient therapist were assigned to the family to attempt to prevent legal proceedings being brought against the family.

In the first in-home session, a family meeting with the whole household was called. Kevin was afraid he was going to be confronted by the in-home treatment team for not attending school. Instead, the case manager asked the whole family what they thought the problems were. The family then told the story about how their father killed himself. The children complained that since their father died, their mother never wanted to come out of her bedroom. Lucy said she did not want to leave her room because she thought her husband's spirit was still there. All the children told how worried they were about their mother. They were afraid she was suicidal like their father. They were all staying home from school to make sure she did not kill herself. They were willing to sacrifice their own educations and social lives to stay close and watch her. This was one of the family strengths that would be drawn upon.

Interactional Patterns and Family Frames

The case manager asked the children to tell Lucy how worried they were about her. They told how Lucy stayed in her room and drank all day and night. That she had not come out of her room in a year. She stayed up all night and slept all day. She had not signed permission slips for school. The older sister was forging her mother's name and calling the brother off from school. Lucy was shocked at how acutely aware the children were of her habits and did not know her oldest daughter was calling her son off from school. Lucy confessed that she was afraid to leave her room because she thought if she did her husband's spirit would leave. All the children said they had seen their dad's spirit, but Lucy had not. The father was cremated, and his ashes were in an urn that the mother kept in her room. She hoped that by keeping the urn close at hand, she would be visited by her husband's spirit. The children were upset that the mother kept the urn in her room. They felt cut off from their father.

The interactional patterns were dominated by Lucy's total disengagement from the family and the children's fear and reluctance to talk among themselves or with their mother about their worries. The session provided a forum for them to be open about their concerns, breaking the pattern of not talking. This alone seemed to provide them with great relief.

Interrupting Patterns and Amplifying Strengths

At the next in-home session, a plan was offered for how the children could best help their mother. Their concern for their mother and desire to help was utilized. The children would take turns watching over their mother. A schedule for who would check in with mom and when was constructed. Each child had a shift. By taking turns checking on mom, the other children could go to school and function normally. Whoever was on duty was to constantly go in and check on Lucy. The children had been afraid to go into Lucy's room fearing they might find her dead. The children reacted to this task with enthusiasm. Lucy, however, did not want her privacy interrupted. The children insisted that they were worried about her life. They were not going to leave her unattended. The therapy team explained that because the children were so worried about her taking her life, Lucy would have to permit them to come in her room and check on her. They all banded together. Lucy had to acquiesce. It was hoped that if the children intruded into Lucy's room, she would come out and become more involved with the children. The children did take their shifts watching Lucy.

After the first session, the children's functioning improved greatly. Those not on duty watching their mother went back to school. However, Lucy was still retreating to her room and isolating herself there. Although the children no longer feared Lucy would kill herself, they were upset that she was still so withdrawn. They wanted her to pay bills, cook dinner, settle arguments between the siblings, and help the group negotiate how to spend the household income. In Lucy's absence, there were frequent screaming matches among the children about money. Lucy remained disengaged. Lucy was strongly encouraged to become more engaged, but she did not.

The children requested another family meeting to help the family set the rules on money. In the family meeting, Tom asked Lucy what she found comforting about staying in her room. She said that is where her husband's ashes were. The children complained that their mother was always in the room with the urn containing their father's ashes. Not only did Lucy stay with the urn, she obsessed about her husband constantly. She would smell his clothes and his deodorant and constantly thought about him. She confessed that she had daily nightmares and flashbacks of the image of her husband in his room as she found him after he shot himself. The children complained they never got a chance to visit the urn. "He is our dad. He is only your husband. You can find a new husband; we cannot find a new dad," they said. Lucy and the children began to argue about how their dad would have dealt with the money issues. When he was living, the father was in charge of finances.

Whole Family Interview: Utilizing Family Frames and the Family Trauma Narrative

The entire family truly believed their father's spirit was in the home. This family frame was utilized. Claiming he had a right to offer his own opinion, the case manager suggested that they should invite the dad to the meeting. The group became silent and looked at their mother. Lucy nodded OK. All three children ran to the bedroom and got the urn. Dad was brought into the room and put on the table. Some family patterns are laden with multiple meanings. Changing these patterns can produce the most profound therapeutic outcomes. For this family, the urn and their patterns around it had multiple and profound meanings. It was anticipated that asking them to change their behavior involving the urn had the potential to produce very meaningful clinical outcomes. Their specific response to the request to bring the urn into the session, however, was not anticipated.

The presence of the urn inspired a family discussion. For the first time, the whole family spoke openly and honestly about the father's death. They talked about how they were angry that he killed himself. They each recounted the story of what happened the night their father took his life. They each talked about the last things they had said to him at the hospital before he died. Kevin said he was mad at his mother for not letting him say goodbye to his dad at the hospital. Lucy said she did not want him to see his father's serious wounds. Kevin said he had already seen him at the house before the ambulance came. Lucy did not know this.

Although this family talk was very helpful for everyone, it exposed troubling narratives. They each were blaming themselves for the father's death. Lucy had a hostile relationship with him for years. She thought he killed himself because of their bad marriage. Tereasa had had an argument with her father earlier that day. She thought he killed himself over the fight. The family narrative was full of self-blame. Lucy did not realize her children were blaming themselves for their father's death. Discovering this resulted in her challenging her own belief that his death was her fault. She said, "How can I tell my children this was not their fault but still blame myself?"

Changing the Family Narrative

After consulting, the therapy team called another family meeting. Lesley and Tom offered a new frame to the children to explain their father's death. They emphasized their father's chronic illness and chronic pain. He was in excruciating, daily pain, with no end in sight. He had no hope of recovering. Tom and Lesley explained that many chronic pain sufferers with no hope of recovery turn to suicide for relief. This is most likely why their father killed himself—to end his misery. This made sense to the entire family. A new narrative was created and accepted.

Tracking Exceptions

After this talk, the urn was permanently placed in the living room. Lucy re-engaged with the family. She began paying the bills and presiding over the family. She started leaving the house, doing grocery shopping, and having a social life. Lucy also decided to go back to school for her GED. The middle daughter and her boyfriend decided it was safe to move to California. Their departure greatly reduced the chaos, fighting, and cramped conditions in the home. Interestingly, Lucy reported she no longer had any nightmares or intrusive thoughts of her husband's dead body. When asked what she thought helped, she said the two family discussions. She said the idea that he killed himself to end his own suffering gave her peace. She stopped having all her nightmares after that discussion.

At a one-year follow-up, all children were doing fine. Lucy had given up some of her husband's belongings and was now dating. She was reading books and not just staring at the TV. She was no longer obsessing over her husband, smelling his clothes and his deodorant. The children were continuing to attend school and the oldest daughter had graduated high school.

CHANGING FAMILY NARRATIVES RELATED TO SEXUAL ASSAULT

When sexual assault is the source of trauma, blaming the survivor is a common and problematic result. Secondary trauma again can interfere with family discussions regarding what happened, and an incomplete knowledge of the assault can allow for unsupportive family narratives. One goal is to develop a nonblaming trauma narrative on a family level. Individual family members' frames regarding the trauma must be assessed. Negative attitudes regarding the survivor must first be reframed before conducting a family session (Sherman et al., 2008). Family frames that increase the risk of expression of trauma symptoms include feelings of powerlessness, sense of failure, and blaming the survivor or each other (Walsh, 2007). Interactional patterns including secrecy, hostel and high conflict levels, denial of abuse, boundary violations, and blocked emotional sharing related to trauma can support these frames (Figley & Figley, 2009; Walsh, 2007). Successful family sessions can change both the interactional patterns of secrecy and help to develop supportive family frames related to the traumatic event(s).

In I-FAST, when sexual assault is the trauma, for whole family sessions to be successful, it is often necessary to proceed in steps leading up to a whole family session. The therapist must establish an alliance with all important family members first. All family members frames regarding what happened must be tracked. The details of the traumatic event must be known. Typically, distorted family narratives are supported by incomplete knowledge of what happened. With sexual abuse, for example, the victim may be blamed if family members only know a fraction of the story. When trauma results from sexual assault, if the full account of what happened is brought to light, it can become more difficult for family members to blame the victim. Changing these narratives, therefore, requires a violation of the "no talk" rule. For a case in which a child has been sexually assaulted and the parents either do not believe the survivor or blame them, a session with the parents only may be needed first, to inform them of the whole story. How they react to this new information then may allow for a whole family meeting in which the parents provide support for the survivor.

A DEFIANT GIRL

Kristen had been sexually assaulted by an older boy at an overnight party when she was 12 years old. She was afraid to tell of the assault. When she began to have behavior problems, her parents, unaware of the assault, misunderstood her and treated her like a defiant girl. After two years of struggle and two residential treatment stays, Kristen told about the assault. Professionals investigated but did not share the details with Kristen's parents, Albert and Barbara. They did not know the details of the assault, and Kristen did not want to share the story. Albert's family framed the assault as either Kristen's fault or as untrue. Albert, stuck between his family and his daughter, did not know what to believe. This devastated Kristen, and her behavior worsened. Ed, an in-home I-FAST practitioner, obtained an agreement from the parents that it was important for them to know the details of what happened to their daughter. Ed was able to obtain the report Kristen gave to the authorities detailing the assault. By using the report, Ed could speak for her, and the parents could finally know what happened to their daughter.

Steps Toward a Whole Family Session

INDIVIDUAL SESSION WITH THE SURVIVOR

The first goal was to convince Albert the assault did happen and help Kristen finally receive support from her father. The family narrative that Kristen was either lying or the assault was her fault would have to be changed. This would require several steps. Ed first collaborated with Kristen's individual therapist, Devaney. Devaney had a very strong rapport with Kristen. She and Ed interviewed Kristen together to talk about the report Ed had obtained. Devaney's presence for this interview helped greatly. Ed read the report to Kristen, and Kristen confirmed everything. Ed told Kristen he wanted to read the report to her parents in a session with them only. Kristen was apprehensive about this saying, "They will not understand." Ed told Kristen that he believed her. He would do his best to help her parents believe her also. Kristen gave permission for Ed to try.

SESSION WITH BOTH PARENTS TOGETHER

Ed set up a meeting with Albert and Barbara to go over the report. The meeting was now one year after Kristen disclosed to professionals what had happened to her. Neither the residential treatment staff or the aftercare outpatient services or the Children's Services investigators informed the parents of what had happened to their daughter. In the absence of knowing the facts, Albert's family were free to blame Kristen for "whatever happened." Albert had to live with doubts about what did or did not happen. And most important, Kristen was not only deprived of support from her father but also had to live in a small town where her own relatives doubted her. She had to encounter the perpetrator and deal with these encounters all by herself. As a result, she was suicidal, self-mutilating, and defiant.

In the session with the two parents, Ed began to read the report word for word to both. After several statements quoting Kristen's account, Albert stopped Ed. He said, "I believe everything. That is how my daughter talks. I know she is telling the truth." Hearing the details of the story for the first time was all that was necessary to persuade Albert.

Ed finished reading the report and spent the rest of the session talking about important details. The abuser was a friend of Albert's oldest daughter. He had threatened to kill Kristen's family members if she told anyone. Kristen may have actually seen the abuser in various locations in the small town they lived in. The discussion focused on posttraumatic stress disorder and how people can respond to trauma. Ed framed the problem: Kristen did not feel safe and felt alone. This explained her nightmares and most likely her suicidal statements and self-harm.

Ed explained that the next step would be a family meeting that included Kristen. She would have to be told that the two parents now know everything. Their job was to let her know that they both believed her and how sorry they were that something so terrible happened to her. Ed gave Albert specific instructions. He told Albert to take the lead in responding to the report and make sure he let his daughter know he believed her. Both parents agreed that this is what should happen next. Ed was pleased with the parents' responses to the report and was confident a family session would go well.

Whole Family Session: Constructing a New Family Narrative

The family session was set and included Ed, Devaney, both parents, and Kristen. Ed purposely set up the seating for Kristen to sit between her Mom and Dad. Ed started by saying that it was very important for there to be no secrets about the abuse that had happened to Kristen. He told Kristen not to worry, that he and the parents had a very good talk about this and that her parents "understood." Kristen was still apprehensive about having the report read during the family session. Albert put his hand on her shoulder and said, "It will be all right, honey." Kristen was very reassured by this. Ed read the whole report with all present. He stressed how the offender threatened to kill family members if Kristen ever told and that initially Kristen believed that. Albert broke down crying. He told Kristen how sorry he was that he had not protected her the way a dad should. They both spontaneously hugged each other. Albert also told her how sorry he was for doubting her about what happened. Kristen was visibly relieved that Albert believed her. Ed had the strong impression that Kristen was anticipating Albert would not believe her. Ed said that by not telling anyone, Kristen sacrificed herself to protect the family. Both parents and Kristen cried together in response to this. The session was very emotional, cathartic, and supportive of Kristen. This session was a great turning point for Kristen and her family. This one session, which could have happened over one year earlier if family treatment had been done, ended the long saga of Kristen exhibiting numerous symptoms and being in and out of various placements.

Tracking Exceptions

After this session, Kristen showed marked improvement in the foster home. Ed conducted another family session. This time Kristen's younger sister also attended. He gave everyone paper and crayons and asked them all to each individually draw a picture of a place where they each felt safe and happy. Without consulting or looking at what they each were drawing, they all drew the same picture. They were all together in their old house in the South. When they showed each other their pictures they all cried. Ed pointed out to Albert that Kristen's drawing showed how connected she was to the family even after spending so much time away in residential treatment and foster care. Albert was very moved. Soon after this session, Albert announced that he and Barbara had decided to move back South after Kristen returned home from foster care.

Kristen now was going home every weekend for family visits. There was no more lying, stealing, defiance, cutting, or nightmares. Ed continued weekly family meetings. After several weekend visits, Kristen was sent home. The family moved back South within a month of her return. One year later, Barbara called Ed to tell him how Kristen was doing. She was off all her medications. Kristen and Albert were getting along very well. There were no more nightmares or cutting or talk of suicide. No more stealing or sneaking out. She did tell "white lies" from time to time. She was dating a nice boy both parents approved of. She had a part-time job and was preparing to graduate. Both parents were employed and were financially stable.

INCLUDING INTRAFAMILIAL SEXUAL ABUSE SURVIVORS AND OFFENDERS IN THE SAME INTERVIEW

Traditionally, there have been strong reservations within the therapeutic community over bringing intrafamilial sexual abuse survivors and perpetrators together for joint interviews (Paige & Thorton, 2015; Stubbs, 2002). Courts often issue no-contact orders between family victims and offenders. Although separating victim and offender provides safety against future abuse, it can also interfere with bringing a sense of resolution for the survivor. Preventing all contact can also result in chronic anxiety for the survivor about the absent offender and their whereabouts (Paige & Thorton, 2015). As time goes on, it is likely that contact between family survivors and perpetrators will occur by accident or at family events such as funerals, graduations, or marriages. These unplanned encounters can be profoundly helpful or hurtful.

Numerous family treatment programs and approaches have utilized family sessions that include both intrafamily sexual perpetrator and survivor in family sessions. Cloe Madanes utilized this approach in her work with juvenile sex offenders at the Family Therapy Institute of Washington, D.C. (Madanes, 1990, 1995). Trepper and Barrett (1989) developed a family treatment program for incest that utilized sessions that included both survivor and perpetrator. Over the last 10 years, the restorative justice movement has focused on in person conferencing between victims of crimes and their perpetrators (Amstutz, 2009; Oudshoorn, Amstuctz, & Jackett, 2015). Restorative justice interventions bring victim and offender together "to resolve collectively how to deal with the aftermath of the offence" (Strang, 2002, p. 44). The restorative justice concepts have been applied specifically to intrafamily sexual abuse and organizing joint family survivor and perpetrator interviews (Julich, 2001; Oudshoorn, 2015). A family treatment approach developed at the Cedar Cottage in Sydney, Australia, has been conducting family sessions with sexual abuse survivors and their family perpetrators, including fathers, for 25 years (Tolliday, Spangaro, & Laing, 2018).

Therapeutic goals for family sessions with survivors and perpetrators include acknowledgement of abuse and the pain it caused and closure and empowerment for the survivor (Grove, 2002; Madanes, 1990, 1995; Paige & Thornton 2015; Tolliday et al., 2018). Some survivors feel a need to transform their relationship with the family offender to co-exist in the same family. Many feel a need to receive acknowledgement of why the abuse was wrong, have the offender take responsibility for abuse, and express remorse for the pain it caused (Julich, 2001). These goals cannot be met by permanently separating survivor and perpetrator.

The role of family relational processes between family offenders and their family victims in the healing of intrafamily sexual abuse was studied by Paige and Thornton (2015). This was an ethnographic study of 35 intrafamily sexual abuse survivors regarding their experiences of contact with their family perpetrator. Survivors who had had encounters with their family perpetrators were interviewed about the helpfulness or harm of these experiences. When the encounters went well, perpetrators were able to take responsibility for the abuse, acknowledge the damage it caused, and express remorse. Survivors reported profoundly positive effects when perpetrators could respond in these ways.

In I-FAST, once it is clear a family is supporting and not blaming the victim, and the perpetrator is willing to take responsibility for abuse and express remorse, family sessions that include both the intrafamily sexual abuse survivor and perpetrator can be organized. The session goals are to create a family narrative that holds the perpetrator responsible for abuse, expresses why the abuse was wrong, and results in an expression of remorse by the offender, which typically includes an apology.

PROCEDURES FOR CONDUCTING FAMILY INTERVIEWS WITH INTRAFAMILY SEXUAL PERPETRATORS AND SURVIVORS

In I-FAST, when the sexual abuser is a family member, before conducting a family interview that includes both the survivor and the abuser, several steps must be completed. The parents must be engaged, and an alliance with them formed. Their frames of the abuse must be ascertained. If they do not believe the victim or if they blame the victim, efforts must first be made to change their view of the abuse before a family meeting can be conducted. Typically, the parents have not been told details of the abuse, and this lack of knowledge allows for distorted views to be maintained. Often, when exposed to the facts of the case, many of these parents will change their frames. As illustrated in the previous case, sometimes it is necessary to obtain a copy of the actual investigative report, which includes the actual statements of both victim and offender. Close collaboration with child welfare professionals is crucial in this regard.

Steps and Conditions Leading to a Whole Family Session

If the parents are supportive of the victim, believe them, and do not blame them, the idea of a family meeting should first be discussed with both parents together. Typically, one of the parents or family adults is the most influential. Who this is must be identified. Their frames regarding the abuse must be understood and their blessings for conducting a family interview must be obtained. Who should attend should be agreed upon. The household members in which the abuse took place are the primary candidates for who should attend a family session in which the abuse will be discussed. Sometimes it is best for very young children not to attend, but this is not a fixed rule. At later stages of the therapy, it may be important to include non-household family members and extended family but not in the first family session.

Once agreements are reached on who should attend the session, the goals of the session should also be addressed with the parents before the actual meeting. The goals of a family session are to make sure there are no secrets about the abuse that have not been stated publicly within the whole family, the offender accepts full responsibility of the offense in the presence of the family, and the offender expresses their sorrow for the pain they caused.

The abuser most often must be interviewed individually. If they are taking responsibility for the abuse and if they are willing to express their sorrow for the pain they caused, then a family interview including the survivor is possible. If the abuser is not admitting to the abuse, is blaming the survivor, or is not remorseful, the family must be enlisted to help the abuser change how they view what happened. This can be done if family members are holding the abuser accountable. It has been our experience that family has far greater influence on persuading offenders to take responsibility for abuse than do legal authorities, therapists, or group members in group therapy.

Finally, the survivor can be seen individually and told the abuser is taking responsibility for the abuse and that a family meeting is being considered. If the survivor is reluctant or feels unsafe having such a session, the parents who are supportive of the survivor can be enlisted to reassure the survivor they are supported and will be safe.

Steps for Conducting the Whole Family Interview

If all the previously discussed conditions are met, a family meeting can be held. Special guidelines should be followed to ensure the meeting is helpful. The first guideline is, No pressure on the survivor. The survivor can speak during the meeting or not, that is their choice. If they do not want to speak, they should not be pressured to do so. Frames should be offered and cultivated by the therapist that promote harmony and healing. These frames can include sexual abuse is an assault on the spirit of the person, not just a physical assault. When an abuser harms someone they love, everyone who loves that person is harmed. As someone who also loves the survivor, the abuse also harms the abuser. These frames stress the harm of abuse on an emotional level and stress healing must happen with all family members, including the offender.

The therapist should begin the meeting with a speech spelling out the goals of the session, emphasizing that everyone will take a turn telling what they know happened, starting with the parents and then the children according to age. The survivor is not required to speak but can if they wish. The therapist should emphasize they are there to help everyone, including the abuser. The therapist should then start by stating what they know already. It is most helpful for the therapist to have a copy of the investigative report and to read the report aloud. This role-models openness for the family and allows the therapist to be the first one to tell the terrible events. Typically, it is then easier for the rest of the participants to be open when it is their turn. Sharing the facts on an investigative report can also minimize denial and manipulation by the offender.

When the session goes well, the survivor receives maximum family support. The family narrative places responsibility of the abuse on the abuser, not the victim. These sessions are often emotional for everyone, including the therapist. When accomplished, the therapist should anticipate substantial postsession improvements and change. Exceptions will be generated spontaneously when sessions go well. When these sessions go well, major healing can occur.

SECRETS

After it was discovered that John had been sexually abusing his stepsister Melinda, his stepmother Cathy had banned him from the home. His father Mark had been seeing him secretly, unbeknownst to Cathy. Mark sought help from the author (DRG) after John had successfully completed sexual offender treatment, had taken responsibility for the abuse, and was remorseful. Mark wanted help to reintegrate John into the family.

Steps for Organizing a Whole Family Session

ALLIANCE WITH THE POWERFUL MOTHER

In this family, Cathy had the most power. She had the power to ban Mark's son from the home. Cathy would have to be engaged and aligned with. Cathy met with me alone and was very open. She confirmed that her position was that John should never have any contact with family members ever again. She explained that when she and Mark were married, John was Mark's favorite son. He let him get away with murder. Cathy described John as very manipulative and Mark as falling for John's manipulation time and again. The couple had fought bitterly about John for the first year of their marriage, and then John sexually assaulted Melinda. Cathy framed John as very sick and incurable and Mark as hopelessly taken in by his son.

I empathized with her about how terrible it must have been to discover what John had done to her daughter. She cried and feared her daughter was forever harmed by this. Despite all the conflict with Mark, Cathy did love her husband and did not want a second failed marriage. I asked Cathy how Melinda was doing. Cathy said Melinda was attending a group for sexual abuse victims. Cathy said she was concerned about Melinda because Melinda did not want to talk about the abuse. No one in the family talked about the abuse. It was too hot of a topic. All feared talking about it could cause a serious fight to erupt between Mark and Cathy.

I asked Cathy if she had considered the possibility that John himself might be able to help Melinda. She was taken aback by this possibility and very skeptical of it. I explained that if John were willing to take responsibility for the abuse and offer his sorrow for the pain he caused, that might help both her daughter and the conflict between she and Mark. Cathy agreed that if John were willing to do that, it would be very helpful but had great doubts that John would do such a thing. I offered Cathy a plan: I would meet with John alone and assess his willingness to help. I would also like to meet Melinda alone and see what she might say about the idea and the abuse in general. If John seemed willing to help and Melinda was OK with the idea, we would then have an all family meeting for John to apologize. First, however, Cathy and Mark and I would meet together to discuss the plan. Cathy was in full agreement. Cathy, Mark, and I met and went over the plan. Mark was also in agreement.

INDIVIDUAL MEETING WITH THE PERPETRATOR

I next met with John alone. He had a lot to share. He did take full responsibility for what he had done and said he felt very bad about it. He even was having nightmares about it. He then told me about how he himself had been sexually abused. After his parents divorced, on a visit with his mother, his mother's live-in boyfriend had fondled his genitals. He put his hand under John's clothes and fondled his penis. John never told anyone this until he was in his group treatment. His group therapist reported it, and John told the story to an investigator. He did not know what happened after that. John did tell his father on one of their secret visits. I told John that the abuse he suffered should not be a secret from Cathy or Melinda. He agreed.

John made a strong impression of being sincere and believable. He did seem genuinely upset with himself over what he had done. He was very willing to come to a family session and apologize in front of everyone. After this meeting, I had a second meeting with the couple to offer them my assessment of John's willingness to help. Cathy was shocked but said she trusted my assessment. I explained that I next wanted to meet with Melinda by herself to make sure she felt OK about the idea of having a family meeting and including John.

INDIVIDUAL MEETING WITH THE SURVIVOR

Cathy brought Melinda in to meet with me alone. After spending a few minutes with Cathy and Melinda together to make sure Melinda was comfortable with me, I spoke with Melinda individually. Regarding the sexual abuse, she said her group helped her, and she did not think it was her fault that John abused her. She did think the fighting between her mother and Mark was her fault. She said that if she had never told, the conflict in the house would not be so bad. She said that on several occasions her mother and Mark had terrible arguments and that her mother yelled that she was getting a divorce. Melinda also believed that Mark was angry with her for telling because his son had to go away as a result. Although Mark had never said anything to her indicating he was angry, it was just how she felt. Finally, Melinda said she too was having bad dreams. She dreamt that she and her mother were alone again. I asked Melinda if she could tell her mother about her fears that the family might break up. She said she dare not tell, fearing it would cause a major fight between her mother and Mark. She said she did not want to talk to her mother about any of this, abuse included, because it could cause a fight.

I told Melinda that I had met with John, that he felt very bad about what he had done and that he was willing to offer his apologies. Melinda said her mother had told her that also. I told Melinda that I wanted to help the family talk about what happened without anyone having a fight. She thought that would be very good. I also asked her what she thought about the idea of having John in a session with the entire family, so that he could apologize for what he had done. Melinda was skeptical that John was remorseful. I asked her if her mom were present would she feel safe with John in the session. She said her biggest fear was not of John but of her mother and Mark fighting.

Melinda agreed to allow me to tell her mother how afraid she was of causing a fight between the parents. I had Cathy join us and explained to her what Melinda's biggest fears were. Cathy was shocked but also empathic toward her daughter. I explained to Cathy how important it was for the family to be able to talk about what happened without fights happening. I would like to help them do that in my office. Cathy reassured Melinda that they would not fight about this at home anymore. Instead, they would come to my office and talk without fighting.

PLANNING SESSION WITH BOTH PARENTS TOGETHER

Before having the family come together, I had one more session with just the couple. I wanted to make sure they both knew about what each child said to me individually. I was hoping the suffering of both John and Melinda could elicit empathy from both spouses and make it possible to have a family session without the couple becoming upset with each other. In the couple session, I explained that John had been molested by his mother's boyfriend. Cathy was shocked by this and in disbelief. I explained that John's group therapist had reported it to the authorities and that John was interviewed by an investigator. She asked Mark if he knew about this. Mark said John did not tell him at the time of the abuse but after the authorities had interviewed John. Cathy asked why he did not tell her about this. Mark said he feared they would just fight about it and that she would accuse him of siding with John again.

I reiterated that Melinda was blaming herself for their fighting and lived in fear they would divorce. I also told Mark that Melinda feared he was angry with her about John having to leave. Mark was shocked by this and adamant that he was not angry with Melinda. I said that the atmosphere in the home was so tense between the couple that the children were afraid to share their feelings with either parent. This was preventing both parents from helping their children or even knowing what they were upset about. To break this pattern, it was very important to be able to have a family discussion about all of this without a fight breaking out. Telling the two together about Mark and Melinda's respective suffering did had the desired effect. They were both very sober and knew they had to stop blaming each other.

Whole Family Interview: Survivor and Perpetrator Together

After seeing each parent individually, John individually, Melinda individually, and conducting three couple sessions, I brought the entire family together. Cathy and Mark sat on the couch with Melinda sitting in between them both. Todd, Mark's youngest son sat in a chair close to the couch. John sat in a chair by himself on the far side of the room. I began with a speech outlining the goals of the session. I explained that today was a day that the family was going to talk about what John had done to Melinda without anyone fighting. It was important that everyone share anything they know about what had happened if they had not already done so. I explained that I had met with everyone alone, except Todd and that I knew that each person either felt bad about what had happened or was afraid that what happened could cause the family to break up. I said that today was a day that they would all have to help each other with what they each felt bad about or were afraid of. At the end of my speech, Melinda volunteered that she did not believe John felt bad about what he had done and feared he would always be a very sick person. I responded that I understood why she felt that way.

I then told the story of what I knew had happened. I told about John going into Melinda's room four times and orally abusing her. I told about John being molested by his mother's boyfriend. I talked about how Melinda blamed herself for the parents fighting and that she was afraid Mark was angry with her for John having to leave. Mark immediately reassured Melinda that he was not angry with her. I then asked each parent if there was any more to the story than what I had told. They both said that was everything. I then asked Todd if he knew anything more. Todd said he did. He said he had seen John come out of Melinda's room on two occasions. He was very afraid to tell anyone this. He felt very bad that he had kept this a secret until this very moment. Both parents offered him support. By now, they both knew their fighting was the major cause of the children not talking.

After all the talk about what John did to Melinda was complete, I said John wanted to make clear to everyone how he felt about what had happened. I told John that because some family members questioned his sincerity, he would have to offer an apology while on his knees in front of everyone. If he were willing to do this, it might help demonstrate his sincerity. John immediately got on his knees. I asked him to go around the room and address each family member individually. He first looked at Cathy and said how sorry he was for harming her daughter. All in the room were instantly crying. He then looked at Melinda and told her how sorry he was for harming her. He looked at his father and told him how sorry he was for causing such problems in his marriage. Finally, he looked back at Melinda and told her their parents' fighting was his fault, not her fault. This was a spontaneous comment by John that he was clearly not coached to offer. The entire sequence was profoundly emotional and obviously therapeutic for everyone. Melinda volunteered that maybe John will be OK after all. Cathy affirmed that she thought John had been sincere.

Tracking Exceptions

I followed up with the couple one week later. Cathy volunteered that "a huge weight and black cloud was lifted from the family" in that one session. She said the abuse was discovered over one year ago, and despite all the previous therapy, they as a family could not talk about what happened without a fight. Now that was all past. The atmosphere in the home was totally changed. There was no more tension or anxiety about a fight breaking out. The couple explained that they had reached an agreement with each other about John's membership in the family. Since John was now 18 and wanted to get his own apartment, it would be OK for John to visit the family for Sunday dinners and on holidays. Mark was free to see his son as much as he wanted. I told the couple I wanted to see them one more time together and they each had an assignment. Mark was to ask John if he was still having nightmares about what he had done to Melinda. Cathy was to ask Melinda if she was still having nightmares about the family breaking up, if she still worried Mark was angry with her, and if she still feared she could cause fighting if she talked about what happened. I gave them a month on this assignment to make sure enough time had elapsed to assess how Melinda and John were doing.

One month later the couple returned. They had already had two Sunday dinners with John and reported both went well. They both talked to their respective child. Remarkably, neither John nor Melinda had had their nightmare since the family session. Melinda reported she no longer feared the fighting and knew that Mark was not angry with her.

9 I-FAST INTERVENTION FOR TRAUMA

CREATING AND TRACKING EXCEPTIONS

I-FAST INTERVENTION

Parents Empowered to Help Their Child

In integrative family and systems treatment (I-FAST), caregivers are put in the lead role to directly help their children overcome the problems targeted for treatment. The goal is to empower caregivers to help their own children. For trauma, parents can be given in-session and between-session intervention procedures focusing on trauma symptoms. The purpose of the intervention procedures is, first, to help ameliorate the trauma symptoms and, second, to change the interactional patterns associated with the symptoms.

DIRECT FOCUS ON TRAUMA SYMPTOMS

Trauma symptoms can be focused on directly in I-FAST when the client is willing to do so and the parents accept the frame that their child is traumatized. Treatment procedures can then focus directly on ameliorating re-experiencing symptoms, withdraw and avoidant symptoms, changing the meaning of trauma, emotional dysregulation symptoms, self-harm symptoms, or obtaining expressions of remorse from abuse perpetrators.

Integrating Interventions from Other Models

As long as the parents are empowered to deliver the interventions, and as long as the interventions require a shift in interactional patterns, any procedure from any evidenced-based trauma-focused therapy approach can be integrated into I-FAST. Procedures aimed at processing trauma experiences and changing their meaning can be integrated into I-FAST if the parents are included in the process, and including them also changes interactional patterns. Exposure techniques can be integrated into I-FAST if parents accept this frame and take the lead at helping the client with the exposure. Avoidance and withdraw symptoms can be addressed again by empowering parents to help their child overcome these symptoms.

Interventions aimed at teaching emotional regulation can be integrated into I-FAST. Caregivers can be given the task of holding, comforting, and rocking a young child struggling to regulate their emotions. Mindfulness can be enlisted to both teach emotional regulation and change family patterns. For a child and an enmeshed, intrusive parent, mindfulness can be prescribed to the child, emphasizing the need for the child to have private time. Mindfulness is employed to help both with emotional regulation and set a boundary between child and parent. With a dysregulated child and a disengaged parent, the emphasis can be placed on helping the child complete their mindfulness by having child and disengaged parent do mindfulness together.

When clients and family are willing to focus on trauma directly, in I-FAST interventions can be borrowed from other models and employed in a flexible way to fit the specific family patterns targeted for change.

INDIRECT FOCUS ON TRAUMA SYMPTOMS

Often clients are not willing to focus directly on trauma symptoms. They may be unwilling to talk about what happened or unwilling to carry out procedures such as exposure interventions. Parents also may be unwilling to focus on trauma, especially if they do not believe the problem they want help with is related to trauma. In these situations, I-FAST can offer help by indirectly focusing on trauma. Whatever goal the family is willing to focus on, changing family patterns associated with trauma symptoms can still be addressed for the purposes of helping with what the family does identify as the problem. Changing strong or weak boundaries, addressing triangulation and coalitions, or reducing hostile family exchanges, all of which may be exacerbating trauma symptoms, can be focused on in the name of helping with whatever problem the family is willing to address. Attachments between adults in the family and the traumatized child can be enhanced as well as enhancing attachments between the adults themselves in the family. Creating a loving, safe environment in the family regardless of the problem being addressed can be an indirect way of ameliorating trauma symptoms.

TRACKING AND ENLARGING EXCEPTIONS: ADJUSTING TREATMENT TO CHANGE

In I-FAST treatment, providers are encouraged to notice and track exceptions throughout treatment and adjust treatment accordingly. If significant change has occurred before the family has begun treatment, the I-FAST clinician must recognize this and begin treatment by reinforcing exceptions that are already occurring. Once interventions aimed at changing patterns are offered, families will often spontaneously produce exceptions. Interactional exceptions are then carefully tracked and enlarged. In I-FAST, therapy procedures are not rigidly employed whether or not the client is improving. We do not have a set of assumptions that require a sequence of procedures to be completed for therapy to be effective. When change does occur, the treatment process is adjusted to accommodate and enlarge those changes. Continued intervention procedures area typically not offered if change has occurred.

Tracking exceptions and adjusting treatment accordingly is one way I-FAST is client feedback–informed. When change and exceptions are observed, feedback is obtained from the family for what specifically has been helpful at producing change and doing more of that is reinforced. An emphasis is placed on what family and client did themselves to produce changes. Ownership of change then goes to family and client. What follows are case examples demonstrating how I-FAST can be employed when focusing directly or indirectly on trauma symptoms.

DIRECT FOCUS ON TRAUMA SYMPTOMS: "MY BRAIN TALKS TO ME"

A single mother, in her early 30s, lived with one son, aged 8, and one daughter, aged 6. Prior to therapy, both children were placed in foster care for two years. Prior to being placed in foster care, both children lived with their mother and father. Their mother was depressed and was not getting out of bed. At one point, the stepfather had attempted to convince the mother to have a sexual threesome. The mother put a knife to her throat threatening to kill herself. Police were called, and when they arrived, they found both children locked in a room with feces smeared on the walls and urine and vomit on the floor. The girl was naked. Both parents were charged with child endangerment, and the children were placed in foster care.

After the children were placed, their mother left the father and moved in with her parents. The father moved in with a new girlfriend. After being placed, the girl told her individual therapist when visiting her father, "her father laughed when she got naked and he does this" and she bent over and patted her buttocks. She told of her brother getting naked. She said she was afraid of the father's girlfriend, saying she had "big boobs." She said she touched her daddy's "winkie." The brother become angry at his sister for saying this. While in foster care, the brother was urinating and defecating himself. He was extremely anxious and had great difficulty separating from his sister. Both were diagnosed with posttraumatic stress disorder (PTSD) and anxiety disorders. Prior to living in foster care, when living with both parents, the abuse by the father was apparently long term. The mother was often passed out on the couch when it occurred.

While the children were in foster care, the mother divorced the father. She moved in with her mother and stepfather. Her mother then died. She went back to school and was studying to be a nurse. Her depression improved when she divorced the husband. After the children were in foster care for two years, the mother became stable enough for a long enough time that children's services reunited her with both children in her own apartment. The father was never charged with abuse; however, his visits with the children were stopped and not allowed to continue after the children went home with their mother.

Presenting Problems and Establishing Alliances With the Parent and Children

Home-based services became involved once the children and mother were reunified. The mother wanted help with the girl being "impulsive" at home and school. At school, she was constantly engaging in attention-seeking. Once she shouted out, "Fire drill! Fire drill!" At home, the girl complained that she missed her foster mother. When returned home she horded food, ate all the time, and complained about not having food. She would ask her mother if she would adopt her.

Collaborating With the Parent and the School and Identifying Strengths

The school wanted the girl on medications for attention-deficit/hyperactivity disorder. The mother was opposed to this. The home-based therapist collaborated with the school and obtained agreements. The school agreed to stop pressuring the mother about medicating the girl and to see if therapy would help first. The mother was very pleased with this agreement. The mother was very nurturing with both children and was given many compliments regarding this. But she was also very insecure about her parenting. She felt very guilty about what her children had gone through and was reluctant to set limits on them. The first several sessions of the therapy focused on helping the mother set more limits. She needed constant reassurance that she was doing fine.

Re-Experiencing Symptoms

The girl was having nightmares and intrusive thoughts. She told her mother and home-based therapist that when she was in school her brain "talked" to her. She said she had thoughts in her brain of being locked in a room with no food. In sessions, the girl would ask the mother why she locked her in the room. The mother apologized and explained that she was sick. The children were encouraged to tell their stories of what happened to them, but neither wanted to.

Tracking Interactional Patterns Associated With the Trauma Symptoms

The mother was afraid of talking with her children about the past, worrying that doing so would make them worse. She also felt very guilty. It was a difficult subject for her. The girl would not spontaneously bring up her nightmares or intrusive thoughts with her mother. When the topic did come up, the mother asked broad questions like if she blamed her (the mother) for the abuse. The girl was asked with whom she would talk about the past. She said only her foster mother, who was her favorite mom. Her frame for who was her "mother" was the woman she could talk to about the past and that was not her biological mother. The brother refused to talk about the past at all. The mother was concerned that trying to get her son to talk about the past would cause him to have behavior problems at school like his sister.

In addition to the girl's trauma symptoms, there were several additional crucial issues. First, the mother felt guilty about not protecting the girl from abuse. These feelings interfered with her parenting and of the mother and daughter being able to talk about what happened. Second, this was a family in a major transition. They were now reunited after a two-year separation. The daughter was more attached to her foster mother than to her own mother. Helping the mother and daughter intensify their attachment was a major goal. Since the girl framed her "mother" as the woman she could talk to about her past, helping her talk to her biological mother about her past might be one way to improve their attachment. This would mean coaching the mother on how to talk to her daughter about her past and putting the mother in the lead role in this process.

Direct Focus on Trauma Symptoms: Mother as Therapist, In-Session and Between-Session Tasks

In school, the girl refused to do schoolwork during class, got out of her seat, and followed her teacher around. Her in-home therapist asked her if she thought about her traumatic events while in school. She said, "All the time." While in a session, the mother was given the frame that the girl might talk about whatever she was upset about if the discussion was focused more directly on her nightmares and intrusive thoughts. Could the girl just tell her mother what happened in the nightmares and what specific thoughts she was having? The suggestion was to focus more directly on the girl's symptoms. The mother was asked to change her habitual way of talking to the girl about her trauma. It could also be classified as an exposure intervention, asking the girl to tell about the nightmares and thoughts she was trying to avoid, but with the mother in the role of therapist, leading the discussion. Instead of insecurely asking the girl broad questions about the meaning of the abuse, the mother would ask focused questions about the content of the nightmares and intrusive thoughts.

After explaining this idea to the mother individually, she was asked to practice asking the girl questions in the session. The mother was asked to have the girl tell her what happened in her nightmare. The mother followed this suggestion, and the girl responded. The girl said in her nightmare her father came back to get her and her mother let him take her. She had the nightmare three times per week. This was all new information for the mother. The mother was asked to reassure the girl her father was gone, and she would not allow him to take her.

Between-Session Task Focusing Directly on Trauma Symptoms

The therapist framed to both mother and daughter that one way to avoid having a nightmare is to tell for the daughter to tell her mother the nightmare before bed and then she would not have to have it. The girl liked this idea. The mother was instructed to have the girl tell the nightmare to her three nights before bed in the next week. This intervention was done for several purposes. First, it could be considered an exposure intervention for the girl, flexibly integrated into I-FAST, with the mother substituting for a therapist. The mother was in the lead role in helping her daughter deal with her trauma symptoms. Second, and perhaps more important, it was intended to help the mother and daughter re-establish a stronger mother–daughter bond. When in foster care, the girl told her nightmares to her foster mother, whom she missed and considered her real mother.

Tracking Exceptions and Changing the Narrative

The mother carried out the procedure. Exceptions then began to occur. On the third night before bed in which the daughter was to tell her nightmare before going to sleep, a major exception occurred. They spontaneously changed their interactional pattern in relation to the girl's trauma symptoms. Instead of saying the thoughts in her brain or telling her nightmare, the girl spontaneously told her mom that she forgave her and that she was afraid her mom would go away again. She then told of a second nightmare of her mom leaving her and her chasing after her mom. Both mother and daughter cried. The mom reassured her daughter that she was very sick before, but she was better now and was never leaving her again.

In the next session, the mother told of this encounter and told how emotional and helpful it was for both she and her daughter. After this encounter, more exceptions occurred. The daughter was more affectionate with her mother at home. They began having fun together. In school, the girl's behavior problems began to improve. She said her brain no longer talked to her at school and she no longer had nightmares. Both children were now more open about the past and talking about their feelings. After his sister improved, the brother was now talking about how his father yelled at him and hurt him. The mother was able to reassure him as well. The case was followed for several additional sessions and the girl remained stable with no additional intrusive thoughts or nightmares. Both mother and daughter reported feeling much closer to each other. The girl said her mother was now her main "mom."

Trauma Symptoms

Danny was experiencing emotional dysregulation, dissociative symptoms, avoidant and extreme behaviors, and severe anxiety after his stepmother repeatedly tapped his mouth shut and his arms behind his back and locked him in a closet for hours. After learning of this, his mother, Melissa, was also traumatized by what happened to her boy. She could not talk to Danny about what happened to him without crying, making Danny reluctant to talk to her about it.

Reframing and the Parent Put in Lead Role

Phil, the therapist, met with Melissa alone to set up an in-session intervention designed to change the interactional pattern between Danny and Melissa of not talking about the trauma. He asked Melissa if she was Danny's therapist, how would she respond to him talking about what happened. By asking this question, Phil was framing Melissa as Danny's therapist. She said she would most likely not cry and would just listen and be supportive. Phil affirmed that was correct. Phil told Melissa that it was important for her son to feel free to talk to her about what happened and what he was afraid of. For him to feel safe talking to her, she had to react to him like she was his therapist: She had to stay calm and exhibit a professional demeanor.

Danny was then brought into the session. Melissa asked him to tell her what he was the most afraid of. She was able to stay calm as a therapist would. Danny responded by telling her he was afraid of seeing his father in public and that his father would then take him to his father's house, and he might be locked in the closet again. At Phil's suggestion, Melissa reassured him that if he did see his father, he would not have to go with him.

Emotional Dysregulation Symptoms: Changing Interactional Patterns

Danny was having intermittent explosive episodes that were not triggered by anything obvious. He may have been dissociating when having these episodes. When Danny's fits occurred, Melissa was uncertain and insecure about how to deal with her son's rages. These responses by Melissa likely intensified Danny's own insecurities and fears. Phil framed Danny's fits as giving him too much power. This would make him more insecure and thus feel more unsafe. Melissa was advised that when Danny threw a fit, she should get him out of the situation, stay calm, hold him, rock him, and comfort him. Phil then had Melissa hold and rock Danny in the session to practice. They both readily did this. Phil suggested they practice this every day for 10 minutes after school. The daily repetition of this intervention was intended to help Danny regain the ability to regulate his emotions as well as give Melissa a new way to respond to his anger episodes. After this session, Melissa felt empowered. She felt she understood what was happening to her son. She had a new confidence in how to respond to him.

Melissa did implement the 10 minutes of holding and rocking Danny every day, fit or no fit. After the session with Phil, Mike, the in-home therapist, observed Danny throw one of his unprovoked fits during a home visit. Melissa reacted just as Phil advised her. She calmly picked up her son, took him to another room, stayed with him, and rocked and comforted him. After five minutes, Danny was calm again and could play with his brother appropriately. This intervention eventually extinguished all of Danny's explosive anger episodes. He did continue to exhibit normal anger in response to obvious upsetting stimuli, but the repeated rocking eliminated the unprovoked episodes in which he looked like he was dissociating.

Avoidant Symptoms

After Danny and Melissa unexpectedly encountered Danny's father in a local store, Danny did not want to play outside and did not want to sleep in his own bed. Melissa lived with fear that Danny's father could come to her house and request a visit. After Danny's father remarried, he became difficult for Melissa to collaborate with. After the abuse incidents, Melissa was afraid to call or talk to Danny's father. This new interactional pattern of avoiding Danny's father made Melissa more afraid of what Danny's father might do. Phil decided to break this pattern by offering to be a go-between for Melissa and Danny's father.

Phil offered to call Danny's father and offer him an appointment to talk over the accusations about his wife putting Danny in the closet. Phil offered to propose to Danny's father that if he wanted to resume his visits with Danny, he would first have to meet with Phil and devise a safety plan of not leaving Danny alone with his wife if Danny visited. Melissa gave Phil permission to talk with Danny's father about this. Phil called Danny's father and offered to see him to discuss Danny's accusations. His father declined the invitation. Phil explained by phone that to ensure Danny's safety and to ensure his wife could not be accused of abuse again, there would have to be an agreed-upon safety plan before a future visit could take place. Danny's father explained to Phil that the accusations caused problems between him and his wife, and they both agreed there should be no more visits. Phil asked if they could have an agreement to meet if Danny's father changed his mind about future visits. The father agreed.

Phil reported the agreement to Melissa. Danny's father did not intend to ask for visits and agreed to talk to Phil first if he changed his mind. Melissa was very relieved by this news. Phil and Melissa planned how Melissa should respond to Danny's father if they saw him in public or if he requested visits and explained the plan to Danny. If Danny's father requested a visit, Melissa should explain to him that he could have no visits unless he took responsibility for the abuse that happened at his house and had a safety plan. She told her son there would be no visits with his father. She told him if they saw his father in public, they would just leave. He would under no circumstances go with his father. This talk put the boy at ease.

Tracking Exceptions

After the mother implemented the comforting procedure and had the talk with the son about the father, the boy began to sleep in his own bed. He became comfortable going out in public again. He reported his bad dreams went away, and he stopped thinking about the abuse every day. His fits at home greatly diminished in both frequency and intensity. These improvements occurred very rapidly. The total number of outpatient and in-home appointments from the time the mother first met with the in-home worker to when his PTSD symptoms abated was, in total, seven sessions.

APOLOGY SESSIONS

Juvenile sex offenders writing apology letters to their victims has been a common intervention in manualized treatment programs. Offenders work on identifying and changing their distortions related to the abuse and on developing empathy for the victims. Once they have achieved these steps, they must write a structured and specific letter of apology, which can then be delivered or not to the victim.

Having offenders apologize to their victims in person has been controversial but offered in several family therapy models. Apology sessions were a major component of family treatment of incest outlined by Trepper and Barrett (1989). Madanes (1992, 1995) used this intervention for juvenile sex offenders and adult offenders when the abuse occurred between family members. This intervention came under much criticism for bringing the offender and the victim together in a session, fearing damage to the victim could result. Fears such as forcing victims to participate in an intervention they were opposed to, or felt unsafe doing, were of serious concern. The possibility that victims could be verbally attacked or blamed by family members in such sessions was also concern. Perhaps for these reasons and others, apology sessions for intrafamily sexual abuse has remained controversial.

Over the last 10 years, the restorative justice movement has focused on in-person conferencing between victims of crimes and their perpetrators (Amstutz, 2009). The restorative justice concepts have been applied specifically to intrafamily sexual abuse (Julich, 2001; Oudshoorn et al., 2015). The role of family relational processes, including apologies from family offenders to their family victims, in the healing of intrafamily sexual abuse was studied by Paige and Thorton (2015). Thirty-five intrafamily sexual survivors were interviewed regarding the helpfulness of contact with their family perpetrator. Survivors who received apologies from family perpetrators who showed remorse for the offense found these encounters very helpful.

In I-FAST, apology sessions for intrafamily sexual abuse can be offered when certain conditions exist. Those conditions are as follows:

- The offender is a family member such as an older sibling or parent.
- The caregivers believe and support the victim and view the offender as responsible for the assault.
- The offender is willing to take responsibility for the abuse.

Sometimes special sessions for the caregivers must be held to help them reach these positions. Helping the offender take responsibility for the abuse may also take special sessions with the offender alone, in-group treatment, or with the caregivers. It can be very effective to enlist caregivers, especially if they are parents, to help the offender take responsibility for the assault.

The survivor must feel safe about the procedure. This may require individual sessions with the survivor but most important, sessions with the survivor and caregivers in which the caregivers can offer reassurance that they will keep the survivor safe.

If these conditions are met, an apology session is possible. In our experience, we have found apology sessions to be profoundly helpful and have had families and survivors report of their healing value. Steps for conducting the sessions that can simultaneously accomplish multiple goals are outlined next (Grove, 2002).

Step 1: A discussion, first, of what happened can be organized with the therapist stating first what they know, followed by the adults stating what they know, and then the children stating what they know. The survivor is given the option of speaking or not. This discussion breaks all secrets about the abuse, the major interactional pattern often occurring with sexual abuse. Uncovering details in a family session often makes it very clear that the offender is responsible.
Step 2: A discussion of why this was wrong can create a family narrative that puts responsibility for the assault on the offender. In this discussion, an emphasis must be placed on the emotional pain and harm the offense caused for the victim and those who love the victim, including the offender.
Step 3: An apology from the offender to each individual in the family, including the victim can be offered. The apology itself is defined not as a request for forgiveness, but as an expression of sorrow by the offender for the pain they caused. When the sessions are done this way, they are typically very emotional and therapeutic for all involved. Interactional patterns of secrecy are broken, a family narrative defining the offender as responsible is created and remorse is expressed by the offender.

BROTHER–SISTER SEXUAL ABUSE

Carla had been sexually abused by her older brother for three years. When told, both her parents believed her and took steps to protect her. Despite this, she was still having nightmares about the abuse and felt the need to lock her bedroom door at night to keep her brother out of her room. Her continued fears could be explained by family patterns and frames. Her father had been a peripheral, inconsequential family member and so she could not view him as a protector from her brother. Second, her brother was not taking responsibility for the abuse but framed it as consensual. Since the abuse had been disclosed, he had had several violent episodes at home, all of which his mother, not his father, had to respond to.

After assessing that both parents were supportive of Carla and that Carla felt safe having a family session, Karen Grider, the therapist organized a whole-family session. The goal of the session was to break all family patterns of secrecy about the abuse, change the brother's frame that the abuse was consensual to totally his responsibility, and set up a strategy to help the father have more of a role in the family. Prior to the session, the family had not discussed the abuse as a family. Aaron was denying intercourse or rape ever happened. He was insisting his sister was always a willing participant and that the abuse had only gone on for one year.

Changing Interactional Patterns in the Session

Karen took several steps and offered numerous frames to the family to ensure a successful family session. Once all the frames Karen offered were accepted, she addressed the issue of secrets. She stated the goal of the session was for everyone to share all they knew about what happened between the siblings, starting with herself. She began the discussion by reading aloud the police report outlining what both children reported. The report was gruesome and detailed. Sex abuse happened for three years, all in Carla's bedroom while the parents were asleep or away or downstairs watching TV. Intercourse occurred three times. On one occasion, Aaron pinned Carla's arms behind her back and raped her. Karen began the discussion by stating all the terrible things herself. This was done for two reasons. First, by Karen going first, all the worst things were already said, making it easier for the rest of the family members when it was their turn. Second, Karen was role modeling having no secrets. She was open about what she knew.

While reading the report, Aaron sat slumped down in his chair. It was obvious having details of what he had done to his sister read aloud in front of both of his parents was very difficult for him. Carla on the other hand, sat upright, next to her mother. At one point during Karen's sharing, Melinda raised her hand and corrected what she thought was an error. It was obvious Carla felt safe having this discussion and was not retraumatized by it. She felt safe because she was believed and supported by her mother and father.

Brenda went next. She recounted the entire story of what she learned from Carla and from the interviews between Carla and the investigators. Brenda explained that the reason Carla told her in the first place was because Carla was concerned about why Aaron had run away from home. Carla believed Aaron ran away because he felt guilty about what he had done. Carl was concerned about her brother's emotional well-being. Steven went next. He told of a time when he went upstairs to check on the two children. When he went upstairs, the two children were startled. Carla was all sweaty, and Aaron was very disheveled. At the time Steven did not think anything of this. He told Brenda what he had seen, and she did not think anything of this. Now looking back, he realized he had interrupted an abusive episode, and he was very upset with himself for not realizing it at the time. Brenda explained that the two siblings had always played together. One of their games was to make a tent out of the covers. Both parents just thought this is what they were doing at the time Steven interrupted them.

After Karen read the report, Brenda had given her account, and Steven had added his example, it was now Aaron's turn. He continued to insist that the abuse had only gone on for one year and that Carla was a willing participant. Karen had Aaron describe in detail several abuse incidents. Aaron would begin his description with what Carla had done, leaving out a description of what he had done. Karen patiently, relentlessly, calmly, with no judgment in her voice, got Aaron to describe in detail what he himself had done in all the encounters. He admitted that on three occasions he inserted his penis into her vagina. He did not frame this as intercourse, but he agreed he did this. He also admitted to the episode in which he pinned Carla's arms behind her back and raped her. He did not frame this as rape because the encounter began in a playful way. By having Karen and both parents go first and by Karen pressing Aaron for details of exactly what happened, Aaron was now openly admitting to everything he had been accused of except the duration of the abuse. During all of this, Aaron slumped further and further down in his chair.

Finally, it was Carla's turn. She was given an option to not speak. She insisted she wanted to talk. She gave details that supported the timeline of the abuse. Aaron agreed with the details and was now admitting the abuse had gone on for three years.

Changing Frames and Establishing Family Narratives: Parents Take the Lead

Karen then turned to the topic of why this was wrong. Aaron went first, then Steven, then Brenda. Aaron agreed it was wrong. Karen asked him if there were differences between him and his sister. He said he was older, and his sister did not "know much." Karen emphasized that it was an older brother's job to protect his younger sister, not to confuse her. Brenda gave numerous reasons why this was wrong. She framed the incident of Aaron pinning Carla's arms behind her back and forcing himself on her as "pure rape." She explained a woman has the right to say no, and a man must accept that no matter what. Finally, Karen gave her reasons for why this was wrong. She agreed with everything that was said but emphasized one last thing. Karen emphasized the emotional pain this caused. She stated that when sex abuse happens in a family, everyone in the family, including the offender has intense emotional pain. Aaron himself agreed that he also was in emotional pain over what he had done.

Apology: An In-Session Task

Karen then asked for an in-session task. She framed the task as something Aaron could do to help everyone in the room with their emotional pain. Aaron was asked to get on his knees and apologize to each person in the room one at a time. Aaron did not hesitate. He got on both knees and apologized to each member. He spontaneously emphasized apologizing for the "pain" he had caused. To his father, he also apologized for "looking down on him," something he spontaneously added to his apology. The family all agreed Aaron's apology was sincere, stating he had never before apologized for anything.

Therapy Strategy: Changing Patterns That Predated the Abuse

At the end of the session, a therapy strategy was agreed to. Steven would be in charge of helping Aaron learn to respect women. He and Aaron would come to sessions together, and Steven would become more involved with Aaron at home. This was done to break up the enmeshment between Aaron and Brenda and to give Steven an important role in the family. Brenda was put in charge of spending more time with Carla and to make sure her self-esteem was not harmed. Carla and Brenda would also come to therapy together to focus on this issue.

Tracking Exceptions

After this session, all of Aaron's violence at home stopped. He still clashed with his mother and had a period of continued poor motivation for school. Steven got more involved with him. They both came to therapy together and had many talks about respecting women.

The most stunning exceptions came from Carla. After the apology session, she had no more nightmares. She also decided it was no longer necessary to lock her door at night. She now felt totally safe at home. Brenda and Carla did come to counseling together. Brenda was convinced Carla did not feel bad about herself over what her brother had done to her. Many discussions were had over how to keep herself safe in the future. The therapy with this family continued for 10 months after the apology session. Periodically, Karen met with Carla alone to ensure she continued to feel safe and that her brother had not tried anything with her. No further abuse or violence had occurred. By the end, Aaron continued to do poorly academically.

SHE WANTED HER FATHER

Marleen was 14 years old and lived with her single mother. Her parents had been divorced since she was a young child. When beginning her freshman year in high school, her functioning dramatically deteriorated. She went from an honor roll student and a girl who was not in any trouble and not sexually active, to a girl who was seriously using drugs, having sex with older boys, and failing all her subjects in school. After several months of this behavior, she was put on juvenile court probation. Marleen was assigned Lindsay Davis, a young female case manager who developed a very powerful rapport with her. When asked by the case manager why she went from doing so well to doing so poorly, she offered a straight forward explanation. Marleen explained that after her parents divorced, she lived with her father. Her father remarried a few years later. Marleen said that when she was 12 years old, she had a girlfriend spend the night. She, her girlfriend, and her father were watching TV together one evening. While watching TV, Marleen's father fondled her. He put his hands under her clothes and fondled her breasts and vagina. Marleen froze and said nothing at the time. She told her school guidance counselor the next day, who reported the abuse. When interviewed, the father said he was drunk and could not remember anything. However, he said his daughter never lied and if she said he did this, he believed her. Marleen was then moved to her mother's house. Her father was court-ordered to have no contact with Marleen and was sentenced to prison.

It was now two years later, and the father was released from prison. Marleen explained that from her standpoint, this was still her father. She wanted to have a relationship with him even though he did terrible things. She said she was "on strike" and would continue to misbehave until the authorities allowed her to see her father again. The author (DRG) was providing supervision.

Collaborating With the Court and Engaging and Assessing the Abuser

The author instructed Lindsay to call the court and ask for two things: First, to allow us to evaluate whether the father might be willing to help his daughter, and, second, if he were willing and did help her, would the court consider allowing him to have supervised visits with Marleen. The court agreed to both suggestions. Lindsay then met with the father alone. It was clear he felt guilty about what had happened and was very willing to help his daughter.

A Family Session: Changing Interactional Patterns

Lindsay was given very specific instructions on how to conduct a family session in which the father would take responsibility for the abuse and offer his apology for the pain he caused. Attending the session were the father, the mother, the father's second wife, Marleen, and Lindsay. In the session, the father got on his knees and apologized. Everyone cried, including Lindsay. The session had a profound effect on everyone.

The family agreed that with the court's permission, both mother and stepmother would supervise brief, public visits between father and daughter. The court was informed that the father had done what was asked of him to help his daughter and of the family's plan to supervise visits. The court order was changed to allow supervised visits.

Tracking Exceptions

After this one session, Marleen stopped using drugs, stopped having sex with boys, and eventually went back to an honor roll student. The family did set up supervised visits for Marleen and her father. Marleen and her father met twice a month at a public place such as McDonalds. Both mother and stepmother collaborated and were present at every visit. As Marleen's behavior stayed consistently improved, the court took her off probation. Lindsay kept in touch with Marleen until she graduated from high school three years later. She graduated with honors.

INDIRECT FOCUS ON TRAUMA SYMPTOMS: SUICIDAL MOTHER

Carl had serious anxiety, nightmares, and self-injurious behavior. His mother, Rebecca, had made a near lethal suicide attempt. When he was initially brought to treatment by his father, Robert, he would not talk to his therapist, Letta, about his trauma symptoms. With great effort and persistence, Letta convinced Robert, who framed Rebecca as crazy and the main source of Carl's problems, to allow Rebecca to participate in Carl's therapy. The therapy was stuck, and it became clear that adding Rebecca to the treatment might allow for progress. Rebecca was recruited into the sessions and great progress was made. Her participation resulted in Carl opening up. Letta instituted a procedure in which she would see Carl and his mother jointly and then see Carl individually after his session with his mother. This resulted in Carl talking and processing what was discussed in the session with his mother. Including his mother in treatment solved the problem of Carl not talking. Once he began to talk, the family patterns associated with Carl's symptoms were identified.

Carl's anxiety and other symptoms could be attributed to several interactional patterns. His two parents were at war with each other, fighting over Carl. Carl was stuck in the middle, not wanting to take sides. He could not tell his father about his fears related to his mother without his father using this information against his mother. Rebecca had weak boundaries with Carl and told him everything, including about potentially unsafe behavior. This intensified Carl's anxiety and made him worry more that she was unsafe. Finally, Carl had been Rebecca's care taker when he lived with her. She had multiple sclerosis, and Carl tended to her. Now that Carl was at his father's house, he could not assess her daily needs and feared no one was looking after her.

Blocking Conflict Between the Parents

To attempt to persuade the parents to collaborate and end their fighting in front of Carl, Letta held a joint interview. It was a disaster. Both fought bitterly for the entire session. Letta could hardly talk. She did her best to prevail upon them how their conflict was affecting Carl but to no avail. After the session, they continued to fight in the clinic parking lot. Letta had to go to the parking lot to tell them to go home. Their fighting would have to be dealt with another way.

Utilizing Parent Frames

Rebecca and Robert were competing with each other to prove to the court that the other was a bad parent. They both framed each other as bad for Carl. When it became clear they both were entrenched in this competition, their negative frames for each other were utilized to block their fighting. Each was seen for an individual session and offered an idea. They each were told that they should restrict their communication to text messages and emails only. That way they each would have a "paper trail" of how the other was conducting themselves. They each could use any insulting or hostile texts by the other to show the court. They each independently liked this idea and began restricting their communication to texts and email. To avoid giving the other any ammunition to use in court, they both became civil in their communication. Carl was no longer subjected to hostile phone calls or fighting between the parents at visit exchanges.

Engaging a New Family Member Into Treatment

Although adding Rebecca to the therapy helped Letta understand Carl's symptoms, the therapy was at an impasse again. Rebecca framed her openness with Carl as "normal" and continued to frighten him with her stories about her behavior and health condition. Letta could not persuade Rebecca to have stronger boundaries between with Carl. There was one more potential participant that could be added to the treatment to attempt to break the impasse, Rebecca's live-in-boyfriend, Steven. Steven was invited to join Rebecca in a session with Carl. His participation would prove to be the turning point on the case.

Enlisting Mother's Boyfriend to Strengthen Mother–Son Boundaries

Letta reiterated with Steven present that she feared Rebecca telling Carl too much intensified Carl's anxiety. She gave examples of what information frightened Carl. Steven agreed that Rebecca had no boundaries with Carl. He said Carl was Rebecca's entire life. He gave his own examples of poor boundaries between Rebecca and Carl. If Rebecca had a bad day while Steen was at work, she would not call him, but would call Carl to tell about her upsets.

Steven was asked to help Rebecca be more aware of this at home and to help her be more careful about what she shared with Carl. Steven was empowered by Letta to help Rebecca have more boundaries. He was very willing to help with this. From this session on, with Steven's help, Rebecca gradually strengthened her boundaries with Carl. Rebecca was also asked to call Steven if she had a bad day, not Carl. She agreed with this suggestion and followed it. These changes helped alleviate some of Carl's anxiety, but he continued to be very anxious of her health and if she was being cared for. One more request would be made of Steven.

Framing the Main Issue and Changing Who Has the Caretaker Role

Leta framed the problem to Steven; namely, Carl did not trust that Steven could take care of Rebecca. Because Carl felt he was responsible to keep his mother safe, he was plagued with constant anxiety and fear. To convince Carl that Steven could take care of his mother, a special session with Carl, Steven, and Rebecca would have to occur. In that session, Carl would have to provide Steven with caretaking lessons. Carl would have to officially turn his mother over to Steven. This made sense to Steven and Rebecca, and they agreed with the plan.

The session was organized. Leta framed it to Carl that it made more sense for Carl to let Steven take care of his mother. Steven lived with his mother and so could look after her much more than Carl could. But, first, Carl would have to teach Steven how to look after his mother. In the session, Carl was asked to instruct Steven on how to take care of his mother. An official list was made outlining all of Steven's official caretaking duties. Carl told Steven he would have to get her things when she needed them. If she is feeling weak or looked upset, he must physically help her get around the house. He gave several specific instructions. Steven was then officially put in charge of keeping Rebecca safe.

Tracking Exceptions

Steven took his new care taking duties seriously. He made sure he followed the suggestions on Carl's list. The list was posted on the refrigerator. On visits at his mother's, Carl would ask her if Steven was properly helping her. Rebecca would affirm that he was. Steven would also share with Carl how he was helping Rebecca. While visiting, Carl would also observe closely if Steven actually was taking adequate care of Rebecca. After several visits, Carl was convinced that it was safe to transfer the role of protector of mom to Steven. He then calmed down completely. All his anxieties and nightmares went away completely.

All the interactional patterns associated with Carl's symptoms had now changed. Robert and Rebecca no longer fought in front of Carl. Boundaries between Rebecca and Carl were stronger. Rebecca no longer told Carl anything that caused him concern for her safety. Steven was now taking care of Rebecca to Carl's satisfaction. Carl no longer worried about his mother.

Leta readministered the Child PTSD Symptom Scale with Carl. This time he reported his nightmares, images, and unwanted thoughts were totally gone. He reported never feeling as if the event were happening again, not having feelings in his body when thinking of what happened, and never having to try not to think of what had happened. There was no more self-mutilation and no more worries that his mom would hurt herself. Two years later, Letta conducted a follow-up. Robert described his son as well-adjusted. He thought helping his boy talk was the helpful. Carl still had visits with his mom. He was doing well after his visits, with no anxiety or nightmares.

Indirect Focus on Trauma Symptoms

In this therapy, the client was exposed to a very serious traumatic event, the suicide attempt of his own mother. He presented with a complex and intensive array of trauma symptoms. The therapist was highly trained in trauma-focused cognitive-behavioral therapy (TF-CBT). Her TF-CBT training on this particular case, however, was useless because the client refused to talk about his trauma narrative or cooperate with any of the other standard treatment procedures offered in TF-CBT. The therapist was flexible, however, and adapted a treatment strategy that the client would cooperate with. Instead of offering TF-CBT, the therapist focused on identifying interactional patterns that contributed to the trauma symptoms and at interrupting those patterns and changing the family on a structural level. Boundaries between mother and son were created. The frequency of interaction between mother and son was increased. They spoke by phone every day. Chronic fighting between the two biological parents was interrupted, and most important, family roles were changed. The client was moved out of a protector role for his mother and replaced in that role by the mother's live-in boyfriend. All the client's trauma symptoms were totally ameliorated by the family interaction and organizational changes. No traditional trauma interventions were offered. The client never talked about his nightmares, or his trauma narrative. The meaning of the trauma to the client was never directly addressed.

Summary

One of the many I-FAST concepts this case exemplifies is the decision regarding whom to include in treatment. Changing this variable often can have profound influence on the outcome of a stuck treatment. There were two major breakthroughs in this case. Both occurred after inviting a new family member into the treatment. The first breakthrough occurred after brining the client's mother in. Obstacles had to be overcome to do this, the biggest being obtaining an agreement from the client's father to include her. Instead of viewing the mother as a trigger for the boy's symptoms and protecting him from her, she was included in the therapy and her interactions with the boy were changed. A second breakthrough that led to the resolution of the case was inviting the mother's live-in partner. The rule in family therapy of "When stuck, add people" was utilized to resolve the case.

FOLLOW THE PHONE CALLS

Thirty-one-year-old Monique, her 7-year old daughter Lilian, and her 10-year old son lived together in a small town. They were referred to children's services by Lilian's school because Lilian had very serious and chronic lice. She was not allowed to go to school until her lice problem was solved. Children's Services referred Monique for intensive in-home treatment with an emphasis on providing parenting classes.

Engaging and Aligning With the Parent

Mike was assigned the case and was able to quickly engage Monique. On his first visit, Mike observed that the house was in disarray and very dirty. Mike won Monique's trust, and she opened-up about her background. She moved to her current town to get away from her parents. Prior to this, with the exception of two brief periods where she lived with each of her children's fathers, Monique and her children had always lived with her parents. This was the first time in her life she had lived separately from her parents without living with a man. She was trying to learn how to be a mom without interference from her parents.

Growing up, both her parents were heavy alcohol and meth addicts. She grew up in a house of drug addicts in and out, her parents fighting with each other, observing chronic domestic violence between her parents and enduring repeated physical abuse from her father and emotional abuse from her mother. When she was an adult, both parents were very controlling of her. They would not allow her to discipline her children and were overbearing regarding how to parent her children. Her parents treated her as a sibling to her children. Her mother in particular, interfered with her parenting. Her father was a chronic substance abuser and would constantly demand money from Monique so he could purchase drugs or alcohol.

The main consequence of all of the childhood exposure to trauma was that Monique had very low self-esteem. She felt completely unloved and unsupported by her parents. She had very serious self-doubts. She did not make good choices in men. Her children had two different fathers, who were both abusive toward her and were serious substance abusers.

Tracking Interactional Patterns

Once moved, her father, who could not drive, left her alone. Her mother, however, was still very involved with her. On one of Mike's home visits, Monique's mother called. Monique and her mother got into a major fight on the phone in front of Mike. After the call, Monique was angry and shaken. She told Mike her mother called constantly. Sometimes, to avoid having to fight with her mom, Monique would give her daughter the phone. The grandmother would then instruct Lillian to not listen to her mother. Afterward, her children would be very hard to manage. If Monique stayed on the phone with her mother, her mother would insult her, and the two would end up in a screaming match. These calls happened seven or eight times per day, every day. Monique either lived in constant anxiety about the next call or would be very angry about the most recent call. In either case, she was emotionally absorbed by these calls, filled with anger or anxiety, all day. Her children lived in a hostile and anxious environment. Her emotional state interfered with her parenting and attentiveness to her two children.

Strengths-Based Approach

Child Protective Services wanted parenting classes for Monique. There were two reasons we felt this would be an error. First, Monique had very low self-esteem resulting from years of emotional abuse from her parents. Suggesting she needed to be taught parenting would not be a way to boost her self-esteem. Second, her mother constantly berated her, telling her she was a bad parent. For us to offer parenting classes would be putting us in agreement with Monique's mother that she was a bad parent. We would be reinforcing the pattern we were trying to break.

I-FAST is organized around a strengths-based philosophy. We assume clients and parents are capable of a more functional range of behavior than they may be exhibiting. In this case, we did not assume Monique was limited in her parenting knowledge or abilities. We did not assume she had deficits that inhibited her parenting, requiring us to teach her parenting skills. Instead, we assumed that she was stuck in an interactional pattern, in this case primarily with her mother, that interfered with her utilizing her parenting abilities. We further assumed that if we could help liberate her from these patterns, she would be empowered to exhibit a wider range of parenting skills than what she was showing without us having to focus at all on her parenting.

Empowering the Mother to Change Her Side of the Pattern

After Mike had learned of Monique's past and of how her mother constantly harassed her, a therapy plan was constructed. The interactional pattern occurred on the phone. It was assumed that Monique knew how to parent her daughter and would if she was not distracted by the calls with her mother and the emotional upset afterwards. We hoped that if we could change these calls, Monique would spontaneously connect with her children. Interventions were devised to help empower Monique to change her side of the interactional pattern between she and her mother.

Use of Between-Session Tasks

When Mike next saw Monique, he talked about the calls. Mike said he wanted to help Monique take charge of these calls and help change how her mother was treating her. Monique was very receptive to this idea. Mike offered three options for how to handle the calls: (a) She could call her mother first and not wait passively for her mother to call; (b) when her mother called, Monique could criticize herself; or (c) when her mother called and criticized her, instead of becoming angry, Monique could respond by just saying "I love you, Mom." Monique did not like any of these options. Mike said that was OK; she could think them over and perhaps come up with an option of her own. The important thing was for Monique to change how she was responding to the calls and see if doing so would have an impact on how her mother treated her.

Tracking Exceptions

At the next home visit, Monique told Mike everything had changed. When her mother called and criticized her, she decided to try the option of telling her mother she loved her. When her mother said something horrific, Monique simply responded with "I love you, Mom." Monique's mother was stunned. She was silent for several seconds. She then made a second feeble attempt to be critical. Monique again responded with "I love you, Mom." Her mom was speechless and just hung up the phone. Monique was ecstatic. She felt empowered. Instead of dreading the next call, she was looking forward to it. When the next call came, her mother was even more horrific than in the first call. Again, Monique responded with "I love you, Mom." Again, her mother just hung up the phone. After these two calls on this first day, Monique's mother did not call anymore on this day. She tried again in the morning of the next day, but again, Monique responded with "I love you, Mom." This time, confident her response would work, Monique tried to be as sincere and loving as possible. On this try, her mother began to cry and then hung up. She did not call back again on the second day. Finally, on the third day, when Monique told her she loved her, Monique's mother said, "I love you, too." Monique said this was the first time her mother had told her she loved her since Monique was 13 years old.

The phone call intervention did not just interrupt the hostility between Monique and her mother, it transformed Monique's relationship with her mother. From this point on, Monique's mother no longer called to criticize her, try to control her, or undermine her with her children. The two began to talk about a wide range of topics and their relationship began to totally change. The effect on Monique was twofold. First, her self-esteem increased substantially. Evidence of this was a plan that she began to implement, of starting her own candle shop business. She said had always wanted to do this but was too afraid to try. Second, all her anxiety and anger went away. The atmosphere in the home was noticeably more relaxed and cheerful. Now that she did not live in fear of calls from her mother or was emotionally upset from a call, she naturally began to attend to both her children. She started playing outside with them. She started cooking on a regular basis and having family dinners. She began to help both children with their homework. Finally, she cleaned up her house. As we were hoping, with the calls from her mother no longer upsetting her or distracting her, with no suggestions from Mike, she focused on her children and was a good mom who did not need any parenting classes.

One final change occurred. After two months of an improved relationship with her mother, her relationship with her father also improved. First, on a phone call, he too told Monique he loved her. More impressively, he volunteered to come over to Monique's house and fix her car. He did not ask her for money to buy drugs; instead, he did something nice for his daughter.

Summary

In this case, the client had endured a childhood of exposure to domestic violence and chronic fighting between her parents and continuous emotional and physical abuse from her mother. The result took a serious toll on her self-esteem and interfered with her ability to emancipate in a functional way from her parents. When she finally did strike out on her own, the weak boundaries and constant hostile contact with her mother continued by phone. As with the last case of the suicidal mother, changing the family patterns was an indirect way of addressing the client's low self-esteem and her neglect of her two children. The goal was to change these patterns and observe the resulting changes in self-esteem and parenting.

SPECIAL POPULATIONS AND TRAUMA

III

10 TRAUMA AND SUBSTANCE ABUSE

As discussed in Chapter 1 of this volume, there is a high correlation of adult substance abuse and childhood sexual assault, particularly intrafamilial sexual assault. To cope with posttraumatic stress disorder (PTSD) symptoms, sexual abuse survivors are vulnerable to the medicating effects of abusing substances.

We have already noted the importance of family support after intrafamilial sexual abuse as a major protective or risk factor in developing PTSD. When sexual or physical abuse of a child becomes a secret or when a child is not believed or blamed for abuse, family support is not forthcoming. Of particular importance is the mother's reaction to sexual abuse. For daughter survivors of intrafamily sexual abuse, the mother believing or not believing and blaming or not blaming the daughter is a major moderator for PTSD and substance abuse. Lacking family support, substance abuse can then become one way the survivor copes. The survivor's substance abuse problems can then become the focus of family interactions, replacing and/or precluding family discussions about past abuses.

Postabuse lack of family support can come in several forms. We observe two common patterns. One pattern is chronic conflict between the survivor, often a daughter, and a parent, often a mother. The parent may not believe the abuse occurred or may blame the victim. This sets in motion chronic hostile and perhaps volatile interactions. When the victim abuses drugs as a coping strategy, the victim and parent may then fight about issues related to drug abuse. This substance abuse conflict replaces the conflict about sexual abuse. Survivor and parent fight about survivor drug use,

not past sexual abuse. Chronic fighting then becomes a habitual interactional pattern that blocks the survivor from obtaining family support regarding the abuse.

Conflict avoidance is a second pattern we observe and is a major impediment to obtaining family support. Emotional disengagement between the survivor and key family members, usually a parent or parents, blocks family support. Minimal contact between the survivor and family and never discussing the abuse when there is contact prevents the survivor from obtaining support.

In both types of patterns, the substance abusing client has an abnormal emancipation. If the substance abuser is a young woman, either cut off from or in on-and-off hostile exchanges, she is without a family to support her and rely on as she attempts to become independent. Lacking emotional support from family, these women can desperately attempt to replace family with intimate partners. The desperation to attach to someone can result in the woman connecting with violent and/or substance abusing partners, setting in motion a new pattern of going in and out of abusive relationships, heaping trauma upon trauma.

Both interactional patterns are demonstrated in the following two cases.

HOT MESS IN BOOTY SHORTS

A common phenomenon over the last 20 years has been grandmothers having to raise the children of their drug-addicted daughters. With the recent opioid epidemic, this phenomenon has become even more common. A percentage of these situations begins with a daughter who is sexually abused or assaulted and a mother who does not believe or support her. The daughter then responds by turning to drugs, and when she has children, her mother must end up raising them. Many of these cases originate because of sex abuse with no family support in response to the trauma. The following case is an example.

Case Background

Angela was grandmother to her two granddaughters, Tammy, aged 9, and Bernice, aged 12. She sought mental health services for both girls when she gained custody of them five years earlier. Over a five-year period, both girls had seen multiple therapists and case managers, and both had, over time, ended up on numerous psychotropic medications. All the therapists either worked with the girls individually or included Angela in their treatment. None ever included or even contacted Anna, the girls' mother and Angela's daughter. Angela originally described Tammy as having attention-deficit/hyperactivity disorder (ADHD) and in need of medications and Bernice as depressed and missing her mother. Angela brought both girls in for a new round of therapy after she discovered that Bernice had sent naked photos of herself to random boys via her smart phone. Lisa Harper became the new therapist and enlisted Jennifer as an in-home intensive case manager. The two worked closely as a team.

Engaging and Establishing an Alliance With the Caregiver

Angela explained that she had had both girls for many years. Her daughter, Anna, had been addicted to drugs for years and was in a lesbian relationship, which Angela did not approve of. Anna moved back and forth with her partner between Angela's town and Columbus, Ohio. Anna was unstable and unpredictable. It was never clear when she would either move away to Columbus or back to Angela's home town. Just as Angela would get the two girls situated, their mother would either move away or move back. When Anna was in town, Angela and Anna would fight frequently about Anna's drug use and lifestyle.

Anna had become addicted to drugs and in serious legal trouble before graduating from high school. She became pregnant with Bernice at age 20. She moved home with Angela and stayed for three years. During this period, she was on and off drugs. Whether on or off drugs, however, Angela and Anna had a very hostile and argumentative relationship. Anna became pregnant with her second child, Tammy, and moved in with Tammy's father. She and Tammy's father became heavy drug users. Tammy's father went to jail, and Anna moved back with Angela.

Soon after moving back with Angela, Anna decided she was lesbian and found a lesbian partner. Angela strongly disapproved of this lifestyle, and so Anna and her partner moved away from Angela's hometown. Angela then won custody of both girls. This began the period of Anna moving back and forth between Columbus and Angela's home town.

Lisa suggested that Anna also participate in the girls' therapy. Angela was opposed to this saying the girls needed to be protected from their mother. Lisa did not push the issue since Anna was living in Columbus at the time. To help gain rapport with Angela, Lisa decided to try to help without including the mother at first. If Anna followed her pattern, she would soon be back in Angela's town, and Lisa could raise the issue of Anna participating again.

Reframing the Granddaughters and an Initial Overarching Frame

Lisa began by seeing the girls individually and with their grandmother. She suggested Tammy did not have ADHD but had a problem mother. Angela agreed. Lisa proposed an overarching frame that would organize the first phase of treatment. Rather than putting Tammy on additional medications, Lisa suggested helping Angela find new ways to help Tammy focus and do better in school. For Bernice, Lisa also offered to help Angela find new ways to help change Bernice's behavior. Lisa proposed parenting instead of medications. Angela was parenting primarily by yelling and lecturing and not following through with rules and consequences. Lisa and Jennifer helped Angela change these patterns, and both girls improved. As expected, Anna and her partner moved back to town, and everything went downhill again.

Decide Whom to Include in Treatment: Recruiting and Engaging the Mother

Lisa again raised the issue of including Anna in the therapy. Angela was again reluctant. By this time, Lisa had established a very good rapport and understanding of Angela. Lisa offered to help Angela obtain a better relationship with Anna to better help her granddaughters. The latest round of hostility and fighting between Angela and Anna had undone all the girl's improvements. Lisa offered a new frame to Angela. Lisa proposed that if she could help Angela and Anna get along then Anna could not undo Angela's parenting. Angela accepted this idea and gave Lisa permission to contact Anna.

Anna came alone the first time. Her appearance was striking. She was dressed in very short shorts and was covered in tattoos and body piercings. She had lost most of her teeth due to chronic use of meth. She looked older than her age. Anna described herself as "a hot mess in booty shorts." Lisa began by asking Anna her opinion of how her girls were doing and if she had any concerns for them. Anna was taken aback by these questions. She told Lisa no one had ever asked her opinion about her daughters. Everyone just blamed her. She was expecting Lisa to be another person who would blame her for her daughter's problems. No one had ever cared about what she thought. Lisa won Anna over just by taking a collaborative, strengths-based position.

Sexual Abuse History and Lack of Family Support

Anna gave Lisa her side the story. Anna told Lisa she had been sexually abused during her childhood by two different perpetrators. The first perpetrator was her mother's brother, her uncle. He raped her on two occasions when Anna was 13. The rapes happened when Angela took Anna to her brother's house to be supervised while Angela worked. She told Angela when it first happened, but Angela did not believe her. Anna was crushed. The abuse stopped, but the damage was done. Anna was now very angry at her mother for not believing her.

The second perpetrator was an older male cousin. Anna was now 16 and her cousin was in his early 20s. He came to visit and stayed for several days. He pressured Anna into having sex against her will. This time Angela discovered the abuse when she entered Anna's bedroom and witnessed her nephew having sex with her daughter. Anna made her nephew leave, and he was never allowed to return. Anna did not report the abuse to the authorities, however. Anna and Angela then had a fight. Anna told Angela she tried to tell her mother about her uncle but was not believed. Angela still did not believe Anna about the first abuse. After this fight, Anna began to use drugs. She dropped out of school and became promiscuous. She started to get in trouble with the juvenile courts. Her pattern of hostility with her mother and an unstable life began. It began exactly after the fight over sexual abuse.

Interactional Pattern Between Grandmother and Daughter

Once Anna's drug use and legal problems began, these issues dominated interactions between Anna and Angela. When they were in contact with each other, Angela assumed Anna was always lying and was always hiding something about illegal behaviors. Angela would confront Anna, and Anna would become angry and storm out. Anna would then move away. While gone, she would miss her daughters and move back to Angela's town, and the pattern would repeat.

Anna explained that now that she was back in town, she and her mother were not getting along again and were fighting. Lisa told Anna she wanted to help her and her mother learn to get along better. She invited Anna to a joint session with her mother. Anna agreed to attend. Lisa then set a meeting with Angela to prepare her for a joint meeting. Angela agreed, complaining about the fighting with her daughter and said both granddaughters were acting up again.

Changing Interactional Patterns: Focusing on Past Abuse

Lisa had now done what no other therapists had done in the previous five years. She persuaded Angela to include Anna in the girls' treatment. She successfully recruited and engaged Anna. She learned Anna's side of the story. And finally, she set up a meeting with both Anna and Angela to attempt to help them improve their relationship.

Lisa organized the session with both Anna and Angela by giving a speech to offer new frames and try to set the stage. She said how important it was for the two women to reach agreements for the sake of the two girls. The speech had no effect, however. The session was a cat fight. Both women blamed each other for the hostility between them. Angela attacked Anna for being a lesbian, a drug addict, and a chronic liar. Anna told Angela she was a terrible mother. Lisa asked Angela why she thought Anna was mad at her. Angela said she did not know. Anna then brought up the sexual abuse and a discussion about what happened ensued. Anna accused her mom of not believing her and not protecting her. Angela said she did not know what to believe.

Lisa became Anna's spokesperson in the session and told Angela the story Anna had told her. Lisa said she believed Anna. She asked Angela to apologize for not believing Anna and for not being able to protect her. Angela would not apologize for not being able to protect Anna. She did apologize for not getting her help, however. Angela's response was not ideal. She did not apologize for the terrible things that happened to Anna. But she did take a big step for her. Angela's apology for not getting Anna help was not just an apology; it was also an acknowledgment that

Angela believed Anna. This was the first time Angela ever said anything to Anna that indicated she believed her daughter. A major step had been taken.

Although the sexual abuse was addressed and Angela offered an apology, the overall session was so hostile that Lisa wondered if it was helpful to bring the two together. Lisa later learned from Anna, that several days after this session, Anna and Angela spontaneously hugged each other and cried together. No words were spoken. Both knew what it was about. Anna confirmed that Angela being willing to talk about the abuse, acknowledging that it did happen, apologizing for not getting Anna help and especially the emotional hug, all helped greatly.

Changing Interactional Patterns: Replacing Criticism With Compliments

To change the pattern between Angela and Anna, Lisa decided to work with Angela alone. Lisa saw first-hand how the two interacted. Individually with Angela, Lisa recounted some of the exact statements Angela said to Anna in the joint session. She asked Angela what she was trying to say to her daughter. Angela would tell Lisa what she wanted Anna to hear. Lisa asked Angela how she thought Anna interpreted what was said. Lisa and Angela processed various statements Angela had said to Anna. Angela realized that the message she intended to send was not the message her daughter received. Lisa was able to persuade Angela to change how she communicated to Anna. She coached Angela to be less critical and more positive and complimentary. As Angela became more positive with Anna, the two fought less, and Anna was more consistent with visiting her daughters. The two women were getting along much better.

Tracking Exceptions and Consolidating Change

A few months passed with Anna not moving back to Columbus. Then an unexpected event occurred. Angela had to have surgery. She would need help to recover. Anna agreed to stay with Angela and help her recover. This was a major exception by Anna. Angela agreed to allow Anna's lesbian partner to stay in the house as well. This was a major exception for Angela. Although their relationship had already improved greatly, Anna agreeing to stay to help and Angela allowing Anna's partner to stay as well helped to further heal all wounds. Anna had stopped all drug use when she and her mother began to get along better. She remained sober.

After Angela recovered from surgery, it was time for Anna and her partner to move out. Anna's partner wanted to move back to Columbus. Another major exception occurred. Anna announced she was not leaving her two daughters ever again. Anna and her partner found an apartment in Angela's town. They both found work and obtained stable income and stable housing—a first in many years. Neither were using drugs. Anna was visiting her daughters regularly and not fighting with her mother. Both girls were doing very well. Angela decided they no longer needed therapy.

Follow-Up

At one-year follow-up found both granddaughters doing very well. Both were off all psychotropic medications. Anna and her partner still resided in Angela's town. All were getting along. After another six months, Angela agreed for both girls to go live again with their mother. Anna regained legal custody of both her daughters. The two ladies worked out a custody change on their own. Angela was now functioning as a grandmother again, not a caregiver. Six months after the change in custody, all were getting along very well. Anna was stable and taking care of her daughters. Angela was having them all over for visits and being a grandmother. Both girls were doing well in school and at home. The family was functioning normally.

THE PSYCHIC

A second major interactional pattern that can develop post intrafamilial sexual abuse is extreme disengagement between the abuse survivor and their family. As a result of abuse and lack of family support, an abnormal emancipation occurs. The survivor completely cuts off the family. This pattern can have several disastrous consequences. First, a young woman alone with no family may be both vulnerable and desperate to find a partner. She may attach to partners with serious problems, such as substance abusing and/or violent men. She may turn to abusing drugs to cope with PTSD symptoms. The following case is an example.

Case Background

Katrina, age 47, had two teenage daughters, Sara,16, and Katy, 17. Their father died when they were seven and eight years old. Katrina had just separated from their father, and he became very depressed. He committed suicide by overdosing on heroin. He left a note telling how losing Katrina had devastated him, saying, "You took my girls from me."

Two years prior to treatment, Katrina lost her apartment and became homeless. Katrina and both girls all found different living arrangements. Katrina moved in with a friend and slept on the couch. Sara was living in her 27-year-old boyfriend's car. She had been going from boyfriend to boyfriend and living in their cars for two years. Katy was living in the home of a girlfriend in another town.

One evening, Sara had a car accident. She had to be taken to the hospital. She tested positive for high levels of methamphetamine and marijuana. Shortly before Sara's car accident, Katrina, found an apartment. She was no longer homeless. She began encouraging both girls to live with her again. Katrina was trying to rescue Sara from her drug use and dealing. Sara, however, was not interested in coming back home. After the car accident, the hospital referred Sara to Children's Services. Children's Services referred Sara to drug treatment and placed her back home with her mother.

Establishing Alliances and Addressing Basic Needs

Katy's drug treatment counselor was Merinda. When Merinda drug-tested Sara, she again tested very high on methamphetamine and marijuana. Sara made it known to Children's Services that she did not want to live with her mother. Merinda knew she would need a strong rapport with Sara. Merinda told Sara it was her treatment. Sara was in charge of what she wanted help on. Sara loved that she was in charge of the treatment. She giggled and said, "I am in charge of my treatment!" "Yes," explained Merinda, who gave Sara a tablet and asked her to write down her goals. With her mother sitting next to her, the first item Sara wrote was she wanted to like her mom again. Merinda asked what had to change for that to happen. Sara complained her mother did not cook, did not keep food in the house, and always dated bad men. By allowing Sara to set the goals, Merinda made a strong and immediate connection. Sara confirmed that she did not want to live with her mother. Her main complaint was that she was terrified of the neighborhood. She was afraid to leave the house and go anywhere. The neighborhood was indeed very unsafe. Sara's fears were justified.

The first family session lasted three hours. Katrina would not stop talking about herself. Katrina volunteered that in the past she had had serious drug problems. She was addicted to crack for almost 15 years. She had now been sober for over 10. Katrina talked a lot about wanting to find a man. With her daughter present, she had no boundaries. She began to talk openly about her sex life, even describing her favorite sexual acts. Merinda had the impression that Katrina was lonely. Although Katrina had no boundaries and would talk about everything in front of Sara, she was open and receptive to receiving help for herself.

Katrina said Sara would become angry, scream, and throw things. Katrina classified Sara as psychotic because of these intense fits. Katrina was calling Children's Service daily, insisting that Sara was psychotic and that she be removed. Sara was withdrawing from methamphetamine. The fits were withdraw symptoms. The problem for Merinda was that Katrina now wanted Sara out. Sara had survived on the street for two years. Sara was back with her mother only because Children's Services placed her there. Both Sara and her mother did not want Sara to be there. The fear was Sara would flee and again live on the street, vulnerable to trafficking.

The priority was for Sara and Katrina to agree to stay together. Katrina had a low income and had difficulty paying bills. Merinda pointed out that if Children's Services placed Sara somewhere else, Katrina would have to pay child support. Katrina was shocked and insisted Sara should stay with her. She never again brought up the idea of Sara living somewhere else.

The problem now was helping Sara feel safe. To accomplish this, Merinda called upon Sara's sister Katy. Katy was living with a friend in another town. Merinda called Katy from the session and explained to her how afraid her sister was. Katy needed to come home to escort Sara out of the house and help her feel safe in the neighborhood. Merinda told Katy she was desperately needed at home. Katy liked the idea of being needed and agreed to move home. She was back home within one week. All three were now living together for the first time in two years. Merinda was able to accomplish a huge intervention in the first two sessions. She persuaded mother and both daughters that it was best for all to live together again.

In the first session with Katrina and both girls, the girls informed Merinda of their mom's problems. Their main complaint was about Katrina going from man to man. They described Katrina as more concerned about men than about them. They said Katrina was too trusting and took up with any man. All of Katrina's boyfriends were criminals. They also complained there was never food in the house. Katrina spent her money on unneeded items like getting her nails done or buying candy. The girls complained Katrina would not even enroll them in school. Katrina affirmed she did not think it was her job to get the girls in school.

Tracking Client Frames

Katrina told Merinda that she was a psychic. She had visions and could foretell the future. She had visions about future boyfriends. While the girls were listing all their complaints, Katrina was telling Merinda about her visions. The girls' complaints were not even registering. Katrina was very open about her visions with other professionals involved. In a meeting with the Children's Services Case Worker, Katrina began talking about her visions and was scolded and put down by the worker. The worker said, "We are here about your daughters, not your visions." She was dismissed and framed as crazy by the other professionals on the case.

To join with Katrina, Merinda asked about her visions in more detail. Merinda expressed a genuine interest in Katrina's visions. Katrina talked on and on about them. She was very appreciative that Merinda had taken an interest in them. Merinda framed Katrina as having a special talent that put her in touch with the spirit world. Katrina was very complimented by this.

Utilizing Client Frames

Merinda suggested that since Katrina was focusing on the more important aspects of the spirit world, perhaps the girls could be in charge of the mundane day-to-day things. The girls could be in charge of food. Katrina agreed. From this point on, Katrina gave the girls money, took them to the store, and allowed them to decide what food to buy. Sometimes Katrina would want to buy candy, but the girls would not allow her. They made sure the money was spent wisely on nutritious foods. From here on, there was always appropriate food in the house.

Katrina signed papers brought by Merinda to enroll the girls in school. Both girls attended school regularly from this point on. After living with Katrina and her sister for several weeks and going to school, Sara's drug screens improved dramatically. She stopped using methamphetamine, and her marijuana use reduced. Both girls now lived with their mother, had a roof over their head, had adequate food, and were enrolled in and attending school.

Assessing Interactional Patterns

Merinda then focused on learning about the family interactional patterns. Katrina rarely interacted with her daughters. She stayed in her bedroom, obsessed with Internet dating sites. The girls told Merinda that in their entire lives, they had never sat down with their mother to have a meal together. Katrina had five children, two sons and three daughters, including Sara and Katy. Except for Sara and Katy, all her children were removed by Children Services when they were young. All had different fathers. Her older children were now grown. One son lived in California. One son was married and lived in Columbus. The oldest daughter was married, had two children, and lived in Columbus. Katrina had not seen or interacted with her son in California since he was three years old. Katrina did have sporadic contact with her son and daughter in Columbus. Sara and Katy stayed in regular contact with their brother and their sister in Columbus via Facebook. They did not talk to their brother in California.

Katrina's mother was in a nursing home. Katrina loved her mom but did not wish to visit her. Her father lived in California. She had not spoken to him in 20 years. The family patterns were dominated by disengagement. Katrina did not interact with either of her parents, two of her adult children, and until Children's Services intervened, she had not lived with her two minor daughters, both homeless, for two years. Katrina herself was living hand to mouth financially and going from man to man with no stable adult relationships in her life.

Initial Interventions: Frames, Tasks, and Changing Interactional patterns

Katrina was now interested in a man at a local gas station. The girls complained that she did not even know this man and was too trusting. It was decided to put the girls in charge of helping Katrina find an appropriate man. Merinda framed it to the girls as, "You two are more in tune with the real world and how it works. Your mom is in tune with the psychic universe. She needs help being in touch with the real world." Katrina loved the idea of her daughters helping her find an appropriate man. At first the girls were reluctant, but that evening they began looking at proper dating sites and became totally enthused with the idea. It was hoped this task would break the pattern of disengagement in the house.

The next session focused on the qualities a man for mom should have. The girls listed several qualities. Mom needed a man who is mentally stable because mom is not. He must have a steady income and a good job. He should not have children but should like children. Mom, on the other hand, wanted someone who was attractive and liked to go out and have fun. The girls pointed out that their mom was like a 16-year-old. Katrina complained that she never got to have fun when she was young. She had extremely strict parents and then had children at an early age. When she escaped her parents, she immediately began a serious drug career that lasted 15 years. She had missed out on dating and having fun.

Trauma History: Breaking the "No Talk" Rule

The next session was again focused on Katrina and boyfriends. When Merinda arrived, Katrina and the girls were already talking about it. The girls emphasized that their mom needed be less trusting. They emphasized the man should have a "clean record." Merinda asked what that meant. Katy said he could not have any criminal background. All of mom's past boyfriends had a criminal background. Merinda asked what kind of criminal background. "We want someone who will love us and not do bad things to us," they said. Merinda asked if anyone had done bad things to them. The sky then opened up and the seas parted.

Katy said she was touched sexually by an adult male perpetrator. Sara said the same perpetrator had touched her also. It was her oldest sister's first husband. The girls were 9 and 10 at the time. It happened just after their biological father died. Their sister began babysitting them. When at the sister's home, her husband would touch them sexually and masturbate. Katrina was told about Katy's abuse only and did not believe her. Later, the sister's husband was caught molesting another child. Katrina then believed Katy but never talked about what happened. This session was the first time the three ever talked about the abuse in detail. Both girls said the abuse happened several times while their sister's husband was babysitting. Katrina knew none of this. She only knew he had touched Katy and thought it was just on one occasion.

The girls then reported that their older sister was raped by her father from age 8 to 14. When the girls accused her husband of molesting them, their sister believed them and told what had happened to her. Katrina knew none of this. Katrina was shocked. All three of her daughters had been sexually abused. She only knew about one of them. Katrina said if she had known she could have helped because she herself had been molested by her own father.

Katrina then revealed that she too had been sexually abused. She told that her father had molested her when she was nine years old. He had intercourse with her when he was drunk. The abuse went on until she was 17 and left home. She told her mom just before she left home, but her mom did not believe her. She was having nightmares and flashbacks. She started to use drugs to try to help herself forget what had happened. She started with alcohol and marijuana and then went to cocaine and crack. She developed a very serious addiction to crack.

This was the first discussion Katrina and her daughters had ever had about sexual abuse. Katrina learned for the first time that both her girls were molested by her older daughter's husband. She learned for the first time that her oldest daughter had been molested for years by Katrina's second husband. The girls learned for the first time that their mother had been molested for years by her own father. There was a tremendous sense of relief in the session after all this had been shared. They were all in shock and awe but also giddy that they could finally talk about what happened and share the terrible secrets that they had kept from one another for so many years. Merinda asked, "How can we stop this pattern and make sure it does not happen to the girls' children." The girls said, "We are not going to choose men like fucking mom."

Exceptions and Breaking Long-Standing Patterns of Disengagement

After this session, Katrina called Merinda. She told Merinda that she had been in deep thought since the session focusing on the past abuse and had decided to forgive her father. Over the years he had attempted to contact her several times, but she never returned his calls. She said he was old now. She wanted to find out if he had changed. He was still her father. She called him and spoke to him for the first time in 20 years. Katrina learned that he was married. They began to speak again regularly and tell about their lives. Her father then sent money to Katrina unsolicited. He wanted his granddaughters to have a good Christmas. This was the first of what would be many steps for Katrina and both her girls to reconnect with several family members.

Thanksgiving was coming. Merinda asked what the plan was for Thanksgiving. Katrina usually did nothing. She had no one over. Merinda asked if they could each invite a family member who would it be. Katrina said her mother and her son in Columbus. Merinda asked about the older daughter. She was remarried. She had Thanksgiving with her husband's family and would not be available. The girls both said they wanted their brother in California to come. He was the only sibling they did not know. Merinda asked how could they make this happen? The girls found their California brother on Facebook and contacted and invited him.

After this session, Katrina decided she should go see her mother in the nursing home. She had not been to see her in years. She and both girls went and invited her to thanksgiving. The dinner took place in the Columbus brother's home. Katrina's mother did come. The brother from California also came. He stayed in town for one week. It was the first time Katrina had seen him since he was three years old. The girls were excited to meet their brother. They all took pictures together. When it was time to eat, they all sat at the table together, the first time in their entire lives they sat at a table together to eat a meal.

Identifying and Changing Frames That Support Interactional Patterns

KATRINA AND HER MOTHER

In an individual session with Katrina, Merinda asked if it was difficult for her to see her mother. Was she angry with her mother for what her father had done to her? Katrina said that she did not tell her mother about the abuse until just before she left home. Initially, her mother did not believe her. But after Katrina moved out, her mother divorced her father. When her mother divorced her father, Katrina felt supported and believed by her mother. She forgave her mother. After Katrina quit drugs, her mother moved close by and frequently asked Katrina to visit. Katrina avoided her mother, however. She told Merinda that her mother did the right thing and left her father. Katrina became a drug addict anyway. She was ashamed to face her mother. She wanted her mother to be proud of her and felt she was disappointed with her. That is why it was hard for her to see her mother. They had never spoken about the abuse. Katrina was assuming her mother was ashamed of her. Merinda told Katrina that she was being too hard on herself. Her father had abused her for many years. She took drugs to try to forget and to cope with what happened. To no avail, Katrina had not forgiven herself.

From Katrina's mother's perspective, we suspected that her mother might believe Katrina avoided her because Katrina was angry with her for not protecting her from abuse. Katrina decided on her own to contact her father after the session focusing on sexual abuse. We therefore suspected she might also initiate a talk with her mother if we suggested the idea to Katrina that her mother might believe she (Katrina) was angry with her. This idea may compel Katrina to call her mother to clarify that she was not angry with her. This is, in fact, what happened. Merinda suggested to Katrina that her mother might think she was angry with her. Katrina did call her mother, and they had their first heart-to-heart talk about the abuse. Katrina told her mother she was not angry with her. She avoided her because she was ashamed about her drug use. Her mother told her she was not ashamed of her.

CLIENT RESPONDS WITH EXCEPTIONS

After this call, Katrina began to call her mother one time per week. They began to have many heart-to-heart talks, and their relationship began to transform. They became much closer to each other. Instead of asking Merinda for advice on different matters, Katrina began to ask her mother for advice on many issues. Katrina's self-esteem greatly improved as a consequence of these talks. As she and her mother became closer, Katrina's obsession with finding a man began to diminish. Katrina was replacing superficial relationships with random men with a new more heartfelt relationship with her mother.

KATRINA AND HER DAUGHTERS

Katrina did not react to the reunion with her son as her daughters did. She was sad that she had lost her son and missed out on his life. After the Thanksgiving dinner, she relapsed and spent her next check on unneeded things. The girls could see their mother was sad about missing her son but were unmoved. They framed her as an ex-drug addict who had made irresponsible choices in her life and had been a terrible mother to them. Despite hearing her story of horrific abuse and how she took drugs to escape the memories of her past, they had no compassion for her. Clearly, a new goal was to help them see their mother in a more compassionate light.

Merinda met with Sara alone. They talked about why Sara thought her mother was sad. Sara said it was her own fault. She was a drug addict and was irresponsible. Merinda asked Sara how she thought the sex abuse Katrina endured from her father affected the course of her life. Merinda pointed out that Katrina began to use drugs to help her forget her past. Sara began offering her own ideas about how hard it must have been for her mother to be on her own with no help from her parents. Sara began to have more compassion for her mother. She began to reframe her from irresponsible to a young person who was damaged and trying to survive.

EXCEPTIONS BETWEEN MOTHER AND DAUGHTERS

After this, both girls began to interact more with their mother. Before, they just came and went without informing their mother where they were going or when they would return. Now they were spontaneously letting her know where they were going, who they were with, and when they would be home again.

The girls' seating arrangement for the sessions changed. Before, both girls sat together on one side of the room and Katrina sat alone on the opposite side of the room. Now, they all spontaneously sat on the couch together. Katrina had joined her daughters on the couch. From this point on, the three sat together in all the remaining family sessions.

Enlarging Exceptions and Consolidating Changes

Both girls were now motivated to be more family-involved. They began to plan future family meetings with their siblings and grandmother. Initially, neither wanted a job or were interested in school. Now they both began to actively look for work and apply for jobs. They both began to seriously focus on school. They both reconnected with their sister. They all Facebooked regularly. They pushed their mom to take them to see their grandmother.

For months after the session in which the sexual abuse was talked about, both girls and Katrina were very dependent on Merinda. They did not want her to go away and could not imagine her not around. During this period, Merinda was concerned about how she could ever terminate the case. After Katrina and her mother had reestablished a better relationship and after Katrina and both girls had become more involved with each other, their reliance on Merinda reduced. Katrina had replaced Merinda with her mother, and the girls had replaced Merinda with their mother. A parallel process had ensued. As Katrina and her mother became more engaged with each other, Katrina and her girls also became more engaged with each other.

Sara and Merinda reviewed the goals Sara had written down in her first appointment. Regarding liking her mother again, with Katrina sitting next to her, Sara looked at her mother and affirmed she did indeed like her again. Merinda asked Sara if there was anything that made her think about her meth days. Sara said her teeth. They were all black from years of meth use, some needed caps and fillings. Katrina, hearing this, without being told to do so, set a dentist appointment the get Sara's teeth cleaned and fixed. The same mother who did not think it was her job to enroll her girls in school was now spontaneously responding to her daughter's dental needs. They had five appointments. Her teeth and smile became wonderful. The terrible stain of the past had been washed away.

After this, Sara's confidence soared. She became very interested in finding a nice boyfriend. She became confident she could find a job. Merinda took her to apply at a local Wendy's. Several prostitutes were being arrested across the street. The neighborhood had not changed, but Sara had. Termination was now possible.

Collaborating With Professionals

Several meetings had occurred throughout this treatment between Marinda and the Children's Service case worker. Katrina's initial insistence that Sara be removed made a lasting negative impression on the case worker. Now that all the treatment goals were met, Marinda discussed termination with the family. They were all afraid of Marinda terminating, fearing that without her, the case worker would remove both daughters from the home. The case worker was, in fact, skeptical that meaningful change had occurred. In I-FAST, when change occurs, all parties, including other professionals, must agree. A meeting was set with Marinda; her supervisor, Kim; the case worker; and the case worker's supervisor. At the meeting, the case workers concerns were heard. Marinda then listed the many changes that had occurred over the past six months. The case worker's supervisor was very impressed. All agreed Child Protective Services were no longer needed. After this meeting, Children's Services closed their case.

Marinda met with the family for one last time. It was a very emotional session. Everyone cried. All were very grateful to Marinda. Marinda gave credit for the changes to all of them and stressed the courage they all displayed in facing the abuse they had all endured.

SUMMARY

Both the discussed herein cases are examples of childhood abuse survivors not obtaining family support, particularly from their mothers, who then turned to serious drug abuse as a coping strategy for PTSD. In the first case, the survivor and her mother developed a chronic pattern of hostile arguing. They fought over the survivor's drug use. The childhood sexual abuse was not talked about. The survivor lost custody of her children to the very person she was in conflict with. This conflict affected the children who were then brought to treatment by the grandmother.

In the second case, the survivor totally cut off her family, avoiding interaction with both her father, the perpetrator, and her mother. She too turned to drugs to cope with her PTSD symptoms, and she too lost custody of her first three children, this time to foster care. She had an adult life of desperately going from man to man, all criminals, at the expense of her children.

In both cases, engaging the survivors and their mothers in a treatment process and helping the survivors to finally receive family support from their mothers lead to major reduction, if not total resolution, of trauma symptoms and their consequences. In the first case, instead of only including the caregiving grandmother in the granddaughter's treatment, the therapist recruited the drug-abusing mother into the treatment and helped her finally obtain support from her mother regarding the sexual abuses she endured. This led to a reconciliation of the mother and grandmother's relationship. Several major changes followed. First, the mother became sober. Second, she obtained stable housing and stable employment and established a stable relationship with her two daughters. Finally, she and her mother agreed for her to regain custody of her two girls.

In the second case, when the survivor was able to obtain support from her mother, she and her mother re-established their relationship. The survivor's desperation to be with a man went away. Her pattern of going from one criminal to another stopped when she and her mother came to terms with the abuse perpetrated by the survivor's father.

In both cases, one of the principal family participants had to be recruited and engaged in treatment. In the first case, the mother, the abuse survivor, had to be recruited and engaged in treatment. In the second case, the mother of the children was the survivor, and her mother had to be reached out to and re-engaged with the survivor. To resolve both cases, a wider observational field than just caregiver and children was needed and outreach by the therapist was required.

Both cases exemplify both the terrible consequence of a daughter not receiving support from her mother after having been sexually abused by a family member and the powerful therapeutic value in helping them finally receive support from their mothers. Despite both women being well into adulthood, it was not too late for a profound impact to result from their mothers finally supporting them regarding past abuse.

STORIES OF VIOLENCE AND RESILIENCE

11

Dominique is in her early 30s, married, and has a master's degree and professional career. She and her husband both grew up in poor, urban, predominantly African American neighborhoods. Both look back and marvel that they were able to escape their neighborhoods and make the life they have now. Dominique explained,

> You never knew what you might be a witness to or what might happen near you that you do not want to be blamed for or be a part of. You see someone get shot or you hear about someone who got shot, and they are your friend and that person did not make it home that day. You wanted to go outside and play but you knew when you did, bad things could happen. Just trying to get to school or go to the store for your mom could mean serious trouble. You wanted to tell someone, but what could they do? These things will keep happening every day if you tell or not. I do not know how I made it out. It is very painful thinking of those times and what I experienced in the neighborhood. I worked after school to stay off the streets. I always knew this was not right. I was not going to live like this forever. My mom made sure I believed in myself, that I could have a good life in the future. I always had the expectation that someday life would be different. I would not be living like this forever. My mom gave me that belief.

Dominique's mother gave her hope and the expectation that she could survive her neighborhood.

STREET VIOLENCE AND TRAUMA

Poor urban area crime rates, including violent crimes, shootings, murders, and drug related crimes are well documented. In 2002, 3,365 youth died from urban gunshot wounds, and 13,000 to 16,000 sustained nonfatal injures (Bertram & Dartt, 2008). Children are living in these neighborhoods—walking to school, playing outside, walking to the store. The chances of a particular child in such a neighborhood, witnessing or being victimized by a crime are substantial. They must live with this possibility every day. They must learn how to be safe in a very unsafe environment every day. School shootings have been happening in these neighborhoods for decades. Children have been getting shot in these neighborhoods for decades. Parents in these neighborhoods must live in constant fear of their children being seriously harmed or killed.

Studies have been devoted to the connection between "neighborhood context" and adverse childhood events (ACEs; Wolfe, Cuevas, Intravia, Baglivio, & Epps,

2018). A strong connection has been established between low socioeconomic status (SES) and high ACE scores. The connections point out an increased risk of family as the source of ACEs. Increased exposure to parental drug use, divorce, domestic violence, sexual and physical abuse, and child neglect are documented. Children living in families in low SES neighborhoods are at risk for developmental and behavioral problems (Aneshensel & Sucoff, 1996; Brooks-Gunn et al., 1993, Elliot et al., 1996; Leventhal & Brooks-Gunn, 2000; Wolfe et al., 2018). These researchers are correlating low SES neighborhoods as presenting increased risk for exposure to *family* violence and neglect. Families are scrutinized as the source of trauma.

What is the effect of the neighborhood itself on children? There seems to be less attention paid to neighborhood violence as a source of ACEs. Ellis (2017) has found a diminished focus on this population. In the trauma literature, great attention is paid to inside the home, less so out among the neighborhood. Several recent major publications offering broad overviews of trauma and trauma treatment do not include special attention to neighborhood violence or list neighborhood violence as a major category of trauma exposure for children (Beck & Sloan, 2012; Classen & Clark, 2017; Friedman et al., 2014). Studies that have focused on the effect of violent neighborhoods on the children living in them show a devastating impact.

Epidemiology

Violence and its psychological toll have reached epidemic proportions in our poor urban neighborhoods (Chen, 2014; Huston, 2014). Over 80% of children in poor, urban neighborhoods have witnessed chronic community violence, encompassing hearing gunfire, observing drug deals and seeing a dead body on the street (Fitzpatrick & Boldizar, 1993; Kliewer et al., 1998). Other estimates of directly witnessing serious neighborhood violence such as robbery, stabbing, shooting, and murder range from between 60% to 75% of youth in poor urban neighborhoods (Sheehan, DiCara, LeBally, & Christoffel, 1997). Seventy percent of children in poor, urban neighborhoods are directly victimized by neighborhood violence, being beaten, stabbed, or shot (Kliewer, Lepore, Oskin, & Johnson, 1998).

Effects of Chronic Exposure to Neighborhood Violence

Children exposed to chronic neighborhood violence through witnessing or victimization are at increased risk of developing posttraumatic stress disorder (PTSD), generalized anxiety, depression, and suicidal ideation (Aisenberg & Mennen, 2000; Dyson, 1990; Horowitz, Weine, & Jekel, 1995; Kerig, Wainryb, Twaali, & Chaplo, 2013; Post et al., 2014). One study estimated that as many as one third of all children living in urban neighborhoods have PTSD, twice the rate reported for soldiers returning from combat (Tucker, 2007). A moderate effect size (0.39) has been documented for the relationship between exposure to or victimization from community violence and PTSD symptoms (Boney-McCoy & Finkelhor, 1995). One study showed that both witnessing neighborhood violence and being victimized resulted in 27% of 7- to 18-year-olds meeting all three PTSD diagnostic criteria. One third of 10-to 15-year-olds exposed to community violence displayed PTSD symptoms (Overstreet, Dempsey, Graham, & Moley, 1999). Perceived safety or danger in the neighborhood is one moderating factor. In one sample, 29% of the participating children felt unsafe (Overstreet & Braum, 2000). Those children were much more likely to develop PTSD if exposed to neighborhood violence. Fifty-two percent of urban adolescents hospitalized psychiatrically reported exposure to multiple incidents of neighborhood violence. Hospitalized patients who witnessed community violence presented with significantly higher rates of PTSD, drug use. and violent behavior than those patients who did not report exposure to neighborhood violence (Fehon, Grilo, & Lipschitz, 2001). A sample of elementary school children living in high-violence neighborhoods displayed worries about safety, nightmares, blunt affect, and recurrence of upsetting thoughts (Osofsky, 1995). African American women living in poor urban neighborhoods are particularly vulnerable (Alim, Charney, & Mellman, 2006).

A growing body of research is identifying similarities between exposure to combat among war veterans and urban gang members (Chen, 2014; Ellis, 2017; Huston, 2014; Post et al., 2014). Recent studies are also finding similarities between urban youth and children in globalized war zones (Kerig et al., 2013). Both groups have been exposed to traumatic events such as shootings, homicide, and hand-to-hand combat. Kerig et al. (2013) observes that both child soldiers and gang members have had exposure to serious and chronic trauma and that this exposure influences decisions to join gangs, perhaps to stay safe.

Effects of living in violent neighborhoods on conduct, school performance, and physical health have also been shown. Serious negative effects of exposure to violence on academic performance have long been documented (Dyson, 1990). Witnessing a shooting or stabbing was linked to increased fighting among elementary-aged children (Bell & Jenkins, 1993). Day-to-day stress of exposure to neighborhood violence may be linked to development of headaches, asthma, allergies, and ulcers in youth (Miller, 1995). It has also been linked to increased risk of infectious diseases (Miller, 1995).

Children living in violent neighborhoods may feel hopeless, developing beliefs that they lack resources to achieve socially approved goals. They then are more likely to engage in high-risk sexualized or criminal behavior (Wallach, 1993).

Effects on Parents and the Family

Coping with stress of community violence diminishes parents' ability to provide protection and guidance (B. James, 1994). When parents themselves are afraid of neighborhood violence, they become less able to moderate the effects on their children of exposure to neighborhood violence. Children of parents who are traumatized are more likely to develop PTSD symptoms themselves (Foy, Madvig, Pynoos, & Camilleri, 1996). Neighborhood violence may undermine a child's trust in their parent's ability to protect them (B. James, 1994).

An interesting relationship between neighborhood violence, family conflict, and development of PTSD has been documented. Living in violent neighborhoods can increase family violence (Cicchetti & Lynch, 1993). Family members can be in conflict over how to stay safe. In turn, children exposed to family conflict and who live in violent neighborhoods feel less safe and are then more likely to develop PTSD if exposed to neighborhood violence (Overstreet & Braum, 2000). Two moderators have been examined: mother's presence in the home and family size. Both moderated development of depression in children, but neither moderated the development of PTSD (Overstreet, Dempsey, Graham, & Moley, 1999).

CODE OF THE STREET

To understand the world of impoverished urban neighborhoods, we turn to ethnographic studies, conducted in a large inner-city metropolitan areas (Anderson, 1999; Ellis, 2014; Horowitz, McKay, & Marshall, 2005). Growing up and having to survive in a violent Toronto neighborhood, Adam Ellis graphically describes the violence he experienced and the survival strategies he employed (Ellis, 2014). Fear of being killed and a desire to stay safe motivated him to join a gang. In the gang, he participated in urban warfare. Participants lost limbs and lives.

Horowitz et al. Study

Horowitz et al. (2005) interviewed 23 parents and 28 children (17 girls and 11 boys). Focus groups were conducted and participants were asked the following questions:

- What is it like growing up/raising children in your neighborhood? Does it feel safe?
- Do you/your children feel safe at school? Who can your children talk to at school?
- Do you/your children confide in friends? Is it safe?

The following are some of the findings and responses.

PARENTS' CONCERNS

Parents reported having serious concerns for their children being exposed to neighborhood violence. Parents worried about their daughters being exposed to unknown men while visiting in their friends' homes. They worried about their sons falling prey to money offered to them to get involved with drug deals. Parents felt helpless to protect their children from neighborhood violence and hopeless that they could escape the problems. Comments included: "I've heard of kids get raped just going from their apartment to the first floor"; "There are a lot of men snatching girls up"; and "The money is fast money, but it is fast death" (Horowitz et al., 2005, p. 359). One parent told of a six-year-old boy killed where she lived and that her child witnessed the killing and saw the dead body.

CHILDREN

Children reported they viewed their neighborhoods as very unsafe, feeling in danger when playing outside. Parks, empty buildings, places where gang members stand, and their own apartment buildings were viewed as very dangerous: "Around my block is very dangerous. Every day someone gets killed"; "In my building there is a lot of drug dealing. I saw three of them get killed"; and "To live around here you have to be scared to walk in the streets at any time" (Horowitz et al., 2005, p. 360).

Parents noticed their children had many fears and worries. They worried about being "jumped," gangs, having to fight, and their own parents' safety. They reported both they and their children had nightmares. Children reported having nightmares of being raped and stabbed.

OUTSIDE HELPERS

Parents reported a serious lack of trust of police or social service providers. Police were described as unavailable and not protective. Parents reported police delaying responding or not responding at all due to their own fears of entering the neighborhood. When not called upon, police were viewed as intrusive and provocative. Parents reported multiple incidents of police arriving at their homes unexpectedly and without respect for tenants' rights.

Parents also did not trust social workers. They did not want their children talking to unrelated adults because of the belief that authorities will remove them from their homes.

PARENTS' AND CHILDREN'S PERCEPTION OF SCHOOLS

Parents described schools as providing inadequate supervision and poor education and lacking resources and school personnel as unresponsive to needs of families. Parents also felt schools were unsafe for their children. Parents wanted more security in school hallways and more screening of entrants into the buildings. Some parents felt teachers acted out their own anger against their students.

Children's beliefs about their schools paralleled their parents'. Children reported not feeling safe at school, observing that many students bring knives to school, and reported a belief that teachers also armed themselves to stay safe. Children also reported not feeling supported by the adults in the schools and that they found it difficult to concentrate on schoolwork due to violence inside and outside of the school building.

PROTECTIVE BEHAVIORS OF PARENTS AND CHILDREN

Parents' attempts to keep their children safe included carefully screening their children's close friends, rarely allowing them to go to other children's homes and keeping them within a line of sight as much as possible. One mother described her efforts to keep her daughter safe: "I let her go to the store only with another child, and I time her. She cannot go in or out of the building by herself, and she cannot ride the elevator. She has 10 minutes to get home from school. She cannot come up the elevator; she has to ring the bell and come up the steps." The parents knew that at some age it was important for their child to learn more independence but also knew independence was very dangerous.

Children had their own ways of staying safe including attitudes about physically fighting, staying close to home, friendships, and how to and not to interact with adults. Boys felt a need to fight back if fought with first. "You have to fight until you prove yourself. If you don't, they'll keep coming until you finally do fight." Girls recognized the importance of staying close to home. "I cannot go outside alone. I have to call someone. I stay inside so I don't get hurt." To avoid problems many children reported just having one close, trusted friend and only confiding in their parents and trusted family. One girl reported, "Friends spread rumors. It backfires. I don't trust nobody." Both parents and children reported family as the greatest source of support. Children reported confiding primarily in their mothers.

Anderson Study

In his 1999 study Elijah Anderson provides further insights into the dangers and coping strategies of families in these neighborhoods:

> Of all the problems of the poor inner-city black community none is more pressing than interpersonal violence. This phenomenon wreaks havoc on the lives of community residents. Muggings, burglaries, car-jackings and drug related shootings may leave victims or innocent bystanders dead. (Anderson, 1999, p. 32)

Anderson writes:

> The violence springs from the lack of jobs that pay a living wage, limited basic services (police not responding to emergencies, building maintenance, trash pickup) the stigma of race, fallout from rampant drug use and trafficking and the absence of hope for the future. Living in such neighborhoods places young people at risk of falling victim to aggressive behavior. (p. 33)

Anderson (1999) notes two groups in these neighborhoods: One group, the "decent," represent the most powerful force to counteract the negative influences of the street: a strong, loving family committed to following the rule of law. The other group "street people," consists of those who are overcome by the despair of the neighborhood and who have "spawned an oppositional culture." The disillusionment of those taken in by the street can be attributed to "the alienation from mainstream society felt by poor inner-city black people, particularly the youth" (p. 34). These two groups, "decent" and" street," organize the community.

The residents of the neighborhoods Anderson studied themselves used the terms "decent" and "street" families. Any given family can have both "street" and "decent" members. Both parents may be "street," but there may be an uncle or grandparent who is "decent." Youth from the families that reflect mainstream values must still learn to survive in the neighborhood itself. Families who are opposed to the "street" values must still reluctantly teach their children to understand the "code of the street" to enable them to survive the poor urban environment.

To stay safe outside their home, urban youth must understand the "code of the street." On the street, if the rules are broken, there will be penalties. Knowing the code is paramount for safely operating in public. *Respect* is at the heart of the code. "The rules of the code provide a framework for negotiating respect" (Anderson, 1999, p. 33). Respect allows one to be left alone while in public. To stay safe, whether one is "street" or "decent," it helps to have respect. On the other hand, disrespecting someone can be interpreted as an act of aggression resulting in a violent response. The code of the street is an adaptation to lack of trust and faith in the police or justice system and is fueled by a belief that mainstream White society does not care about the urban Black poor (Anderson, 1999). That the issue of neighborhood violence has been minimized in the trauma literature in favor of blaming the families for the increased ACEs of youth in these neighborhoods could be taken as evidence of this lack of caring.

ROBERT

Robert grew up in a poor, urban, predominantly African American neighborhood in a large metropolitan area. When he graduated from high school, he decided he would be safer if he enlisted in the army and went to the Vietnam War than he would be if he stayed in his neighborhood. His attempt to escape the violence of his neighborhood would prove to be disastrous. While in Vietnam, Robert used heroin to help him cope with the war. When he returned, his addiction continued. He married and had a son and a daughter. As an addict, he committed several drug-related crimes. He was in and out of prison for various drug-related offenses. At some point, due to multiple offenses, he was sentenced to prison for many years.

He was sent to a prison in Indiana. While in prison, he continued with his heroin addiction. He wanted to be transferred to a prison in Ohio where his children lived, hoping they would visit. After many years, he was transferred to an Ohio prison. By this time, his son was grown and did not want to visit him. His daughter was a teenager and did visit him. On her visit she said, "Dad you have missed your son's entire childhood. Are you now going to miss my entire childhood?" His daughter's question had a profound effect on Robert. He decided he was going to overcome his addiction and turn his life around.

Robert did quit heroin and was eventually released from prison. He became an addictions counselor working with urban, African American adolescents. Although he has stopped using heroin, he continued to have his Vietnam nightmares. One meeting with his daughter in prison changed his life. The power of family was greater than the power of his addiction. The power of his relationship with his daughter helped him turn his life around. Robert had his family therapy session in jail with him and his daughter and no therapist. Using Anderson's classification, when Robert returned from war, he joined those of the "street." His encounter with his daughter turned him away from the "street" and back into the hands of the "decent."

GANGBANGING

Lana grew up with her mom, older sister and her aunt. She views her early childhood with fondness. In first grade, she beat up two girls on the way home from school. No other children ever bothered her after this. She had respect and was feared. She was very proud of this. She did not misbehave in school. She felt loved, wanted, and cared for by her mother, her aunt, and her sister. She remembers a positive childhood until "trauma hit."

When Lana was eight, her mother moved the family to a different city to live with her mother's new boyfriend. The new boyfriend was "controlling and violent." He was jealous, possessive, and suspicious of Lana's mom. By moving to a new city, Lana's mom became disconnected from her family and friends. She had no support system in the new city. By contrast, her boyfriend's entire family lived there. He also had many friends who would "spy" on Lana's mom. Lana's mom and her daughters had to "sneak" out of the house to socialize. After three years, Lana's mom decided she needed to get away from the boyfriend. She saved money secretly. The family was then able to move away unexpectedly, in the middle of the night.

After Lana's mom left, the boyfriend stalked her. He did things like put sugar in her gas tank. It took years to obtain a total break-up. Lana's mom would talk to her now ex-boyfriend on the phone or he would show up outside the house, and her mom would talk to him. Because Lana's mom had no support system in the ex-boyfriend's town, she was vulnerable. She had no one to protect her, was lonely, and only had the boyfriend and his family.

When Lana was 11, the boyfriend showed up at the house unexpectedly. He beat Lana's mom severely. She was seriously injured. Lana was holding her mother in her lap and feared for her mother's life. This incident is what Lana defines as traumatic. She is still haunted by this scene today.

When Lana and her sister were teenagers, Lana's mom got away from the boyfriend completely. Lana remembers the next few years as an ideal time in her life. Her mom joined a church and met other people. She befriended other women. Lana had positive experiences in school. She had many friends who were not in trouble. She was a cheerleader and ran track.

Lana's life took a major turn after she graduated from high school and emancipated from home. She met an older boyfriend who introduced her to cocaine. She became very addicted. This began her life in gangs. She joined a gang and lived a life on the street for decades. She described herself as a "gangbanger." She and her gang got into physical fights with other gangs. No one was killed. Guns were not involved. Just very violent, physical, group brawls. During this period, Lori had two children, a son and a daughter.

After she had her son, she wanted to get out of the drug and gang life. She thought if she moved away, she could start over. She moved to Ohio intending to have a fresh start. But she was drawn back into the drug and gang life. Finally, a turning point arrived. Lana was court-ordered into inpatient drug treatment. While in inpatient drug treatment, she was still getting in trouble. Her daughter was not permitted to come visit. She called her nine-year-old daughter to tell her she could not come and visit. Her girl said, "When are you going to stop getting into trouble. We cannot even come to see you." This was a turning point for Lana. Like Robert, Lana was deeply moved by her daughter. The power of her relationship with her daughter convinced her to finally get out of the gang and drug world.

When she got out of the drug treatment program, she stopped using drugs. She started to go to church. Church helped her realize she also had to get out of the gang. She gradually replaced her support system from gang members to church friends. She was and still is very close to her sister, who was not in gangs and encouraged her to stay off drugs. She was very supportive and helpful to her at this time in her life. She eventually went back to school and obtained training as a drug treatment counselor. She then obtained a job as a drug treatment counselor. She has now been sober for over a decade.

Although Lana was exposed to serious violence as a child and is still haunted by events of those times, she does not believe this history influenced her to become addicted to drugs and join gangs. She felt loved by her mother and sister. She views her early childhood, the years before her mother moved to the new city with her boyfriend as an ideal childhood. She believes she gained strength from her early childhood experiences. In the end, her love for her young daughter, like the love she received from her mother when she was a young girl, provided her with the motivation to change her life.

Lana offered her own views of what it is like for African Americans in urban poor neighborhoods:

> African Americans in poor neighborhoods believe nobody cares about them. Because they are Black, they are labeled as bad, as criminals and drug users. Just because you have a single mom does not mean you are not going to make it. It hurts. Because

> your pants sag does not mean you sell drugs, or do not have a good mom or dad. The sagging pants signal that you might be in a gang, so you are given respect and are left alone. The police single out African Americans. They pulled my daughter over for a broken tail light. They made her get out of her car and searched her body. She was afraid for her life. If you have dreams, Blacks who are stuck are envious. You are looked down on by Whites and pulled down by Blacks.

"MAN-UP" TREATMENT

Presenting Problems and Family Frames

Devin was 11 and lived with his paternal grandmother in a poor, urban, predominantly African American neighborhood. He attended sixth grade at his neighborhood middle school. At the request of his grandmother, Devin was receiving counseling from his in-school therapist, Sarah. Devin was getting poor grades and was bullied. His grandmother wanted him to receive "man-up" therapy. She described him as "flamboyant." She was afraid his emotional reactions in public and his "flamboyant" presentation would result in him being a victim of violence. At school, he would easily become upset and cry. He showed vulnerability. His grandmother was very concerned showing "weakness" in his neighborhood was dangerous. She feared he would be seriously hurt on the way to and from school or even not make it home at all. He had no respect from the other boys. His grandmother explained, "Because he is an African American male, he has to learn how to stand up for himself." Devin was not following the "code of the street."

Intervention Strategy

Devin's father was in and out of his life. He had been in and out of jail and so had difficulty finding work. Devin's father and mother were never married. His grandmother labeled his mother as "schizophrenic." When Sarah first became involved, Devin's father lived with his mother and Devin. Devin's father agreed Devin needed to learn how to "man up." Devin's father did not believe in counseling or trust counselors. Sarah never met with him, but indirectly involved him by obtaining agreements with Devin's grandmother and coaching her to interact differently with her son. Sarah was following the "go to and through power" rule (Haley, 1996). When trying to change an organization, such as Devin's family, a therapist can go to and through power. Devin's grandmother was in charge.

To get Devin's father more involved with him, Sarah convinced Devin's grandmother that Devin's father could teach him how to "man up." With the grandmother's permission, Devin's father was asked to help his son learn how to be a man. Sarah suggested that to help Devin with this, the father just needed to spend time with Devin. If he did this, he would rub off on Devin, and Devin would learn how to "man up." Devin's grandmother did talk this over with Devin's father, and Devin's father did spend more time with him. After school, his father taught him boxing and football.

Interactional Patterns and Exceptions

Devin's father and grandmother generally did not get along. They had a pattern of Devin's father living with Devin's grandmother, the two fighting, the father moving out and not coming around at all, and then eventually moving back in again. When he was not living with his mother, Devin's father did not spend time with Devin, but when he was living there, he did spend time with Devin. Soon after Sarah became involved, Devin's grandmother kicked Devin's father out of the house. He went to live with his girlfriend. Sarah emphasized to the grandmother that it was very important for Devin to continue to have time with his father even though the father was now out of the house and not on speaking terms with Devin's grandmother. She persuaded the grandmother that Devin's father was still important so Devin could complete his "man up" lessons. Devin's father did continue to stay involved with him, seeing him on weekends. This was a change. They went to a haunted house together for Halloween, they played laser tag together, and went to go-carts and movies together.

Exceptions

His time with his father helped Devin. Previously, Devin would become extremely emotional at school, crying, punching lockers, walking out of class, screaming, and threatening to hurt himself. He also displayed the "flamboyant" presentation of himself. Both his father and grandmother were concerned Devin would be beaten by the other boys for behaving this way. Now, after his "man up" lessons, Devin had much better control of his emotions. The therapist observed an exception at school. Two boys were yelling and swearing at Devin in class. Devin became upset but stayed in control of his emotions. He asked to be excused from class. With the teacher's permission, Devin took a time out, got himself under control, and went back to class five minutes later, with no emotional outbursts.

Devin's grandmother also noticed changes in Devin. She observed that out in public Devin did not behave "flamboyantly." He did at home, but the grandmother was not concerned about this since he was not in danger at home. When asked by Sarah, Devin's grandmother affirmed that the time his father was spending with Devin was helping him. Despite her upset with her son, she gave him credit for helping Devin.

The Children Take Charge

Devin rode his bicycle to school every day. One day, it was raining. His grandmother did not want him to take his bike to school. Devin snuck his bike to school anyway. When his grandmother found out, she instructed Sarah to address his "disrespect" in counseling. Sarah discovered that Devin was trying to stay safe. Devin and several other sixth graders were being escorted to school every day on bicycles by several eighth-grade boys. To get to school from his house, Devin had to get by a notorious corner where drug deals and violence were a regular occurrence. The eighth-grade boys had taken it upon themselves to help Devin and other sixth grade boys get to school safely. School officials were unaware of this. The boys did not tell either their parents or adults at school about this. Even if they had, the parents and adults at school did not communicate with each other.

When winter came, the bike riding escort stopped. Devin had to find a new safe way to and from school. He had one trusted friend. The two boys joined forces to escort each other to and from school. They had a secret route that avoided dangerous areas. Despite the new plan, a boy harassed Devin on the way home from school, calling him "fag" and beating him up. Devin's father and grandmother were in conflict regarding how Devin should respond. His father insisted Devin would have to fight the boy or risk being viewed by the neighborhood as weak and lose “respect”—a dangerous problem to have. Devin spent the next week suffering serious anxiety over the idea of having to fight this boy. He was caught using the school library Internet attempting to order a hand gun. He did not trust the adults to keep him safe. He attempted to take matters into his own hands. Sarah intervened with the school to prevent his expulsion. Finally, Devin’s father and grandmother reached an agreement. They decided Devin would not have to fight the boy, but in the future if another boy tried to fight him, he would have to fight back. Devin was quite relieved at not having to fight the boy. He felt out of harm’s way. For now.

SYSTEMIC INTERVENTION

In these stories, whether there are family problems or not, serious problems and safety issues are in the neighborhood. To address these problems, a wider, macro approach is required. These stories and Anderson’s description of “street” versus “decent” families provide several concepts for integrative family and systems treatment (I-FAST) treatment providers who work with youth from these neighborhoods.

Family Motivations

Both the youth and families living in these neighborhoods are highly motivated to stay safe. Some of these youth may be court-ordered into treatment for using drugs or exhibiting conduct problems such as committing petty crimes. The youth and families themselves may not be motivated to focus on what the court wants. But both the youth and families may be highly motivated to focus on keeping their youth safe. Robert left his neighborhood and went to Vietnam hoping to stay safe. Devin’s grandmother and father both wanted him to have “man up” therapy to teach him how to survive on the street. Many of the youth themselves are highly motivated to stay safe. This might mean a youth carrying a gun, or having baggy pants, or groups of children escorting each other to school every day. In I-FAST, collaboration is emphasized. The families pick the problem and goal they wish to focus on. For youth in dangerous neighborhoods, in many cases that would be how to stay safe.

Frames

Mainstream society does not care and cannot be trusted is a common frame according to Anderson. Lana’s commentary illustrates this frame. The police cannot be trusted to help when help is needed. Social Services cannot be trusted. They will take the children. The school personnel do not care and cannot be trusted to keep the children safe. On the other hand, the school personnel often frame the adults in the family negatively. The mutual negative frames reinforce the two sides not collaborating. Treatment providers must overcome these frames if they are to develop rapport and engage families and youth from these neighborhoods.

Hopelessness and despair are also common frames. How to reframe the situation from hopeless to hopeful becomes a major therapeutic task. “Decent” and “street” are frames that come from the neighborhood residents themselves and provide organizing principles for how to understand the neighborhood residents. “The code of the street,” the rules for survival, are also known among the residents of these neighborhoods. “Respect” is a very important frame. Having it or not can be life or death.

Family Patterns and Structure

African American youth, compared to White youth, maintain more extensive social networks, which include fictive or informal kinship, and report more frequent contact with members from their social networks (Ajrouch, 2001; Rhodes et al., 1994). Formal and informal kinship networks can be a strong source of social support for urban youth (Jones, 2007; Leshem, Haj-Yahia, & Guterman, 2016). Formal kinship consists of biological family members. Informal kinship networks (nonblood relatives) can attain family status and titles such as "uncle" or "aunt" and provide additional support and protection to urban youth. An assessment of a given youth's "family" and their protective potentials must be expanded to include informal kin.

Anderson (1999) describes how many families may have family members from both the "decent" and "street" categories. On any given case, a parent may be "street," but an uncle or grandparent may be "decent." On any given case, finding family members who are "decent" may be possible even if the primary caretakers may not fit this description. Anderson also described great despair and hopelessness among families who have succumbed to the street. Restoring hope for these families could help move them out of the "street" category.

The story of the boys escorting the younger children to school outside the awareness of all the adults illustrates a common interactional pattern. The children may be more organized than the adults. Parents and adults at school may blame each other and not interact. Professionals on these cases may blame parents. When multiple professionals share these cases, they often are in conflict over how to work the case. The adults can either be disengaged from each other or in conflict with each other. While the adults are busy not interacting, the children can take matters into their own hands. That could include arming themselves or joining gangs.

Strengths and Resilience

FORMAL AND INFORMAL KINSHIP NETWORKS

Frequent, consistent, and proximal contact with formal and informal kinship networks is a documented strength and source of support for African Americans (Hill, 1999; McAdoo 1997). This support has been found to moderate behavior problems of youth (Jones, 2007). High levels of support from formal kin were found to be associated with less behavior problems and better psychosocial adjustment among African American teens (R. Taylor, 1996). Jones found a moderate effect size of formal kinship support on preventing PTSD (Jones, 2007).

SPIRITUALITY

Spirituality is an important element in many African American families (Jones, 2007). A reliance on religiosity and spirituality can assist urban African American families cope with the violence that surrounds them in their neighborhoods (Haight, 2002). Prayer was shown to reduce stress in African American communities (Jennings, 1991). Consistent church attendance was found to reduce oppositional behavior, depression, and immature behavior among African American youth (Christian & Bararin, 2001). In contrast, Garbarino, Dubrow, Kostelny, and Pardo (1992) found that parents who lacked religious beliefs had more difficulty helping their children make sense of exposure to violence. Spirituality can help give meaning to experiences of urban violence (Garbarino et al., 1992).

Spirituality and formal and informal kinship connections have been shown to moderate exposure to complex trauma in poor urban neighborhoods (Jones, 2007). Although all three have shown to have independent moderating effects, Jones (2007) speculates that it may require a combination of all three to have the strongest protective influence on chronic exposure to neighborhood violence.

Flexibility

Both Lori and Robert moved in and out of the "decent" and "street" categories. They demonstrated there is flexibility in movement between these categories. The idea is common that once in a gang, one cannot get out. Both Robert's and Lori's story do not validate this idea. Their stories provide reason for hope, even if a youth has been absorbed by the "street."

The Power of Family

Anderson (1996) proclaimed the most powerful force opposing the "street" was a loving family. Dominique, Robert, and Lana are testimonials to this power. The love they received from their mothers and the love of and for their children motivated all three to avoid or escape the street. Their stories are why we do family therapy. The power of family can destroy or heal. For I-FAST providers working with youth in dangerous neighborhoods, how can the power of family to heal be brought to bear?

ORGANIZING THE ADULTS

When the problem is the neighborhood, a larger observational field and intervention plan than a focus only on family is required. A more macro approach is required that includes adults in the home, extended family, informal kin, adults at school, church, and other community institutions. One treatment task, therefore, is to organize the grown-ups from all these groups.

Several family approaches focus on this wider observational field and intervene intentionally to organize the adults. Jerome Price has documented his work with urban Detroit youth (J. Price, 1999). A major component of Price's work with urban youth involves helping the youth's parents organize other adults in their child's life. Parents are advised to identify the other parents and caregivers of the youth their son or daughter are spending time with. They are helped to determine if other parents and caregivers will work with them or not. Adults who are "street" or "decent" are identified and either utilized or marginalized. Parents are helped to join forces at helping each other's children avoid trouble. Parents are also helped to align and work with adults in their child's school. Adults from both home and school are encouraged to work together.

Mathew Selekman has done considerable work with urban Chicago youth and their families (Selekman, 2017). Selekman focuses on organizing groups of key adults in the youth's life in two major ways. First, Selekman places great emphasis on helping adults involved in the youth's life to resolve conflicts with each other and work as a team on the youth's behalf. These adults include adults in the home, caregivers and extended family, and caregivers and professionals, as well as conflicts among the professionals themselves. Second, Selekman emphasizes identifying and mobilizing a collaborative family team. The family is encouraged to identify key concerned adults in the youth's and family's life who can participate in keeping the youth safe and out of trouble. These adults can include those in the home, caring teachers, coaches, clergy, extended family, and family friends. Both these methods take a more macro approach to providing safety for youth in dangerous neighborhoods.

Aspects of both approaches can easily be incorporated into I-FAST. Both approaches are identifying and changing interactional patterns. Their attention is not limited to interactions within the homes of their clients. Several sets of adults are helped to collaborate: adults in the home, extended family, adults in the schools, and adults in the neighborhood.

What follows is an example of a mother who utilized concepts that both J. Price (1999) and Selekman (2017) outline, without any professional mental health intervention.

SHE HAD A VILLAGE

Dana was African American, married, had two girls, 13 and 16, and one boy, Isaiah, aged 7. She and her husband lived in a nice suburb. After an 18-year marriage, her husband divorced her. He "changed his lifestyle choices." The father told the two daughters of his lifestyle but not Isaiah. Both parents decided to "shield" Isaiah from this until he was old enough to know. Before leaving, the husband had mismanaged the finances. The couple had bad credit. After the divorce, Dana's income would not allow her to stay in the area she lived. She was forced to move to an inner-city urban area where street crime was serious. Although the new neighborhood had problems, Dana's mother and father lived in the area, and her childhood church was nearby. She would call upon both parents and the church for support. She was worried for the safety of all her children but particularly her son. Her main concerns were him succeeding in school, staying out of trouble, and not getting killed in the neighborhood.

Dana struggled emotionally after the divorce. She lost face and felt great shame. Her frames were that she was not woman enough, she failed to keep her man, how would she make it alone, she did not see the divorce coming, and what would people say. One result of all these ideas was that Dana was suicidal for the first year after her divorce. She felt abandoned by her friends. For 18 years, her identity was "his wife." Now she had to find herself again. Dana had to accept that her husband was not coming back. She realized that she had to pick herself up.

Dana was devastated emotionally and now lived in a very dangerous neighborhood. She lived in a neighborhood where many of the African American boys were in gangs and there was serious gun violence. Many of the boys had seen killings. One of her main concerns was to keep Isaiah out of this. This problem went beyond the difficulties in her family. To keep her son safe, she would need both her family and neighborhood support.

Dana was aware of neighborhood danger. At 19, a man put a gun in her side. She was working at a hair salon alone. A man came in posing as a customer. He pointed the gun at her and demanded money. He demanded that she take her clothes off. The phone rang, and Dana told the man that was her co-worker calling. The man ran out of the store. After this incident, Dana's boyfriend bought her a gun and insisted she carry it. She did not. Instead she found a new job.

To help her son survive the neighborhood, Dana organized support from multiple family members and neighborhood resources. Dana had a village. One of the deacons in her church helped her. He owned property and allowed her to rent from him at a reduced rate. Although her parents were not together, Dana had a relationship with both. Her father lived close by and kept her son after school until Dana got home from work. Her father had a business and employed her son during summers. This was one way she kept Isaiah off the street.

Dana described her son as "hyper." He was suspended for what Dana believed was "silly stuff." Although Dana did not agree with how the school was handling her son, she collaborated with school personnel and established a working relationship with the teacher and the principle. She gave Isaiah a stress ball to squeeze during class to help with his "hyperness." She gave him a daily to-do list to tape to his school desk. She came to the school randomly, walking into her son's classroom unexpectedly. These random visits and the fact that her son had to face a unified group of adults had a profound impact on his behavior. The suspensions ended. Dana's dedication kept her son in school. The boys in the neighborhood who did get suspended ran the streets. They could end up in gangs or get killed. Keeping Isaiah in school helped keep him safe.

Despite Dana's efforts, the neighborhood still took its toll. One day while playing basketball, Isaiah witnessed a stabbing at the basketball court. One boy became angry about a call on a play. He pulled out a knife and stabbed one of the other players. Isaiah and his friend were worried about what else might happen, so they left. Isaiah would later tell Dana that he had nightmares for years related to witnessing this stabbing.

Isaiah told Dana of the stabbing incident when it occurred. He did not tell her his solution for staying safe until after he was an adult. Isaiah's friend decided to join a gang after the basketball incident. He convinced Isaiah, who wanted to stay friends with the boy, to join the gang also. Isaiah did not fully join the gang but joined the "entry level" status. To be initiated, he had to take a beating from several gang members. He was 14. Dana remembers him coming home one day limping but did not realize at the time why he was limping. Isaiah denied anything was wrong. Isaiah's duty in the gang was to drive around with other gang members, looking for enemies to beat up. While in the gang, Isaiah bought a gun and carried it. All the gang members had guns.

Dana knew Isaiah's friend was trouble. The police were always being called to his home. There was much violence in that home. Dana did not allow Isaiah to go there. At this time in Dana's life, her oldest daughter became pregnant. The daughter also was in a violent relationship. Dana had to now occupy herself with helping her daughter. She got the daughter out of the violent relationship, moved her home, and helped with her grandchild. One result of this was that Dana's attention was now focused on her daughter. She could no longer be solely focused on Isaiah. It was during this period that Isaiah joined the gang.

After one year in the gang, Isaiah decided to get out. The gang caused him "stress." He did not approve of what he had to do. He was not into the gang deep enough to be trapped. He got out before he knew too much, before he could be labeled a "snitch." He weighed the pros and cons and decided the risks of staying in were too high compared to what was "right." Dana was unaware of Isaiah's gang involvement. Despite all Dana's efforts and devotion, the neighborhood almost absorbed her son. But her involvement with him, their time going to church, and his grandfather's involvement with him all were factors influencing his decision to get out.

As an older teen, Isaiah began to use marijuana. Although he was now not in a gang, he was still spending time with gang members and drug users. This represented the majority of the boys in his area. He would go to parties at night and not come home until morning. When he did come home, he would be angry, hit walls, and destroy things. To try to shock him, Dana threw him out of the house. She wanted to "scare the hell out of him so he would straighten up." Isaiah had to stay away for one week. However, he did not miss one day of school. Dana called the school every day to make sure. Dana reported to the police that she kicked him out but that she knew where he was. He went to the family of one of his female friends. Dana also suspended his phone. After one week he came home. This "intervention" helped but not completely.

At the end of the school year, Dana decided to send Isaiah to Florida to live with his father for the summer. The first two years after the divorce Dana and her children's father had no contact. Then he began to call the children periodically. As the years past after the divorce, Dana believed Isaiah was struggling with low self-esteem. Dana's theory was that the trouble Isaiah was making was an attempt to be accepted by peers. Dana thought something was missing for Isaiah. What was missing was a father. Dana put her issues with her ex-husband aside and ask him to help with his son. This was a major decision for Dana, one that many mothers do not make. Dana called her ex-husband and told about the trouble Isaiah was having. Isaiah's father suggested he take him for the summer. Dana struggled with this idea because Isaiah's father was gay and had a live-in relationship. This was against Dana's religion, and the children were taught this was wrong.

Over time, Dana overcame her misgivings as she met gay people in her work life. In her church world, this was forbidden. Her work world was more tolerant. She herself challenged her church beliefs. She put her misgivings aside and thought what was best for her son. She agreed to send him. When Isaiah returned at the end of the summer he had changed. His father was a hard worker and took care of himself and his home. He was very consistent with rules and consequences. Isaiah's father had him on a tight schedule. Isaiah had to be up and dressed by nine. He could not sit around and watch video games. He had to go to the library and improve his mind. He had to go to the gym. He had to look for a job. Isaiah's father was stricter than Dana.

At the end of the summer, both parents were concerned about Isaiah moving back to his dangerous neighborhood. His father suggested to Dana that Isaiah stay in Florida until after high school. Both parents proposed the idea to Isaiah, but Isaiah did not want to stay. Both parents worked out expectations for Isaiah if he went back to Dana. They offered Isaiah a deal. If he went home to Dana, he had to comply with expectations, or he would have to go back to Florida. When Isaiah returned home, he kept his part of the bargain. Isaiah was able to finish high school in his home neighborhood. He stayed out of gangs, off drugs, and followed his parents' rules.

Dana's story offers a formula for success for helping African American children stay safe in very violent neighborhoods. Both Dana and Isaiah either witnessed or were victims of serious violence in their neighborhood. Because Dana herself had been victimized, she knew the risks of living in the area, especially for an African American male. Dana organized a group of adults to help keep her son safe. She was a dedicated mother who was willing to take serious steps to keep her son out of trouble. She organized support from her church and her father, and she collaborated with school professionals. She tried to keep her son busy after school by having him work for her father. Even so, Isaiah witnessed a stabbing at age 14 and joined a gang. He then became a victim and perpetrator of violence. But he knew it was wrong, thanks to the strong influence of his mother and family. He got out of the gang. But he still was in trouble in the neighborhood. Dana and her ex-husband then joined forces. Dana attributes their joint efforts as what made the difference of saving their son from the violence of his neighborhood.

Dana's son is now 25 years old. She recently asked him if he still had nightmares about the stabbing. Isaiah explained that his nightmares went away years earlier. He attributed the change to his mother's tradition of what Dana described as "meditative family prayer." Every day the entire family would spend time together engaged in "meditative prayer." This family ritual helped her son feel secure. It fit within the family beliefs and carried with it the power of that belief system. Isaiah's nightmares went away without him telling his trauma narrative or processing it with a mental health professional.

12 TRAUMA AND CHILDREN

OUT-OF-HOME PLACEMENT

General Statistics

As of 2016, the Children's Bureau (2016), a department within the US Department of Health and Human Services, estimated there were 437,465 children in foster care nationwide. In that year, 273,359 entered and 250,248 exited foster care. Forty-five percent were in nonrelative foster family homes, 32% were in relative foster family homes, 7% were in institutions, 5% were in group homes, 5% were on trial home visits, and 4% were in preadoptive homes (U.S. Department of Health and Human Services, Administration for Children and Families, Administration on Children, Youth and Families, Children's Bureau, 2016).

Many of the children placed in out-of-home settings come with exposure to trauma most at the hands of one or both parents. In 2012, the Children's Bureau (2013) reported that, of children placed in care, 18.3% were physically abused and 9.3% were sexually abused. Four fifths (81.5%) of victims were maltreated by one or both parents. The parent(s) could have acted together, acted alone, or acted with up to two other people to maltreat the child. Nearly two fifths (36.6%) of victims were maltreated by their mother acting alone. One fifth (18.7%) of victims were maltreated by their father acting alone, one fifth (19.4%) of victims were maltreated by both parents, and 12.0% of victims were maltreated by a perpetrator who was not the child's parent.

Length of stay statistics were as follows: 10% were in care less than 1 month, 35% were in care for 1 to 11 months, 28% were in care for 12 to 23 months, 15% were in care for 24 to 35 months, 9% were in care for three to four years, and 4% were in care for five or more years (Children's Bureau, 2016).

Of the children remaining in care for more than one year, placement stability is a serious problem. In 2008, for example, the National Adoption and Foster Care Analysis and Reporting System reported that for children remaining in care for an average of 15.3 months there were 3.2 placements per child. One study found 32.3% experienced eight or more placements throughout their child welfare experience (Pecora et al, 2005; Williams et al., 2009). One study found that 30% of children in kinship care and 52% of children in nonrelative care experienced three or more moves after the first year in care. Children in kinship care had fewer placement moves than those in nonkinship care (Webster, Barth, & Needlle, 2000).

Children coming into care who have experienced trauma then also endure moving from placement to placement, compounding the effects of whatever maltreatment they may have endured prior to placement. Magnetic resonance imaging scans of traumatized children show damage not just resulting from trauma, but also damage due to multiple placement disruptions. There is evidence that atypical hypothalamic–pituitary–adrenal (HPA) axis activity are higher for foster children than the general population. One study found that disruptions in care altered the HPA axis due to receiving inconsistent, insensitive care and/or frequent transitions in caregivers (Fisher, Gunnar, Dozier, Bruce, & Pears, 2006).

Many of these children are referred by child welfare workers to mental health services for trauma-related symptoms or other behavioral problems. Considering the trauma histories of these children and the added instability of foster placements and the additional risk of being abused again while in foster care, these cases present considerable challenges. First and foremost, these children must feel safe and secure in the home they are placed before embarking on work on past trauma. Treatment providers must make stabilizing the child's placement a priority. At a minimum, this requires collaborating with child welfare case workers and engaging foster parents in treatment.

Frames

Often children in out-of-home placement are framed as defiant or having conduct problems either by caregivers and/or professionals. Many of these children have serious behavior problems. They may be angry at adults for not recognizing they have been mistreated or because they have been moved from their family or because they have had no stable life since placed out of their home. Their behaviors can evoke hostile reactions from involved adults, only resulting in more anger from the child, putting their placement at risk. Framed as defiant, but with histories of serious trauma and instability, they are being seriously misunderstood.

These children also tend to carry serious diagnoses as defined by the fifth edition of the *Diagnostic and Statistical Manual of Mental Disorders* (American Psychiatric Association, 2013), considered frames in I-FAST. They may be framed as borderline personality disorder or bipolar disorder. These diagnoses can result in the child being heavily medicated. In Ohio, children in care are more heavily medicated than any other child group. Many are prescribed multiple psychotropic medications. It could be argued that they are being sedated so they are more manageable while in care. Despite having endured mistreatment, separation from their family, and perhaps going through multiple placements, they are framed as having a serious mental health diagnosis. The child is framed as the problem, not what has happened to them or the environment they are currently in.

Interactional Patterns

Tracking interactional patterns for children in out-of-home care requires a large observational field. If placed in foster care, interactions of those in the foster home must be tracked. Interactions between the placed child and their biological family must be tracked. Interactions between foster and biological family must be tracked. And interactions involving key professionals, especially those with power over determining placement, must be tracked.

In our work, we have observed several common patterns. In the foster home, caregivers may interact with the placed child with hostility if they view them as defiant. If the child reacts with hostility, then these homes become verbal war zones. During hostile exchanges, the child may be threatened with being expelled from the home. Both the hostility and threats of expulsion can intensify the exchanges. The pattern becomes one of escalating symmetry with each side responding to the other side's anger with more anger. For a child with a trauma history, this hostile environment can be retraumatizing and intensify their symptoms.

If it is a two-parent home, a common issue can be that one of the caregivers wants to foster and the other does not. This disagreement can produce a disengaged caregiver and conflict between the two caregivers with the placed child caught in between. Sometimes the parent that does not want to foster is pressuring the other parent behind the scenes, complaining about the placed child. When faced with pressure from the other parent, the parent who brought the child into the home may become more vigilant with the child. The child may be under pressure to be perfect and be criticized for minor infractions.

Regarding the child and biological parents, disengagement is often the pattern. With long-term placements, biological family may have been disengaged for many years. In these cases, it is important to understand who the child most wants contact with. It could be a parent, a sibling, or an extended family member. Often tracking family members down and just getting them to call can help stabilize the placed child.

With smart phones, a child and one or more of their family can easily stay in contact. Social media create the possibility of secret communications between the placed child and their family members, delineating a cross-generational coalition. In these instances, the foster parents are left out of the interactions. There is no adult-to-adult interaction between the two families. This can easily contribute to undermining a placement.

Patterns between the two homes can often involve conflict between the two sets of adults with the placed child triangulated and caught in a loyalty bind. These patterns are often played out when there are phone calls between the placed child and their family members or during, before or after visits between the placed child and biological family members.

For a child struggling with issues related to trauma, all these patterns can result in them feeling unsafe and/or conflicted, exacerbating whatever symptoms they may be expressing.

Whom to Include in Treatment

A wider and more complex cast of characters for out-of-home placement children results in more possible choices for whom to include in therapy. Should the treatment focus on the child and their caregivers, the child and biological family members, members from both biological and foster care families? In I-FAST, all options are possible and are decided upon on each case.

CONFUSED ABOUT LOVE

Brittany was 13. She lived with her foster mother, Tammy; her foster father, Mike; and their 23-year-old son Tyler. She had lived there for 10 months after living with her biological mother her whole life. After being placed with her foster parents, Brittany's mother withdrew from her life entirely. Brittany's biological mother had serious drug problems. She had been in and out of relationships with drug-using men. Brittany was sexually abused by one of these men. She was also sexually abused by an older cousin. She had witnessed much domestic violence between her mother and her mother's partners. What was most upsetting to Brittany was serious physical abuse perpetrated by her mother. She was unsure if her mother loved her.

Brittany was having multiple problems both in the foster home and at school. At school, she was belligerent with adults and getting suspended. She was causing problems on the bus and was threatened with being expelled from riding on the bus. The foster father said if he or his wife had to drive Brittany to school, Brittany could not live with them. Brittany was also going from boyfriend to boyfriend, all older than her. When she broke up with one, she would threaten suicide and cut herself on her arms. At home, the situation was very bad. Brittany and Mike would argue constantly. Brittany and Tammy would also argue. At times, the whole household would gang up on Brittany.

Treatment Goals

Corrine had seen Brittany individually and included Tammy in many sessions. Although heavily recruited by Corrine, Mike never came. Every week Tammy was upset about a different Brittany problem. Corrine could not get Tammy to stay focused on any problem. The treatment had no focus. To address this problem, Corrine scheduled a live supervision session supervised by David Grove, in which Mike was invited. The goal of the session was to get an agreement from the family to focus on one problem for a month, or until it was resolved. They had to pick just one. Corrine and Dave agreed this might take an extra-long session to accomplish.

The family arrived without Mike. Only Tammy and Brittany came. Three chairs were arranged for the family, one for the missing dad. Brittany and Tammy sat next to each other. Corrine asked Tammy to summarize what the treatment was about. She listed a total of 14 different problems. Corrine asked Tammy to pick just one problem that treatment could focus on for one month. Both Tammy and Brittany laughed and said, "ONE!!"

Family Frames

The session unfolded with Brittany and Tammy interacting like two combatants. During the discussion, Tammy said several times that if Brittany could not follow the rules, she could not live with them. It was assumed that if Tammy said this in a therapy session, she said it more emphatically at home. Brittany was under the threat of being expelled. This threat was likely intensifying the emotional hostility. Regarding Brittany's abuse history, Tammy said she herself had been abused and Brittany had to learn to move on. Brittany's trauma history drew no compassion from Tammy. Tammy's frame was, "She knows right from wrong." Tammy was framing and treating Brittany like a defiant child, not a hurt child.

Choosing a Goal

After failing to choose one problem to focus on, Tammy was asked what problem Mike would want to focus on. Tammy said Mike was upset about disrespect at home. Corrine asked for an example. Tammy told about a recent night: "Brittany was told to give me the TV remote. She started screaming at me, and I had to scream back. Then Mike began to yell at her. He tried to grab the remote from her. She hit him in the face. He then pushed her down on the couch and took it from her." Corrine asked what their son was doing. "Yelling at her too," Tammy said.

Interactional Patterns

After learning of this example, improving the home environment had to be a priority. The foster father wanted her out. Tammy was threatening to send her to juvenile detention. In the example Tammy gave, the whole family was yelling. A physical altercation occurred between Brittany and Mike. If this continued, Brittany would not last in this home. The constant yelling, the hostile environment, and the threats of expelling Brittany were no doubt exacerbating her symptoms. If feeling safe is a priority for trauma clients, Brittany could hardly feel safe.

It was unclear what the state of the marriage was. It was suspected there were problems. Mike never came to treatment. Tammy never referred to him by name, only calling him, "my husband." It was also suspected that Mike was on a campaign behind the scenes insisting Tammy to send Brittany away. To appease Mike, Tammy had to become hypervigilant about setting limits on Brittany. This was magnifying the hostility and threats coming from Tammy to Brittany.

After hearing the example fight and being informed that Mike's number one problem was lack of respect at home, it was agreed that the focus of treatment should be to improve how Brittany was behaving at home.

Changing Patterns in the Session: Eliciting Compassion

Given the verbal combat and hostility between Tammy and Brittany in the session, changing the mood of the session to one of compassion and empathy became a priority. The treatment team was waiting for a topic, or a statement to be made, that could be used to transform the session. The topic changed to what rules and consequences Brittany was accustom to when living with her mother.

Tammy explained that when Brittany lived with her mother there were no consistent rules. If Brittany wanted to do something, and her mother said "no," an argument would ensue. The argument would end with Brittany's mother "beating the daylights out of her." After the beating, her mother would then allow Brittany to do whatever she wanted in the first place. Tammy then explained that she thought Brittany was purposely trying to provoke her (Tammy) to see if Tammy would ever beat her like her mother did. Tammy said sometimes when Brittany was very angry, she called Tammy "Alice," Brittany's biological mother's name. The family had now brought up a subject that could be utilized to change the mood of the session.

Corrinne asked Brittany: "What did you want from your mother, her anger or her love?" Everyone became silent. Brittany immediately began to cry. She said softly, "Her love." Corrinne asked, "If you could not get her love, was her anger better than nothing." "Yes," Brittany said, as the tears flowed down her cheeks. Corrinne then asked, "What do you want from Tammy, her anger or her love?" "Her love," Brittany replied. Tammy then began to talk compassionately about how Brittany's mother beat her. She also talked about how much fun she and Brittany had doing simple things like laying on the couch eating popcorn and watching movies. Tammy gave several examples of fun things she and Brittany did together. The entire tone of the session had dramatically changed. Instead of fighting with each other, the topic changed to loving exchanges that had occurred between Brittany and Tammy. Tammy was now expressing empathy and compassion for Brittany.

Corrine asked Brittany, "Do you find it difficult to believe that Tammy loves you?" "Yes," Brittany replied. Tammy then told of a necklace she gave Brittany with a stone heart. Tammy told Brittany she was giving her a piece of her heart. Tammy then also told of a letter Brittany had written her. In the letter Brittany wrote about having to choose between her biological mother who beat her and Tammy, who was not her real mother but who would not abuse her. In the letter, Brittany said she chose Tammy. The tone of the session had been completely transformed, and the stage was now set to change the direction of the treatment.

End of Session: Compliments, Reframes, Tasks

A plan for how to end the session was organized. An ideal I-FAST session ends with compliments offered to the family first, followed by task frames to set up interventions, and finally with tasks for between sessions. The frames offered must be accepted by the family. The tasks offered must make sense to the family and focus on the presenting problem while requiring changes in the identified interactional patterns. Corrine spent the last 10 minutes with Tammy individually. First, Corrine complimented Tammy. She used Tammy's frame and said, "I do think Brittany knows right from wrong. You have done a marvelous job teaching her that." Tammy nodded in the affirmative. Corrine then offered a reframe, "Based on how she reacted to wanting anger or love from her mother, I think Brittany is confused about love. She is confused about what love looks like." Tammy agreed whole heartedly. We had successfully used Brittany's response to the question of wanting her mother's anger or love to reframe Brittany as a *confused* girl, not a *defiant* girl. Brittany's reaction in the session was so powerful and dramatic, it was hard to argue with the idea that she was confused about love. Corrine followed, "I think she wants your love, but the way she tries to get it is to provoke you. Then when that happens, she gets the whole household upset, and it all backfires. She wants your love, but she is confused about how to get it, so she makes you mad instead." Tammy agreed.

Tammy agreed to all the frames. It was now time to give her tasks. Corrine suggested that the main task was for Tammy to remain calm and become loving when Brittany became provocative. If Brittany yelled and said something horrific, Tammy should realize that at that moment, Brittany wanted her love. Instead of becoming angry, Tammy should say something loving. After the earlier discussion, in which Brittany had cried and said she wanted love when she became provocative, this suggestion made sense to Tammy.

To assess the marriage, Tammy was asked to talk this over with Mike. The two of them should develop their own plan for remaining calm or loving when Brittany became provocative. They should help each other with this since Brittany was so skilled at getting everyone upset. How Tammy and Mike responded to this task would help understand the state their marriage. Tammy agreed to all the tasks. Before the session ended, she and Corrine were laughing together. Tammy was leaving the session in a very positive mood. There would be a nice drive home with Tammy and Brittany.

Tracking Exceptions

For the next session, Mike still did not attend. Tammy reported that she was able to respond to Brittany's provocations by remaining calm, and a few times telling her she loved her. Tammy said Brittany immediately calmed down. The mood in the house was much improved. Tammy felt empowered and had a way to respond to Brittany that did not lead to an all-household uproar. Regarding Mike, she said she forgot to tell him what was talked about in the session. She had no interaction with him about any of the ideas discussed. She did say that if she and Brittany did not argue, Mike stayed out of it. If Tammy and Brittany got along, there was peace in the house.

Corrine continued to see Brittany individually and to include Tammy in her sessions. There were setbacks. As time went on, Tammy was able to stick to staying calm or becoming loving when Brittany became upset. Brittany's behavior at home improved. Brittany and Tammy already spent positive time together. The problem was these positive times were undone by the frequent horrific arguments. It was understandable why it was difficult for Brittany to believe Tammy loved her. One minute they were sitting on the couch watching movies, and the next minute they were in a fight with Tammy threatening to send Brittany to juvenile detention. It was hoped that if the arguments could be interrupted, all that would remain would be the positive times. Their relationship would then strengthen. This is, in fact, what happened. With Brittany and Tammy getting along, gradually Brittany's school problems settled down also. Once their relationship strengthened, Brittany's infatuation with boys diminished.

Follow-Up: Big Family Changes

Several months went by. In one session, Tammy wanted to see Corrine alone. She told Corrine that Mike had moved out. They were divorcing. She said they had had problems for years. Mike had had affairs. Regarding Brittany, Tammy confessed that Mike did not want to take her in and was "on my back any time Brittany made the least amount of trouble." The pattern was now clear. Mike was on a campaign to send Brittany away. Tammy had to exaggerate her limits on Brittany to try to appease Mike. She said that since Mike left, the mood of the house had become more relaxed and Brittany had settled down even more. It has now been several years since Brittany was placed with Tammy. Brittany still lives with Tammy and will soon graduate from high school.

Discussion

Numerous approaches focus on helping foster or adoptive parents respond more lovingly to traumatized children placed in their homes. The interactional pattern in this family is believed to be common. Foster or adoptive parents can treat the placed child like a defiant child, and the home atmosphere is characterized by hostile and intense exchanges. Changing these hostile interactions to those of compassion, empathy, and love become a major therapeutic task for these cases. In I-FAST, we share this goal. However, I-FAST differs from many other approaches in at least two major ways. First, in I-FAST, the unit of analysis is triadic. We do not just focus on assessing interactions between caregivers and the traumatized client. We also focus on interactions between the adults in the home. In this case, the foster father was in the background pressuring the foster mother, and this contributed greatly to how the foster mother interacted with the client.

Including the foster father in our unit of analysis led to indirectly including him in the therapy. Although he never came to a session, his presence was felt. First, by asking what his opinion of what the treatment goal should be, we were able to reach an agreement with the foster mother on a goal to focus on. Bringing the foster father into this discussion resolved what had been an impasse. Second, by including the foster father in one of the tasks the foster mother was given, we were able to indirectly assess if there were marital problems. This was confirmed later when the foster mother confessed that her husband was on a campaign to expel the client. The value in knowing this was that it allowed the therapist to have more empathy for the foster mother, who was originally viewed as a very hostile and uncaring parent.

Second, in I-FAST, we do not have specific procedures or frames. Instead, we utilize frames that come from the family, or in this case the session itself, to set up changing interactional patterns. In this case, framing the client as confused came out of everyone's actual experience in the session. This frame was utilized to convince the foster mother to change how she was interacting with the client. In another case, a different frame, one that arose from a different family and a different session might be offered. The actual frames offered in this type of case will vary from case to case, but the category from which the frames are selected from will remain the same. What frame can be utilized from the family that promotes compassion and empathy for an abused client? The frame varies, but the category of compassion and empathy stays the same.

HIDING HER POOP

Background

This case illustrates the consequences of generational family abuse and long-term placement in the child welfare system. The story begins with Margret and her three siblings. Margret and her siblings were physically abused by both of her parents, and her father was habitually violent toward her mother. Starting when Margret was a preteen, all the children were moved several times to numerous foster homes, were eventually separated from one another, and lost to each other. At 18, Margret emancipated from her last foster home. Like many who age out of foster care, she had no one. This made her vulnerable. Like many girls in this situation, one choice is to find any man.

She found a man to marry and then soon after divorced. She had her first daughter with this man. She then moved in with a new boyfriend who became the father of both of her younger daughters, Belinda and Carmen. This relationship was unstable. The couple separated many times. One of the separations left Margaret and her two younger daughters homeless. Her oldest daughter was now 18 and emancipated. Margaret asked her oldest daughter to take the two younger daughters until she could find stable housing.

Multiple Placements

The two girls lived with their older sister for two years. After two years, Margaret and the two youngest girls' father split permanently. Margaret now had a new live-in boyfriend. She also had stable housing. She convinced her oldest daughter that her situation was improved. The two younger girls returned to their mother and her new boyfriend.

The girls were removed again one year later due to sexual abuse of both girls by Margret's boyfriend. Margaret did not leave the man, so the girls were placed in foster care. Children's Services did not view the older sister as an appropriate placement for the girls since the older sister allowed the girls to go back to their mother one year earlier.

Margret was diagnosed with bipolar disorder and/ordered into treatment. The diagnosis ignored her background of trauma, instability, and her current circumstances.

She had no connections with any of her biological family or any appropriate elders and was dependent on any man to take care of her financially. Margaret was vulnerable to be preyed upon by problem men. She had to live a life of dependency on one inappropriate man after another.

She was able to get away from the sexually abusive boyfriend by finding another man with whom to live. She got her two younger daughters back. Both girls were removed again, however, due to physical abuse, by Margaret herself. Her new boyfriend was intolerant of the girls. To keep her new boyfriend happy, Margaret had to keep a tight leash on both girls. The girls remember this as a time when their mother changed and became very angry and hostile. The girls had to stay in their rooms at night, even if they had to go to the bathroom. If they made noise and woke the boyfriend, Margaret would beat them. Once Carmen wore a red dress that the boyfriend disapproved of. Margaret ripped the dress off and beat her with it.

Carmen was now 9 years old, and Belinda was 15. They were in their fourth placement away from their mother. The new foster mom was a single parent and was good to them. Both did well in this home and were very attached to the foster mother. After one year, however, the foster mother became engaged. Her fiancé said that she could either be a foster parent and not marry him or she could give up fostering. The foster mother decided to give up fostering. Both girls had to be placed elsewhere again.

Adoptive Home

Both girls were moved to a foster-to-adopt home, with Brenda, aged 60, and Tom, aged 68. Tom was in poor health. He had a stroke and did not fully recover. He could not walk and had trouble sleeping. Everyone had to be extra quiet to not disturb his sleep.

After being removed from the foster mother they both loved, both sisters' functioning deteriorated. Belinda decompensated badly. After only one month, Brenda informed Children's Services that she could not keep Belinda. Belinda was placed in residential treatment where she decompensated further. The residential therapist did not think she should have visits with Carmen. After Belinda was placed in residential treatment, Carmen never saw her again. Brenda decided to adopt Carmen. With this, all records of Carmen's and Margaret's pasts were sealed.

"Behavior Problems"

Soon after being adopted, Carmen started having "behavior" problems. Brenda's biggest complaint was that Carmen was not making her bed. No matter what punishment Brenda employed, she could not get Carmen to make her bed. Brenda explained, "Can you believe she will pull the covers up and say the bed is made when there are dirty clothes in the bed!" Carmen would put her clothes in her toy box. Brenda would check the toy box every day and take the clothes away proclaiming, "She does not need clothes if she cannot take care of them."

Another serious infraction, according to Brenda, was that Carmen would not wear a red dress Brenda bought her for Christmas. After having her red dress ripped off her and beaten with it by her biological mother, Carmen never wanted to wear a red dress ever again. Brenda was unaware of this history. Her position was, Carmen just needed to do what she was told.

Patterns and Frames

Brenda was framing Carmen as a defiant child. She punished her for minor infractions, she screamed at her, and threatened to unadopt her if she did not "do what she was told." As a girl who had suffered serious trauma, this type of treatment exacerbated her symptoms. She did not feel safe. The more Brenda screamed and threatened to remove her, the more Carmen did not comply with the rules. This then resulted in more screaming and threatening from Brenda.

Starting Treatment

Brenda was advised to get counseling for Carmen. She was assigned to Lesley, a young woman with no children. Brenda immediately disqualified her. Brenda said she had fostered over 30 children and did not need parenting advice, especially from a young woman who had no children. Brenda kept a journal of Carmen's weekly violations and brought it to therapy to report how bad Carmen behaved during the previous week.

Lesley met with Carmen alone. She was a very pleasant, well mannered, eager to please little girl. Lesley described her as superficially engaged. She would smile and say all the right things, while projecting an emptiness. She had a dead, empty look in her eyes. She had a hard time staying focused on any topic. The first time she met her, Lesley told Carmen she liked her shoes. For the next year, every time Carmen saw Lesley, she mechanically complimented Lesley's shoes. With Brenda, Carmen would say, "I love you. I want to be in this home," with a dead look on her face. It was as if there was no soul behind those eyes.

Lesley naturally empathized with Carmen. She would attempt to point out Carmen's positive attributes to Brenda. This backfired. It resulted in Brenda thinking Lesley did not appreciate how bad Carmen was. Brenda would respond to Lesley's compliments of Carmen by becoming even more upset at Carmen to demonstrate to Lesley that Carmen was bad, not good.

With Brenda's punitive style, Carmen got worse. She started urinating on the carpet at night. Brenda discovered this when she stepped in it in the morning. This resulted in screaming and threatening. Carmen responded with more bizarre symptoms. She began defecating in a plastic bag at night and hiding it in the toy box, beneath the clothes she stuffed there. When Brenda searched the tool box for clothes that were not supposed to be there, she found the poop. Screaming and threatening then ensued. Lesley asked about her pooping. Carmen said while crying, "I don't know why I do it. I'm a bad girl."

Aligning with the Parent:

After consulting about the case, Lesley changed her approach with Brenda. She took a one-down position, acknowledging Brenda's superior knowledge of parenting. She also validated and empathized with Brenda, pointing out how awful and unacceptable Carmen's behavior was. Lesley was able to convince Brenda to keep a chart with rewards and punishments clearly laid out. Brenda was persuaded to focus on the urinating and defecating and temporarily ignore other infractions. There was to be no screaming or threatening, just a punishment or reward. Brenda followed this, and Carmen improved. When Carmen improved, Brenda returned to yelling and screaming. Carmen then relapsed to urinating and defecating.

Reframing the Child

After consulting a second time, Lesley again changed her approach with Brenda. The new therapeutic goal was to shift Brenda away from rewards, punishments, and behaviors to emphasizing an affectionate motherly relationship with Carmen. To accomplish this, Carmen would be reframed from a noncompliant child to a damaged, traumatized child.

Lesley learned details of the sexual and physical abuse Carmen suffered from Rachel, the Children's Services case worker. She shared this with Brenda and suggested that Carmen might be suffering from posttraumatic stress disorder. She encouraged Brenda to research the subject, which Brenda did. Lesley was able to persuade Brenda that Carmen was a damaged child.

Between-Session Tasks

Once Brenda accepted the idea Carmen was damaged, not defiant, she asked how best to deal with a damaged child. This was the first time Brenda had asked Lesley for advice. Lesley explained Carmen had to feel safe. If Carmen could feel safe, she may settle down and be more compliant. For a child who endured such terrible mistreatment to feel safe, Brenda would have to exaggerate being motherly with her. Brenda was willing to try this new approach. Brenda was asked to "exaggerate" being motherly, so she could not claim she was already being motherly and not change anything.

Changing Interactions, Compliments

Lesley obtained an agreement from Brenda to compliment Carmen. Brenda could discus infractions in the middle of the session, sandwiched between compliments at the beginning and end. The sandwich approach allowed Brenda to complain about Carmen, but with compliments mitigating the effects of the complaints. Carmen was very pleased to receive compliments from Brenda. This was a big change that had a positive effect.

Lesley suggested some changes for Brenda to implement at home. She had to exaggerate her "mommy" time with Carmen. This meant changing the bedtime routine. Brenda began reading Carmen stories before bed and tucking her in at night. Lesley also suggested the frame that "developing young girls need extra mom time to help them understand how to become a proper lady." Brenda ate this up. Brenda and Carmen started to have "girl" days together. They would go shopping or to movies or get their nails done together. Carmen lapped the attention up.

Tracking Exceptions and Changes

All of Carmen's problem behaviors went away. She no longer pooped or urinated in her room at night, she made her bed properly, and she put her clothes away properly. As she improved, Brenda warmed up to her even more. In sessions, instead of sitting across from each other and commencing a face-off, they sat next to each other on the couch. As Brenda talked to Lesley, she would play with Carmen's hair and stroke her. Brenda became much more relaxed. The two would laugh together. Amazingly, as Brenda became more affectionate and attached to Carmen, Carmen's entire demeanor changed. Instead of having an empty lost look about her, she came to life. Her eyes sparkled. There was a human being in there after all.

After Carmen improved, Lesley met with her alone. Carmen explained most of her symptoms. When living with her biological mother, if she ever woke up her mother's boyfriend, she would be severely beaten. She was not ever allowed to get out of bed. At Brenda's, Brenda stressed how important her sick husband's sleep was. To be a good girl and not wake anyone up, she went to the bathroom in her room.

Months went by and the improvement continued. All agreed everything was OK. Lesley terminated the therapy. Four months later, Lesley got a call from Brenda. The defecating and urinating in the bedroom had resumed. Carmen was not following instructions again.

Disrupted Adoption

Brenda brought Carmen back to Lesley. Major family changes had occurred. Brenda took in two additional foster children. One was an infant with serious medical needs. Brenda became absorbed with the care of the medically fragile infant. She was on a mission to keep the baby alive. She no longer had time for "girls' day" or story reading. Carmen would have to grow up and fit into the new situation. It appeared to Lesley that Brenda was not just angry at Carmen again, but that she had lost interest her. Lesley made numerous attempts to encourage Brenda to become reconnected with Carmen. All failed. Brenda was going to save this new foster child. That was more important than helping Carmen. If Carmen could not grow up and carry her own weight, she would have to go. Now living under a renewed threat of expulsion, Carmen became worse. and Brenda contacted Children's Services and insisted they disrupt the adoption.

Rachel, the Children's Services adoption worker insisted Brenda honor her obligation to Carmen as her adoptive mother. She suggested that the new foster children be placed in a foster home with no other children, so the infant could get full attention. Brenda insisted the infant was already receiving her full attention. There was a financial incentive for Brenda. The infant was classified as medically fragile. Brenda received the maximum per diem for his care. By contrast, she received very little financial assistance for Carmen.

Rachel tried to persuade Brenda to keep Carmen but all failed. After months of struggle, Brenda disrupted her adoption of Carmen. Carmen was removed from yet another failed placement and placed in a new foster home. The new foster mother was kind to her. Her bazaar symptoms did not occur there, but Carmen was now a very sad, downtrodden child. She had no idea what her future was. The plight of this child is a common story for many traumatized children in the child welfare system. Treated as defiant children, they feel unsafe and exhibit defiant behavior. This results in multiple moves, each one of which creates more damage.

Discovering and Reconnecting With Family

Rachel talked to Carmen about her past and discovered that Carmen had an older sister, who would now be in her late 20s. When Carmen was adopted, her family records were sealed. Neither Lesley nor Rachel had access to these records. Rachel asked Brenda if she knew of this sister. Brenda did know of the older sister and told Carmen the rule was to never talk about her biological family. Carmen was so afraid of incurring Brenda's wrath she tried to forget her past. Rachel learned from Carmen about the time she had lived with her older sister. Rachel was then able to have Carmen's sealed file opened and learned the entire history.

Rachel found Carmen's sister's phone number in the sealed record. Amazingly, the phone number was still correct. Rachel called, and the sister answered. The sister cried on the phone and told how much she regretted allowing her sisters to go back to their mother. Rachel conducted a home study. Carmen's sister was married. Both she and her husband worked and were financially stable. Both the sister and her husband wanted Carmen to come live with them.

The plan was for Carmen to have several weekend visits and go from there. Rachel took Carmen to the first weekend visit. When Carmen's sister first laid eyes on her, she looked at Carmen like she was her own child. Carmen lit up and was amazed that someone loved her. The older sister had a photo album with many photos of the time all the girls were together with their mother. Many of the photos were before their mother changed and became so hostile. The older sister even had baby pictures of Carmen. They began to reminisce about what it was like before their mom became so angry. They talked about birthday parties and family get togethers. They sat next to each other and looked at every photo in the album together.

After several weekend visits, an extended stay was arranged. All went well. Carmen ended up going to live with her older sister. She has been there now for three years. She has started high school and is doing well academically and socially. To Rachel's knowledge, she has no serious mental health symptoms.

MINUCHIN'S FAMILY-TO-FAMILY MODEL

To prevent patterns of disengagement of biological family from a placed child and to prevent conflict between the biological family and the foster family, Patricia Mincuhin developed a family-to-family model for foster care (Minuchin et al., 1990). In this model, biological and foster families are connected at the beginning of placements and encouraged to interact during the placement. Foster parents are trained how to interact respectfully with biological parents and to even mentor them if they are receptive. The first author (DG) implemented this model with a foster care agency he consulted with. Intake procedures were set up to connect the foster and biological families at the outset of placement. Foster parents were trained to work with biological families while the child was in their home. The model was employed in the following cases. The author viewed the foster parents as co-therapists for both the children in their homes and their biological families.

Isiah's Village

BACKGROUND

Ten-year-old Isiah was found by police in an abandoned crack house in an unsafe neighborhood laying in a puddle of his own urine. Children's Services placed him in foster care with Larry and Cheryl. Isiah's parents were both active cocaine users and had a volatile and violent relationship. Isiah's father had children with two separate women. He went back and forth between the two mothers. Isiah's parents were court-ordered to complete drug treatment. Neither parent was complying.

Isiah told Cheryl of life with his parents. They frequently had terrible arguments. Sometimes they would hit each other. Isiah became afraid they would hit each other every time they argued whether they hit or not. Sometimes after a bad argument, his father would leave and be gone for months. Then his father would return, and the arguments would start again. Whether his father was home or not, there would always be extra people in the house. He and his mother moved a lot, sometimes into other peoples' homes. Once he went to live with his aunt in Florida and stayed there until his mother came and got him and brought him back to Ohio.

Isiah was a quiet, well-behaved but troubled boy. He had nightmares several times per week. He would wake up frightened, and Cheryl would have to help him get back to sleep. Cheryl and his therapist, Dave Grove, asked him to tell about his nightmares. Isiah did not want to talk about them. Isiah had witnessed chronic domestic violence between his parents. He lived in constant fear of violence occurring. He did not report being physically or sexually abused but his children's services case worker suspected it. His parents' relationship was unstable and had a chronic pattern of separations. Anxiety about not having a place to live also upset Isiah. He was very unmotivated in school. He would go to school, but he did no school work at school or at home. This was very disturbing to Cheryl, who placed a great emphasis on education.

INTERACTIONAL PATTERNS

Both Larry and Cheryl were committed to having Isiah. There was no conflict between the two over Isiah's stay in the home. Because Isiah was troubled but not a troublemaker, both caregivers had great empathy for him. He was in no danger of being moved. One troubling interactional pattern was total disengagement of the biological family. Cheryl had a phone number for Isiah's mother, but no one ever answered. Isiah told Cheryl he not only missed both his mother and father, but his whole family. Isiah had an entire village.

CHANGING INTERACTIONAL PATTERNS

Isiah said he was close to his aunt in Dayton, Ohio, his aunt in Florida, and to both his grandmothers. Dave gave Cheryl the task of tracking down everyone's name and phone number and establishing phone contact. Children's Services had the phone number of the paternal aunt in Dayton. Cheryl contacted her first. From this aunt, she obtained the paternal grandmother's number, also in Dayton. The paternal grandmother knew the maternal grandmother's number in Massachusetts. The Maternal Grandmother knew the Maternal Aunt's number in Florida. Cheryl quickly tracked down everyone. None of the relatives would talk to Children's Services. All would talk to Cheryl. She had their boy. They were grateful to talk to Cheryl and re-establish contact with Isiah by phone. Once the mother's side of the family was contacted and they realized Cheryl cared, Isiah's mother called Cheryl. After this, she called sporadically, but unpredictably throughout the rest of Isiah's stay with Cheryl. Through these phone calls with the relatives, Isiah was able to re-establish contact with his village. The impact of this was to reduce but not eliminate the frequency of his nightmares and generalized anxiety. His school performance was not affected.

THE FAMILY ATTEMPT TO SOLVE THE PROBLEM

Cheryl was able to learn much history. Both mother and father had a long and serious history of drug abuse. At one time, the mother's family attempted to intervene on Isiah's behalf. Isiah's grandmother persuaded his mother to place him in the custody of his aunt in Florida. Isiah then went to live with his aunt for almost one year. Before legal custody could be officially transferred, his mother went to Florida and took him back. She took Isiah to his paternal aunt in Dayton. She told terrible stories to the paternal aunt in Dayton about the maternal aunt in Florida. The two ladies had never met so they did not talk. Isiah's mother managed to temporarily hide Isiah from both the authorities and from the maternal side of the family.

ENGAGING BIOLOGICAL FAMILY

Dave challenged Cheryl to get the entire group to come to Ohio to make a plan for getting Isiah out of foster care. Cheryl got both grandmothers, both aunts, and both parents. All came for one week. Cheryl met all of them individually and in small groups for coffee outside of her home. Members from the maternal and paternal sides of the family met and befriended each other. Future attempts by either parent to manipulate the group were now less likely.

FAMILY SESSION

The entire group met in Dave's office. Everyone came including both biological parents. Cheryl kept Isiah at home for the initial part of the meeting to protect him from any conflict that might occur. Dave began to start the meeting, but Cheryl interrupted. Everyone had to pray first. All held hands and Cheryl led the prayer. Dave was then permitted to begin. He started by saying how lucky Isiah was to have so many family members who loved him. After offering compliments, he explained that everyone hoped Isiah's parents would be able to complete their case plan and have Isiah returned to them. If his parents were not able, however, what would the family plan be? The goal of the session was for the family to discuss and make that decision.

The grandmothers were asked to speak first. They both said the authorities were not being hard enough on the parents. If they were in charge, they would demand more than just each parent completing drug treatment. For an African American family to speak ill of the parents to a White therapist indicated that Dave had their complete trust. He owed that to Cheryl. Although the grandmothers were hard on both parents, because the matriarchs of each clan were speaking, no one contradicted them. A discussion ensued about who should take Isiah in case either parent could not. They all agreed the aunt in Florida should. Fences between the two sides of the family had been mended in the meetings Cheryl organized before the big family meeting.

FAMILY AGREEMENTS: CREATING EXCEPTIONS

Dave wrote a document outlining the family plan. The document stated that the family wished Isiah to go with the aunt in Florida if the parents could not have him. Either parent would be welcome to visit him in Florida. All signed—both grandmothers, both parents, and both aunts. The document was given to the Children's Services case worker and eventually to the judge. The author has consulted for 20 years with two separate Children's Service agencies. No case worker or judge in either agency had ever received a document with the signatures of both parents and four extended family members outlining a family placement plan for a child in foster care.

ISIAH AND FAMILY REUNITED

After the family agreements were obtained, it was time for Isiah to come. Cheryl brought him to the office. One of the most moving and gratifying moments in the author's career happened when Isiah opened the door and saw his entire family, his whole village, there to see him. Everyone cried. Cheryl knew exactly what to do. A family photo session ensued. Isiah took a photo in both of his parents' arms. Another in the arms of both of his grandmothers. Another group photo with all his family. And one final photo with his aunt from Florida, whom his grandmothers told him he would go with if he did not go back to his parents. After the meeting, before everyone left town, Cheryl had the entire group to her house for dinner.

TRACKING EXCEPTIONS

From this point on, Isiah's nightmares stopped. His anxiety and troubled demeanor went away. His school work improved greatly for the first time in Cheryl's home. Isiah's parents did not complete their case plan, and Isiah did go with his aunt in Florida. Cheryl stayed in touch with him for the next several years. For as long as Cheryl and the author worked together, Cheryl would announce how Isiah was doing after every phone call she made to Florida. He was on the honor roll in school, something Cheryl was most proud of. He had no repeating nightmares. He had very good friends in his neighborhood. The most interesting development involved his mother. One year after Isiah went to his aunt, his mother moved to Florida to be near her son. She was off drugs. Instead of interfering with his placement at his Aunt's, his mother accepted a role of "godmother." She visited Isiah and re-established a relationship with him but was totally respectful of her sister's role as primary caretaker.

DISCUSSION

Isiah is a child who could have ended up in the child welfare system until 18, having to live in numerous placements, with every move exacerbating his symptoms. Instead, because of Cheryl, Isiah was reconnected with his family. Instead of his symptoms worsening, phone calls to family members lead to the partial improvement of some of his symptoms. Cheryl recruited Isiah's entire extended family to stay connected with him by phone. It is believed that the family session helped Isiah feel more secure, both because everyone made the effort see him and because they all agreed where he would go if he could not go back to his parents. Finally, Cheryl and Larry became extended kin. From the family visit on, Isiah was already with family, Cheryl and Larry. His symptoms went away when he felt secure. Most important, involving all his relatives led to the family getting organized and devising a family plan for Isiah. He went to his aunt. His mother did not attempt to disrupt the placement. Instead, she re-established a relationship with her son, which continued for the years in which Cheryl stayed involved.

Sex and Affection

BACKGROUND

Gerald, aged 10; Ronny, aged 8; and Rebecca, aged 6 all lived with their single father, Mr. S. Their mother left the family and had no contact since her departure. One day, Rebecca told her school guidance counselor that her father and brothers were sexually abusing her. She described intercourse by her father on multiple occasions. She also said her father was having sex with her brother Gerald. A medical examination showed that Rebecca had been violated vaginally many times. Although both Mr. S. and Gerald denied abuse, because of the medical evidence, all three children were placed in separate foster homes. Gerald was placed with Phyllis and Arthur.

ENGAGING THE BIOLOGICAL PARENT

Children's Services was required by law to have a plan for reunification of the children with their father. All, including Mr. S. were required to receive therapy. Because the initial plan was for Gerald to return to his father, Mr. S. was invited to attend a meeting with Phyllis and Arthur. It was explained to Mr. S. that while Gerald was in foster care, Mr. S. could help by coming regularly to counseling with Gerald and his foster parents. Mr. S. was agreeable. Although he completely denied all the sexual abuse allegations, Mr. S. presented himself as very mild mannered and affable. He met every other week with Phyllis and Dave to get updates on Gerald. The rapport established with Mr. S. at these meetings would become very important.

Gerald was very well-behaved at Phyllis and Arthur's; however, after he was there for two months, he began to behave strangely. He asked Arthur if he could have sex with him. Both Arthur and Phyllis were bewildered by this request. Phyllis discovered he was humping stuffed animals in his bedroom. Phyllis had established a very nice relationship with Gerald. She asked him why he was humping the animals. Gerald then spontaneously confessed to sexually abusing his sister. He admitted to everything she accused him of. This was all reported to the authorities.

INTERACTIONAL PATTERNS

Secrets are the main interactional pattern with sexual abuse. Professionals can participate in this secrecy by not informing family members of discovered abuse. If one therapy goal for trauma and sexual abuse is to break the interactional patterns that perpetuate it, when abuse is discovered, family must be informed.

A session with all three children was requested so Gerald could apologize for abuse and both siblings could know he was confessing. This session was blocked by Rebecca's individual therapist. Rebecca's therapist feared it would be traumatic for her to receive an apology in person from Gerald. Gerald was asked to write an apology letter instead. With no coaching, Gerald produced a very moving and emotional document. He drew a picture of himself and his sister. Both were crying. On the picture he simply wrote, "I am very sorry." The letter was spontaneous and sincere. It was sent as it was to Rebecca's case worker, who gave it to Rebecca.

Mr. S. was also invited to a session to be informed Gerald was confessing. Phyllis, Gerald, and the therapist met with Mr. S. Gerald confessed to his father that he had sexually abused his sister. Mr. S. was very forgiving. Gerald was asked to apologize to his father for harming his sister, his father's daughter. By asking Gerald to apologize to his father, a man who was also accused of sexually abusing Gerald, Dave was holding Gerald to a higher standard than what his father was being held to. Dave did not know what would happen by doing this, but he thought Gerald would react in some way that would lead to something new. Gerald offered an apology to his father, for hurting his sister.

On his car ride home with Phyllis, Gerald opened up about what his father had done to him. It was extensive and intensive abuse. Gerald slept with his father every night. His father abused him with oral sex and anal intercourse. Gerald did not experience this as unwanted or abusive behavior. Instead, he thought it was his father being affectionate and loving. He was totally confused. Gerald thought that if you loved your father, you had sex with him. That is why he asked Arthur if Arthur wanted to have sex with him.

Gerald's accusations were reported to his case worker. Gerald was interviewed by an investigator. He was examined medically and found that he had been anally violated. Gerald was very upset by the police involvement. He felt he had betrayed his father. He was worried his father would be angry with him and not love him anymore for telling on him. There were now two siblings accusing Mr. S. of serious abuse and the medical evidence from both that they had been violated. It seemed likely that Mr. S. would be arrested for sexually abusing his children.

Before Mr. S. was arrested, however, Dave wanted to see if he would be willing to help his son, despite the terrible things he had done to Gerald. Dave did not want Mr. S. to go to jail with Gerald believing his father was angry with him and hated him. Gerald was tormented by the idea that his father now hated him. A special session was set up with Mr. S. Phyllis brought Gerald and stayed at a fast-food restaurant near the office. While Phyllis and Gerald were at the restaurant, Dave met with Mr. S. to assess if he would be willing to help his son. If so, Phyllis would bring Gerald to the meeting. If not, Phyllis would take Gerald home.

UTILIZING FAMILY FRAMES

Dave met with Mr. S. in what was one of the most unforgettable therapy sessions Dave had ever conducted. Dave told Mr. S. all the accusations Gerald had made against him. He was already aware because he had been interviewed by the police. Following the "no secrets about sex abuse" rule, Dave did not accuse Mr. S. of anything or ask him if he had done anything to his son; he just informed Mr. S. of the accusations. Dave had learned from previous meetings with Mr. S. that Mr. S. was a Star Trek fan. Dave posed to Mr. S. that if something terrible happened on the Enterprise, who was ultimately responsible? Mr. S. said that as captain, Captain Kirk was ultimately responsible for whatever happened under his command.

The rapport established with Mr. S. during Gerald's placement with Phyllis and Arthur was now called upon. Dave explained to Mr. S. that, like Captain Kirk, as captain of his family, he should offer his apology to Gerald for whatever happened that Gerald would make such terrible accusations. Mr. S. was being asked to apologize, not confess. By asking for an apology, not a confession, Mr. S. was being given an opportunity to help his son without putting himself in legal jeopardy. Mr. S. responded by giving Dave an unforgettable look. It was clear to Dave that Mr. S. understood Dave was not attempting to investigate him but was sincerely offering him a chance to help his son. There was an understanding conveyed in that look. Mr. S. said he would most assuredly apologize. Dave told him that Gerald was worried Mr. S. was angry with him and did not love him anymore. Mr. S. said that was not true. He was not angry with Gerald, and he loved him very much. Mr. S. was obviously a very disturbed man for perpetrating such terrible abuse, but he knew he had seriously hurt his children and was willing to help them.

APOLOGY SESSION

Now that it was clear Mr. S. would offer help, Gerald joined the session. Dave told Gerald that his father was aware of all the things Gerald had accused him of. Dave told Gerald that his father wanted to say something to him. Mr. S. asked Gerald to sit across from him. He reached out and took Gerald's hands and said, "I am so sorry. I am not angry with you. You are my son. I love you very much. I love all three of you." Dave has conducted many apology sessions in his career. All were very emotional. This apology session was the most emotional session Dave had ever been a part of. Everyone, including Dave, cried. A lot.

After saying what he needed, Mr. S. hugged his son. The two said goodbye and parted. Gerald went home with Phyllis. Two days later, Mr. S. was arrested. He was eventually tried and found guilty of multiple counts of sexually abusing a child. He was sent to prison for many years. For as long as Dave knew Gerald after this, Gerald never spoke to his father again. This session was the only opportunity for anything therapeutic to happen between father and son, perpetrator and victim. After this session, Gerald's strange sexual behavior stopped. He was no longer tormented by the idea that his father hated him.

FOLLOW-UP

Several months after this session Phyllis and Arthur decided to not foster children. Gerald had to be moved to a new home in another county. Dave lost touch with him. One year later, Dave was consulting for a new foster care agency. Incredibly, although they were in different homes, Gerald and both his siblings were all in the new foster care network. Dave was asked to offer treatment to all three children. Dave could now meet both Ronny and Rebecca and have the three children together if that looked to be helpful. None of the three children had seen each other since they had been taken from their father's custody almost two years earlier.

Dave met Ronny and Rebecca each individually. His session with Rebecca was very moving. Rebecca brought her "life book" to the appointment. This is a photo album that children in the child welfare system are encouraged to keep. It is meant to provide something permanent when the children go from foster home to foster home. They may have to change families, but they can keep their life book. Rebecca was unaware Dave had been Gerald's therapist. She opened her life book to the first page. On the very first page was the apology letter Gerald had sent to her two years earlier. Rebecca told Dave, "My brother did bad things to me, but he sent me this nice letter." Dave asked if she wanted to see one or both of her brothers. She said she would like that. She had not seen either in years and missed them both very much.

A session for all three siblings was set. It was labeled a therapy session. Dave viewed it as a visit. All attended. The session was awkward at first. None knew what to say to each other. Dave asked if they wanted to play games that were available. None did. After 15 minutes of small talk, with no warning, Ronny asked Gerald if Gerald thought their father was angry with them for telling what he had done to them. Gerald immediately answered confidently, "No. He told me he was sorry, that he loved us and was not angry." Ronny was not expecting this answer. He asked if Gerald was sure of this. Gerald looked at Dave. He knew Dave was there when his father apologized. Dave reassured both Ronny and Rebecca that he had witnessed their father telling Gerald he loved them and was not angry.

Soon after this meeting, Rebecca was adopted by a family in another state. She had to move away. Neither brother would see her again. Both Gerald and Ronnie began to have behavior problems. Both had to be moved to new foster homes. Dave lost touch with both. One year later, Children's Services called Dave and asked him if he would do a one-time emergency session with Gerald. Gerald was disrupting from yet another foster home and would soon be moved again. Gerald asked if he could see Dave before he was sent to a new home.

Gerald was now 13 years old. He was a very angry boy. He had a cross and serious look on his face. He told Dave he was angry at his father. Dave asked if he was angry about what his dad had done to him. Gerald said he was not mad about that. Dave asked if he had bad dreams or unwanted thoughts about what his father did to him. He said he did not. Dave said he was happy to hear that and asked why he thought that was. Gerald said simply, "Dad apologized for that." Gerald was angry because he and his siblings could not be together. They had no place to stay. Dave asked Gerald why he continued to make trouble and get thrown out of all the different homes? Gerald said that is what he wanted to tell about. He had lost his sister. Since she was adopted, he could never see her again. Now he also was up for adoption. He was not going to let that happen because then he would also lose his brother. He was going to continue to make trouble so no one would want him. He would never be adopted. He would at least be able to see his brother. That was his plan. He wanted Dave to tell the case worker that he did not want to be adopted. Dave said he would tell her, but it may not make a difference This session was the last time Dave ever saw Gerald. It is not known if he or Ronnie were ever adopted. All three children would be grown by now. It is not known if the brothers were ever able to reunite with their sister.

DISCUSSION

Although the apologies from Gerald to Rebecca and from Mr. S. to Gerald had enduring therapeutic impact, the saga of long-term placement in the child welfare system eventually overshadowed the problems that originally resulted in the removal from the biological father. Mr. S. lived an isolated life. He did not volunteer names of extended family nor did any of the children know their relatives. Unlike Isiah, there were no aunts or grandparents to call upon. Keeping Mr. S. engaged while Gerald was placed with Phillis and Arthur did provide the opportunity for him to apologize before he was incarcerated. Many sexual abuse victims whose disclosures send family to jail suffer tremendous long-term guilt. Hopefully, Gerald was spared that fate by his father's apology and reassurance that he was not angry with him. Many in the treatment community assume perpetrators of such heinous abuse are of no therapeutic use to the victim. If approached correctly, the first author (DG) has found otherwise. If approached as a human being in pain over what they have done to a loved one and it is clear the therapist is not asking the perpetrator to put themselves in legal jeopardy, some perpetrators will step forward to be helpful to their children. Mr. S. is one example.

13 INTERGENERATIONAL TRAUMA

In earlier chapters we reported research outlining several challenges for working with adult trauma survivors. To summarize, it is estimated that adult trauma survivors make up a majority of adults in the social service system; however, many trauma survivors do not seek treatment for trauma. They may end up in substance abuse treatment, they may seek treatment for their child, or they may be mandated to seek treatment for themselves or their child or children. When trauma survivors do end up in treatment either for themselves or their children, special engagement procedures are required. A collaborative approach is needed in which treatment choices are offered and the choices requested by the trauma survivor are respected.

Children of trauma survivors can end up in treatment partly due to severe impairment of parenting resulting from their parents' serious trauma symptoms. Avoidance symptoms can result in severely disengaged parents. The belief that the world is unsafe can produce overprotective and intrusive parents. Intrafamilial sexual abuse can result in the survivor cutting off extended family, leaving them alone and unsupported. Their children are then subject to the consequences of this vulnerability. Many women who endure intrafamily sexual abuse end up seriously abusing substances and/or in and out of one domestic violence relationship after another, with obvious serious consequences for their children.

When a trauma survivor's child also becomes a victim of trauma, the parent's trauma history can create serious barriers to the capacity of the parent to help their now-traumatized child. The parent may become too upset when hearing about the child's trauma resulting in the child being reluctant to tell their parent what happened. Or, because the parent has endured some terrible past, they may have little empathy for their child, expecting their child to "suck it up," since the parent may feel they were able to do so.

When a parent trauma survivor ends up in treatment for whatever reason, this provides an opportunity to correct all or most of these parenting issues. Unfortunately, if the parent is unable to perform the therapeutic tasks the treatment approach requires, the common practice of numerous child treatments is to refer the parent to their own trauma treatment. The child may then be seen individually, losing the opportunity to correct the trauma symptoms that impair the parent. The opportunity to help the adult may also be lost since many trauma survivors will not engage in treatment that focuses directly on their trauma history.

Treatment must be flexible and offer choices that keep the trauma survivor engaged in therapy. Above all other groups, these parents and their children need a flexible approach that can adapt to client choices and help with their trauma symptoms. Because many are not willing to focus on their trauma histories, indirect nontrauma-focused methods of helping are required. Some may eventually trust a clinician to help them with their trauma symptoms. This requires an approach that begins with focusing on their initial request and adjusting the treatment to focus on trauma in later stages. The following cases will demonstrate how integrative family and systems treatment (I-FAST) can adapt to these cases and offer the flexibility required to help both child and parent resolve their respective symptoms.

INDIRECT FOCUS ON TRAUMA: ANIMAL KINGDOM

Background

Monique, aged 33, and her two teenagers, Mark aged 15, and Lilian, aged 14, lived in 34-year-old boyfriend Robert's home. The juvenile court referred them for in-home therapy because the teens would not come home from school. They would either wander the streets until the early morning hours or the police would find them and take them home. Both were on juvenile probation for truancy from home and serious behavior problems at school.

When Charles and Maria first went into the home, the house had an intense urine odor. The smell was so intense, the urine smell lingered with Charles for two days. Charles asked how many pets the family had. Monique said about 1,000. Robert angrily corrected her proclaiming that if the baby animals were counted it was 1,300. Almost all the animals were hamsters in the basement. The mother had rescued them from a pet store. Monique and the children fought over the chores. The teens were on animal clean up detail. Although it was his house, Robert stayed away as much as possible because of the smell.

Establishing Alliances

Charles and Maria asked to see the animals. Monique told them they would have to see them next week. The family was out of flea spray. No one could go to the basement without receiving a full body spray of flea repellant. The next week Charles and Maria got their flea spray and went to the basement. It was full of cages of hamsters. One third were dead. The litter had not been changed for a while. The dead animals were identified. The family agreed to remove the dead hamsters while Charles and Maria were there. There were arguments about whether some of the hamsters were dead or just sleeping. Cages had to be shaken to determine.

Engaging the Boyfriend

Because the family lived in his home, Robert needed to be engaged. It was assumed we might engage Robert if the animals were removed. There was concern that if the animals were not removed, Robert might not allow Monique and her children to stay. If that were to occur, then on top of all the other problems, the family would be homeless. Charles called the U.S. Department of Agriculture. The U.S. Department of Agriculture informed Charles that the hamsters could not be sold as pets, the mother's intention. They had to either be euthanized or sold as snake food. It violated several codes for so many animals to be in the house.

At the next home visit, Monique was on her couch crying. She and Robert had a fight about the animals. Robert announced that she and her children would have to move if she wanted to keep the animals. The only place she could go was Alaska. Charles informed Monique of what he had learned from the U.S. Department of

Agriculture. Reluctantly, Monique decided to sell all the hamsters as snake food. The animals were removed from the house. It took weeks. Once the animals were gone, the smell in the house dramatically improved. Robert was very pleased that the animals were gone from his home. From this point on, Robert was completely engaged.

Winning the Mother's Trust and Learning Her Story

Charles asked Monique why she was thinking of moving to Alaska. Monique told Charles her whole family background. As a child, Monique lived with her two biological parents and older brother in Ohio. As a young teenager, both her brother and father molested her separately and on multiple occasions. She told her school guidance counselor her father was molesting her. An investigation was done. The parents and brother all denied the abuse. To punish her for telling or to keep her safe, it was not clear which, Monique was sent to live with her father's brother in Alaska. While she lived in Alaska, her father died and her brother moved out of her parents' house. She went back to Ohio to live with her mom. She was sexually abused multiple times by both her father and brother. Her mother blamed her for everything. Then, as a senior in high school, she was gang raped at a party. The boys got her drunk and all raped her. She became pregnant with what would be her oldest child. Later in her life she would look at all the photos of her high school year book, trying to figure out which boy was the father of her son.

Her mother's response to her being gang raped was to kick her out of the house because she was pregnant. Monique found an apartment and a young man to move in with. This man would become the father of her second child. He mistreated her, and she eventually left him for another man. She was mistreated by him also and eventually got away from him as well.

There were multiple consequences of this trauma. Monique did not trust men. She would only get so close. However, without a man she was financially unstable. This resulted in her having superficial live-in relationships to provide housing for her and her children. Because they were superficial, they did not last. Over time, she and her children never maintained stable housing. She admitted that because of the sexual abuse, she did not trust men. She never married and she never would. It was not clear what impact the sexual assaults had on her sexual relationships.

PTSD Symptoms and Interactional Patterns

Monique cut herself off from all family. She had no elders in her life. Her father had been a Christian minister. She therefore rejected Christianity and church. She had her own spiritual beliefs, but the communal aspects of religion were not part of her life. She did not have any relationships with adults besides whatever man she lived with. She avoided all non-household family and social relationships. She had nightmares of her brother molesting her and of the gang rape she endured. She was depressed and stayed in her room—classic posttraumatic stress disorder (PTSD) avoidance symptoms.

Monique would dissociate when too angry and have subsequent loss of memory. There was conflict between Monique and Lilian. They would have intense arguments. Sometimes Monique would say things to her daughter in these arguments that she could not remember saying. Lilian told Charles her mother called her a "fucking cunt." Charles had Lilian repeat this to Monique. Monique was stunned. She did not remember saying this. She apologized and hugged her daughter. Charles's impression was that she truly did not remember. Lilian told Charles her mother claimed to not remember many terrible things she said to her. Monique seemed to only forget things when she was very angry. Charles concluded that Monique was dissociating.

To cope with her trauma symptoms, Monique smoked marijuana. Avoidance was another method of coping. On an interactional level, Monique was disengaged from all relationships in the house, among extended family, and within her local community. Monique just stayed in her bedroom. She and Robert were not close. He stayed away as much as possible. The children were left to fend for themselves. The two teenagers either stayed away or were out of control.

Establishing Goals

Monique did not want trauma treatment. She and Robert wanted help to settle Mark and Lilian down. They were upset that the two teens would stay away from home and were both on probation. It was decided to focus on the goals Monique and Robert wanted as an indirect way of helping Monique with her trauma. To achieve the goals of settling the teens down, many of Monique's withdraw symptoms would have to change.

The family patterns were characterized by disengagement, serious conflict between Monique and her two oldest children, instability between Robert and Monique, and no meaningful relationships outside the household for Monique. The children had to go to extremes to get their mother out of her bedroom. When Robert was home, he was so upset about the state of his house, he threatened to throw everyone out. Monique was either totally disengaged from her children or fighting with them about their extreme behavior. To get the children settled down, these interactional patterns would have to change.

Our goals were to help Monique become more engaged with her children, to stabilize the couples' relationship, to get Robert more engaged with both Monique and her children, and to help the couple establish meaningful relationships outside the family. We assumed that for Monique to establish loving relationships with her children and with Robert, she would have to exorcise most of her trauma demons.

Strategy for Changing Interactional Patterns

The couple would be helped to work together to settle the children down, the problem they wanted help on. Helping them work together would hopefully result in them getting closer emotionally and help both to get closer to the children. What was not anticipated was the struggle that ensued getting the children to accept and adjust to these changes. There were consequences to many years of Monique being disengaged from her children and to her never committing to one man. The two teens were accustomed to raising themselves. They made and followed their own rules. Years of this produced two out-of-control teenagers who were comfortable exhibiting bizarre behaviors. They learned to regard the given man Monique lived with as temporary. The idea that their mother would stay with and even marry a man never occurred to them. They disregarded whatever man their mother was with. Although Monique and Robert would change their sides of the patterns early in treatment, it would take one and a half years and numerous incidents for the children to settle down and adjust to an improved mother. Over this period, Charles and Maria had three separate treatment episodes with the family.

Utilizing Crises to Change Patterns and Reinforce Exceptions

The interventions for each teen will be presented separately. They did not occur in the sequence described, but one after the other, with each teen alternating having serious issues. Each incident either teen presented was an opportunity to offer Monique and Robert suggestions that simultaneously addressed the children's issues and required Monique and Robert to become more involved with the children and with each other. The cumulative effect of helping Robert and Monique work together to address these dilemmas was to both gradually produce a family in which all were positively engaged with each other and a more meaningful relationship between Robert and Monique. By the end of treatment, the patterns of disengagement and conflict were changed, and Robert was integrated fully into the family.

The Daughter's Problems

UTILIZING THE DAUGHTER'S MOTIVATIONS AND INTERESTS

Lilian had a strong motivation to prove her mother wrong about anything. This motivation was put to good use. Lilian told her mother that she saw dead people. Lilian was infatuated with anything Gothic. She had a reputation at school as being strange. In one session, Monique told Charles about the "gypsy" curse. Monique explained that according to the gypsy curse, the women in the family had a special connection to "the other side" and could communicate with the dead. Mom's theory was her daughter was cursed. Charles had Monique tell Lilian the theory that she was cursed. Lilian insisted she was not cursed. To prove to her mother she was not cursed, Lilian stopped claiming to see dead people and gave up her obsession with death. This improved her reputation at school and resulted in her having new friends.

ENGAGING THE ADULTS WITH EACH OTHER AND WITH THE DAUGHTER

Monique informed Charles that Lilian was cutting herself. Lillian had a history of self-harm. Charles instructed Lillian to give her favorite piece of glass used to cut herself to Monique. Charles proposed a safety plan for Lilian that included both adults taking turns supervising Lilian and locking up any objects she could use to harm herself. Initially, Monique objected to having to supervise Lilian so intensely but carried out the plan when Robert insisted it was necessary and volunteered to take shifts himself. The plan was followed, and Lilian stopped cutting completely. Charles believed these interventions were effective because they required Monique to get more involved. It got her out of the bedroom. They also involved Robert becoming more engaged with both Monique and the children.

NOTICING AND UTILIZING EXCEPTIONS

Lillian and Mark were both suspended from school. Mark defended Lillian when she was attacked by another student. Monique was upset over this. She told Charles that the family rule was "You only fight with each other, and you only fight at home." Robert joined the session and proclaimed that this "was not a rule I want for my family." He was now framing the group as "my family." Charles took advantage of this exception by Robert to promote a discussion of how they were all becoming a family. Charles instructed Robert and Monique to agree on a new rule for "their family." A compromise was reached that the kids could argue at home but not physically fight, and they could fight at school but only for "noble reasons."

Lillian began huffing aerosols. She passed out in the living room with a can of bug killer. Robert found her and took her to the hospital. She was released with the recommendation to stop huffing. To persuade Lillian to stop, Monique collected all the aerosols in the house and threw them out. She and Robert went shopping for nonaerosol toiletries and cleaning products. Monique called Charles from Wal-Mart when an argument ensued. Robert was refusing to stop using an aerosol body spray and had placed his regular product in the cart. Charles explained to him that Lillian could die by abusing aerosols. Robert agreed to try another product. Lillian responded well to this and stopped huffing. A few weeks later she asked Robert to buy an aerosol product. He refused, telling her he loved her and did not want her to die. Again, Charles enlarged this exception by promoting a family discussion. Robert was becoming more engaged with the children. Robert and Monique were now collaborating with each other. All family members were gradually becoming more bonded with each other.

IMPROVING MOTHER AND DAUGHTER'S EMOTIONAL CLOSENESS

Lillian requested to go to a church youth group. Monique became incensed. She called Charles crying, "I always knew she would do this to me!" Monique's father was a Christian minister. She did not want her children to become Christians. With Charles's encouragement, she allowed her daughter to attend the youth group, provided she did not go to the actual church service. Charles framed it as a positive youth activity. Monique admitted she wanted her daughter to be happy, even if it meant taking a different spiritual path than herself. Lillian did not enjoy the youth group and only went once. However, this initiated a change in which Monique and Lillian began doing more mother–daughter activities together. They began shopping and getting manicures together. This was a change that became permanent. It not only increased the bond between Monique and Lillian; it also involved Monique breaking her pattern of avoidance. The church episode also represented a newfound willingness of Monique to negotiate and challenge her hatred of Christianity. She was giving up some of her trauma distortions.

Although Lillian was not interested in the church youth group, she did become interested in joining girls' soccer at school. Monique went to her games. This was another activity that interrupted Monique's withdraw pattern and intensified her bond with Lillian. In addition, Lillian made new friends on the soccer team. She was invited for sleepovers and had her new friends sleep over. The sleepovers and soccer team produced additional exceptions. First, when Lillian had sleepovers, Monique was out of her bedroom and involved with the girls. Second, by going to Lillian's soccer games, Monique met other mothers whom she befriended and began socializing with. She now had new relationships outside of the family—a major change for Monique.

Focusing on the Son's Problems

From the beginning of the case, Mark was totally out of control. It took several weeks to dispose of the hamsters. During this period, it was winter. The dead hamsters were outside and frozen. Mark would use the frozen hamsters for batting practice. He would batt the frozen hamsters into the neighbors' yards. On one occasion, he batted a frozen hamster, and it hit the windshield of a neighbor man trying to drive to work. The neighbors were upset about this. Mark would cut up furniture in the house, put holes in the walls, or cut the woodwork in the house with axes. On one occasion, he disassembled the kitchen sink and made a marijuana pipe.

CHANGING FAMILY PATTERNS

Responding to one of Mark's infractions, Monique confiscated his video games and locked them in the garage. To retrieve his videos, Mark took a sledge hammer and pounded a hole in the garage wall, making a "new door." Robert repaired the garage and under Charles's suggestion, the entire family made the garage into a family game room. One night per week the entire family would go to the garage and play Dungeons and Dragons. This became a new family activity that they kept going long after Charles had terminated his time with them.

CHANGING PATTERNS: STRENGTHENING THE COUPLE RELATIONSHIP AND PROMOTING FAMILY TIME

Charles suggested that when Monique fought with either teen she call Robert to ask his advice. They should reach an agreement on the phone for how Monique should respond. Monique and Robert followed this suggestion. They became more involved with each other and began talking by phone regularly, child problems or not. Doing this reinforced a process of the couple collaborating, compromising, and reaching agreements. It strengthened their relationship.

Children's Services reported to Charles that Mark was locked out of the house and was being forced to live in the doghouse in the backyard. Mark was indeed living in the doghouse and had been for two days. He was not locked out. He was in the doghouse voluntarily. He refused to come in the house. Monique wanted him to come in to talk about a minor behavioral incident. Mark decided to wait her out. In the doghouse, he had a sleeping bag, mattress, candles, and a Mark Twain book. He was sneaking back in the house at night to shower, use the bathroom, and eat. Charles coached Monique on how to get him to come inside. Monique was to make his favorite breakfast: pancakes, eggs, and sausage. After a few days of smelling his favorite foods wafting from the kitchen window, he returned to the house without incident, got ready for school, and sat down for breakfast. After this, Monique began to cook breakfast every morning for all three children and for Robert when he was home.

Mark bought a BB gun and was caught shooting ducks in the city park. He had to appear in court. The judge was threatening to send him to long-term juvenile jail. Monique went to court to plead for him to remain in her custody. Charles coached her on how to be appropriate in court. She had a history of being uncooperative with court staff. When the judge asked her why he should not send Mark to the Department of Youth Services, she replied, "Because that would be a cake walk compared to what I am going to do to him." The judge seemed surprised. He was expecting a plea for leniency. He replied, "I have no choice but to return him to your custody."

COLLABORATING WITH PROFESSIONALS

Charles had a collaborative relationship with Mark's probation officer. He called upon this relationship to help the court be a resource for Monique. With agreement of the court, Monique designed Mark's community service plan. Monique's plan for her son became court orders. For two months, Monique had Mark wash and detail police cars every Saturday morning.

UTILIZING PARENT FRAMES AND SKILLS AND IMPROVING MOTHER AND SON'S EMOTIONAL CLOSENESS

Monique framed the problem as Mark being bored. She included as part of his court orders extra reading at home and, as a further consequence, a special activity. Charles discovered that Monique knew how to sword fight. This was an astonishing and unique skill. As part of Monique's court-ordered community service plan for Mark, Monique could teach Mark sword fighting. He could be taught the proper manner of handling blades. To fulfill his community service requirement, Mark had to sword fight with his mother. We were reasonably certain this had never been a part of any juvenile's community service plan. Besides further empowering Monique by putting her in charge of devising Mark's community service plan, this was a way to get Monique involved with her son in a proactive way. This activity helped change interactions. Mark and Monique had regular sword fighting lessons in the backyard, only if Mark behaved.

Consolidating, Reinforcing, and Enlarging Changes

After a year and a half of many incidents, both teens settled down. Monique became engaged in positive ways with both of her children and Robert. She was able to overcome her social avoidance symptoms. She cooked breakfast every morning for her family. She and Mark continued their sword fighting competitions. She and Lillian continued spending time together. Robert became much more engaged with both children. Monique genuinely involved Robert in the solving of her children's issues. After having to involve himself with each child multiple times over a year and a half, the three were now very connected. Family Dungeon and Dragon night was now a family tradition. Monique was now socializing with her own friends. Finally, the couple were much more connected. Through the process of reaching compromises and sticking to the agreements they made, the couple were much closer. Monique learned to trust a man and to love her children. It was not known if her nightmares went away.

Summary

In this therapy, the parent suffered intense childhood trauma and was seriously impaired. Her impairment rendered her unavailable to her children, to relationships with men, and to friends outside the family. She did not want trauma treatment. She wanted help for her out-of-control teenagers. What she did and did not want was completely respected. The focus was on helping her help her children. Doing this required her to overcome her avoidance symptoms. She had to expose herself to what she was avoiding—social relationships and a committed relationship with a partner. She had to confront and change many of her beliefs associated with her trauma history.

One powerful belief related to her trauma background changed. She became more open to Christianity. This was demonstrated in a very dramatic way. Several months after terminating the case for the last time, Charles was invited to Robert and Monique's wedding. They had a small Christian ceremony at a venue that had spiritual significance to Monique.

FLEXIBLE USE OF TRAUMA INTERVENTIONS

The Caged Animal

Marleen, aged 37, a single mother, requested child care for her 14-year-old developmentally delayed son, Thomas, during her upcoming hysterectomy surgery and recovery period. Marleen told Charles, the case manager, that she required the surgery due to the severe damage that years of sexual assault had done to her sexual and reproductive organs. Marleen explained that at age 13, her mother sold her to a couple to be their sex slave. For the remainder of her childhood Marleen was sexually assaulted by the couple and numerous of their friends. The physical damage was so severe that on one occasion while going to the bathroom her intestines partially came out. Charles suggested Marleen see a therapist who specialized in trauma treatment. Marleen did not want trauma treatment; she just wanted child care for her son after she had her surgery.

CASE BACKGROUND

Marleen was in serious need of trauma treatment. She lived alone with her son. She did not work. She had no relationships with other adults. She avoided leaving her apartment. Marleen had panic attacks when she left the house. When living with the couple who had abused her, if Marleen left the house too long, she would be beaten when she got home. At home, Thomas would terrorize her. Frightened of her son, she would lock herself in the bathroom. On occasion, Thomas would parade around the house naked, sometimes with an erection. When this occurred, Marleen would black out and find herself hours later locked in her bedroom. Her reaction of fear to her son, her dissociative symptoms, her panic level anxiety, and her pervasive pattern of avoidance were classic trauma symptoms. Marleen had been in individual treatment for years. Evan after years of treatment, she refused to tell her trauma history.

RESPECTING PARENT GOALS AND WINNING TRUST

Since Marleen only wanted help with care for Thomas through the recovery of her surgery, Charles was advised to respect her wishes and focus solely on what she was requesting. It was hoped that if Charles did this, he might earn Marleen's trust. She then might ask help on some of the other problems she and Thomas were experiencing. This is what happened. Charles helped Marleen with what she wanted, and then after she recovered from surgery, she asked Charles to help with managing Thomas's behavior. Not only did Marleen isolate herself in her apartment; she was extremely protective of Thomas. Other than allowing him to go to school, Marleen kept Thomas inside all the time.

AN OVERARCHING FRAME AND TREATMENT STRATEGY

Charles framed Thomas was a "caged animal." As long as he had to stay inside all of the time, at 14 years old he was not going to settle down. This frame made sense to Marleen. Charles then pointed out that Marleen would have to get Thomas out of the house. At this point, Marleen admitted for the first time to Charles that she was herself afraid to go out and that she had panic attacks if she did. Charles then offered to accompany her.

UTILIZING PARENT MOTIVATIONS AND FLEXIBLE USE OF EXPOSURE PROCEDURES

This task could be viewed as exposure therapy for Marleen. To get her son out of the house, she had to break her very entrenched pattern of isolation and avoidance. It was assumed that if she did this, there could be profound therapeutic effects for her. Marleen was not willing to break her patterns for her own personal benefit, but to help her son, she was willing.

For their first venture out, Charles took Marleen and Thomas to a book store. When they arrived, Marleen wanted Charles to accompany them inside. Charles explained, "He is not my son; you should go in without me." Marleen took Thomas into the book store and re-emerged after 12 minutes. This is when Charles learned that Marleen had an internal clock set at 12 minutes—the amount of time she could be away from home earlier in her life without receiving a beating.

Charles took Marleen and Thomas to the book store and the library. Marleen was able to stay inside for longer and longer durations. After she became comfortable taking Thomas to these locations, Charles took them to the mall. Charles explained to Marleen, "Thomas needs to learn to go to places where other teenage boys go." Marleen was terrified of going to the mall, but in the interest of helping Thomas, she agreed. After going to the mall several times, Marleen allowed Thomas to go on his own. As he got out of the house more, Thomas's behavior improved.

MAJOR EXCEPTIONS AND PROCESSING THE TRAUMA NARRATIVE

After months of this exposure therapy, Marleen decided to take Thomas to a movie on her own. She and her son went together to the first place she had left the house to go to without Charles. Marleen was astonished at the price of popcorn and a soft drink. This was a major breakthrough for Marleen, which she initiated on her own without any input from Charles.

After the movie trip, Marleen complained to Charles that her therapist was firing her because she would not tell her trauma narrative. She told Charles fragments of the story but never the whole story at once. She had never told anyone the story. She herself only remembered it in disorganized fragments unattached to any unifying context. Charles asked Marleen if she would tell him the story. Her telling the story for the first time would also be a major exception.

To tell Charles, she had to tell the whole story and/organize it. She only had a fragmented story in her mind. Marleen had to organize her thoughts, feelings, and beliefs about what had happened to her. Marleen's was a story of severe betrayal by her own mother, serial sexual assaults including being gang raped on multiple occasions, and a first marriage with chronic and serious domestic violence. Finally, after months of respecting what Marleen herself wanted help on, Charles had gained the trust for Marleen to tell him her "trauma narrative."

At age 13, Marleen was sold by her mother to a married couple. The husband raped Marleen on several occasions while the wife restrained her. Marry had two daughters that were products of rape. She suspected that the couple were unable to have children and that her purpose was to provide them. If Marleen left the house for more than 15 minutes, when she returned, she was beaten. Marleen lived with the couple until age 17. She escaped when the husband was sent to prison for molesting other children. By this time, Marleen's parents had divorced. Marleen left her daughters behind and went to live with her father whom she did not blame for being sold to the couple. Marleen blamed her mother for this offense. There was a tradition in her mother's family of selling children. She went to live with her father and no longer associated with her mother.

Marleen lived with her father until her early 20s when she got married. Her first husband was domestically violent, jealous, and possessive and would beat her if she left home. While married to this man, Marleen's father died. After a few years, Marleen's husband unexpectedly died of a heart attack. Marleen then married Thomas's father. This was a good marriage. Her second husband did not mistreat Marleen. He died, however, when Thomas was three years old. She then got into yet another abusive relationship. To escape this relationship, Marleen moved to Ohio, away from all the abuse, and began her period of isolation and avoidance.

Charles responded to this story by being impressed with how resilient and strong Marleen was to have been able to move on after enduring such horrible and extensive abuse. Marleen had not thought of herself this way. Marleen had not considered herself to be a strong person.

TRACKING AND REINFORCING EXCEPTIONS

Marleen told Charles her trauma narrative. It was not clear if there was an "index trauma." Charles reported that Marleen's trauma history was so severe he was concerned he could not be of help. It was suggested that since he was the first human being Marleen had ever told her story to, the act of telling him might have already been very helpful. Charles was advised to wait and observe the effect of Marleen telling him her story.

Marleen telling Charles her story was indeed a breakthrough. Her functioning greatly improved. On her initiative, Marleen decided she wanted to work. She found a part-time job and began working 20 hours per week. She also began communicating more with her two adult daughters and other relatives. All exceptions initiated by her with no input from Charles.

REINFORCING EXCEPTIONS AND ADJUSTING FAMILY MEMBERS TO CHANGE

The main problem now was helping Thomas, a developmentally disabled child, adjust to a mother who was suddenly making major changes. Thomas's behavior problems re-emerged in response to Marleen's changes. Marleen's spontaneous response was to want to quit her job and stay home with Thomas. Charles persuaded her to not react this way. Instead, Thomas was helped to find a "job" at the mall with a vendor he had befriended. The vendor gave him odd jobs and paid him token wages. Both Thomas and Marleen were proud of this "job," and Thomas settled down after this.

After one year, Thomas and Marleen had undergone dramatic and life-changing improvements. Marleen had overcome her anxiety regarding leaving her home. She could go shopping, go to entertainment events, and work part-time without having panic attacks or the desire to return home after 12 minutes. Because these changes produced profound changes in her routine, Thomas had to be helped to adjust. Marleen went from being very overprotective of Thomas to allowing him to leave the house and do a multitude of age-appropriate activities on his own. She no longer viewed the outside world as dangerous or her participation in it as threatening.

Thomas's behavior at home improved immensely. He no longer terrorized his mother or paraded around the house naked. Charles helped Marleen by respecting what she initially requested, and Marleen then allowed Charles to help her with her trauma symptoms.

FOLLOW-UP

Two years after Charles had begun working with Thomas and Marleen, a major family development occurred that helped Marleen make even more dramatic improvements. Her mother became ill with cancer. Marleen decided to go to help her. This was the first time she went home since her move to Ohio. Marleen visited her now-adult daughters and grandchildren, the first time she had seen her daughters since she moved to Ohio and the first time she had ever seen her grandchildren. One daughter lived in the house of the couple who abused her. It was a dramatic discovery for Marleen that she could visit that house without having panic attacks or flashbacks. While visiting to help her mother, Marleen found that her brothers could not care for her mother. When she returned, Charles asked if she had forgiven her mother. Marleen said she did not, but that it was her mom and she had to help. After this trip, she decided to move back home.

Well after her move home, Marleen came back to Ohio to visit. She looked up Charles. By this time, Marleen had no need for any mental health services. She had a live-in boyfriend who was a very nice man. Thomas was doing very well. Marleen was apparently free from any trauma symptoms that interfered with her functioning. Her mother had passed away. Marleen gave Charles a book of photos of islands near her father's home. She told Charles to show the book to his clients who have trauma. Marleen instructed Charles to tell them they can choose how they want to remember their pasts. Marleen choose to remember these islands and the time with her father and not remember anything else.

Marleen periodically called Charles to report how she was doing. On her last call, Charles told Marleen of this book and that her story would be told in it. Marleen cried and affirmed that her story needed to be told.

SUMMARY

In this case, a severely traumatized mother was initially requesting childcare services only. Although she had been in individual therapy for years, she had never told her trauma story. Nor did she want help focusing on her trauma symptoms. Following the principals of trauma-informed care, the parent's request for child care only was respected. Respecting this request resulted in the parent then asking for help with her developmentally delayed son.

In I-FAST, parents are put in the lead role at helping their children with the problems the parents are requesting help on. This is done partly to break the interactional patterns between and among family members. In this case, the mother had to help the son leave the house. This task was exposure therapy for a traumatized mother, a task she would have rejected if posed as something to help herself but was accepted as something done to help her son.

In the process of helping her son, numerous classic trauma interventions procedures such as exposure, processing trauma narratives, and changing the meaning of trauma were employed in a flexible, nonprescriptive way when the client was receptive to cooperating with them. The result was a complete amelioration of all the parent's extreme trauma symptoms, including nightmares, flashbacks, panic attacks, and dissociative symptoms. She was able to reconnect with family, establish a loving relationship with a man, and go back to work.

No One Leaves the House

BACKGROUND

Eleven-year-old Cindy lived with her biological parents Anne and Andy. She was referred for intensive in-home treatment by juvenile court because she had not attended school in over one year. Unless either her mother or father accompanied her, she had serious panic attacks if she left the house. Cindy would not bathe fearing a monster would kill her while in the bath tub. She would not go up or down stairs in any location including her home. She would not leave the house to play with other children.

Anne described herself as agoraphobic. She could not leave the house without having panic attacks or go up and down steps. Anne had been taking Xanax for 14 years. She was on an extremely high dosage and was clearly addicted. Anne had been sexually abused repeatedly as a teenager. Her father sold her sexually to his friends. At 17, she was also raped by an 18-year-old boy. After the boy raped her, Anne's mother took her to a pediatrician who prescribed Xanax. Ever since, her Xanax dosage gradually increased over time to what was now an alarming amount. Anne lived with her parents until age 20 when she met Andy. The two married, and Anne thought she had escaped her father's grasp.

Andy was also severely impaired. He worked with his father as an automobile mechanic. He was a very good husband until his father unexpectedly died three years prior to this treatment episode. Andy and his father were very close. After his father died, Andy became depressed. He quit working and stayed at home. He spent most of his time either on the couch watching TV or in his room watching pornography. His porn addiction gave him an interest in sexual activities that he wanted to do with Anne. This would then trigger Anne's PTSD reactions to her rape history. When treatment began, no one in the home ever left the house except Andy to get food and other necessities. Andy was in the process of applying for social security disability income. He thought he would never again be able to work. Anne's dysfunction worsened significantly after Andy became depressed and isolated. Charles and Mike, a team of intensive in-home I-FAST treatment providers, worked together on the case. They received supervision from Phil Washburn and consultation from David Grove.

ESTABLISHING ALLIANCES AND IDENTIFYING STRENGTHS

Mike and Charles established a very powerful rapport with the whole family. They did this by being genuinely accepting of the family despite the serious impairments of everyone. Both parents appreciated Mike and Charles treating them like "normal" people. Mike and Charles were strengths-based and found ways to offer sincere compliments. The parents were complimented for having a nice house that they kept very clean and that they were very hospitable. They were complimented for being loving parents. They had a dog that both Charles and Mike let lick them. The family also played video games, which allowed them to create representations of themselves as characters in the games. During the initial sessions, both Mike and Charles would play the video games with the family. A powerful rapport resulted from this and put Mike and Charles in a position to offer interventions that would eventually transform the entire family. Mike and Charles won their trust and were allowed to help in massive ways over the next 12 months.

At some point, Mike and Charles asked the family, "What happened? How did you come to be in this predicament?"

SETTING INITIAL GOALS

The initial goal that the parents wanted to focus on was helping Cindy go back to school. It was observed that Cindy's and Anne's anxiety symptoms paralleled each other. We therefore assumed that Cindy would go to school if her mother took her. This was a problem since Cindy insisted she could not leave the house. She did offer the exception that at times she could leave the house if Andy went with her. It was then suggested that both parents drive Cindy to school in the morning, drop her off, go into the building with her, get her settled, and go back home, leaving Cindy in school. They could then pick her up after school. The parents followed this plan, and Cindy was quickly back in school regularly.

OVERARCHING FRAME AND INITIAL INTERVENTIONS

Although Cindy was back in school, the pervasiveness of her anxiety symptoms remained. She would not bathe, go up or down stairs, or go outside and play. The parents were very concerned about all this impairment. The problem was framed as fears that would require much courage by Cindy to overcome. It was suggested to Anne that it would be very helpful to Cindy if Anne could role-model courage for her daughter by focusing on overcoming some of her own fears. If Anne would focus on her fears, it might inspire Cindy to focus on hers. Anne was agreeable. Anne offered an example of a traumatized parent who would not engage in treatment for herself but would agree to push herself on behalf of helping her child.

Anne was asked if she had ever gone to a restaurant, or a movie, or Bob Evans for coffee, or gone to the mall for a pretzel. She had not done any of these things. Anne was offered two methods to overcome her fears. She could do shock therapy and overcome her worst nightmare fear first. This would result in her simultaneously overcoming her lesser fears. Or, she could choose an incremental, step-by-step process in which a list ladder would be made and each item would be focused on one at a time, starting with a minor fear and working gradually toward the larger fears. This was a choice in which the client picks which method to change and bypasses the issue of if change is possible. Anne chose step-by-step change.

A systematic desensitization list was made with Anne and with Andy's participation and approval. Studies have shown that agoraphobic wives will cooperate more readily with such a list and not relapse if husbands participate in the making of the list (Grove, 2002; Haffner, 1977, 1983). With Andy accompanying, Mike and Charles started taking Anne to a park for 10 minutes. After three weeks, she was able to stay at the park for 30 minutes. Next, all went to the mall together.

INITIAL EXCEPTIONS

An exception occurred when the couple decided to go to the mall on their own for a pretzel. From then on, both would go out of the house together on dates. Anne improved and was able to go out of the house, up and down steps, and to places she had never gone to. Cindy also improved parallel to her mother. As Anne and Andy began to go out on dates, Cindy began to go out and play. When Anne overcame her fear of going up and down steps, Cindy overcame her fear of going up and down steps. After Cindy was able to go out of the house, the couple decided to start going to church. From this point on, the whole family attended a church every Sunday.

COLLABORATING WITH PROFESSIONALS

Anne's Xanax addiction was addressed simultaneously to the systematic desensitization procedure. Anne was asked what the severity of her anxiety was when she first started on Xanax. She said it was far less then it was currently. For example, although she had anxiety before she was prescribed Xanax, she could leave the house without panic attacks. Anne was asked if Xanax really helped with her anxiety. How could she explain that she was far worse now even on a maximum dosage? Anne became quiet. On the next appointment, Anne said she had thought about the Xanax and asked if Charles and Mike would help her get off.

Charles contacted the doctor and informed him that Anne herself wanted off and was now receiving behavioral treatment to overcome her anxiety. The doctor was very concerned about the high dosage and was agreeable to make a plan to taper Anne off. Because Anne had been on Xanax for so long and was on such a high dosage, the doctor was worried that Anne could have seizures and die while coming off. A plan was constructed for the doctor to gradually take her off with Charles and Mike both going to the home two times per week to monitor her withdrawal symptoms. Anne herself saw the doctor every Friday for additional monitoring. To prevent seizures, Klonipin was substituted for the Xanax. She was gradually switched from Xanax to Klonipin, then gradually taken off Klonipin. The entire process, which ended with Anne medication free, took nine months. As she got off the medications and got out of the house doing more normal things, her mood and confidence improved. Because she was coming off the medications, improvement in her anxiety symptoms could be attributed to Anne herself overcoming her fears, not to medications. It allowed Anne to take ownership of the change.

TRAUMA NARRATIVE

Over a period of months, Anne told Mike and Charles her trauma narrative in segments. Beginning at age 12, her father had his male friends come to the house. The men would drink and get drunk. After drinking, the father's friends would pay him money to have sex with Anne. Her father would also have sex with her in positions in which they would not face each other. This went on for years. The drunken gatherings would occur approximately once a month when Anne's mother would stay with her own mother for a weekend. Anne lived in terrible fear of the weekends her mother went away. Anne's father threatened that if she ever told her mother he would hurt Anne and her mother. It was unclear if the mother knew what was happening.

When a senior in high school Anne went to a party with other high school–aged teens. At the party, she was raped by one of the boys. Anne told her mother about this rape. Her mother believed her and took her to the doctor. The doctor examined her for sexually transmitted diseases and did a pregnancy test. Anne was then referred to a psychiatrist who prescribed Xanax. Anne did not want to talk to a counselor about her trauma history. She just ended up taking Xanax. To make sure no one ever harmed her again, Anne's mother stopped her weekend visits with her mother. The sex abuse by her father and his friends then stopped.

INTERACTIONAL PATTERNS: WEAK BOUNDARIES BETWEEN ANNE AND HER FATHER

When Mike and Charles met Anne, her mother had died. Her father was still alive and tormented her. One trigger to Anne's trauma symptoms was the lack of boundaries between her father and her family. Her father would come over to the home unannounced and walk in without knocking. He would randomly drive his truck by the house and make sure he was noticed. When these things happened, Anne would hide in her bedroom, dissociate, or have flashbacks. Both she and Andy were afraid to set limits on Anne's father. They had the belief that he had murdered people. Charles and Mike began to believe this also and were themselves afraid to suggest the couple set limits on Anne's father.

The consultant was concerned the murderer idea was just a frame, not a fact. Mike and Charles were seeing it as a fact. It was suggested that they do a background check on Anne's father. They discovered the worst crimes Anne's father had ever been charged with were traffic violations. Charles and Mike were now convinced that it was a frame, not a fact, that Anne's father was a murderer. They told the couple the father had only been accused of traffic violations. Andy became convinced it was safe to set limits on his father-in-law. Andy explained to Anne's father that he could only come over if he called first and was told it was OK. He was told to stop driving by in his truck and making a ruckus. Anne's father followed this new rule, and no one was murdered. Creating this boundary helped Anne to become more relaxed at home. Prior to this she lived in fear that her father could intrude at any time.

IMPROVING THE COUPLES' RELATIONSHIP: SEX THERAPY

Anne's trauma symptoms interfered with sex between her and her husband. When her husband requested sex in a way that reminded her of her past, she would have flashbacks, shake, and cry. Eventually the couple had no sex, and the husband became more and more addicted to pornography.

The last item on Anne's desensitization list was sex with her husband. Anne wanted to reconnect with her husband sexually. Andy was enthused about the goal of reconnecting with his wife sexually. To start, Andy was persuaded to burn all his pornography. Next, the couple was asked to practice being civil and affectionate with each other. They were asked to not worry about having sex for a while. They had to learn how to trust each other first. Andy was asked to give Anne a back rub twice a week with all clothes on. Once Andy attempted to put his hands under her shirt but Anne stopped him and he complied. Charles then had to scold Andy for not following the procedure. From then on, Andy followed the procedures.

After the back rubs, Charles and Mike educated the couple on the Master's and Johnson's technique of sensate focus. The consultant had experience using this procedure. In the consultant's experience, the procedure often acted as a restraint from change in which couples respond by spontaneously reconnecting sexually. The couple were instructed to get in the nude and learn how each one liked to be touched in any area other than sexual organs. Initially, Anne would not do the procedure and asked Andy to go into the bathroom and masturbate. Charles then had to scold Anne for not following the procedure. The couple did stick with the procedure and, as expected, after a few times following it, they spontaneously reconnected sexually. They could have sex in multiple positions without Anne having flashbacks. Andy's mood and self-esteem improved greatly after being able to have a normal sex life with his wife. Anne was extremely proud of herself for learning to have a sex life with her husband. Her self-esteem improved greatly. As the parents' sex life improved, the mood of the house became more cheerful, and the daughter's mood went from depressed and morose to happy and cheerful.

MOTIVATING THE HUSBAND TO WORK AGAIN

After months of improvements in functioning with everyone in the home, Andy volunteered to Mike that he had a doctor's appointment to sign up for long-term disability income. Mike replied, "Andy, you are 32 years old. If you go on disability at your age it is over for you. You will never get off the couch." Andy became angry and insisted he was keeping the appointment. Mike left the session worrying he had pushed Andy too hard and would be fired. In the next appointment, however, Andy had completely reversed himself. He had decided to cancel his appointment for the disability application and had begun looking for work. He thanked Mike for confronting him. His self-esteem had improved dramatically as a result of this decision. He was an auto mechanic by trade before his father died. He did go back to work, initially finding work as a mechanic. One year later, he had his own automobile mechanic business.

TERMINATING

Andy was not on disability and back to work instead. Cindy was back to school and having a normal social life for a girl her age. Anne was able to leave the house and do normal activities with no anxiety. Anne was completely off all medications. The couple were reconnected sexually. Anne was having no PTSD symptoms, and Anne had a normal boundary with her father. After one year, it was time for Charles and Mike to end services. The family were having a hard time letting them go. Mike and Charles then created images of themselves on the video game the family played. They now joined the family as additional characters in the video game. They were both waving hello. Anne and Andy could visit Mike and Charles anytime they wanted on the video game.

SUMMARY

This case again illustrates how a parent, seriously impaired by her own trauma history, who had rejected trauma treatment for herself, would cooperate in treatment that benefited her if it was in the interest of helping her child. The mother would engage in a treatment intended to help her child while simultaneously focusing on her own impairment.

This case also illustrates the flexibility of I-FAST on a procedural level. Procedures from other models such as systematic desensitization and sensate focus were integrated into this treatment. They could be integrated into I-FAST by utilizing them to change interactional patterns. To change how the couple were interacting with each other, the husband was included in the implementation of the systematic desensitization. Sensate focus was also utilized to change how the couple were interacting. The case is one more example of how improving the quality of family relationships impacts trauma symptoms. The disengaged husband became closer emotionally to his wife and daughter. The wife, with all her severe trauma symptoms, improved in part due to the improved quality of her relationship with her husband and with her daughter.

FAMILY RESPONSES TO IMPROVEMENT

When a presenting problem is resolved, there are many ways family can respond to improvement. One response is that everyone acknowledges improvement, is pleased, and ready to terminate services. Another response is that improvement is not acknowledged. Treatment then has to focus on helping family agree that improvement has happened. A less common response to improvement, but one that does occur and has been reported in the classic family therapy literature (Haley, 1980; Stanton & Todd, 1982), is that the patient gets out of the patient category, but then another family member goes in to the patient category. Someone improves but then someone else decompensates. When this last response to change happens, it can be thought of as the family having problems adjusting to the patient no longer being in the role of patient. In any organization, a change of role requires multiple changes on multiple levels. For a family, these changes may become very difficult to make especially if changes occur rapidly. The following case is an example of this last response to improvement.

"You Don't Lose Your Memory"

INITIAL PRESENTING PROBLEM

Brenda was a 38-year-old single mother of one child, 13-year-old Keith. Keith's father had never been involved. Brenda's parents were deceased. She had an older brother with whom she had minimal contact and a younger sister who had a child Keith's age, with whom Brenda did interact. The therapist, Marilyn Hartline, soon learned from Brenda that she had a horrific history of sexual assault. Brenda's father died when she was six. She grew up with her mother and her two siblings. Brenda's mother was a severe alcoholic. The family always needed money. When Brenda turned 13, her mother began prostituting her to obtain money for her alcohol addiction. The sexual abuses continued until Brenda left home at age 18 when she married. After escaping her mother, Brenda then divorced at the age of 20. A result of all this abuse was that Brenda became very withdrawn and avoidant of social relationships. She avoided all relationships with men. She also had no interest in women friends. She had no life outside of work and her son Keith. She functioned well at work and was a very reliable employee. But she came straight home from work every day and was a devoted mother to Keith. She only interacted with her younger sister and occasionally had her nephew for overnight visits because he and Keith were close. Brenda was also very protective of Keith. She rarely allowed him to associate with his friends. She was busy keeping herself and her son safe from a dangerous world.

ESTABLISHING ALLIANCES AND TREATMENT GOALS

Brenda was not requesting help on trauma. Brenda sought services for her son, describing him as defiant and rebellious. Keith was sneaking out of the house at night, smoking marijuana, and failing many subjects in school.

INTERACTIONAL PATTERNS

The interactional patterns between Brenda and Keith were characterized by enmeshment. Brenda considered Keith her best friend. She also treated Keith like a small child. She still tied his shoes, ran his bath water and cut his meat and spaghetti at the dinner table. The most dramatic sign of enmeshment was that Brenda and Keith still slept together. Keith was ahead of schedule in his physical development. He was almost six feet tall and had already grown hair on his chest. Brenda rarely issued consequences for Keith's misbehavior, and when she did, Keith could quickly talk her out of them. By respecting Brenda's wish to focus on her son and not on her trauma background, Marilyn was able to establish a very strong therapeutic relationship with Brenda. Brenda became very receptive to suggestions regarding parenting Keith.

CHANGING PATTERNS AND RESOLVING INITIAL COMPLAINTS

Marilyn worked for numerous sessions helping Brenda set and stick to consequences. Marilyn helped Brenda treat Keith like a 13-year-old. The shoe-tying, meat-cutting, and bath water running all stopped. Marilyn pointed out that during the night, Keith could have an embarrassing "accident." Brenda understood this meant Keith could have a wet dream. She had never thought of this possibility. Once given this idea, Brenda had Keith sleep in his own bed. Marilyn also helped Brenda allow Keith to do normal activities with his friends when he behaved appropriately. Keith responded very positively to this. Finally, Marilyn helped Brenda have more boundaries with Keith. Instead of talking to Keith as a friend, Marilyn helped Brenda have these types of talks with her sister. Keith responded by settling down completely. His grades improved in school, he stopped smoking marijuana, and since he was now allowed to associate with friends away from home, he stopped sneaking out at night. All these changes and new boundaries meant Brenda no longer needed to be so devoted to Keith. She had to pull away from him emotionally. He could no longer be her best friend. He could no longer be the center of her whole life outside of work. This meant that Brenda now had a very empty life. Once Brenda no longer needed to function in a role that required total devotion to Keith, she began reporting bazar occurrences.

ADJUSTING TO CHANGE

Things were happening that Brenda could not explain. She began discovering that her car was not parked where she left it the night before. In the morning it was parked on the street, not in the driveway. She began to keep track of the odometer and in the morning discovered 50 miles would be added. She suspected that Keith was sneaking out again but quickly eliminated that possibility. Then things got more bazar. Every evening Brenda dressed in her pajamas and went to bed at 9:00 PM. One morning she woke up and was not in her pajamas. She was wearing a red dress. She was also not under the covers. When she took a shower, she discovered a bruise on her neck as if someone had kissed her. She discovered a man's name and phone number on her match book. A few nights later, she went to bed at 9:00 PM. The next thing she knew it was 1:00 AM, and she was in a bar, in her red dress, sitting next to a man. She asked the man how long she had been there. The man was confused and said she had been talking with him for the last hour.

Brenda realized she was driving the car at night. She was frightened by this. To prevent herself from leaving at night, she gave her car keys to her neighbor with instructions to not give them back until morning even if she asked for them. To prevent herself from "sleepwalking," she put bells up on the doors, thinking if she tried to go out, the bells would arouse her.

FOCUSING DIRECTLY ON THE PARENT'S PROBLEM

Brenda told this to Marilyn. All these events happened after Keith had improved. Many child treatment programs are designed to help children improve and then terminate services. If a family member struggles after the child client improves, the parent is often referred for adult services. In I-FAST, we encourage more flexibility. Especially in the case of parents impaired by trauma histories. If focusing on the child gains the parent's trust, and then the parent is referred to someone else for adult services, an opportunity to help that parent may be lost. I-FAST advocates that the original clinician remain involved and help the parent with their problems. This is what Marilyn did.

Marilyn asked Brenda if she had an explanation for the bazar events. Brenda did. As a child she was soft spoken, shy, and unassertive. When her mother began to abuse her, these traits were not helpful. She invented an imaginary persona named Tabitha. Tabitha was assertive and did not stand for abuse. When Brenda was in situations in which she needed to be assertive, she called herself "Tabitha" and stood up for herself. As a child, she was always aware of what she was doing when she "became" Tabitha. When she got away from her mother, she no longer assumed the role of Tabitha. Brenda's theory of what was happening now was that Tabitha had developed a life of her own, was taking over her body and going out at night. Brenda explained, "I thought I was finished with Tabitha, but she is in my memory. You don't lose your memory."

Brenda was describing herself as having dissociative identity disorder, what in earlier times was diagnosed as multiple personality disorder. Although multiple personality disorder is now less common, what is not uncommon is an adult parent, severely impaired by their trauma history, who seeks treatment for something other than their trauma history. In a broader sense, this is a common case.

Brenda had had no previous therapy where she might have gotten exposed to the idea of multiple personalities. She was terrified of what was happening to her. She told no one but Marilyn. She was not acquiring what Freud would term "secondary gains" from her symptoms, that is, special treatment or privileges. Marilyn was at first skeptical. Brenda mentioned that when she was in high school, Tabitha wrote love letters to boys. Brenda still had some examples. At Marilyn's request, she brought them in. Marilyn was astonished to discover that the letters were not in Brenda's handwriting. Marilyn then consulted with David Grove on the case.

AN OVERARCHING FRAME AND DEVISING A TREATMENT STRATEGY

Grove was consulting with Jay Haley at the time (Grove, 1993; Grove & Haley, 1993). Haley described a Milton Erickson method for working with multiple personality clients. Erickson treated 22 multiple personality clients. Erickson did not approach the problem of two personalities as pathological but as a natural condition of the client. He framed the problem as two personalities occupying the same body and not agreeing on how to conduct their daily lives. Typically, one personality avoided the other. Treatment procedures involved getting the two personalities to interact with each other and reach compromises on how to organize their daily lives. This method fits into I-FAST on several levels. First, it focuses on interactional patterns between the personalities and aims at changing those patterns. Instead of avoiding each other, they must interact. Second, the focus of the treatment ends up on clear behavioral goals that each personality wants to focus on. Instead of focusing on how many personalities there may be or on personalities fusing, goals common for multiple personality treatments, in this method, goals each personality want to focus on are pursued. Treatment ends up being about what type of man to date or how they should dress. These are specific behavioral goals that are especially important in a case of multiple personalities. These clients' inner lives can be so complex a therapist can easily get lost in the mind of such a client. The therapy can lack a focus that does not have clear behavioral goals.

ESTABLISHING NEW GOALS AND FORMING AN ALLIANCE WITH TABITHA

This strategy was adopted for Brenda and Tabitha. We knew what Brenda was upset about. She did not want to do anything she was not consciously aware of. She did not want to pick up men in bars and have sex with them. She wanted to sleep through the night in the comfort of her own bed. To follow Erickson's approach, Marilyn would have to meet Tabitha and find out what her goals were. (Note: For a detailed discussion on the clinical procedures employed for meeting Tabitha and for helping Brenda and Tabitha communicate with each other, see Grove, 1991; Grove & Haley, 1992.)

With Brenda's consent, Marilyn met with Tabitha. Brenda wore glasses. She was severely near-sighted. She could not see across the room without her glasses. When Tabitha came, she immediately removed the glasses proclaiming, "I hate these darn things." Without her glasses, Brenda said she "was blind as a dingo bat." Tabitha, on the other hand, was driving at night with no glasses. In her first meeting with Marilyn, Tabitha proclaimed that Brenda did not tell her everything. She told Marilyn a story of a night in which the mother was physically abusive. Marilyn confirmed Brenda had not told the story. Tabitha then observed that although neither she nor Brenda knew why, after that night they both believed Brenda's mother hated her.

Tabitha listed several of her complaints. Brenda was overweight and Tabitha complained bitterly about that. She said, "When I was in charge of our body, we did not have a weight problem." She complained, "It is hard to pick up guys with a body like this." Marilyn said, "Can you understand why Brenda put on weight? She did not want her mother to prostitute her." Tabitha said, "Yes but I have my needs too." Tabitha was also very upset that Brenda did not let her come out anymore. Without even knowing it, Brenda was "pushing me (Tabitha) away."

When asked what Tabitha wanted Brenda to change, she said, "We are opposites. She is a homebody. I like to go out. I like men and sex. She wants nothing to do with men. I want her to lose weight, and she wants to stay large." Tabitha explained, "She leads a boring life." Brenda was indeed bored and lonely. Boredom could be described as stimulus deprivation. All types of symptoms can arise out of stimulus and social deprivation. Since giving up her devotion to Keith, Brenda did not know what to do with herself. Now Tabitha was coming, possibly to address those issues. The goals of both Tabitha and Brenda were now clear. The issues they needed to compromise on were clear. What should their bodily appearance be? What role should men play in their life? What should they do with their free time? These goals fit I-FAST.

IDENTIFYING PATTERNS

In the next session, Marilyn explained that Tabitha had come and was angry about several things. Brenda became upset at the idea that Tabitha was angry with her. Brenda said, "She is just my imagination! She is just a teenage girl's imaginary person! I just want to get rid of her." Brenda's habitual way of dealing with Tabitha was to "push her away." Brenda was avoiding Tabitha. Instead of having nightmares or flashbacks or intrusive thoughts, Brenda had Tabitha. Tabitha was her trauma symptom. Instead of avoiding anything that might trigger a nightmare or intrusive thought, Brenda was avoiding Tabitha. Erickson's procedure of having the two personalities talk would require Brenda to be "exposed" to Tabitha. She had to be exposed to what she was avoiding. This would require some persuasion on Marilyn's part, but as with many trauma clients, if they are willing to face what they are avoiding, major changes can ensue.

OFFERING REFRAMES AND CHANGING PATTERNS

A change in Brenda's interactional pattern with Tabitha would be for her to interact with her and reach agreements on the day-to-day issues they differed on. This would require Brenda to change how she was framing Tabitha. Marilyn offered her a reframe. Marilyn suggested that Tabitha's existence represented a special ability that Brenda had. To create Tabitha required a "special ability." In addition, Tabitha's purpose originally was to help Brenda survive. Brenda agreed with all of this. Marilyn suggested that instead of trying to get rid of Tabitha, Brenda should accept her. Brenda said she never looked at it that way. She agreed maybe she should accept Tabitha. Marilyn proposed to help Brenda and Tabitha talk directly to each other. Although she found this idea difficult, Brenda agreed. Brenda told Marilyn, "I trust you. That is all that matters." Clearly, it would have been an error to transfer this case.

Brenda and Tabitha did talk directly in the next session. They argued about men. Brenda asked why Tabitha picked up men. Tabitha spelled out the word, "HORNEY!" The interaction itself was comical, but the topic was very serious. Marilyn stated that a major issue between them was what role men should play in their lives. Marilyn gave the assignment for them to continue this discussion before the next session and try to reach an agreement.

TRACKING EXCEPTIONS

Brenda returned to the next session having made major changes. She had changed her hair style and color. She now wore contact lenses not her glasses. She explained that she and Tabitha had had many talks and had reached many agreements. They agreed Brenda should change her appearance and lose weight. Brenda explained, "We decided I need to go back to who I was originally. This is my natural hair color. I am going to lose weight. For me to become me, I have to go back to who I was before. I cannot hide under weight or hair color."

Marilyn asked Brenda if there was anything she might be avoiding that Tabitha might know. Brenda said yes. Tabitha had told her to go back to the night Brenda made Tabitha. All her answers were there. Brenda then remembered a terrible night when she was 13. She and her two siblings were all home. Her mother came home drunk and tried to kill her. Her mother looked at her "with such hatred in her eyes." She told Brenda, "I will see you dead before the night is through." Indeed, her mother made what Brenda interpreted as three attempts to kill her that night. Brenda said she only weighed 120 pounds. She was not big or strong enough to fend her mother off. The weight was not just there to deter men. The three children had to survive a night in which they all believed their mother intended to murder them. Finally, Brenda and her older brother subdued their mother. Brenda barricaded herself in her room for the rest of the night with all the abuse she had endured up to that point rushing back to her. Brenda said, "After all of the years of sexual abuse, after being called stupid, and being told repeatedly that she hates you, to have her then try to kill you not once but three times. That has an effect." Tabitha told Marilyn that she was not going to leave Brenda alone until Brenda faced that night.

This was Brenda's index trauma. The narrative attached to it was that her mother hated her. As Tabitha pointed out earlier, both Tabitha and Brenda believed the mother hated Brenda and both were unsure why. Clearly, a reframe was needed to address this very upsetting belief. Before a reframe could be offered, Marilyn had to take six weeks off work for medical problems. After Brenda and Tabitha had begun to interact, Tabitha agreed she would not leave the house. Brenda no longer was terrified of this possibility and was no longer giving her wallet and car keys to her neighbor. Brenda's situation no longer seemed urgent. It was decided to postpone a next meeting with Brenda until after Marilyn returned to work.

REINFORCING AND CONSOLIDATING CHANGE

Six weeks later Brenda returned. Further dramatic changes had occurred. She had lost weight—around 10 pounds. She had gone back to adult education and passed a test for her high school diploma. Most important, she decided her mother did not hate her. After remembering the terrible night, Brenda went on a mission to try to understand her mother. She interviewed all of her surviving relatives. She learned her mother was very bitter that her husband, Brenda's father, had died and left her alone to raise three children. Brenda's mother hated Brenda's father. Brenda also learned that she looked just like her father and reminded her mother of her father. Brenda had decided to change her interactional patterns with her relatives. Instead of avoiding them, she sought them out and interviewed them about her mother. When she broke this pattern, she learned new frames. Brenda decided that when her mother looked at her that night with hatred in her eyes, she did not see Brenda, she saw Brenda's father. Brenda's mother hated her father, not her. This idea gave Brenda peace of mind. After realizing this, she visited her mother's grave for the first time since her mother had died, 10 years earlier. After all this progress, we decided to set the next appointment for two months, to see what Brenda could accomplish in that amount of time.

Two months past and Brenda returned for the seventh and last session since the focus shifted to her amnesia episodes. Brenda had lost an additional 10 pounds. Her appearance had changed dramatically. She had now enrolled in a community college. She would become the first person in her family to obtain a college degree. When asked about men, she told of the compromise she and Tabitha had reached. They decided Brenda would have a man friend. He would be a friend, not a sexual partner. Tabitha agreed. This was a half-way point between avoiding men altogether and picking up strangers and having sex with them. Brenda had, in fact, met a man with whom she had become friends and was socializing with regularly. Tabitha was brought in one last time. She was satisfied with all the compromises made. She said Brenda was no longer bored or lonely. When asked what would become of her now, Tabitha explained, "I will be a voice in the back of Brenda's mind."

CONCLUSION

In this chapter, four cases of severely traumatized parents seeking help for their child were presented. All had endured serial sexual assaults from a family member, with some enduring serial gang rape and later domestic partner violence. All were seriously impaired by trauma symptoms. All had rejected treatment focusing on those symptoms. Instead of referring the parents to their own individual treatment and working with their child individually, a trauma-informed approach was offered of respecting their wish to help their child and including the parent in this treatment. In each case, the parent's trust was won by respecting their choices. This ultimately led to a treatment that did indeed resolve their trauma symptoms. The cases all illustrate the flexibility of I-FAST at adapting to client choices. They illustrate how to integrate intervention procedures from various approaches into I-FAST. Procedures from any approach can be used in I-FAST if those procedures serve the goal of changing interactional patterns associated with problems clients wish help on. In each case, parent goals were respected, overarching frames were constructed that utilized family beliefs, interactional patterns related to the problems were tracked and changed, and intervention procedures that made sense to the trauma survivor were offered.

RESEARCH

IV

SUPPORTING EVIDENCE FOR I-FAST TREATMENT OF TRAUMA

14

Mo Yee Lee, Xiafei Wang, and Pamela Scott

Integrative family and systems treatment (I-FAST) is initially developed as a home-based treatment for at-risk children and adolescents with diagnoses from the *Diagnostic and Statistical Manual of Mental Disorders* (DSM; American Psychiatric Association, 2013) to prevent out-of-home placement. Currently, I-FAST has been expanded to be used in outpatient mental health settings with both children and adult populations who have mental health and substance use problems. Efficacy of I-FAST has primarily been established for children and adolescents. Five published studies have been conducted on different aspects of I-FAST focusing on its efficacy on child- and family-level outcomes, role of systems collaborations, and I-FAST training model in treatment efficacy. Table 14.1 summarize findings of these studies.

In addition to the evidence of I-FAST on improving child outcomes, this chapter describes two studies to further provide supporting evidence for I-FAST trauma treatment. The first study examined the impact of I-FAST on family functioning. Chapter 3 of this volume clearly highlights the important role of family environment in trauma treatment. As discussed, family support outweighs other protective factors in preventing or minimizing posttraumatic stress disorder (PTSD). In addition, family support moderates the development of PTSD after traumatic experience. For children exposed to trauma, a nurturing family environment can have healing and positive effects on their brain development (Ludy-Dobson & Perry, 2010). The second study explored the impact of I-FAST on breaking the cycle of intergenerational transmission of trauma from the perspective of families who had received I-FAST treatment.

STUDY 1: EFFICACY OF I-FAST ON FAMILY FUNCTIONING

This is part of a larger study that examined I-FAST efficacy on child-, family-, and systems-levels outcomes. The study was funded by two state departments in Midwest from 2014 to 2018. This study only focused on efficacy of I-FAST on family functioning. We hypothesized that effective I-FAST treatment would lead to improved family functioning in the dimensions of family cohesiveness and family adaptability, family communication, and family satisfaction. This study was approved by the institutional review board of a university in a Midwestern state.

Research Participants

Research participants were from a mental health agency in a Midwestern state that serves five counties. Participating families were all low-income families with treatment costs covered by Medicaid and other public funds. The court, Children's Services, hospitals, or other mental health agencies referred families to the programs.

Table 14.1.

SUMMARY OF FINDINGS OF PUBLISHED STUDIES ON I-FAST

Citations	Research Design and Purpose	Samples	Reporting Sources	Measurements	Results
Lee et al. (2009)	Single-group longitudinal design with 3-assessment points at pretreatment, posttreatment, and 6-month follow-up to examine I-FAST efficacy on child- and family-level outcomes	77 families with children who had DSM diagnoses	• Parents • Children 12 or above • Case managers	The Ohio Scales (Ogles et al., 2001) • Problem severity • Functioning FACES II • Family cohesion • Family adaptability Parental Competence Family Participation Systems Collaboration Scale (Lee & Greene, 2002)	Paired-sample *t* tests, repeated measures, analysis of variance, and Wilcoxon signed-rank tests indicated the following findings: • Significant decrease in child's level of problem severity from pretreatment to posttreatment • Significant increase in child's level of functioning from pretreatment to posttreatment as measured • Significant increase in parental competence to address their children's issues • Significant improvement in family functioning in terms of family cohesion and adaptability • Significant decrease in the number of children in out-of-home placement • Consistently high level of family participation in treatment Children maintained positive changes that had made at the time of termination at six-month follow-up
Lee et al. (2012)	Qualitative study to explore I-FAST process and skill components involved in systems collaboration	26 agency collaborators across 11 counties in a Midwestern state	• School: 14 • Court: 5 • Children Services: 4 • Parent visitation center: 1 • Domestic violence shelter: 1 • MRDD staff: 1	Eight focus groups	Qualitative findings highlighted the process of developing collaboration, which consisted of making initial contact, a trial period and developing trust, and the key ingredients of collaboration, which focused on interpersonal and professional qualities.

Lee, Greene, Fraser, Grove et al. (2013)	Noninferiority trial to compare treatment efficacy of I-FAST and MST	79 youth who have received I-FAST and 47 youth who have received MST	• Parents • Children 12 or above, • Case managers	The Ohio Scales (Ogles et al., 2001) • Problem severity • Functioning	Using noninferiority test and a noninferiority margin 15%, I-FAST is not inferior to MST in reducing problem severity and improving functioning in youth clients based on parents, youth, and I-FAST case managers' reports. I-FAST was superior to MST in reducing problem severity and functioning in youth based on youth assessments, and superior to MST in improving functioning based on workers' assessments.
Lee, Teater, et al. (2013)	Structural equation model to examine how systems collaboration with schools influenced child- and family-level outcomes.	38 child clients with DSM diagnoses who had received I-FAST service	• Parents, • Children 12 or above, • Case managers	The Ohio Scales (Ogles et al., 2001) • Problem severity • Functioning Parental Competence Systems Collaboration Scale (Lee & Greene, 2002)	Final SEM model accounted for 31% of the variance in problem severity, 38% of the variance in level of functioning, 30% of the variance in parental competence with children, and 41% of the variance in family functioning. Final SEM model indicated systems collaboration with schools positively influenced parental competence with children, which positively predicted the level of functioning in children and negatively predicted problem severity in children.
Lee et al. (2015)	Quasi-experimental design to examine efficacy of I-FAST training model on clients' treatment outcomes	63 clients in one undertraining agency that received ongoing consultation and 147 clients in an I-FAST agency that received no ongoing consultation	• Parents, • Children 12 or above, • Case managers	The Ohio Scales (Ogles et al., 2001) • Problem severity • Functioning	Chi-square analyses and independent samples *t* test analyses indicated no significant differences between the client outcomes of the two agencies who had achieved reliable change on problem severity and functioning based on parents' assessments.

Notes: FACES II, Family Adaptability and Cohesion Scale; DSM, *Diagnostic and Statistical Manual of Mental Disorders*; I-FAST, integrative family and systems treatment; MRDD, Mental Retardation and Developmental Disabilities; MST, multisystemic therapy; SEM, structural equation model.

Eighty families completed I-FAST treatment and provided data at pretreatment, six-week assessment, and termination. Among the 80 children, 38.8% were males ($n = 31$) and 61.3% females ($n = 49$). The majority of participants were students at elementary school (39.5%) and high schools (31.6%) while 14.5% middle schools and 14.5% were in kindergartens or preschools. Child participants were predominantly White (92.5%), with 3.8% Hispanic/Latino Americans, 1.3% Native Americans, and 2.5% biracial. The ages of the children ranged from 3 to 26 (mean 11.4, SD 4.6). Mental status examination was conducted by licensed mental health professionals. Using the fourth edition of the *Diagnostic and Statistical Manual of Mental Disorders* (American Psychiatric Association, 2000) criteria, the majority of participants had a diagnosis of mood disorders (43.6%). In addition, participants had the following diagnoses: attention-deficit/hyperactivity disorder (15.4%), adjustment disorder (12.8%), bipolar disorder (10.3%), oppositional defiant disorder (5.1%), conduct and disruptive disorder (5.1%), PTSD (5.1%), and developmental disorder (2.6%).

Treatment Fidelity

Treatment fidelity was measured by the I-FAST Checklist, which is a 67-item measure that assesses core treatment components of I-FAST: Creating Alliance (items 1–34, including Engagement, 1–11; tracking interactional pattern, 12–15; tracking interactional exception, 16–17; problem definition, 18–24; and goal consensus, 15–34), Facilitating Change (item 35–54, including developing frames, 35–40; developing procedures, 41–46; and systems collaboration, 47–54), and Tracking Change, Building Resilience, and Closing (item 55–67 including tracking change, 55–61, and building resilience and closing, 62–67). The I-FAST clinical consultant who provided regular biweekly consultation to the participating case managers/therapists rated the adherence and competence of the interventions of each core treatment component on a 5-point Likert scale: absence (0), a few (1), some (2), always, (3), and a lot (4). The I-FAST Checklist was scored by summing individual items and averaging the total score by the number of applicable items with higher mean scores indicating greater adherence to and competence of the assessed skills when implementing I-FAST by participating case managers/therapists.

Measurements

The study used the Family Adaptability and Cohesion Scale (FACES IV) to assess family functioning in terms of cohesion and flexibility, family communication, and family satisfaction (Olson, 1985; Olson & Gorall, 2006). FACES IV comprises six subscales (42 items), in addition to the family communication subscale (10 items) and the family satisfaction scale (10 items), for a total of 62 items (Olson & Gorall, 2006). It assesses the dimensions of family cohesion and family flexibility based on the circumplex model (Olson, Russell, & Sprenkle, 1980, 1983). All family members over the age of 12 are eligible to complete the FACES IV. Respondents are requested to rate how frequently the described behavior occurs in his or her family on a 5-point Likert scale that ranges from 1 (almost never) to 5 (almost always).

FAMILY COHESION AND FAMILY FLEXIBILITY

The 42-item scale that assesses the dimension of family cohesion and family flexibility consists of six 7-item subscales. There are two balanced scales (balanced cohesion and balanced flexibility) and four unbalanced scales (disengaged, enmeshed, rigid, and chaotic). The cohesion dimension score and flexibility dimension score are calculated based on the scores of these six subscales and range from zero to 100. Specifically, a percentile score of zero to 15 indicates "disengaged"; 16 to 35, "somewhat connected"; 36 to 65, "connected"; 68 to 85, "very connected"; and 86 to 100, "enmeshed" on the cohesion dimension. A percentile score of 1 to 15 indicates "rigid"; 16 to 35 "somewhat flexible"; 36 to 65 "flexible"; 68 to 85 "very flexible"; and 86 to 100 "chaotic" on the flexibility dimension. Olson, Gorall, and Tiesel (2007) reported satisfactory Cronbach's alpha of 0.77 to 0.89 for the subscales measuring family cohesion and adaptability. Good concurrent and discriminant validity was also established for FACES IV (Olson et al., 2007).

FAMILY COMMUNICATION

Family Communication is a 10-item scale that is developed based on the Parent–Adolescent Communication Scale, which is a 20-item scale developed to measure communication in families with an adolescent (Barnes & Olson, 1982, 1985; Olson & Barnes, 2007). The raw score of the Family Communication Scale ranges from 10 to 50 that can be transformed into a percentile score with higher score indicating higher level of family communication. Using the percentile scores, there are five levels of family communication: very low (10–20), low (21–35), moderate (36–60), high (61–85), and very high (86–99). The mean raw score for this scale is 36.2 (SD 9.0) based on a national sample of 2,465. The internal consistency reliability of the scale is 0.90 with a test–retest coefficient of 0.86 based on the same national sample (Olson & Barnes, 2007).

FAMILY SATISFACTION

Family Satisfaction is a 10-item scale that is based on a 14-item scale developed by David Olson and Marc Wilson (1982) to assess family members' satisfaction with various aspects of family functioning including family closeness, flexibility, and communication. The score of the Family Satisfaction Scale ranges from 10 to 50 that can be transformed into a percentile score with higher score indicating higher level of satisfaction. Using the percentile scores, there are five levels of family satisfaction: very low (10–18), low (21–35), moderate (40–58), high (66–84), and very high (87–99). The mean raw score for this scale is 37.5 (SD 8.5) based on a national sample of 2,465. The internal consistency reliability of the scale is 0.92 with a test–retest coefficient of 0.85 based on the same national sample (Olson, 2007).

Data Analyses

Data collected from various instruments were checked and coded for data processing and statistical analyses. The Statistical Package for Social Sciences was used for this purpose. Regarding treatment fidelity, the study used descriptive analyses to assess the level of adherence and competency of I-FAST skills as demonstrated by case managers and therapists when providing I-FAST treatment. The study used repeated measures analysis of variance to assess the within-subject changes during the three assessments of pretreatment, six-week assessment, and termination (or six months whatever come earlier). To address the problem of attrition, we had used multiple imputation method to simulate value for the missing assessments to reduce the adverse effect of missing observations in the data analyses (Allison, 2000). When there were two valid assessments, we imputed the

Table 14.2.

I-FAST FIDELITY (*N* = 10)

Treatment Component	N	Mean	SD
Total scale	***10***	***3.43***	***0.23***
Creating Alliance	**10**	**3.50**	**0.19**
Engagement	10	3.62	0.17
Tracking interactional patterns	10	3.76	0.24
Tracking interactional exceptions	10	3.23	0.36
Problem definition	10	3.44	0.21
Goal consensus	10	3.44	0.19
Facilitating Change	**10**	**3.44**	**0.27**
Developing frames	10	3.35	0.38
Developing procedures	10	3.34	0.26
Systems collaboration	10	3.59	0.27
Tracking Change, Building Resilience and Closing	**8**	**3.26**	**0.32**
Tracking change	8	3.28	0.32
Building resilience and closing	8	3.23	0.33

Notes: Mean fidelity scores for clinicians as rated by expert consultant. I-FAST fidelity is rated from 0 to 4 for each technique or clinician behavior, with higher scores indicating greater use of the specified skill.

Source: I-FAST Fidelity Scale was developed by Mo Yee Lee, Scott Fraser, David Grove, Gilbert J. Greene, and Andy Solovey, 2003, revised 2014.

missing assessment with available valid results of other variables. Details for the imputation were attached at the footnote of Table 14.2 and Table 14.3. We used multiple imputation from SPSS to create five imputed datasets and combined these results to simulate value for the missing observations (Graham, Cumsille, & Elek-Fisk, 2003; Schafer & Olsen, 1998).

FAMILY COHESION

Data were obtained from 72 parents and 30 youth regarding family cohesion at pretreatment, six-week assessment, and termination. Parents in general perceived the family as more cohesive than their children at pretreatment (61.7 vs. 37.3). Specifically, more parents' perceived the family as "connected" and "very connected" while over 20% children perceived the family as only "somewhat connected." In addition, only 3.9% parents perceived the family as disengaged while almost 20% of children perceived the family as "disengaged" Figure 14.1 and 14.2 shows the distribution of families for each family type at pretreatment, six-week assessment, and termination or six months based on parents and youth's reports. Based on parents'

Table 14.3.

DESCRIPTIVE ANALYSIS OF FAMILY COHESION, ADAPTABILITY, COMMUNICATION, AND SATISFACTION PERCENTILE SCORES

	Pretreatment		Six-Week Assessment		Termination (or 6-month)	
	Mean	S.D.	Mean	S.D.	Mean	S.D.
Parent (*N* = 72) Family cohesion	61.86	18.94	60.97	17.18	65.01	14.73
Family adaptability	46.96	11.54	48.53	12.00	49.67	10.10
Family communication	36.00	0.84	36.51	0.86	36.98	0.74
Family satisfaction	31.99	1.16	33.63	1.02	34.62	0.87
Youth (*N* = 30)						
Family cohesion	37.26	25.22	39.80	24.05	44.28	21.67
Family adaptability	39.20	13.72	45.38	14.81	45.46	13.68
Family communication	29.71	1.65	30.38	1.53	33.17	1.41
Family satisfaction	27.55	1.84	29.03	1.84	32.57	1.70

Notes: Parent survey: 52 completed all three assessments; 2 missing in 6-week only, 17 missing in 6-month only

Youth survey: 20 completed all three assessments; 2 missing in pre-assessment only and 8 missing in six-months only

report, more families become very connected from pre-assessment (39.7%) to termination (49.4%).

Findings based on pairwise comparisons indicated there were positive changes in family cohesion from six-week assessment to termination (or six months) based on parents' and youth's reports, and the positive changes were statistically significant based on parents' report.

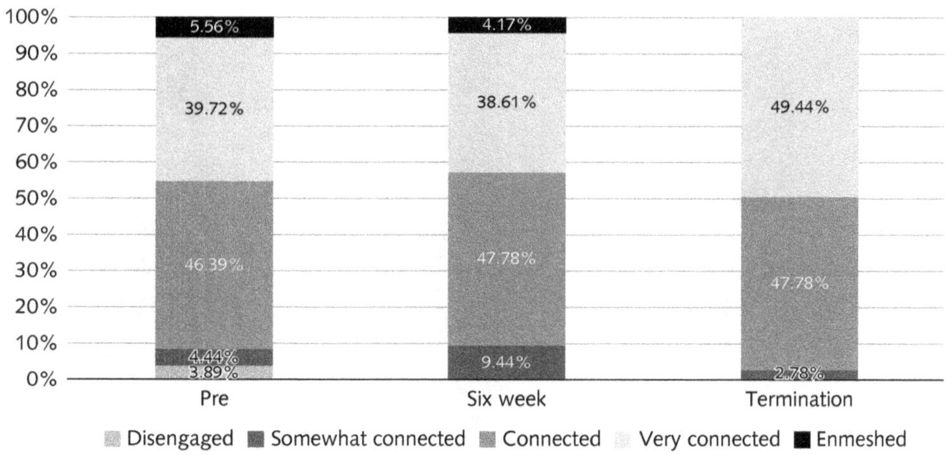

FIGURE 14.1.

PARENTS' PERCEPTIONS OF FAMILY COHESION (*N* = 72).

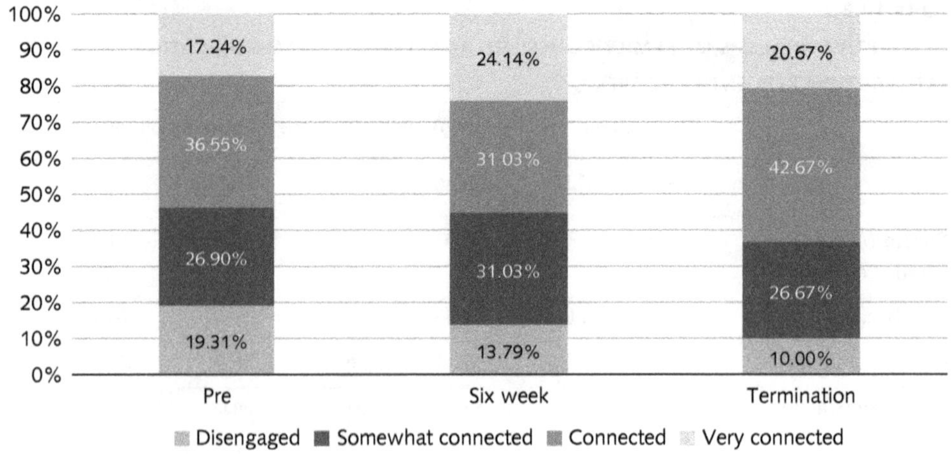

FIGURE 14.2.
YOUTH'S PERCEPTIONS OF FAMILY COHESION ($N = 30$).

FAMILY ADAPTABILITY

Data were obtained from 72 parents and 30 youth at pretreatment, six-week assessment, and termination (or six months). Parents in general perceived the family as more flexible than their children at pretreatment (50.0 vs. 39.2). Specifically, Figure 14.3 and 14.4 shows the distribution of families for each family type at pretreatment, six-week assessment, and six months follow-up based on parents and youth's reports. Based on parents' report, more families become flexible from preassessment (78.3%) to termination (88.3%). Based on youths' report, more families become flexible from preassessment (64.0%) to six-week assessment (73.3%), and termination (78.0%). No families belonged to rigid at six-month assessment, compared with 6.7% in pretreatment and 3.33% at six-week assessment.

Findings based on pairwise comparisons indicated that families showed a trend of becoming more flexible with I-FAST treatment. There were positive changes from pretreatment to six-week assessment to termination (or six months) in family adaptability based on both parents' reports (47.0, 48.5, and 49.7, respectively) and youth's

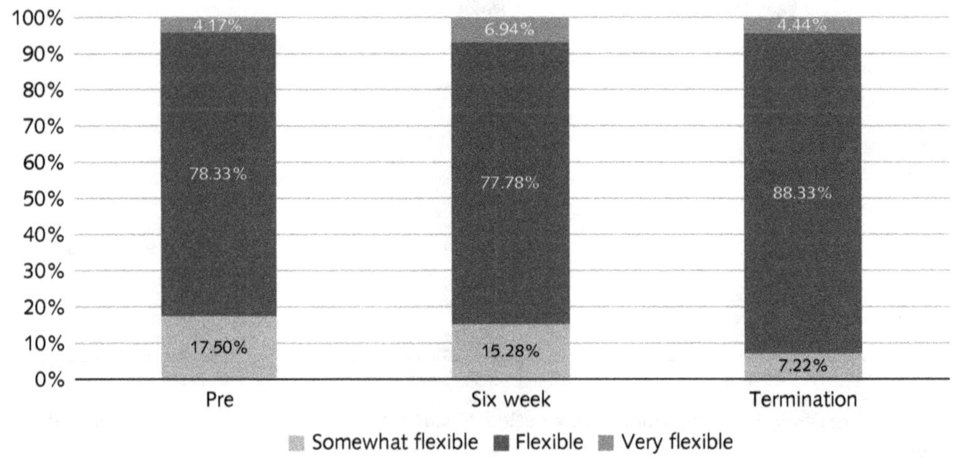

FIGURE 14.3.
PARENTS' PERCEPTIONS OF FAMILY FLEXIBILITY ($N = 72$).

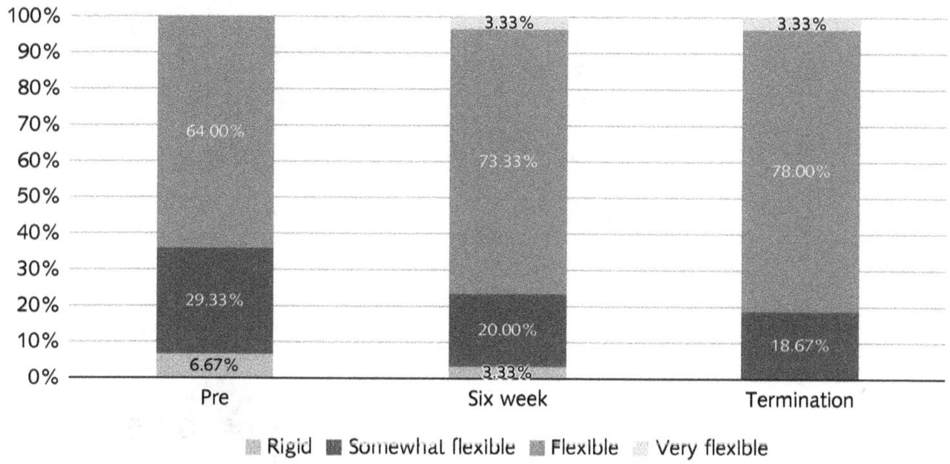

FIGURE 14.4.
YOUTH'S PERCEPTIONS OF FAMILY FLEXIBILITY ($N = 72$).

reports (39.2, 45.4, and 45.5, respectively). In addition, there were statistically significant changes in family adaptability from pretreatment to six-week assessment based on youth's report.

FAMILY COMMUNICATION

Parents and youth appeared to have different assessment of family communication with parents having a more positive evaluation of family communication than youth at pretreatment (36.0 vs. 29.7). The mean score at pretreatment of 36.0 based on parents' report indicated a moderate level of communication; that is, parents generally felt good about their family communication but have some concerns. However, the mean score at pretreatment of 29.7 based on youth's report indicated a low level of family communication, indicating their concerns about the quality of their communication. Despite the low level of family communication at pretreatment, findings based on youth's report showed a positive and significant change in family communication from pretreatment (29.7) to six-week assessment (30.4) at termination or six months (33.2), moving from low level of family communication at pretreatment and 6-week assessment to a moderate level of family communication at termination or six months. Based on parents' report, there was a trend of positive improvement in family communication from pretreatment (36.0) to six-week assessment (36.5) and termination or six months (37.0), but this change was nonsignificant and stayed at moderate level of family communication (Table 14.3 and 14.4). In addition, there were a decrease in the percentages of parents and youth with low or very low level of family communication from pretreatment to termination (or six months) (Figure 14.5 and 14.6).

FAMILY SATISFACTION

Majority of parents (67.4%) and youth (76.7%) reported low or very low level of family satisfaction at pretreatment with youth reporting a lower level of satisfaction than parents (32.0 vs. 27.6). In other words, both parents and youth were somewhat dissatisfied and have some concerns about their family. Figures 14.7 and 14.8 shows the distribution of families for each level of satisfaction at pretreatment,

Table 14.4.

PAIRWISE COMPARISONS OF PARENTS' AND YOUTHS' ASSESSMENT OF FAMILY COHESION, FAMILY ADAPTABILITY, FAMILY COMMUNICATION AND FAMILY SATISFACTION AT PRETREATMENT (T0), SIX-WEEK ASSESSMENT (T1), AND TERMINATION OR 6 MONTHS (T2)

	T0–T1			T1–T2			T0–T2		
	Mean Difference	Std. Error	95% CI	Mean Difference	Std. Error	95% CI	Mean Difference	Std. Error	95% CI
Parent Family cohesion	0.89	1.70	[–2.44, 4.23]	**–4.04***	1.81	[–7.59,–0.49]	–4.20	5.51	[–14.99, 6.59]
Family adaptability	–1.57	1.58	[–4.66, 1.52]	–1.15	1.51	[–4.11, 1.81]	–2.71	1.70	[–6.05,0.62]
Family communication	–0.52	0.66	[–1.82,0.78]	–0.48	0.79	[–2.02,1.07]	–0.99	0.79	[–2.54,0.55]
Family satisfaction	**–1.64***	0.69	[–3.00,–0.28]	–0.98	0.80	[–2.55,0.58]	**–2.63****	0.94	[–4.47,–0.79]
Youth									
Family cohesion	–2.54	3.84	[–10.07, 4.99]	–4.48	3.62	[–11.60,2.64]	–7.02	4.56	[–15.98,1.94]
Family adaptability	**–6.18***	3.08	[–12.22, –0.14]	–0.07	3.15	[–6.47,6.33]	–6.26	3.38	[–13.03,0.51]
Family communication	–0.67	1.25	[–3.12,1.79]	–2.79	1.57	[–5.86,0.28]	**–3.46***	1.57	[–6.54,–0.37]
Family satisfaction	–1.48	1.51	[–4.45,1.48]	**–3.54****	1.40	[–6.28, –0.80]	**–5.03****	1.51	[–7.98,–2.07]

Notes: Parent survey: 52 completed all three assessments; 2 missing in 6-week assessment only, 17 missing in 6-month assessment only. Youth survey: 20 completed all three assessments; 2 missing in preassessment only and 8 missing in six-months assessment only.

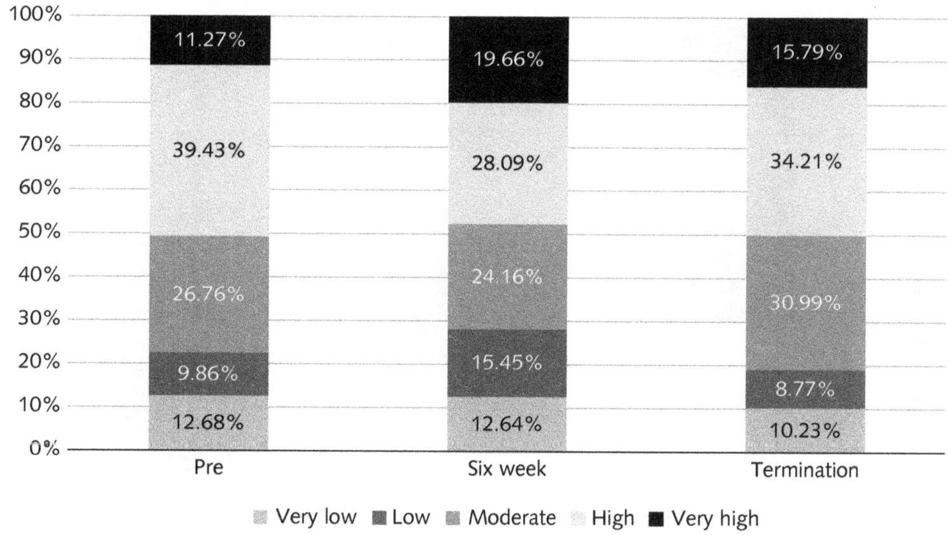

FIGURE 14.5.
PARENTS' PERCEPTION OF FAMILY COMMUNICATION (N = 72).

six-week assessment, and termination or six month based on parents and youth's reports.

I-FAST treatment had a positive impact on family satisfaction. Findings based on both parents' and youth's report indicated a positive change in family satisfaction from pretreatment (32.0 and 27.6, respectively) to six-week assessment (33.6 and 29.3, respectively) and termination or six months (34.6 and 32.6 respectively). This change was statistically significant from pretreatment to six-week assessment and pretreatment to termination (or six months) based on parents' report and significant from pretreatment to termination and 6-week assessment to termination (or six months) based on youth's report. Youth moved from "very dissatisfied" to "somewhat dissatisfied" while parents moved from the low end of "somewhat dissatisfied" to the high end and approaching a moderate level of satisfaction from pretreatment

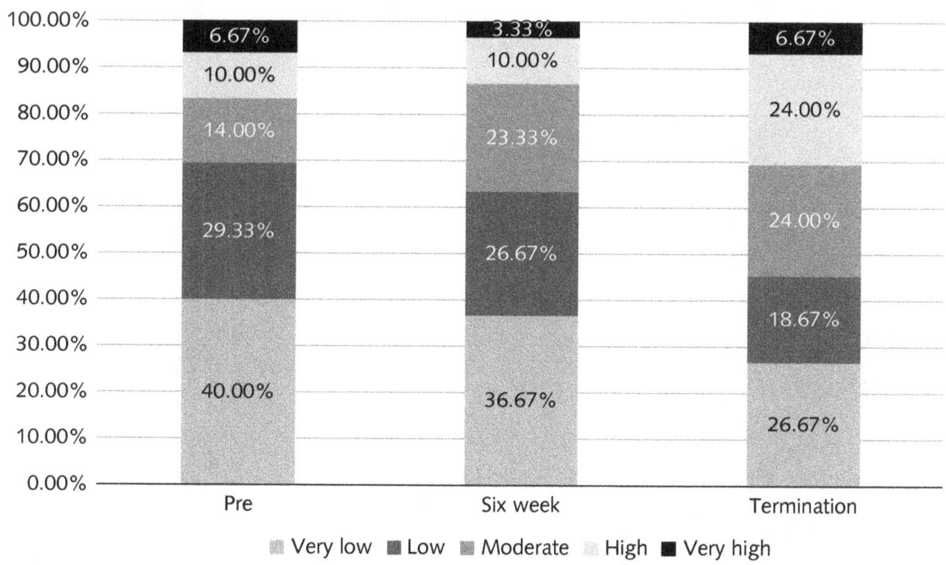

FIGURE 14.6.
YOUTH'S PERCEPTION OF FAMILY COMMUNICATION (N = 30).

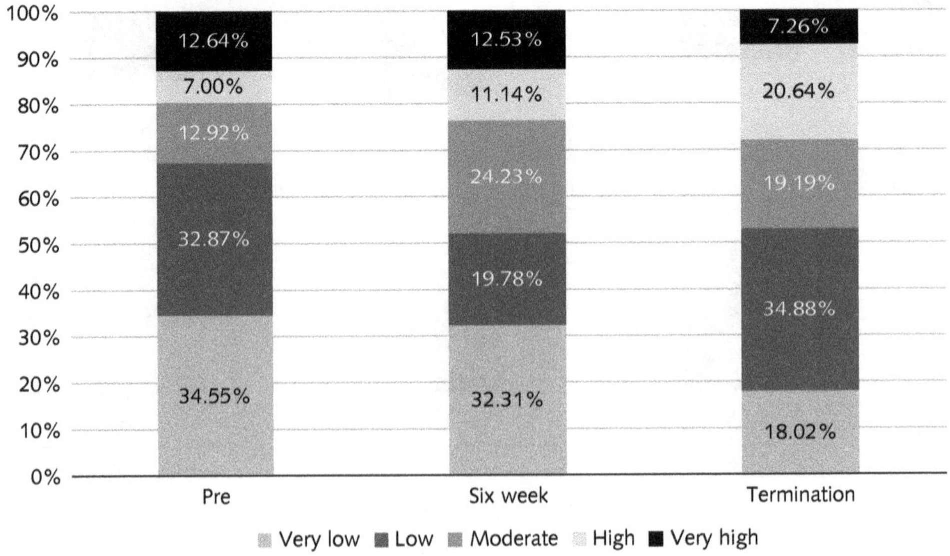

FIGURE 14.7.
PARENTS' PERCEPTION OF FAMILY SATISFACTION ($N = 72$).

to termination (or six months; Table 14.3 and 14.4). Also, there were a decrease in the percentages of parents (34.6 vs. 18.0) and youth (59.3 vs. 25.3) with a very low level of family satisfaction from pretreatment to termination (or six months) (Figures 14.5 and 14.6).

Discussion and Summary

Findings of this study provided initial empirical evidence that supported the efficacy of I-FAST in improving family functioning in the domains of family cohesion, family adaptability, family communication, and family satisfaction based on parents and youth's self-reports. In general, youth were less satisfied with all domains of family functioning at pretreatment than their parents. However, the treatment impact

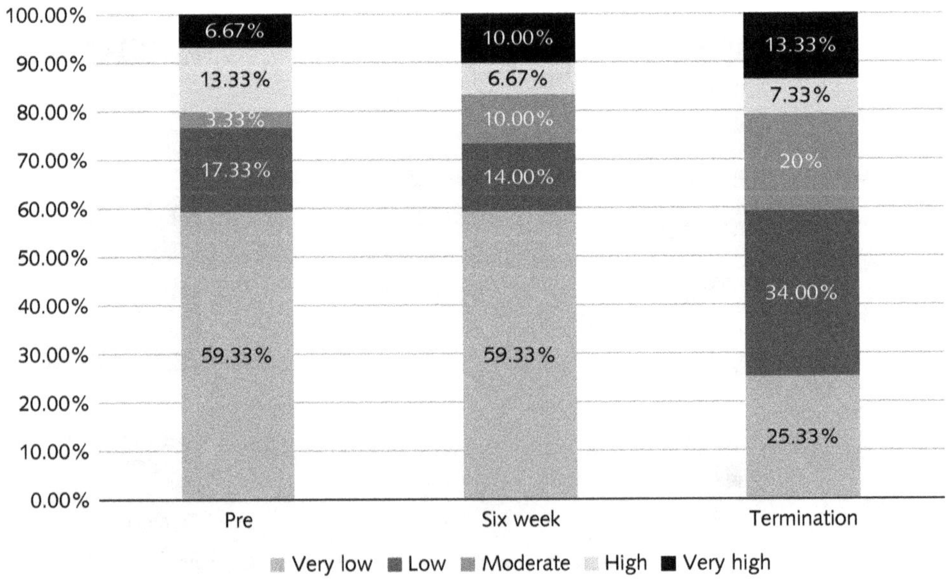

FIGURE 14.8.
YOUTH'S PERCEPTION OF FAMILY SATISFACTION ($N = 30$).

appeared to be more prominent for youth than parents as they reported greater and also significant changes in the dimension of family adaptability, family communication, and family satisfaction. Parents also reported positive changes in all assessed dimensions and significant changes in family cohesion and family satisfaction although the magnitude were slightly smaller than the changes reported by their children.

STUDY 2: I-FAST AND TREATING FAMILIES TO BREAK THE CYCLE OF TRAUMA TRANSMISSION

This is a qualitative study that used a grounded theory approach to explore families' lived experience of trauma transmission and parents' perception of helpful I-FAST treatment components that counteracted the transmission of trauma and reduce the negative intergenerational effects of trauma on their children. The study was approved by the institutional review board of a university in a Midwestern state.

Background and Significance

Although the connection between trauma exposure and negative health and mental health outcomes (Friedman, Keane, & Resick, 2007) has gained increased recognition in recent decades recognition of the cascading impact of early childhood trauma on family systems is only beginning to emerge. For example, the seminal Adverse Childhood Experiences (ACEs) study has significantly contributed to our understanding of the ways in which early childhood adversity can affect individuals, with profound deleterious effects shown on a variety of physical and behavioral health outcomes. The public is gradually understanding "how your biography becomes your biology," and researchers have made enormous progress in untangling the links between toxic stress and biopsychological well-being (Nakazawa, 2015). However, intergenerational effects have received less attention (i.e., few studies have considered ACEs in the context of family and parenting). Current clinical and research evidence suggests that children living with parents who have trauma histories are more likely to develop trauma symptoms with compromised developmental outcomes (J. E. Lambert, Holzer, & Hasbun, 2014). A meta-analysis of 42 studies suggested a moderately positive association between parents' PTSD severity and children's psychological distress (effect size = 0.35; J. E. Lambert et al., 2014). There is also an emerging line of studies in pediatrics to link maternal ACEs with infant development (Racine, Plamondon, Madigan, McDonald, & Tough, 2018).

Given that the family provides the primary environment in which a child develops and socializes (Gallarin & Alonso-Arbiol, 2012), it is necessary for those attempting to work with families to consider the impact of intergenerational trauma on the family system. Certain treatment models have been developed to specifically treat compromised parent–child attachment relationship to address intergenerational trauma (Copping et al., 2001; Skinner & McLean, 2017; Suchman et al., 2017), This emerging research is demonstrating the potential to break the cycle of intergenerational trauma by changing interactional patterns, including multiple family members into the treatment and being nonjudgmental and affirming to parents.

To better serve the population experiencing intergenerational trauma, further research is necessary to identify meaningful components of family therapy through the lens of clients' lived experience. In fact, understanding clients' experience is fundamental in revealing how parents' trauma history interacts with parenting and the development of child's mental health conditions. Clients' perceptions of helpful and unhelpful treatment strategies are essential to define the characteristics of services that constitute trauma-informed family therapy. Consistent with I-FAST assumptions, clients know better about their lives and have a deeper understanding of what works for them, compared to either service providers or policymakers.

The complex nature of families that are served in community mental health settings present significant barriers for knowledge building utilizing randomized controlled studies (Tcheremissine et al., 2014). To better understand what approaches are most effective for families with generational trauma histories the authors engaged in a qualitative study giving voice to the families who received I-FAST treatment for their child. The study asked the following questions: (a) What are families' lived experience of trauma transmission? (b) How did the parent experience the process of receiving treatment for their child? and (c) What aspects of I-FAST treatment were helpful to counteract the transmission of trauma and reduce the negative intergenerational effects of trauma?

Participants

The study used purposive sample to recruit informants. Criteria of inclusion were a parent who (a) had trauma histories; (b) had a child involved with a behavioral health service agency; and (c) had either completed I-FAST treatment or had been in I-FAST treatment for an extended period. This study recruited 12 parents from a large community child mental health agency in a Midwest state that has adopted I-FAST in providing family-based mental health services for children, young adults, and families. The agency daily serves approximately 2,200 youth and families to promote their success in families, schools, and communities.

Data Collection

Data were collected by conducting 90 minutes in-depth semistructured interviews with participants. Participants were asked by the researcher to share their experiences of ACEs and perceived effects of ACEs on their parenting. Attention was also paid to participants' perceptions of helpful and unhelpful treatment strategies and changes in their families after the completion of therapy. Each participant received a $100 gift card incentive, and participants consent was obtained before the interview. The recruitment process stopped when achieving theoretical saturation, meaning the researcher had already identified certain repetitive patterns of themes based on participants' lived experience.

Data Coding and Analysis

Interviews were recorded and transcribed verbatim by professional transcribers. A grounded theory approach was used to analyze data. Grounded theory aims to discover and develop knowledge on the lived experience of people, particularly those groups of people for whom there is limited understanding or stereotypical thinking (Corbin & Strauss, 2008). Before starting coding, the researcher had familiarized herself with the content of the interviews by reading each interview four times. The coding process employed ATLAS.ti 8, starting with the open coding. Special attention was paid to the text related to parents' trauma histories, the effect(s) of trauma on their parenting, and their child's symptoms and functioning, as well as clinical strategies and service resources they had received to facilitate changes. After coding for first four interviews, the researcher developed a coding list and used the coding list to code the rest of the interviews and recoded the first four interviews. Second, the researcher classified codes denoting similar themes to develop a higher level of conceptualization through axial and selection coding processes. The entire process of data collection, coding, and analysis included key components of grounded theory, such as theoretical sensitivity, constant comparison, and theoretical sampling (Corbin & Strauss, 2008).

Trustworthiness

Trustworthiness strategies were employed to enhance the rigor of data collection and analysis (Lincoln & Guba, 1985; Padgett, 2016). Experts reviewed the interview guides before starting the first interview to ensure dependability. In terms of confirmability, an audit trail documented the entire process of data collection. The researcher wrote field notes, memos, and self-reflection, as well as initiated peer briefing during the processes of data collection and data analysis to increase the credibility of the research findings. Finally, for the sake of transferability, the research findings were shown in the way of "thick description," which means using verbatim quotes from the participants' narratives to buttress each theme and provide sufficient details of the phenomenon.

Results

Twelve parents who had trauma histories shared their experiencing of trauma transmission and their perceived helpful and unhelpful treatment. Two participants (16.7%) were African Americans, and 10 (83.3%) participants were White Americans. All participants were from low-income families because the agency only served families receiving Medicaid. No Asian American, Hispanic American, or other races were represented in the sample. All interviewed participants were mother figures, including two grandmothers, nine biological mothers, and one stepmother who participated in the study together with her husband (the child's biological father joined for a while in the interview). The families were involved with social service systems to address their child's behavioral and emotional disorders. The traumatic events mothers experienced included childhood physical abuse, emotional abuse, sexual abuse, having a family member having mental health conditions or substance abuse, domestic violence, and witnessing neighborhood violence.

IMPORTANCE OF FAMILY ENGAGEMENT

Consistent with the overarching assumptions of I-FAST, participants identified the value of including the family in the treatment process rather than focusing only on the child. Some compared their experience of family therapy against previous treatment episodes in which they were not included.

> It was like a family thing because she got to know like my whole family. Like she got to know all the kids. And at that time, my sister was living with me, so she had a time to know my sister and her newborn and son. So she actually got to know all of us, and she didn't, I didn't feel like she was just my daughter's counselor, I felt like she was our family counselor. (Participant 1)

> One of the things that were really important to me is helping us as a family, not just me or [client], but helping my other two children, or helping me learning how to explain to my other two children why [client] is the way he is, and how to communicate with him without misunderstanding what he's trying to mean or what he's trying to do or the way he's trying to be. (Participant 7)

> So I think just the whole family involvement. Where if he was just going somewhere and going back in a room like he does for occupational therapy, I don't think the results would have been as good. So I think that the home therapy. (Participant 8)

> When we were at other agencies, it's not the same. They have plans, and they have graphs and different things that they have to do. And when I got, when I am with them, and they come to see me on the first visit, and they tell me, oh, this is what we have to do, and this is all the plans and everything, and I say, you are not doing that in my family. . . . I was like, I don't want to do this book with you and waste an hour of time when we need to figure out why that child just smacked that child. . . . So I'm sorry it's not based upon what they want to do, it needs to be based on what we need. (Participant 1)

HELPFUL I-FAST TREATMENT COMPONENTS

Participants' experiences revealed four components of I-FAST that were helpful to break the intergenerational trauma, including "changes of parent–child interactional patterns," "therapeutic alliance," "strengths-based approach," and "intersystems collaborations."

Changes of Parent–Child Interactional Patterns

Some participants indicated a cycle of trauma occurring in the family context, which had been maintained through compromised parent–child interactional pattern. Receiving I-FAST enabled families to change the previous problem-maintaining interactional patterns to break the trauma transmission. The following case illuminated the process of I-FAST addressing intergenerational trauma by changing parent–child unhealthy interactional patterns caused by the parent's childhood trauma.

This mother shared her story of being used as a tool to make her mother happy since childhood, resulting in her extremely low self-esteem. She developed co-dependency and entered an abusive relationship with a partner who shared the same predatory characteristics with her mom. Because of abuse both in childhood and adulthood, she tended to seek emotional comfort from her son and to repeat her mother's way of parenting.

> People who have been abused as a child or abused in an adult life will look to other people for their emotional reassurance and their worth. I had it in childhood, and then I had it in an adult relationship, and then my child was most likely to have it. Things kept going. (Participant 8)

Without a solid self, she admitted that she treated her child as her own possession and did not allow her son to relate to other people. She said she felt threated if her son "showing affection to other people, women especially, like teachers and therapists."

On the other hand, although the emotional entanglement was intensive between this mother and her son, it was not healthy parent–child bonding and did not beget a safe environment for the mother to consider the child's unique needs as an individual person. She said, "We were there together, and we loved each other, but we were not really connecting" (Participant 8).

Change happened when the mother observed the way the therapist connecting with the child and began to change the perception of her child. By connecting with her son in a way of communicating with an independent person (e.g., see his loving part, seeing him as an independent person from herself), this mother achieved a real bonding and connection with her child. She described the details:

> I think the therapist helped with perceiving him more for who he was and not just my baby, you know. This is a person here who, you know, has a sense of humor and has this and that and just kind of getting in there, where I was so disconnected. He was just my little cuddle of love baby, I really didn't have that bond or connection with him just as another person. He was, you know, my little, almost like, oh, God, wow, almost like a dog or a cat or something, you know. Wow. Wow.
>
> I think when the therapist started to talk with him, and tickling him, and getting him to kind of open up, I kind of did get to see more of who he was than just, my little baby. I knew his likes and dislikes but just, he wasn't really reachable. But I didn't really know how to try, you know. I wasn't really trying when I was in that environment to get in there like she did and pull him out. So yeah, I would say that my perception did change. Mostly, it's self-reflective, but also just that my child being an individual.

Because of the updated perception of her child as an individual person, the mother also changed her attitude towards her son's relationship with her and with other people.

> I am opening up to allowing my child to love other adults and not feeling threatened by that. Also kind of coming to terms with the fact that my child doesn't have to love me. It's not his job to love me. I also kind of came to terms with it, that he's not my possession. He's my responsibility, which is a whole different kind of thing, because I had co-dependency issues. I guess I always will, you know. He's, my son is not there to provide me with love. It's my job to provide him with love and safety.

She also realized the necessity of setting the boundary and discipline her child:

> Yeah, and then when he's, you know, a teenager and he says, I hate you. Well, like okay, well, too bad you still can't stay out until midnight, you know, I won't. Where, in the situation I was in before, if he had said that, I probably would have let him go do whatever it is I didn't want him to do because he said he hated me, and I can't have him hate me. But now, you know, I know kids will say that, but. He was likely to be, you know, in a bad relationship, drug abuse, everything, you know, everything I went through if I didn't get this worked out myself.

Therapeutic Relationship

For families experiencing intergenerational trauma, a good therapeutic relationship consists of three components, including clients' psychological safety, clients' feeling cared for as a person, and the therapist–client personal connection.

Psychological safety. Participants stated that having their histories and predicament being understood meant a lot to them, but they would only share their stories when they perceived psychological safety. Participants said,

> Don't want to tell you our deepest darkest secrets if we don't feel comfortable with you. (Participant 1)
>
> Just me being open to it and not feeling defensive, because she wasn't sitting there and saying, you are a bad mom. That was all in my head. But, once I started opening myself up to trying the things that she was telling me to try, and I saw the results. (Participant 8)

Building a sense of psychological safety for clients hinged on a nonjudgmental attitude from therapists, as shared by the participants:

> We have been in the system a lot, and you find it really hard to trust people because it is like are you trying to take my kids away from me? Are you coming and looking for key phrases to say, she is not a good mom? I never feel judged by her. That allows me to really open up to her about how I feel. I can tell her that I am aggravated with my son and feel overwhelmed without her saying, maybe we should take him away. (Participant 10)

Meanwhile, being nonjudgmental relied on making efforts to understand the history of trauma for clients, which usually required an inquisitive attitude from therapists that suspends their prior assumptions. One participant shared this insight:

> You might see that they were unable to take care of their kids, and then they fell right back into drugs or some type of routine, and their kids ended up getting taken from them. It is easy to judge people by their experience, that person over there is on drug, and they didn't do this, or they didn't do that. But what you don't see is that, their dad raped them, and their mom beat them, and they have never seen the good example of what work ethic is about. What you don't see is that they had lice their whole childhood, because their mom wouldn't address it. Because of that, they didn't have friends because nobody would play with them. They never had a good example of education, so they never valued education as something significant. They never had anybody to help them with their homework, so they were always in trouble at school. They dropped out early, because they feel so far behind. They didn't enjoy school. ***Those are things people don't think about. They judge that people because of the choices that they make, but the choices that they make are anything that they know.*** (Participant 6; emphasis added).

"I'm a person too." It is common that services are designed around children's and adolescents' needs when behavioral health service agencies work with this population. Hence, therapists only see parents as a role to fulfill their parental responsibilities to help their child to recover, while their own needs or past experiences remain unaddressed. However, for families experiencing intergenerational trauma, it was important to engage and care parents as a person not just because of the role as a parent. Some participants shared that they needed someone to acknowledge them as individual persons.

> That makes me feel really amazing because they are not just acknowledging that this is about the child, but ***they acknowledge that I'm a person too***, and I may not be feeling good enough. And there is been times where I'm in there and I'm just zoned out. I am just not myself and she is like are you with me? I'm just like, not today. I just feel like, I think I have a lot of stuff going on. And she's like, you need a session? I'm like, yeah. (Participant 1; emphasis added)
>
> ***I wanted to be recognized as a person***, you know, not just as a mother or like a caretaker or provider, but just me as a person. I'm used to taking care of my kids, and people saying, oh it must be hard as a parent. (Participant 6; emphasis added)
>
> She helped me just as much as she helped my son because even though she was here for him and the whole thing was based around him, she was still very attentive to me. How are you doing, how are you handling things, just things like that. And having that trust is even bigger. ***That is an issue for my son, and that is always been an issue for me.*** (Participant 11; emphasis added)

"She doesn't come in as a therapist." It seems paradoxical that a good therapeutic relationship results from not acting as a therapist, but a personal level therapist–client connection did create good therapeutic outcomes. Meanwhile, clients' well-being improved through activities outside professional settings.

First, some degree of self-disclosure from therapists facilitated a personal-level connection between the therapist and the client. Some participants pointed out that they enjoyed the part of knowing the individual experiences of the therapist.

> We've had one or two sessions where she just comes in, and it's like having a family member come over to visit. I like that because it is not always just work, work, work, work, work with her. ***To have a casual conversation with another adult, that is therapeutic itself.*** I feel relaxed around her, that it is just because she comes in as a real person. ***She doesn't come in as a therapist.*** She will link it to a personal story. She will tell us funny things that her kids did. She gives us like a glimpse into her own life. She is not robotic. (Participant 10; emphasis added)
>
> She made us feel comfortable. She had stories of her own. (Participant 9)

Second, building a personal connection means therapists genuinely caring clients by seeing them as a real person, rather than treating them as a work task or a paycheck. Some participants shared the bad experiences of having therapists who were like a "robot," who were too "professional," and being treated as a paycheck, all of which prevented clients being expressive.

> Really personal. Down-to-earth, shake your hand, how you doing, and actually, genuinely care about how you're doing. Whereas, previous situations or previous experiences has been more automated, like please answer the following questions

> yes or no, or sometimes, always, and maybe things like that. Not really looking for an individual answer, but more so looking for the test score. . . . Some people they get so into their job that they forgot to act like a person, and you feel like you're talking to a robot. And if you feel like you're talking to a robot, you're going to have automatic responses. You are not going to feel like you can open up and be expressive. (Participant 6)
>
> She realized life happened. She realized it is that thing, there are just things that are out of your control. People I've dealt with were more robotic like or very textbook, were very this is my job, I have to be professional. You know that doesn't work for everybody. Sometimes you just need somebody to get you to laugh, because once you get somebody to laugh, typically, you are good. (Participant 11)
>
> They have to gain my trust. Because if I don't trust you, I'm not going to give you 100% of everything. I'm not going to open up to you with everything. And be patient and persistence in, I need to feel that you are willing to invest that time in me, because I am worth it. I am not just a paycheck. (Participant 7)
>
> I can actually, honestly say that she cares. And really, nobody ever, in my lifetime, as a, to this point, that has ever cared for me or my kids. (Participant 1)

Finally, the minor and ordinary efforts therapists made beyond the professional setting exerted a substantial effect on clients' lives and were highly appreciated by clients.

> She walked us into the shelter. She sat while we ate, she comforted me while I was bawling my eyes out. She stayed there with me for almost all night. She had to go home at one point and get some rest and get back up, but she stayed with us for a couple hours. I just feel like nobody else would have did that. (Participant 3)
>
> She'll stay late if she has to meet up with us. I feel like they are always there for us. No matter what, they will make the time to help you with anything. (Participant 4)
>
> She helped us with a Thanksgiving dinner. (Participant 10)

A Strengths-Based Approach

Considering parents' sense of self was compromised by their traumatic experience, particularly low self-esteem and confidence, which influenced their parenting and caused detrimental effects on their child development, using a strengths-based approach in a therapeutic setting helps families in terms of (a) increasing parental competency to discipline children and (b) modeling a strengths-based family communication style.

Parental competency. It was common that parents worried they were hurting their child and believed that they were incapable of being a good parent. A strengths-based approach is a cure for building parental competency for parents who were trauma survivors. One parent described the process in which the therapist helped the family by first addressing her issue of self-esteem.

> She has really helped with my self-esteem. I can sit here and tell you that I'm a really great person and I do love myself. I feel that I'm as good as other person. I'm not different. She is affirming me that I'm on the right track, that I am not giving advice

that is detrimental to these kids. She's helped me with building my confidence in speaking to the girls. (Participant 7)

In another case, a strengths-based approach means affirming parents' efforts to make the change and reminding of them what they have already achieved in such a challenging environment, which encouraged parents not to easily give up. One mother shared her experience of gaining perseverance:

There's been times the counselors have come, and I am packing my stuff. I'm leaving. I cannot do this because I am going to lose my mind. I am hurting them more. I'm not doing them any good. But her words were very encouraging. She says you're in this position where it feels impossible, and you guys are doing it and you continue to do it and every day is going to be different. She says you are doing the best you can, and more than most people can. The mere fact that you're worrying whether you're doing a good job is telling us you're doing a good job. I don't think I would've lasted this long if she hadn't been here. I would have given up a long time ago if it hadn't been for her encouraging. (Participant 9)

Moreover, parents carried immense feelings of guilt with them because of their experience of being involved with the social service systems, particularly the involvement with the child welfare system, which highly prevented them from effectively disciplining their child. Therapists' affirmation hence plays a role in encouraging parents to set the boundary to discipline their child. Some parents pointed out their changes:

No body telling me you're doing the right thing. I had CPS on me, I had the school on me, they were just on me, but not helping. I had the agency telling me you're doing the right thing. Keep going. Move forward. (Participant 4)

I see me being a little bit not second-guessing myself as a parent and the decisions that I make. I've been more confident as a parent. I've been more strict as a parent. (Participant 3)

I learned ways to punish them when they do things, they got no business doing, helping me to not constantly feel everything that happens is my fault. (Participant 12)

Modeling a strengths-based communication style. Therapists also model a strengths-based approach for parents to effectively communicate with their children, and embrace positive attitudes toward their everyday life, particularly for challenging situations.

I made sure to tell my son last night before bed how wonderful he was the entire day, how great he was, how good he was to his brother. That really helped, because before I would say things like, when you're not here, we don't have these issues. You are the issue. And that would just make things worse, and my therapist pointed out that is not helping. (Participant 5)

If something really negative that was going on, she always made sure to follow up with something like, but you guys are doing really good with this, but we need to work with this. Positive reinforcement is needed for anybody. People don't get that recognition that they need. She was always finding something positive. That

> was something I noticed from her, and I loved it. So, from that point on, I always made it, where is the positive? Something is horrible, but where is that positive? Let's find that one positive thing. Let's take that positive, and let's make it grow. (Participant 11)

> Because I felt like with some of the other places he was at, they just repeated the same information. They didn't really seem to be working with him therapeutically. It was always just telling me about his bad behaviors, you know, so. . . . So once we went to the Ranch, it was a lot of, yes, [client] is still having struggle with this. However, he's doing really well with this. And so like learning the things that he was doing well with made it easier to try and figure out how we could implement different structure in the house for when he returned. (Participant 10)

Intersystems Collaboration

Families experiencing generational trauma usually have multiple family members involved with different social service systems, including school, child protection systems, and mental health and substance abuse services. Therefore, intersystems collaboration among different social service systems to provide holistic services can effectively address clients' needs. Additionally, parents with their own history of childhood trauma may have had negative experiences and perceptions of social services, which directly impacts how they interact with service providers.

> Because the Children Service lady wasn't, didn't like me and wasn't very nice to me, and I just told her, you know, this is how it's going to be. I'm the mom. You don't know what it's like raising these kids, and you're not going to take my kids, and, you know, if you got a problem, you can get the . . . out of my house. You know, like get out. You got a problem, get out. You're not going to look at me and smirk at me and say you're going to take me to court and expect me to keep my cool. (Participant 2)

One parent said it was helpful that the therapist communicated with school systems and occupational therapists to have a more accurate understanding of the child's problems.

> The therapist has also been involved in some of his other therapies. For example, in school. She comes to the IEP [individual education plan] meetings; when he was having trouble going to OT [occupational therapy], she went. She stayed for a session there. So, she got talk with another therapist that was working with him or a teacher that's working with him so that the care is all kind of on the same page. So that was something I think that was really important, that she knew what was his challenges were in school, if there were any. (Participant 8)

One mother emphasized the importance of the integration of behavioral health and health services, because her son suffered from severe side effects of taking the medications prescribed for controlling his behavioral symptoms.

> Even if they don't like teach you about the medication itself, if they give you ways to learn about the medication, or if they can get you linked up with maybe another appointment with the doctor. Coordinating with them to where maybe you get

Table 14.5.

BACKGROUND INFORMATION OF INFORMANTS (N=12)

	N (%)
Parental Roles	
Biological mother	9 (75%)
Grandmother	2 (16.7%)
Stepmother (with child's biological father)	1 (8.3%)
Race	
White American	10 (83.3%)
African American	2 (16.7%)
Marital Status	
Single	6 (50%)
Married	6 (50%)
Parents' Traumatic Experience	
Physical abuse	1 (8.3%)
Sexual abuse	2 (16.7%)
Emotional abuse	4 (33.3%)
Family members suffering from mental health problems	1 (8.3%)
Family members having substance abuse problems	1 (8.3%)
Domestic violence	6 (50%)
Neighborhood violence	1 (8.3%)

> an extra 20 minutes with the doctor to really be able to talk about what are the side effects. Meeting with a nutritionist is also important, because people don't understand the way, the role, the food, and what you put in your body alters the chemicals in the medication that they're taking too. And I know it's a lot, it's so helpful because I would have never known that him drinking caffeine while taking his medication would just make it seem like it wasn't working. (Participant 10)

Discussion and Summary

Based on clients' lived experience, this study demonstrates the importance of utilizing a strengths-based, family systems approach when treating children who have family histories of generational trauma. From the participants' stories of their experience in treatment, this research identified four effective components of I-FAST treatment to break the cycle of intergenerational trauma. They are changing parent–child interactional patterns, building therapeutic alliance, employing strengths-based approach, and facilitating intersystems collaborations. The compromised family functioning and family relationship can be improved by altering problem-sustaining parent–child interactional patterns, which are primarily driven by parents' personal traumatic experience. Treating parents' trauma history, as well as its effects on their parenting issues, in an interaction context, can be viewed as the unique advantage of I-FAST. The study findings also highlight the importance of building an authentic therapeutic alliance to treat families experience generational trauma. The key components include (a) providing clients with psychological safety by showing a nonjudgmental attitude and adopting an inquisitive stance to understand clients' trauma histories; (b) incorporating parents' needs when treating child's problems; and (c) building a personal connection with the families. Moreover, it is necessary to employ a strengths-based approach to increase parental competency, which has been largely compromised due to parents' trauma histories. Given the challenges and cumulative stressors those clients may face in their everyday life, it can also be helpful to model a positive attitude for parents to embrace their child's problems and life demands. Finally, facilitating intersystem collaborations among different social service agencies were also important for effectively working with families experiencing intergenerational trauma.

CONCLUSION

This chapter summarized findings of previous efficacy studies on I-FAST, presented findings of two additional studies that examined the impact of I-FAST on family functioning, and explored the impact of I-FAST on breaking the cycle of intergenerational transmission of trauma from the perspective of parents who had received I-FAST treatment. While we have initial supporting evidence for the positive impact of I-FAST on family functioning and behavioral outcomes, future efficacy studies will have to include trauma-specific outcomes. In addition, trauma includes a wide range of adverse experiences. For instances, ACEs include both abuse and household dysfunction as two distinct constructs. As such, it will be helpful to examine the impact of I-FAST on different types of trauma because of their differential impact on a person's experience, which will have implications for treatment. Other specific recommendations for future research will include (a) the adoption of rigorous research designs including randomized clinical trials using representative samples to establish effectiveness of I-FAST for treating trauma; (b) using multiple research sites that serve ethnically/racially diverse populations; and (c) using multiple research methods, both quantitative and qualitative, to identify the mechanisms of change associated with I-FAST for treating trauma.

EPILOGUE

In this book, we have identified and attempted to address what we believe is a major gap in the trauma treatment literature: how to bring the potential healing power of family relationships fully to bear on the damage and aftermath of trauma. The emphasis on trauma in the field of psychotherapy was originated by Freud and was focused on the individual trauma survivor. Subsequent trauma theory and treatment has been heavily influenced by this origin. How family fits in to both the suffering and the resolution of suffering for trauma survivors has not been a major emphasis.

We have shown how *interactional patterns*, habitual responses to trauma symptoms between the survivor and family members, and/or family patterns that predate trauma can perpetuate and exacerbate suffering due to trauma. We have shown how to identify these patterns and target them for change in treatment.

We have outlined a *flexible yet structured* treatment framework that can adjust to and engage a wide range of clients. We have devised a treatment approach that can adapt to the client, rather than expecting the client to adapt to the treatment. This flexibility and adaptability is consistent with trauma-informed principles aimed at addressing the barriers of engaging clients with trauma histories into treatment.

We have shown how to track and utilize the client's and family's belief system in treatment, their *frames,* to intensify engagement and to promote family cooperation with a change process. By tracking and utilizing family beliefs, we have shown how to offer a truly cross-cultural treatment approach. Beliefs from any ethnic group are tracked and utilized in the approach we have described. We have shown how the utilization of client, family and ethnic beliefs in treatment can intensify the healing process. When client beliefs are engaged in the treatment process, we believe healing is enhanced.

We have shown how to recruit family into treatment and how they can be of service in the healing process. We have provided an overarching family framework that allows for the *integration of intervention procedures* from the evidenced based trauma treatments and from traditional ethnic healing practices. In the approach described here, any intervention procedure can be utilized as long as it is aimed at the problem(s) the client is motivated to focus on and the implementation of those procedures requires changes in the family patterns that are reinforcing the client's symptoms.

We have shown how to magnify and intensify improvements and modify and adjust the course of treatment accordingly by tracking and utilizing *interactional exceptions*, what the client and family are doing when the symptoms are not occurring, and their goals as they are achieved.

Finally, we have shown how *family treatment as a stand-alone therapy* can focus directly on the amelioration of posttraumatic stress disorder (PTSD) symptoms. When trauma survivors are not willing to focus on their own trauma histories or symptoms, we have shown how to help ameliorate PTSD symptoms by focusing treatment on whatever problem the trauma survivor is interested in receiving help on. In this way we are simultaneously respecting client treatment choices and helping them with their difficulties related to trauma. We have shown how any treatment that focuses on helping families improve relationships and become more harmonious, more loving, more predictable, and more stable can help many clients who suffer from the aftermath of trauma. Finally, we have provided research supporting how integrative family and systems treatment (I-FAST) produces improved family relationships on numerous levels.

REFERENCES

Acoca, L. (1999). Investing in girls: A 21st century strategy. *Juvenile Justice, 6*(1), 3–13.

Afifi, T. O., & MacMillan, H. L. (2011). Resilience following child maltreatment: A review of protective factors. *Canadian Journal of Psychiatry, 56,* 266–272.

Ahmed-Leitao, F., Spies, G., van den Heuvel, L., & Seedat, S. (2016). Hippocampal and amygdala volumes in adults with posttraumatic stress disorder secondary to childhood abuse or maltreatment: A systematic review. *Psychiatric Research: Neuroimaging, 256,* 33–43.

Aisenberg, E., & Mennen, F. E. (2000). Children exposed to community violence: Issues for assessment and treatment. *Child and Adolescent Social Work, 17*(5), 341–360.

Ajrouch, K., Antonucci, T., & Janevic, M. (2001). Social networks among Blacks and Whites: The interaction between race and age. *Journal of Gerontology Series B: Psychological Sciences and Social Sciences, 56*(2), S112–S118.

Alexander, J., Waldron, H., Robbins, M., & Neeb, A. (2013). *Functional family therapy for adolescent behavior problems*. Washington, DC: American Psychological Association.

Alexander, P. (2015). *Intergenerational cycles of trauma and violence: An attachment and family systems perspective.* New York, NY: W. W. Norton.

Alexander, P., Teti, L., & Anderson, C. (2000). Child sexual abuse history and role reversal in parenting. *Child Abuse and Neglect, 24,* 829–838.

Alford, F. (2016). *Trauma, culture and PTSD.* New York, NY: Palgrave Macmillan.

Alim, T., Charney, D., & Mellman, T. (2006). An overview of posttraumatic stress disorder in African Americans. *Journal of Clinical Psychology, 62*(7), 801–813.

Allison, P. D. (2000). Multiple imputation for missing data: A cautionary tale. *Sociological Methods and Research, 28,* 301–309.

American Psychiatric Association. (2000). *Diagnostic and statistical manual of mental disorders* (4th ed.). Arlington, VA: Author.

American Psychiatric Association. (2013). *Diagnostic and statistical manual of mental disorders* (5th ed.). Arlington, VA: Author.

American Psychological Association, Presidential Task Force on Evidence-Based Practice. (2006). Evidence-based practice in psychology. *American Psychologist, 61,* 271–285.

Amstutz, L. S. (2009). *Victim offender conferencing: Bringing victims and offenders together in dialogue.* New York, NY: Good Books.

Anderson, E. (1999). *Code of the street.* New York, NY: W. W. Norton.

Aneshensel, C., & Sucoff, C. (1996). The neighborhood context of adolescent mental health. *Journal of Health and Social Behavior, 37*(4), 293–310.

Armbruster, P., & Kazdin, A. (1994). Attrition in child psychotherapy. In T. H. Ollendick & R. J. Prinz (Eds.), *Advances in clinical child psychology* (Vol. 16, pp. 81–108). New York, NY: Plenum Press.

Asari, T., Konishi, S., Jimura, K., Chikazoe, J., Nakamura, N., & Miyashita, Y. (2010). Amygdalar enlargement associated with unique perception. *Cortex, 46,* 94–99.

Bailey, K., & Stewart, S. (2014). Relations among trauma, PTSD, and substance misuse: The scope of the problem. In P. Ouimette & J. P. Read (Eds.), *Trauma and substance abuse: Causes, consequences, and treatment of comorbid disorders* (pp. 11–34). Washington, DC: American Psychological Association. http://dx.doi.org/10.1037/14273-002

Baranowsky, A. B., & Gentry, J. E. (2015). *Trauma practice: Tools for stabilization and recovery* (3rd ed.). Ashland, OH: Hogrefe.

Bardin, A. (2004). EMDR within a family system perspective. *Journal of Family Psychotherapy, 15,* 47–61.

Barnes, H. L., & Olson, D. H. (1982). Parent–adolescent communication scale. In D. H. Olson (Ed.), *Family inventories: Inventories used in a national survey of families across the family life cycle* (pp. 3–8). St. Paul, MN: Family Social Science, University of Minnesota.

Barnes, H. L., & Olson, D. H. (1985). Parent–adolescent communication and the circumplex model. *Child Development, 56,* 438–447.

Barsaglini, A., Sartori, G., Benetti, S., Pettersson-Yeo, W., & Mechelli, A. (2014). The effects of psychotherapy on brain function: A systematic and critical review. *Progress in Nuerobiology, 114,* 1–4.

Barth, J., Bermetz, L., Heim, E., Trelle, S., & Tonia, T. (2013). The current prevalence of child sexual abuse worldwide: A systematic review and meta-analysis. *International Journal of Public Health, 58,* 469–483.

Bateson, G. (1972). A theory of play and fantasy. In *Steps to an ecology of mind: Collected essays in anthropology, psychiatry, evolution, and epistemology* (pp. 177–193). Northvale, NJ: Aronson. (Original work published 1955)

Bateson, G. (1979). *Mind in nature: A necessary unity.* New York, NY: E. F. Dutton.

Beck, J. G., & Sloan, D. M. (Eds.). (2012). *The Oxford handbook of traumatic stress disorders.* New York, NY: Oxford University Press.

Beeghly, M., Perry, B. D., & Tronick, E. (2016). Self-regulatory processes in early development. In S. Maltzman (Ed.), *The Oxford handbook of treatment processes and outcomes in psychology: A multidisciplinary biopsychosocial approach* (pp. 42–54). New York, NY: Oxford University Press.

Bell, C., & Jenkins, E. (1993). Community violence and children on Chicago's South-side. *Psychiatry, 56,* 46–54.

Belsky, J., Jaffee, S. R., Sligo, J., Woodward, L., & Silva, P. A. (2005). Intergenerational transmission of warm-sensitive-stimulating parenting: A prospective study of mothers and fathers of 3-year old. *Child Development, 76,* 384–396.

Benish, S. G, Imel, Z. E., & Wampold, B. (2008). The relative efficacy of bona fide psychotherapies for treating post-traumatic stress disorder: A meta-analysis of direct comparisons. *Clinical Psychological Review, 28,* 746–758.

Benson, M., Buehler, C., & Gerard, J. (2008). Interparental hostility and early adolescent problem behavior: Spillover via maternal acceptance harshness, inconsistency and intrusiveness. *Journal of Early Adolescence, 28,* 428–454.

Berger, D., Saito, S., Ono, Y., Tezuka, I., Sharahase, J., Kuboki, T., & Suematsu, H. (1994). Dissociation and child abuse histories in an eating disorder cohort in Japan. *Acta Psychiatrica Scandinavica, 90,* 274–280.

Berkowitz, S. J., Stover, C. S., & Marans, S. R. (2011). The child and family traumatic stress intervention. *Journal of Child Psychiatry, 52*(6), 676–685.

Bernardon, S., & Pernice-Duca, F. (2010). A family systems perspective to recovery from posttraumatic stress in children. *The Family Journal: Counseling and Therapy for Couples and Families, 8,* 349–357.

Bertram, R., & Dartt, J. (2008). Post-traumatic stress disorder: A diagnosis for youth from violent, impoverished communities. *Journal of Child and Family Studies, 18,* 294–302.

Berwin, C., Andrews, B., & Valentine, J. (2000). Meta-analysis of risk factors for posttraumatic stress disorder in trauma exposed adults. *Journal of Consulting and Clinical Psychology, 66,* 748–766.

Bick, J., & Nelson, C. A. (2016). Early adverse experiences and the developing brain. *Neuropsychopharmacology Reviews, 41,* 177–196.

Bickart, K., Wright, C., Dautoff, R., Dickerson, B., & Barrett, L. (2010). Amygdala volume and social network size in humans. *Nature Neuroscience, 14,* 163–164.

Blaustein, M. E., & Kinniburgh, K. M. (2017). Attachment, self-regulation, and competency (ARC). In M. A. Landolt, M. Cloitre, & U. Schnyder (Eds.), *Evidence-based treatments for trauma related disorders in children and adolescents* (pp. 293–320). Cham, Switzerland: Springer International.

Bleiberg, K. L., & Markowitz, J. C. (2019). Interpersonal psychotherapy for PTSD: Treating trauma without exposure. *Journal of Psychotherapy Integration, 20,* 15–22.

Boney-McCoy, L., & Finkholer, D. (1995). Psychosocial selquelae of violent victimization in a national youth sample. *Journal of Consulting and Clinical Psychology, 63,* 726–736.

Bowen, M. (1978). *Family therapy in clinical practice.* New York, NY: Aronson.

Bracken, P. J., Giller, J. E., & Summerfield, D. (1995). Psychological responses to war and atrocity: The limitations of current concepts. *Social Science and Medicine, 40,* 1073–1082.

Bradford, K., & Barber, B. (2005). Interparental conflict as intrusive family process. *Journal of Emotional Abuse, 5,* 143–167.

Bradley, R., Greene, J., Russ, E., Dutra, L., & Weston, D. (2005). A multidimensional meta-analysis of psychotherapy for PTSD. *American Journal of Psychiatry, 162,* 214–227.

Bremner, J. D., Elzinga, B., Schmahl, C., & Vermetten, E. (2008). Structural and functional plasticity of the human brain in posttraumatic stress disorder. *Progress in Brain Research, 167,* 171–186.

Bremner, J. D., Randall, P., Scott, T. M., Bronen, R. A., Seibyl, J. P. Southwick, S. M., . . . Innis, R. B. (1995). MRI-based measurement of hippocampal volume in patients with combat-related posttraumatic stress disorder. *American Journal of Psychiatry, 152,* 97–81.

Bremner, J. D., Vythilingam, M., Vermetten, E., Adil, J., Khan, S., Nazeer, A., . . . Charney, D. D. (2003). Cortisol response to a cognitive stress challenge in posttraumatic stress disorder (PTSD) related to childhood abuse. *Psychoneuroendocrinology, 28,* 733–750.

Breslau, N. (2002). Epidemiologic studies of trauma, post-traumatic stress disorder and other psychiatric disorders. *Canadian Journal of Psychiatry, 47*(10), 923–929.

Breslau, N., Davis, G. C., Andreski, P., Peterson, E. L., & Schultz, L. R. (1997a). Sex Differences in post-traumatic stress disorder. *Archives of General Psychiatry, 54,* 1044–1048.

Breslau, N., Davis, G. C., Peterson, E. L., & Schultz, L. (1997). Psychiatric sequelae of posttraumatic stress disorder in women. *Archives of General Psychiatry, 54,* 81–87.

Breslau, N., Kessler, R. C., Chilcoat, H. D., Schultz, L. R., Davis, G. C., & Anreski, P. (1998). Trauma and posttraumatic stress disorder in the community. *Archives of General Psychiatry, 55,* 626–632.

Breslau, N., Wilcox, H., Storr, C., Luciea, V., & Anthonoy, J. (2004). Trauma exposure and posttraumatic stress disorder: A study of youths in urban America. *Journal of Urban Health, 8,* 530–544.

Briere, J., & Elliott, D. M. (2003). Prevalence and psychological sequelae of self-reported childhood physical and sexual abuse in a general population sample of men and women. *Child Abuse and Neglect, 27,* 1205–1222.

Briggs, E. C., Greeson, J., Layne, C., Steinberg, A., Amaya-Jackson, L., Ostowski, S. A., . . . Pynoos, R. S. (2013). Links between child and adolescent trauma exposure and service use histories in a national clinic referred sample. *Psychological trauma: Theory, Research, Practice and Policy, 5*(2), 101–109.

Brooks-Gunn, J., Duncan, G., Kato, P., & Sealand, N. (1993). Do neighborhoods influence child and adolescent behavior? *American Journal of Sociology, 99,* 353–395.

Brown, A., Laitner, C., & Sax, G. (2017). Trauma systems therapy for children and adolescents. In M. A. Landolt, M. Cloitre, & U. Schnyder (Eds.), *Evidence-based treatments for trauma related disorders in children and adolescents* (pp. 363–384). Cham, Switzerland: Springer International.

Brown, D. W., Anda, R. F., Tiemeier, H. Felitti, V. J., Edwards, V. J., Croft, J. B., & Giles, W. H. (2009). Adverse childhood experiences and the risk of premature mortality. *American Journal of Preventive Medicine, 37,* 389–396.

Brown, E. (2005). Efficacious treatment of stress disorder in children and adolescents. *Pediatric Annals, 34,* 139–146.

Bryant, R., Flemingham, K., Kemp, A., Das, P., Hughes, G., & Peduto, A. (2008). Amygdala and ventral anterior cingulate activation predicts treatment response to cognitive behavior therapy for post-traumatic stress disorder. *Psychological Medicine, 38,* 555–561.

Buckner, J., Heimerg, R., Ecker, A., & Vinci, C. (2013). A biopsychosocial model of social anxiety and substance use. *Depression and Anxiety, 30,* 276284.

Buehler, C., Franck, K., & Cook, E. (2009). Adolescents' triangulation in marital conflict and peer relations. *Journal of Research on Adolescence, 19,* 669–689.

Buehler, C., & Gerard, J. (2002). Marital conflict, ineffective parenting and children's and adolescents' maladjustment. *Journal of Marriage and Family, 64,* 78–92.

Buehler, C., & Welsh, D. (2009). A process model of adolescents' triangulation into parents' marital conflict. *Journal of Family Psychology, 23,* 167–180.

Butler, O., Willmund, G., Gleich, T., Gallinat, J., Kuhn, S., & Zimmerman, P. (2018). Hippocampal gray matter increases following multimodal psychological treatment for combat-related post-traumatic stress disorder. *Brain and Behavior, 8*(5), e00956.

Caliso, J. A., & Milner, J. S. (1992). Childhood history of abuse and child abuse screening. *Child Abuse and Neglect, 16,* 647–659.

Capaldi, S., Zandberg, L. J., & Foa, E. B. (2017). Prolonged exposure therapy for adolscents with PTSD: Emotional processing for traumatic experiences. In M. A. Landolt, M. Cloitre, & U. Schnyder (Eds.), *Evidence-based treatments for trauma related disorders in children and adolescents* (pp. 209–226). Cham, Switzerland: Springer International.

Carter, B., & McGoldrick, M. (1989). *The changing family life cycle: A framework for family therapy* (2nd ed.). Boston, MA: Allyn and Bacon.

Catherall, D. R. (1998). Treating traumatized families. In C. R. Figley (Ed.), *Burnout in families: The systemic costs of caring* (pp. 187–215). Boca Raton, FL: CRC Press.

Cattaneo, L. B., & Goodman, L. A. (2010). Through the lens of therapeutic jurisprudence: The relationship between empowerment in the court system and well-being for intimate partner violence victims. *Journal of Interpersonal Violence, 25,* 481–502.

Cattaneo, L. B., & Goodman, L. A. (2015). What is empowerment anyway? A model for domestic violence practice, research, and evaluation. *Psychology of Violence, 5,* 84–94.

Chan, Y. (1994). Parenting stress and social support of mothers who physically abuse their children in Hong Kong. *Child Abuse and Neglect, 18,* 261–269.

Chard, K. M., Schuster, J. L., & Resick, P. A. (2012). Empirically supported psychological treatments: Cognitive processing therapy. In J. G. Beck & D. M. Sloan (Eds.), *The Oxford handbook of traumatic stress disorder* (pp. 439–448). New York, NY: Oxford University Press.

Chen, M. (2014). The PTSD epidemic in our most violent neighborhoods. *Al Jazeera America.* Retrieved from http://america.aljazeera.com/opinions/2014

Chesney-Lind, M. (1989). Girls' crime and woman's place: Toward a feminist model of female delinquency. *Crime and Delinquency, 35*(1), 5–29.

Chilcoat, H. D., & Breslau, N. (1998). Posttraumatic stress disorder and drug disorders: Testing causal pathways. *Archives of General Psychiatry, 55,* 913–917.

Children's Bureau. (2013, December 17). Child maltreatment 2012. Retrieved from https://www.acf.hhs.gov/cb/resource/child-maltreatment-2012

Children's Bureau. (2016, November 30). The AFCARS report (Report no. 24). Retrieved from https://www.acf.hhs.gov/cb/resource/afcars-report-24

Christian, M., & Barbarin, O. (2001). Cultural resources and psychological adjustment of African American children: Effects of spirituality and racial attribution. *Journal of Black Psychology,* 27, 43–63.

Christie, H., Hamilton-Glachristsis, C., Alves-Costa, F., Tomlinson, M., & Halligan, S. L. (2019). The impact of parental posttraumatic stress disorder on parenting: A systematic review. *European Journal of Psychotraumatology, 10*(1), 1550345.

Chu, J. A. (2011). *Rebuilding shattered lives* (2nd ed.). New York, NY: Wiley.

Cicchetti, D. (2013). Annual research review: Resilient functioning in maltreated children; past, present and future perspectives. *Journal of Child Psychology and Psychiatry and Allied Disciplines, 54,* 402–422.

Cicchetti, D., & Lynch, M. (1993). Toward an ecological/transaction model of community violence and child maltreatment: Consequences for children's development. *Psychiatry, 56,* 96–118.

Cisler, J. M., Sigel, B. A., Steele, J. S., Smitherman, S., Vanderzee, K., Pemberton, J., . . . Kilts, C. D. (2016). Changes in functional connectivity of the amygdala during cognitive reappraisal predict symptom reduction during trauma-focused cognitive-behavioral therapy among adolescent girls with posttraumatic stress disorder. *Psychological Medicine, 46,* 3013–3023.

Classen, C. C., & Clark, C. S. (2017). Trauma-informed care. In S. N. Gold, C. J. Dalenberg, & J. M. Cook (Eds.), *APA handbook of trauma psychology, Vol. 2: Trauma practice* (pp. 515–541). Washington, DC: American Psychological Association.

Cloitre, M. (2015). The "one size fits all" approach to trauma treatment: Should we be satisfied? *European Journal of Psychotraumatology, 6.* doi:10.3402/ejpt.v6.27344

Cloitre, M., Khan, C., Mackintosh, M. A., Garvert, D. W., Henn-Haase, C. M., Falvey, E. C., & Saito, J. (2019). Emotion regulation mediates the relationship between ACES and physical and mental health. *Psychological Trauma, 11,* 82–89.

Cloitre, M., & Schmidt, J. A. (2015). STAIR narrative therapy. In U. Schnyder & M. Cloitre (Eds.), *Evidence based treatments for trauma-related psychological disorders: A practical guide for clinicians* (pp. 277–298). New York, NY: Springer.

Cohen, J. A., & Mannarino, A. P. (1996). A treatment outcome study for sexually abused preschoolers: Initial findings. *Journal of the American Academy of Child and Adolescent Psychiatry, 35*(1), 42–50.

Cohen, J. A., & Mannarino, A., P. (1998). Factors that mediate treatment outcome in sexually abused preschoolers: Six and 12-month follow-ups. *Journal of the American Academy of Child and Adolescent Psychiatry, 37,* 44–51.

Cohen, J. A., & Mannarino, A. P. (2000). Predictors of treatment outcome in sexually abused children. *Child Abuse and Neglect, 24*(7), 983–994.

Cohen, J. A., Mannarino, A. P., & Deblinger, E. (2017). *Treating trauma and traumatic grief in children and adolescence* (2nd ed.). New York, NY: Guilford Press.

Cohn, D., Silver, D., Cowan, C., Cowan, P., & Pearson, J. (1992). Working models of childhood attachment and couple relationships. *Journal of Family Issues, 13,* 432–449.

Coiro, M., & Emery, R. (1998). Do marriage problems affect fathering more than mothering? A quantitative and qualitative review. *Clinical Child and Family Psychology Review, 1,* 23–40.

Conners-Burrow, N. A., Kramer, T. L., Sigel, B. A., Helpenstill, K., Sievers, C., & McKelvey, L. (2013). Trauma-informed care training in a child welfare system: Moving it to the front line. *Children and Youth Services Review, 35,* 1830–1835.

Coohey, C. (1996). Child maltreatment: Testing the social isolation hypothesis. *Child Abuse and Neglect, 20,* 241–251.

Copping, V. E., Warling, D. L., Benner, D. G., & Woodside, D. W. (2001). A child trauma treatment pilot study. *Journal of Child and Family Studies, 10*(4), 467–475.

Corbin, J., & Strauss, A. (2008). *Basics of qualitative research: Techniques and procedures for developing grounded theory.* Thousand Oaks, CA: SAGE.

Courtois, C. A., & Ford, J. D. (2013). *Treatment of complex trauma: A sequenced, relationship-based approach.* New York, NY: Guilford Press.

Cougle, J. R., Kilpatrick, D. G., & Resnick, H. (2012). Defining traumatic events: Research findings and controversies. In J. G. Beck & D. M. Sloan (Eds.), *The Oxford handbook of traumatic stress* (pp. 11–27). New York, NY: Oxford University Press.

Cougle, J., Resnik, H., & Kilpatrick, D. (2009). Does prior exposure to interpersonal violence increase risk of PTSD following subsequent exposure? *Behavior Research and Therapy, 47,* 1012–1017.

Coulter, S. (2011). Systemic family therapy for families who have experienced trauma: A randomised controlled trial. *British Journal of Social Work, 41,* 502–519.

Courtois, C. A., & Ford, J. D. (2013). *Treatment of complex trauma: A sequenced, relationship-based approach.* New York, NY: Guilford Press.

Cowan, C., & Cowan, P. (2005). Two central roles for couple relationships: Breaking negative intergenerational patterns and enhancing children's adaptation. *Sexual and Relationship Therapy, 20,* 275–288.

Cox, M., Paley, B., Payne, C., & Burchinal, M. (1999). The transition to parenthood: Marital conflict and withdrawal and parent-infant interactions. In M. J. Cox & J. Brooks-Gun (Eds.), *Conflict and cohesion in families: Causes and consequences* (pp. 87–104). Mahwah, NJ: Erlbaum.

Cozolino, L. (2017). *The neuroscience of psychotherapy: Healing the social brain* (3rd ed.). New York, NY: W. W. Norton.

Cozolino, L. J., & Santos, E. N. (2014). Why we need therapy—and why it works: A neuroscientic perspective. *Smith College in Social Work, 84,* 157–177.

Creamer, M., Burgess, P., & McFaine, A. (2001). Post-traumatic stress disorder: Findings from the Australian National Survey of Mental Health and Well-being. *Psychological Medicine, 3*(7), 1237–1247.

Cronholm, P. F., Forke, C. M., Wade, R., Bair-Merritt, M. H., Davis, M., Harkins-Schwarz, M., . . . Fein, J. A. (2015). Adverse childhood experiences: Expanding the concept of adversity. *American Journal of Preventive Medicine, 49,* 354–361.

Cross, D., Fani, N., Powers, A., & Bradley, B. (2017). Neurological development in the context of childhood. *Clinical Psychology: Science and Practice, 24,* 111–124.

Crum, R. M., La Flair, L., Storr, C. L., Green, K. M., Stuart, E. A., Alvanzo, A. A. H., & Lazareck, S. R. (2013). Reports of drinking to self-medicate anxiety symptoms: Longitudinal assessment for subgroups of individuals with alcohol dependence. *Depression and Anxiety, 30,* 174–183.

Cusack, K., Jonas, D. E., Forneris, C. A., Wines, C., Sonis, J., Middleton, J. C., . . . Gaynes, B. N. (2016). Psychological treatments for adults with posttraumatic stress disorder: A systematic review and meta-analysis. *Clinical Psychology Review, 43,* 128–141.

Dana, D. (2018). *The polyvagal theory in therapy: Engaging the rhythm of regulation.* New York, NY: W. W. Norton.

David, S. (2013). Potential reporting bias in MRI studies of the brain. *PloS One, 8*(7), e70104.

Davies, P. T., & Cummings, E. M. (1994). Marital conflict and child adjustment: An emotional security hypothesis. *Psychological Bulletin, 116,* 387–411.

Davies, P., Harold, G. T., Goeke-Morey, M. C., & Cummings, E. M. (2002). Child emotional security and interparental conflict. *Monographs of the Society for Research in Child Development, 67,* 1–113.

Davies, P., Sturge-Apple, M., Woitach, M., & Cummings, E. (2009). A process analysis of the transmission of distress from interparental conflict to parenting: Adult relationship security as an explanatory mechanism. *Developmental Psychology, 45,* 1761–1773.

Deblinger, E., Lippmann, J., & Steer, R. (1996). Sexually abused children suffering posttraumatic stress symptoms: Initial treatment and outcome findings. *Child Maltreatment, 1,* 310–321.

De Jong, P., & Berg, I. K. (2013). *Interviewing for solutions* (4th ed.). Belmont, CA: Brooks/Cole.

de Shazer, S. (1985). *Keys to solutions in brief therapy.* New York, NY: W. W. Norton.

de Shazer, S. (1988). *Clues: Investigating solutions in brief therapy.* New York, NY: W. W. Norton.

de Shazer, S. (1991). *Putting difference to work.* New York, NY: W. W. Norton.

De Silva, P. (1993). Post-traumatic stress disorder: cross-cultural aspects. *International Review of Psychiatry, 5,* 217–229.

De Silva, P. (2006). The tsunami and its aftermath in Sri Lanka: Explorations of a Buddhist perspective. *International Review of Psychiatry, 18*(3), 281–287.

Dinkzwager, A., Bramsen, I. Ader, H., & Van der Ploeg, H. (2005). Secondary traumatization in partners and parents of Dutch peace-keeping soldiers. *Journal of Family Psychology, 19,* 217–226.

Dorrepaal, E., Thomaes, K., Hoogendoorn, A. W., Veltman, D. J., Draijer, N., & van Balkom, A. J. L. M. (2014). Evidence-based treatment for adult women with child abuse-related Complex PTSD: A quantitative review. *European Journal of Psychotraumatology, 5.* doi:10.3402/ejpt.v5.23613

Dorsey, S., McLaughlin, K. A., Kerns, S. E. U., Harrison, J. P., Lambert, H. K., Briggs, E. C., . . . Amaya-Jackson, L. (2017). Evidence base update for psychosocial treatments for children and adolescents exposed to traumatic events. *Journal of Clinical Child & Adolescent Psychology, 46,* 303–330.

Drozdek, B., Wilson, J. P., & Turkovic, S. (2012). Assessment of PTSD in non-Western cultures: The need for new contextual and complex perspectives. In J. G. Beck & D. M. Sloan (Eds.), *The Oxford handbook of traumatic stress* (pp. 302–314). New York, NY: Oxford University Press.

DuMont, K., Widom, C., & Czaja, S. (2007). Predictors of resilience in abused and neglected children grown-up: The role of individual and neighborhood characteristics. *Child Abuse and Neglect, 31,* 255274.

Dyson, J. (1990). The effect of family violence on children's academic performance and behavior. *Journal of the National Medical Association, 82,* 17–22.

Egeland, B., Jacobvitz, D., & Sroufe, L. (1988). Breaking the cycle of abuse. *Child Development, 59,* 1080–1088.

Ehlers, A., & Wild, J. (2015). Cognitive therapy for PTSD: Updating memories and meanings of trauma. In U. Schnyder & M. Cloitre (Eds.), *Evidence based treatments for trauma-related psychological disorders: A practical guide for clinicians* (pp. 161–188). New York, NY: Springer.

Ehring, T., Welboren, R., Morina, N., Wicherts, J. M., Freitag, J., & Emmelkamp, P. M. G. (2014). Meta-analysis of psychological treatments for posttraumatic stress disorder in adult survivors of childhood abuse. *Clinical Psychology Review, 34,* 645–657.

Elbert, T., Schauer, M., & Neuner, F. (2015). Narrative exposure therapy (NET): Reorganizing memories of traumatic stress, fear, and violence. In U. Schnyder & M. Cloitre (Eds.), *Evidence based treatments for trauma-related psychological disorders: A practical guide for clinicians* (pp. 229–255). New York, NY: Springer.

Elliot, D., Bjelajac, P., Fallot, R., Mrakoff, L., & Reed, B. (2005). Trauma-informed or trauma-denied: Principles and implementation of trauma-informed services for women. *Journal of Community Psychology, 33,* 461–464.

Elliot, D., Wilson, J., Huizinga, D., Sampson, R., Elliot, A., & Rankin, B. (1996). The effects of neighborhood disadvantage on adolescent development. *Journal of Research in Crimean and Delinquency, 33*(4), 389–426.

Ellis, A. (2017). Memories of urban warfare: Trauma, PTSD and gang violence. *Journal of Community Corrections, 2*(26), 1546–7627.

El-Sheikh, M., & Whitson, S. (2006). Longitudinal relations between marital conflict and child adjustment: Vagal regulation as a protective factor. *Journal of Family Psychology, 20,* 3039.

Enoch, M. (2011). The role of early life stress as a predictor for alcohol and drug dependence. *Psychopharmacology, 214,* 17–31.

Epstein, C., Hahn, H., Berkowitz, S., & Marans, S. (2017). The child and family traumatic stress intervention. In M. A. Landolt, M. Cloitre, & U. Schnyder (Eds.), *Evidence-based treatments for trauma related disorders in children and adolescents* (pp. 145–166). Cham, Switzerland: Springer International.

Etkin, A., & Wager, T. D. (2007). Functional neuroimaging of anxiety: A meta-analysis of emotional processing in PTSD, social anxiety disorder, and specific phobia. *American Journal of Psychiatry, 164,* 1476–1488.

Fallot, R. D., & Heckman, J. P. (2005). Religious/spiritual coping among women trauma survivors with mental health and substance use disorders. *Journal of Behavioral Health Services & Research, 32,* 215–226.

Fang, X., & Corso, P. (2007). Child maltreatment, youth violence and intimate partner violence: Developmental relationships. *American Journal of Preventive Medicine, 33,* 281–290.

Fehon, D., Grilo, C., & Lipschitz, D. (2001). Correlates of community violence exposure in hospitalized adolescents. *Comprehensive Psychiatry, 42*(4), 283–290.

Felitti, V., Anda, R. F., Nordenberg, D. Williamson, D. F., Spitz, A. M., Edwards, V., . . . Marks, J. S. (1998). Relationship of childhood abuse and household dysfunction to many of the leading causes of death in adults. *American Journal of Preventive Medicine, 14,* 245–258.

Felmingham, K., Kemp, A., Williams, L., Das, P. Hughes, G., Peduto, A., & Bryant, R. (2007). Changes in anterior cingulate and amygdala after cognitive behavior therapy of posttraumatic stress disorder. *Psychological Science, 18,* 127–129.

Figley, C. R., Ellis, A. E., Reuther, B. T., & Gold, N. (2017). The study of trauma: A historical overview. In S. N. Gold, J. M. Cook, & C. J. Dalenberg (Eds.), *APA handbook of trauma psychology, Vol. 1: Foundations in knowledge* (pp. 1–11). Washington, DC: American Psychological Association.

Figley, C., & Figley, K. (2009). Stemming the tide of trauma systemically: The role of family Therapy. *Australian and New Zealand Journal of Family Therapy, 30,* 173–183.

Fine, J. G., & Sung, C. (2014). Neuroscience of child and adolescent health development. *Journal of Counseling Psychology, 61,* 521–527.

Finger, B., Hans, S. L., Bernstein, V. J., & Cox, S. M. (2009). Parent relationship quality and infant–mother attachment. *Attachment & Human Development, 11,* 285–306.

Finkelhor, D., Ormrod, R. K., & Turner, H. A. (2009). Lifetime assessment of poly-victimization in a national sample of children and youth. *Child Abuse & Neglect, 33,* 403–411.

Finkelhor, D., Shattuck, A., Turner, H., & Hamby, S. (2015). A revised inventory of adverse childhood experiences. *Child Abuse & Neglect, 48,* 13–21.

Fisch, R., Weakland, J., & Segal, L. (1981). *The tactics of change.* New York, NY: W. W. Norton.

Fishbane, M. D. (2007). Wired to connect: Neuroscience, relationships, and therapy. *Family Process, 46,* 395–412.

Fisher P. A., Gunnar M. R., Dozier, M., Bruce J., & Pears K. C. (2006). Effects of therapeutic interventions for foster children on behavioral problems, caregiver attachment, and stress regulatory neural systems. *Annals of the New York Academy of Sciences, 1094,* 215–225.

Fitzpatrick, K., & Boldizar, J. (1993). The prevalence and consequences of exposure to violence among African-American youth. *Journal of the American Academy of Child and Adolescent Psychiatry, 32,* 424–430.

Fivaz-Deqeursinge, E., Lopes, F., Python, M., & Favex, N. (2009). Co-parenting and toddler's interactive styles in family coalitions. *Family Process, 48,* 500–516.

Fonzo, G. A., Goodkind, M. S., Oathes, D. J., Zaiko, Y. V., Harvey, M., Peng, K. K., . . . Etkin, A. (2017). Selective effects of psychotherapy on frontopolar cortical function in PTSD. *American Journal of Psychiatry, 174,* 1175–1184.

Forsythe, C. J., & Compas, B. E. (1987). Interaction of cognitive appraisals of stressful events and coping: Testing the goodness of fit. *Cognitive Therapy and Research, 11,* 47–85.

Fosco, G. M., & Grych, J. H. (2008). Emotional, cognitive and family systems mediators of children's adjustment to interparental conflict. *Journal of Family Psychology, 22,* 843–854.

Fosco, G. M., & Grych, J. H. (2010). Adolescent triangulation into parental conflicts: Longitudinal implications for appraisals and adolescent-parent relations. *Journal of Marriage and Family, 72,* 254–266.

Foy, D., Madvig, B., Pynoos, R., & Camilleri, A. (1996). Etiologic factors in the development of posttraumatic stress disorder in children and adolescents. *Journal of School Psychology, 34,* 133–145.

Frank, J. (1961). *Persuasion and healing: A comparative study of psychotherapy.* Baltimore, MD: Johns Hopkins University Press.

Fraser, J. S., Solovey, A. D., Grove, D., Lee, M. Y., & Greene, G. J. (2012). Integrative families and systems treatment: A middle path towards integrating common and specific factors. *Journal of Marital and Family Therapy, 38*(3), 515–528.

Fraser, J. S., Grove, D., Lee, M. Y., Greene, G., & Solovey, A. (2014). *Integrative family and systems treatment: A strength-based common factors approach.* New York, NY: Oxford University Press.

Freud, S. (1897). The etiology of hysteria. In J. Strachey (Ed.), *The standard edition of the complete works of Sigmund Freud* (Vol. 3, pp. 189–224). London, England: Hogarth Press.

Freud, S. (1898). Sexuality in the etiology of neuroses. In J. Strachey (Ed.), *The standard edition of the complete works of Sigmund Freud* (Vol. 3, pp. 261–286). London, England: Hogarth Press.

Freyd, J. (1996). *Betrayal trauma: The logic of forgetting childhood abuse.* Cambridge, MA: Harvard University Press.

Friedman, M. J., Keane, T. M., & Resick, P. A. (2014). *Handbook of PTSD: Science and practice* (2nd ed.). New York, NY: Guilford Press.

Fritz, P., Slep, A., & O'Leary, K. (2012). Couple-level analysis of the relation between family-of-origin aggression and intimate partner violence. *Psychology of Violence, 2,* 139–153.

Frost, N. D., Laska, K. M., & Wampold, B. E. (2014). The evidence for present-centered therapy as a treatment for posttraumatic stress disorder. *Journal of Traumatic Stress, 27,* 1–8.

Gallarin, M., & Alonso-Arbiol, I. (2012). Parenting practices, parental attachment and agressiveness in adolescence: A predictive model. *Journal of Adolescence, 35*(6), 1601–1610.

Galovski, T. E., Wachen, J. S., Chard, K. M., Monson, C. M. & Resick, P. A. (2015). Cognitive processing therapy. In U. Schnyder & M. Cloitre (Eds.), *Evidence based treatments for trauma-related psychological disorders: A practical guide for clinicians* (pp. 189–204). New York, NY: Springer.

Garbarino, J., Dubrow, N., Kostelny, K., & Pardo, C. (1992). *Children in danger: Coping with the consequences of community violence.* San Francisco, CA: Jossey-Bass.

Gaskill, R. L., & Perry, B. D. (2012). Child sexual abuse, traumatic experiences, and their impact on the developing brain. In P. Goodyear-Brown (Ed.), *Handbook of child sexual abuse: Identification, assessment, and treatment.* Hoboken, NJ: Wiley.

Gaudin, J., Polansky, N., Kilpatrick, N., & Shilton, P. (1993). Loneliness, depression, stress, and social support in neglectful homes. *American Journal of Orthopsychiatry, 63,* 597–605.

Gerard, J. Krishnakumar, A., & Buehler, C. (2006). Marital conflict, parent–child relations and youth maladjustment: A longitudinal investigation of spillover effects. *Journal of Family Issues, 27,* 951–975.

Gil, E. (2016). *Play in family therapy* (2nd ed.). New York, NY: Guilford Press.

Goffman, E. (1974). *Frame analysis: An essay on the organization of experience.* Cambridge, MA: Harvard University Press.

Goldbeck, L., & Jensen, T. K. (2017). The diagnostic spectrum of trauma-related disorders in children and adolescents. In M. A. Landolt, M. Cloitre, & U. Schnyder (Eds.), *Evidence-based treatments for trauma related disorders in children and adolescents* (pp. 3–28). Cham, Switzerland: Springer International.

Goncalves, O. F., & Perrone-McGovern, K. M. (2016). Translating neuroscience into counselling practice. *Canadian Journal of Counselling and Psychotherapy, 50,* 421–440.

Green, R., & Werner, P. (1996). Intrusiveness and closeness-caregiving: Rethinking the concept of family enmeshment. *Family Process, 35,* 115–136.

Greene, G. J., & Lee, M. Y. (2011). *Solution-oriented social work practice: An integrative approach to working with client strengths.* New York, NY: Oxford University Press.

Grove, D. (1993). Ericksonian approaches with multiple personality clients. *Journal of Family Psychotherapy, 4,* 1–18.

Grove, D. (2002). Opening up sexual abuse: Guidelines for helping incestuous families talk openly about sexual abuse. *Journal of Brief Therapy, 1,* 113–129.

Grove, D., & Burnaugh, R. (2002). *Invisible men: Finding, engaging and inspiring men in Therapy.* Phoenix, AZ: Zieg, Tucker & Theisen.

Grove, D., & Haley, J. (1993). *Conversations on therapy.* New York, NY: W. W. Norton.

Guarnaccia, P. J. (1993). Ataques de nervios in Puerto Rico: Culture-bound syndrome or popular illness? *Medical Anthropology, 15,* 157–170.

Gudino, O. G., Leonard, S., Stiles, A. A., Haven, J. F., & Cloitre, M. (2017). STAIR narrative therapy for adolescents. In M. A. Landolt, M. Cloitre, & U. Schnyder (Eds.), *Evidence-based treatments for trauma related disorders in children and adolescents* (pp. 251–272). Cham, Switzerland: Springer International.

Gurwitch, R. H., Messer, E. P., & Funderburk, B. W. (2017). Parent–child interaction therapy. In M. A. Landolt, M. Cloitre, & U. Schnyder (Eds.), *Evidence-based treatments for trauma related disorders in children and adolescents* (pp. 341–362). Cham, Switzerland: Springer International.

Haffner, J. (1977). The husbands of agoraphobic women and their influence on treatment outcomes. *British Journal of Psychiatry, 131,* 289–294.

Haffner, J. (1983). Agoraphobic women married to abnormally jealous men. *British Journal of medical Psychology, 52,* 99–104.

Haight, W. (2002). *African American children at church: A sociocultural perspective.* New York, NY: Cambridge University Press.

Haley, J. (1973). *Uncommon therapy.* New York, NY: W. W. Norton.

Haley, J. (1980). *Leaving home: Therapy of disturbed young people.* New York, NY: McGraw-Hill.

Haley, J. (1987). *Problem solving therapy.* San Francisco, CA: Jossey-Bass.

Haley, J. (1996). *Learning and teaching therapy.* New York, NY: Guilford Press.

Hall, G. (Ed.). (2017). *The psychotherapist's essential guide to the brain.* Brisbane, Australia: Dahlitz Media.

Hall, S. F., & Jones, A. S. (2018). Implementation of intensive permanence services: A trauma-informed approach to preparing foster youth for supportive relationships. *Child and Adolescent Social Work Journal, 35*(6), 587–598.

Hanna, S. M. (2014). *The transparent brain in couple and family therapy: Mindful integrations with neurosciences.* New York, NY: Routledge/Taylor & Francis.

Hanson, R. F., & Lang, J. (2016). A critical look at trauma-informed care among agencies and systems serving maltreated youth and their families. *Child Maltreatment, 21,* 95–100.

Harris, M., & Fallot, R. D. (2001). *Using trauma theory to design service systems: New directions for mental health services.* San Francisco, CA: Jossey-Bass.

Harris, W., Putnam, F., & Fairbank, J. (2006). Mobilizing trauma resources for children. In A. F. Lieberman & R. DeMartino (Eds.), *Shaping the future of children's health* (pp. 311–339). Calverton, NY: Johnson and Johnson Pediatric Institute.

Hashima, P., & Amato, P. (1994). Poverty, social support, and parental behavior. *Child Development, 65,* 394–403.

Heffernan, K., Cloitre, M., Tardiff, K., Marzuk, P. M., Portera, L., & Leon, A. C. (2000). Childhood trauma as a correlate of lifetime opiate use in psychiatric patients. *Addictive Behaviors, 25,* 797–2000.

Helpman, L., Santiago, P., Chhetry, B. T., Shvil, E., Rubin, M., Sullivan, G. M., . . . Yuval, N. (2016). PTSD remission after prolonged exposure treatment is associated with anterior cingulate cortex thinning and volume reduction. *Depression and Anxiety, 33,* 384–391.

Hill, R. (1999). *The strengths of African American families: Twenty-five years later* (2nd ed.). Lanham, MD: University Press of America.

Hitchcock, C., Ellis, A. A., Williamsom, P., & Nixon, R. D. V. (2015). The prospective role of cognitive appraisals and social support in predicting children's posttraumatic stress. *Journal of Abnormal Child Psychology, 43,* 1485–1492.

Hofstede, G. (1980). *Culture's consequences*. Beverly Hills, CA: SAGE.

Hopper, E. K. (2017). Trauma-informed psychological assessment of human trafficking survivors. *Women & Therapy, 40,* 12–30.

Horowitz, K., McKay, M., & Marshall, R. (2005). Community violence and urban families: Experiences, effects and directions for intervention. *American Journal of Orthopsychiatry, 75*(3), 356–368.

Horowitz, K., Weine, L., & Jekel, J. (1995). PTSD symptoms in urban adolescent girls: Compounded community trauma. *Journal of the American Academy of Child and Adolescent Psychiatry, 34,* 1353–1361.

Hughes, K. C., & Shin, L. M. (2011). Functional neuroimaging studies of post-traumatic stress disorder. *Expert Review of Neurotherapeutics, 11,* 275–285.

Huston, T. (2014, April 23). "Chiraq": Chicago becoming more dangerous than terror-torn Iraq. *Brietbart.* Retrieved from http://www.breitbart.com/big-gevernment/2014/04/23

Hyman, S. M., Garcia, M., & Sinha, R. (2006). Gender specific associations between types of childhood maltreatment and the onset, escalation and severity of substance use in cocaine dependent adults. *American Journal of Drug and Alcohol Abuse, 32,* 655–664.

Hyman, S. M., Gold, S. N., & Cott, M. A. (2003). Forms of social support that moderate PTSD in childhood sexual abuse survivors. *Journal of Family Violence, 18,* 295–300.

Hyman, S., Paliwal, P., & Sinha, R. (2007). Childhood maltreatment, perceived stress and stress-related coping in recently abstinent cocaine dependent adult. *Psychology of Addictive Behaviors, 21,* 233–223.

Imel, Z., Laska, K., Jakupcak, M., & Simpson, T. L. (2013). Meta-analysis of dropout in treatments for posttraumatic stress disorder. *Journal of Consulting and Clinical Psychology, 81,* 394–404.

Institute of Medicine of the National Academies. (2007, October). Treatment of PTSD: An assessment of the evidence. Report brief. National Academy of Sciences, Washington, DC.

Jaffee, S. R., Caspi, A., Moffitt, T. E., Polo-Tomas, M., & Taylor, A. (2007). Individual, family and neighborhood factors distinguish resilient form non-resilient maltreated children: a cumulative stressors model. *Child Abuse and Neglect, 13,* 231–253.

James, B. (1994). *Handbook for treatment of attachment-trauma problems in children*. New York, NY: Lexington Books.

James, K., & MacKinnon, L. (2012). Integrating a trauma lens into a family therapy framework: Ten principles for family therapists. *Australian and New Zealand Journal of Family Therapy, 33,* 189–209.

Janoff-Bulman, R. (1992). *Shattered assumptions: Towards a new psychology of trauma*. New York, NY: The Free Press.

Jatzko, A., Rothenhofer, S., Schmitt, A., Gaser, C., Demirakca, T., Weber-Fahr, W., . . . Braus, D. F. (2006). Hippocampal volume in chronic posttraumatic stress disorder (PTSD): MRI study using two different evaluation methods. *Journal of Affective Disorders, 94,* 121–126.

Jennings, A. (1991). The relationships among three factors of prayer, stress, and coping. *Dissertation Abstracts International*, 51(10).

Jones, M. (2007). Exposure to chronic community violence: Resilience in African American children, *Journal of Black Psychology, 33*(2), 125–149.

Julich, S. J. (2001). *Breaking the silence: Restorative justice and child sexual abuse*. Albany, New Zealand: Massey University,

Kagitcibasi, C. (1994). A critical appraisal of individualism and collectivism: Toward a new formulation. In U. Kim, H. C. Triandis, C. Kagitcibasi, S. Choi, & G. Yoon (Eds.), *Individualism and collectivism: Theory, method and applications* (pp. 52–65). Thousand Oaks, CA: SAGE.

Kalmakis, K. A., & Chandler, G. E. (2013). Adverse childhood experiences: Towards a clear conceptual meaning. *Journal of Advanced Nursing, 70,* 1489–1501.

Kalmakis, K. A., & Chandler, G. E. (2015). Health consequences of adverse childhood experiences; A systematic review. *Journal of the American Association of Nurse Practitioners, 27,* 457–465.

Katz, L., & Gottman, J. (1996). Spillover effects of marital conflict: In search of parenting and co-parenting mechanisms. In J. P. McHale & P. A. Cowan (Eds.), *Understanding how family-level dynamics affect children's development: Studies of two-parent families* (pp. 57–76). San Francisco CA. Jossey-Bass.

Kauffman, J. (Ed.). (2002). *Loss of the assumptive world: A theory of traumatic loss.* New York, NY: Brunner-Routledge.

Kerig, P. (2012). Trauma and juvenile delinquency: Dynamics and developmental mechanisms. *Journal of Child and Adolescent Trauma, 5,* 83–87.

Kerig, P., & Alexander, J. (2012). Family matters: Integrating trauma treatment into Functional Family Therapy for traumatized delinquent youth. *Journal of Child and Adolescent Trauma, 5,* 205–223.

Kerig, P., & Becker, S. (2010). From internalizing to externalizing: Theoretical models of the processes linking PTSD to juvenile delinquency. In S. J. Egan (ED.), *Posttraumatic stress disorder (PTSD): Causes, symptoms and treatment* (pp. 33–78). Hauppauge, NY: Nova.

Kerig, P., Vanderee, K., Becker, S., & Ward, R. (2011). Deconstructing PTSD: Traumatic experiences, posttramatic symptom clusters and mental health problems among delinquent youth. *Journal of Child and Adolescent Trauma, 5,* 129–144.

Kerig, P., Wainryb, C., Twaali, M., & Chaplo, S. (2013). America's child soldiers: Toward a research agenda for studying gang-involved youth in the United States. *Journal of Aggression, Maltreatment and Trauma,* 22(7), 773–795.

Kernsmith, P. (2006). Gender differences in the impact of family of origin violence on perpetrators of domestic violence. *Journal of Family Violence, 21,* 163–117.

Kessler, R. C., Sonnega, A., Bromet, E., Hughes, M., & Nelson, C. B. (1995). Posttraumatic stress disorder in the national comorbidity survey. *Archives of General Psychiatry, 52,* 1048–1060.

Kilpatrick, D., Acierno, R., Saunders, B., Resick, H., Best, C., & Schnurr, P. (2000). Risk factors for adolescent substance abuse and dependence: Data from a national sample. *Journal of Consulting and Clinical Psychology, 68,* 19–30.

Kleinman, A. (1982). Neurasthenia and depression: A study of somatization and culture in *China. Culture, Medicine and Psychiatry, 6,* 117–190.

Kliethermes, M. D., Drewry, K., & Wamser-Nanney, R. (2017). Trauma-focused cognitive behavioral therapy. In M. A. Landolt, M. Cloitre, & U. Schnyder (Eds.), *Evidence-based treatments for trauma related disorders in children and adolescents* (pp. 167–186). Cham, Switzerland: Springer International.

Kliewer, W., Lepore, S., Oskin, D., & Johnson, P. (1998). The role of social and cognitive processes in children's adjustment to community violence. *Journal of Consulting and Clinical Psychology, 66,* 199–209.

Knight, C. (2015). Trauma-informed social work practice: Practice considerations and challenges. *Clinical Social Work Journal, 43,* 25–37.

Kolassa, I. T., & Elbert, T. (2007). Structural and functional neuroplasticity in relation to traumatic stress. *Current Directions in Psychological Science, 16,* 321–325.

Kretchmar, M., & Jacobvitz, D. (2002). Observing mother–child relationships across generations: Boundary patterns, attachment and the transmission of caregiving. *Family Process, 41,* 351–374.

Kwong, M., Bartholomew, K., Henderson, A., & Trinke, S. (2003). The intergenerational transmission of relationship violence. *Journal of Family Psychology, 17,* 288–301.

Lacky, C., & Williams, K. (1995). Social bonding and the cessation of partner violence across generations. *Journal of Marriage and the Family, 57,* 295–305.

La Flair, L. N., Franko, D. L., & Herzog, D. B. (2008). Sexual assault and disordered eating in Asian women. *Harvard Review of Psychiatry, 16,* 248–257.

Lambert, J. E., Holzer, J., & Hasbun, A. (2014). Association between parents' PTSD severity and children's psychological distress: A meta-analysis. *Journal of Traumatic Stress, 27,* 9–17.

Lambert, M. J. (1992). Implications of outcome research for psychotherapy integration. In J. C. Norcross & M. R. Goldfriend (Eds.), Handbook of psychotherapy integration (pp. 94–129). New York, NY: Basic Books.

Lang, A. J., & Gartstein, M. A. (2018). Intergenerational transmission of traumatization: Theoretical framework and implications for prevention. *Journal of Trauma & Dissociation, 19,* 162–175.

Langeland, W., & Dijkstra, S. (1995). Breaking the intergenerational transmission of child abuse: Beyond the mother-child relationship. *Child Abuse Review, 4,* 4–13.

Larkin, H., Felitti, V. J., & Anda, R. F. (2014). Social work and adverse childhood experiences research: Implications for practice and health policy. *Social Work in Public Health, 29,* 1–16.

Laugharne, J., Kullack, C., Lee, C. W., McGuire, T., Drummond, P. D., & Starkstein, S. (2016). Amygdala volumetric change following psychotherapy for posttraumatic stress disorder. *Journal of Neuropsychiatry and Clinical Neuroscience, 28,* 312–318.

Lauth-Lebens, M., & Lauth, G. W. (2016). Risk and resilience factors of posttraumatic stress disorder: A review of current research. *Clinical and Experimental Psychology,* 2(2). http://dx.doi.org/10.4172/2471-2701.1000120. doi:10.4172/2471-2701.1000120

Lee, J., Pomero, E., Yoo, S., & Rheinboldt, K. (2005). Attitudes toward rape: A comparison between Asian and Caucasian college students. *Violence Against Women, 11,* 177–196.

Lee, M. Y., Fraser, J. S., Greene, G. J., Solovey, A., Grove, D. (2014). *I-FAST Fidelity Scale* (rev. ed.). Columbus, OH: Lee, Fraser, Greene, Solovey & Grove. Updated ed. (Original work published 2003)

Lee, M. Y., & Greene, G. J. (2002). *Systems Collaboration Scale.* Columbus, OH: Lee & Greene.

Lee, M. Y., Greene, G. J., Fraser, J. S., Edwards, S. G., Scott, P., Grove, D., & Solovey, A. (2013). Common and specific factors approaches to home-based treatment: I-FAST and MST. *Research on Social Work Practice, 23*(4), 407–418.

Lee, M. Y., Greene, G. J., Fraser, J. S., Grove, D., Solovey, A., Edwards, S., & Scott, P. (2013). Common and specific factors approaches to home-based treatment: I-FAST and MST. *Research on Social Work Practice, 23,* 407–418.

Lee, M. Y., Greene, G. J., Hsu, K. S., Solovey, A., Grove, D., Fraser, S., . . . Teater, B. (2009). Utilizing family strengths and resilience: Integrative Family and Systems Treatment (I-FAST) with children and adolescents with severe emotional and behavioral problems. *Family Process, 48,* 395–416.

Lee, M. Y., Hsu, K. S., Liu, C., Greene, J. G., Fraser, S., Grove, D., . . . Scott, P. (2015). Treatment efficacy of Integrative Family and Systems Treatment (I-FAST) with and without consultation: the role of model training in the sustainability of evidence-based family treatments. *Administration and Policy in Mental Health and Mental Health Services Research, 43*(4), 579–591.

Lee, M. Y., Sebold, J., & Uken, A. (2003). *Solution-focused treatment with domestic violence offenders: Accountability for change.* New York, NY: Oxford University Press.

Lee, M. Y., Teater, B., Greene, G. J., Hsu, K. S., Fraser, S., Solovey, A., Grove, D., & Washburn, P. (2012). Key processes, ingredients and components of successful systems collaboration: Working with severely emotionally or behaviorally disturbed children and their families. *Administration and Policy in Mental Health and Mental Health Services Research, 39*(5), 394–405.

Lee, M. Y., Teater, B., Hsu, K. S., Greene, G. J., Fraser, S., Solovey, A., Grove, D. (2013). Systems collaboration with schools and treatment of SED children or adolescents. *Children & Schools, 35*(3), 155–168.

Lee, R. (2001). Ethnomedicine: Ancient wisdom for contemporary healing. *Alternative Therapies in Health and Medicine, 7,* 28–30.

Leerkes, E., & Crockenberg, S. (2006). Antecedents of mothers' emotional and cognitive responses to infant distress: The role of family, mother, and infant characteristics. *Infant Mental Health Journal, 27,* 405–428.

Le-Scherban, F., Wang, X., Boyle-Steed, K. H., & Pachter, L. M. (2018). Intergenerational associations of parent adverse childhood experiences and child health outcomes. *Pediatrics, 141,* 1–9.

Leshem, B., Haj-Yahia, M. M., & Guterman, N. B. (2016). The role of family and teacher support in post-traumatic stress symptoms among Palestinian adolescents exposed to community violence. *Journal of Child and Family Studies, 25,* 488–502.

Leventhal, T., & Brooks-Gunn, J. (2000). The neighborhoods they live in: the effects of neighborhood residence on child and adolescent outcomes. *Psychological Bulletin, 126*(2), 309–337.

Liberzon, I., & Sripada, C. S. (2008). The functional neuroanatomy of PTSD: A critical review. *Progress in Brain Research, 167,* 151–169.

Lieberman, A. F., Ippen, C. G., & Van Horn, P. (2006). Child–parent psychotherapy: 6-month follow-up of a randomized controlled trial. *Journal of the American Academy of Child and Adolescent Psychiatry, 45,* 913–918.

Lieberman, A. F., & Van Horn, P. (2008). *Psychotherapy with infants and youth children: Repairing the effects of stress and trauma on early attachment.* New York, NY: Guilford Press.

Lincoln, Y. S., & Guba, E. G. (1985). *Naturalistic inquiry.* Newbury Park, CA: SAGE.

Lindauer, R. J. L., Vlieger, E. J., Jalink, M., Olff, M. Carlier, V. E., Majoie, C. B. L. M., den Heeten, G. J., & Gersons, B. P. R. (2005). Effects of psychotherapy on hippocampal volume in outpatients with post-traumatic stress disorder: A MRI investigation. *Psychological Medicine, 35,* 1421–1431.

Ludy-Dobson, C., & Perry, B. (2010). The role of healthy relational interactions in buffering the impact of childhood trauma. In E. Gil (Ed.), *Working with children to heal interpersonal trauma: The power of play* (pp. 26–43). New York, NY: Guilford Press.

Lyons-Ruth, K., Melnick, S., Bronfman, E., Sherry, S., & Llanas, L. (2004). Hostile-helpless relational models and disorganized attachment patterns between parents and their young children: Review of research and implications for clinical work. In L. Atkinson & S. Goldberg (Eds.), *Attachment issues in psychopathology and intervention* (pp. 65–94). Mahwah, NJ: Erlbaum.

Madanes, C. (1981). *Strategic family therapy.* San Francisco, CA: Jossey-Bass.

Madanes, C. (1990). *Sex, love and violence: Strategies for transformation.* New York: W. W. Norton.

Madanes, C. (1995). *The violence of men.* San Francisco, CA: Jossey-Bass.

Maljeko, K., Abler, B., Plener, P. L., & Straub, J. (2017). Neural correlates of psychotherapeutic treatment of post-traumatic stress disorder: A systematic literature review. *Frontiers in Psychiatry, 8,* 1–12.

Markowitz, J. C. (2017). *Interpersonal psychotherapy for posttraumatic stress disorder.* New York, NY: Oxford University Press.

Markowitz, J. C., Choo, T. H., & Neria, Y. (2018). Do acute benefits of interpersonal psychotherapy for posttraumatic stress disorder endure? *Canadian Journal of Psychiatry, 63,* 37–43.

Markowitz, J. C., Petkova, E., Neria, Y., Van Meter, P. E., Zhao, Y., Hembree, E., . . . Marshall, R. D. (2015). Is exposure necessary? A randomized clinical trial of interpersonal psychotherapy for PTSD. *American Journal of Psychiatry, 172,* 430–440.

Marriott, C., Hamilton-Giachritsis, C., & Harrop, C. (2014). Factors promoting resilience following childhood sexual abuse: A structured narrative review of the literature. *Child Abuse Review, 23,* 17–34.

Marshall, D., English, D., & Stewart, A. (2001). The effect of fathers or father figures on child behavioral problems in families referred to child protective services. *Child Maltreatment, 6,* 290–299.

Matsakis, A. (2007). *Back from the front: Combat trauma, love and the family.* Baltimore, MD: Sidran Institute Press.

McAdoo, H. (1997). *Black families* (3rd ed.). Thousand Oaks, CA: SAGE.

McClean, C. P., Asnaani, A., & Foa, E. B. (2015). Prolonged exposure therapy. In U. Schnyder & M. Cloitre (Eds.), *Evidence based treatments for trauma-related psychological disorders: A practical guide for clinicians* (pp. 143–160). New York, NY: Springer.

McEwen, B. S. (2000). The neurobiology of stress: From serendipity to clinical relevance. *Brain Research, 886,* 172–189.

McGoldrick, M., Gerson, R., & Petry, S. (2008). *Genograms: Assessment and intervention* (3rd ed.). New York, NY: W. W. Norton.

McNeil, C. B., Hembree-Kigin, T. L., & Anhalt, K. (2011). *Parent–child interaction therapy.* New York, NY: Springer.

Merkangas, K., Avenevoli, S., Costello, J., Koretz, D., & Kessler, R. (2009). National comorbidity survey replication adolescent supplement (NCS-A). Background and Measures. *Journal of American Academy of Adolescent Psychiatry, 48*(4), 367–369.

Milad, M. R., Pitman, R. K., Ellis, C. B., Gold, A. L, Shin, L. M., Lasko, N. B., . . . Rauch, S. L. (2009). Neurobiological basis of failure to recall extinction memory in posttraumatic stress disorder. *Biological Psychiatry, 66,* 1075–1082.

Milani, A. C. C., Hoffman, E. V., Fossaluza, V., Jackowki, A. P., & Mello, M. F. (2016). Does pediatric post-traumatic stress disorder alter the brain? Systematic review and meta-analysis of structural and functional magnetic resonance imaging studies. *Psychiatry and Clinical Neurosciences, 71,* 154–169.

Miller, T., (1995). Stress adaptation in children: Theoretical models. *Journal of Contemporary Psychotherapy, 25,* 5–14.

Minuchin, S. (1974). *Families and family therapy.* Cambridge, MA: Harvard University Press.

Minuchin, P., Brooks, A., Colapinto, L., Genijovich, E., Minuchin, D., & Minuchin, S. (1990). *Training manual for foster parents based on an ecological perspective on foster care.* New York, NY: Family Studies.

Minuchin, S., & Fishman, C. (1981). *Family therapy techniques.* Cambridge, MA: Harvard University Press.

Montgomery, A. (2013). *Neurobiology essentials for clinicians: What every therapist needs to know.* New York, NY: W. W. Norton.

Najavits, L. M., & Anderson, M. L. (2015). Psychosocial treatments for posttraumatic stress disorder. In P. E. Nathan & J. M. Gorman (Eds.), *A guide to treatments that work* (4th ed., pp. 571–592). New York, NY: Oxford University Press.

Najavits, L. M., Hyman, S. M., Ruglass, L. M., Hien, D. A., & Read, J. P. (2017). Substance use disorder and trauma, In S. N. Gold (Ed.), *APA handbook of trauma psychology: Foundations in knowledge* (Vol. 1, pp. 195–213). Washington, DC: American Psychological Association.

Najavits, L. M., Weiss, R. D., & Shaw, S. R., (1997). The link between substance abuse and posttraumatic stress disorder in women. A research review. *American Journal of Addiction, 6,* 273–283.

Nakazawa, D. J. (2015). *Childhood disrupted: How your biography becomes your biology, and how you can heal.* New York, NY: Simon and Schuster.

National Childhood Traumatic Stress Network Core Concepts and Curriculum Workgroup. (2013). Psychological first aid (PFA) field operations guide Appendix A. Available at https://www.nctsn.org/resources/psychological-first-aid-pfa-field-operations-guide-appendix

Nayak, N., Powers, M. B., & Foa, E. B. (2012). Empirically supported psychological treatments: Prolonged exposure therapy. In J. G. Beck & D. M. Sloan (Eds.), *The Oxford handbook of traumatic stress disorder* (pp. 427–438). New York, NY: Oxford University Press.

Neimeyer, R. A. (Ed.). (2001). *Meaning reconstruction and the experience of loss.* Washington, DC: American Psychological Association.

Newcomb, M., & Locke, T. (2001). Intergenerational cycle of maltreatment: A popular concept obscured by methodological limitations. *Child Abuse and Neglect, 25,* 1219–1240.

Nichter, M. (1991). Ethnomedicine: Diverse trends, common linkages. Commentary. *Medical Anthropology, 13,* 137–171.

Nijdam, M. J., Martens, I. J. M., Reitsma, J. B., Gersons, B. P. R., & Olff, M. (2018). Neurocognitive functioning over the course of trauma-focused psychotherapy for PTSD: Changes in verbal memory and executive functioning. *British Journal of Clinical Psychology, 57,* 436–452.

Ogles, B. M., Melendez, G., Davis, D., & Lunnen, K. M. (2001). The Ohio scales: Practical outcome assessment. *Journal of Child and Family Studies, 10,* 199–212.

Ohio Department of Mental Health. (2006). *The statewide report* (Vol. 12). Columbus, OH: Author.

Olfson, M., Mojtabai, R., Sampson, N., Hwang, I., Drus, B., & Wang, (2009). Dropout from outpatient mental health care in the United States. *Psychiatric Services, 60,* 898–907.

Olson, D. H. (1985). *Family inventories: Inventories used in a national survey of families across the family life cycle.* St. Paul, MN: Family Social Science, University of Minnesota.

Olson, D. H. (2007). *Family satisfaction scale (FSS).* Minneapolis, MN: Life Innovations.

Olson, D. H., & Barnes, H. L. (2007). *Family communication scale (FCS).* Minneapolis, MN: Life Innovations.

Olson, D. H., & Gorall, D. M. (2006). *FACES IV and the circumplex model.* Minneapolis, MN: Life Innovations.

Olson, D. H., Gorall, D. M., & Tiesel, J. W. (2007). *FACES IV manual.* Minneapolis: Life Innovations.

Olson, D. H., McCubbin, H. I., Barnes, H., Larsen, A., Muxen, M., & Wilson, M. (1982). *Families: What makes them work.* Newbury Park, CA: SAGE.

Olson, D. H., Russell, C. S., & Sprenkle, D. H. (1983). Circumplex model of marital and family systems: VI. Theoretical update. *Family Process, 22,* 69–83.

Osofsky, J., (1995). The effects of exposure to violence on young children. *American Psychologist, 50,* 782–785.

Oudshoorn, J., Amstuctz, L. S., & Jackett, M. (2015b). *The little book of restorative justice for sexual abuse: Hope through trauma.* New York, NY: Good Books.

Overstreet, S., & Braun, S. (2000). Exposure to community violence and post-traumatic stress symptoms: Mediating factors. *American Journal of Orthopsychiatry, 70,* 263–270.

Overstreet, S., Dempsey, M., Graham, D., & Moley, B. (1999). Availability of family support as a moderator of exposure to community violence. *Journal of Clinical Child Psychology, 28,* 151–159.

Owen, M., & Cox, M. (1997). Marital conflict and the development of infant-parent attachment relationships. *Journal of Family Psychology, 11,* 152–164.

Ozer, E., Best, S., Lipsey, T., & Weiss, D. (2003). Predictors of posttraumatic stress disorder and symptoms in adults: A meta-analysis. *Psychological Bulletin, 129,* 52–73.

Pacela, M. L., & Delahanty, D. L. (2012). Classification of acute stress disorder. In J. G. Beck & D. M. Sloan (Eds.), *The Oxford handbook of traumatic stress disorders* (pp. 28–38). New York, NY: Oxford University Press.

Padgett, D. K. (2016). *Qualitative methods in social work research.* Thousand Oaks, CA: SAGE.

Paige, J., & Thornton, J. (2015). Healing from Intra-family sexual abuse: The role of relational processes between survivor and offender. *Children Australia, 40,* 242–259.

Palfrey, N., Reay, R. E., Aplin, V., Cubis, J. C., McAndrew, V., Riordan, D. M., & Raphael, B. (2019). Achieving service change through the implementation of a trauma-informed care training program with a mental health service. *Community Mental Health Journal, 55,* 467–475.

Park, C. L., Armelz, S., & Tennen, H., (2004). Appraisal-coping goodness of fit: A daily internet study. *Personality and Social Psychology Bulletin, 30,* 558–569.

Pearlman, L. A., & Courtois, C. A. (2005). Clinical applications of the attachment framework: Relational treatment of complex trauma. *Journal of Traumatic Stress, 18,* 449–459.

Pecora, P. J., Kessler, R. K., Williams, J., O'Brien, K., Downs, A. C., English, D., . . . Holmes, K. (2005). *Improving family foster care: Findings from the Northwest foster care alumni study.* Seattle, WA: Casey Family Programs.

Pereda, N., Guilera, G., Forns, M., & Gomez-Benito, J. (2009). The prevalence of child sexual abuse in community and student samples: a meta-analysis. *Clinical Psychology Review, 29,* 328–338.

Perrin, S., Leigh, E., Smith, P., Yule, W., Ehlers, A., & Clark, D. M. (2017). Cognitive therapy for PTSD in children and adolescents. In M. A. Landolt, M. Cloitre, & U. Schnyder (Eds.), *Evidence-based treatments for trauma related disorders in children and adolescents* (pp. 187–208). Cham, Switzerland: Springer International.

Perry, B. (2005). Maltreatment and the developing child: How early childhood experience shapes child and culture. *The McCain Lecture Series, Centre for Children & Families in the Justice System.* Retrieved from http://www.lfcc.on.ca/mccain/perry.pdf

Perry, B. (2006). Applying principles of neurodevelopment to clinical work with maltreated and traumatized children: The neurosequential model of therapeutics. In N. B. Webb (Ed.), *Working with traumatized youth in child welfare* (pp. 27–52). New York, NY: Guilford Press.

Polusny, M., & Follette,V. (1995). Long-term correlates of child sexual abuse: Theory and review of the empirical literature. *Applied and Preventive Psychology, 4,* 143–166.

Porges, S. W. (2011). *The polyvagal theory: Neurophysiological foundations of emotions, attachment, communication, self-regulation.* New York, NY: W. W. Norton.

Porges, S. W. (2017). *The pocket guide to the polyvagal theory: The transformative power of feeling safe.* New York, NY: W. W. Norton.

Porges, S. W. (2018). Polyvagal theory: A primer. In S. W. Porges & D. Dana (Eds.), *Clinical applications of polyvagal theory: The emergence of polyvagal-informed therapies* (pp. 50–69). New York, NY: W. W. Norton.

Post, M., Hanten, G., Xiaoqi, L, Schmidt, A., Avci, G., Wilde, E., & McCauley, S. (2014). Dimensions of trauma and specific symptoms of complex posttraumatic stress disorder in inner-city youth: A preliminary study. *Violence and Victims,* 29(2), 262–279.

Price, J. (1999). *Power and compassion: Working with difficult adolescents and abused parents.* New York, NY: Guilford Press.

Price, M., Pallito, S., & Legrand, A. C. (2018). Heterogeneity in the strength of the relation between social support and post-trauma psychopathology. *Journal of Psychopathology and Behavioral Assessment, 40,* 334–343.

Pruitt, D. (2016). *Beyond the offense: Family involvement and restorative trauma treatment of juvenile sex offenders.* El Paso, TX: LFB Scholarly Publishing.

Pynoos, R. (1993). Traumatic stress and developmental psychopathology in children and adolescents. In J. M. Oldham, M. B. Riba, & A. Tasman (Eds.), *The American psychiatric press review of psychiatry* (Vol. 12, pp. 205–338). Washington, DC: American Psychiatric Press.

Racine, N., Plamondon, A., Madigan, S., McDonald, S., & Tough, S. (2018). Maternal adverse childhood experiences and infant development. *Pediatrics, 141*(4), e20172495. doi:10.1542/peds.2017-2495

Rak, C. F., & Patterson, L. E. (1996). Promoting resilience in at-risk children. *Journal of Counseling & Development, 74,* 7368–373.

Ralph, R. O. (2005). Verbal definitions and visual models of recovery: Focus on the recovery model. In R. Ralph & P. W. Corrigan (Eds.), *Recovery in mental illness: Broadening our understanding of wellness* (pp. 134–145) Washington, DC: American Psychological Association.

Rao, K., DiClemente, R. J., & Ponton, I. E. (1992). Child sexual abuse of Asians compared with other populations. *Journal of American Academy of Child and Adolescent Psychiatry, 31,* 880–886.

Resick, P. A., Monson, C. M., & Chard, K. M. (2017). *Cognitive processing therapy for PTSD: A comprehensive manual.* New York, NY: Guilford Press.

Reyes, V., Stone, B. J., Dimmler, M. H., & Lieberman, A. F. (2017). Child–parent psychotherapy: An evidence-based treatment for infants and young children. In M. A. Landolt, M. Cloitre, & U. Schnyder (Eds.), *Evidence-based treatments for trauma related disorders in children and adolescents* (pp. 321–340). Cham, Switzerland: Springer International.

Rhodes, J., Ebert, L., & Meyers, A. (1994). Social support, relationship problems and the psychological functioning of young African American mothers. *Journal of Social and Personal Relationships, 11*(4), 587–599.

Riggs, D. S., Monson, C. M., Glynn, S. M., & Canterino, J. (2009). Couple and family therapy for adults. In F. B. Foa, T. M. Keane, M. Friedman, & J. A. Cohen (Eds.), *Effective treatments for post-traumatic stress: Practice guidelines from the International Society for Traumatic Stress Studies.* London, England: Guilford Press.

Rodriguez, N., Kemp, H. V., & Foy, D. (1998). Posttraumatic stress disorder in survivors of childhood sexual and physical abuse: A critical review of the empirical research. *Journal of Child Sexual Abuse, 7,* 17–45.

Saito, S. (1998). Childhood sexual abuse and dissociation in Japan: A clinical overview from an outpatient clinic standpoint. *Psychiatry and Clinical Neurosciences, 52*(Suppl), S151–S155.

Sameroff, A. (1998). Environmental risk factors in infancy. *Pediatrics, 102,* 1287–1292.

Sar, V., Kundakci, T., Kiziltan, E., Bakin, B., & Bozkurt, O. (2000). Differentiating dissociative disorders from other diagnostic groups through somatoform dissociation in Turkey. *Journal of Trauma & Dissociation, 1,* 67–80.\

Saxe, G., Ellis, H., Fogler, J., & Navalta, C. (2012). Innovations in practice: Preliminary evidence for effective family engagement in treatment for child traumatic stress-trauma systems therapy approach to preventing dropout. *Child and Adolescent Mental Health, 17,* 58–61.

Schauer, M., Neuner, F., & Elbert, T. (2017). Narrative exposure therapy for children and adolescents (KIDNET). In M. A. Landolt, M. Cloitre, & U. Schnyder (Eds.), *Evidence-based treatments for trauma related disorders in children and adolescents* (pp. 227–250). New York, NY: Springer.

Schickedanz, A., Halfon, N., Sastry, N., & Chung, P. J. (2018). Parents' adverse childhood experiences and their children's behavioral health problems. *Pediatrics, 142,* 1–9.

Schnyder, U., Ehlers, A., Elbert, T. Foa, E., Gersons, B., Resick, P., . . . Cloitre, M. (2015). Psychotherapies for PTSD: What do they have in common. *European Journal of Psychotraumatology, 6.* doi:10.3402/ejpt.v6.24750

Schuler, E. R., & Boals, A. (2016). Shattering world assumptions: A prospective view of the impact of adverse events on world assumptions. *Psychological Trauma, 8,* 259–266.

Schwarz, B. (2009). Interparental conflict and adolescents' depressive mood in separated families: The role of triangulation. *Psyhologie in Erziehung und Unterrict, 56,* 95–104.

Schwarz, S. (1990). Individualism–collectivism: Critique and proposed refinements. *Journal of Cross-Cultural Psychology, 21,* 139–157.

Schwartz, J., & Steffensmeier, D. (2012). Stability and change in girls' delinquency and the gender gap: Trends in violence and alcohol offending across multiple sources of evidence. In S. Miller, L. Leve, & P Kerig (Eds.), *Delinquent girls: Contexts, relationships and adaptation* (pp. 3–23). New York, NY: Springer.

Selekman, M. (2017). *Working with high-risk adolescents: An individualized family therapy approach.* New York, NY: Guilford Press.

Sevel-Brooks, S. B., & Rice, K. F. (1997). *Families in recovery coming full circle.* Baltimore, MD: Brooks.

Shaffer, A., & Sroufe, L. (2005). The developmental and adaptational implications of generational boundary dissolution: Findings from a perspective longitudinal study. *Journal of Emotional Abuse, 5,* 67–84.

Shah, S. A. (2007). Ethnomedical best practices for international psychosocial efforts in disaster and trauma. In J. P. Wilson & C. S. Tang (Eds.), *Cross-cultural assessment of psychological trauma and PTSD* (pp. 51–64). Boston, MA: Springer.

Shapiro, F., & Laliotis, F. (2015). EMDR therapy for trauma-related disorder. In U. Schnyder & M. Cloitre (Eds.), *Evidence based treatments for trauma-related psychological disorders: A practical guide for clinicians* (pp. 205–228). New York, NY: Springer.

Shapiro, F., Wesselmann, D., & Mevissen, L. (2017). Eye movement desensitization and reprocessing therapy (EMDR). In M. A. Landolt, M. Cloitre, & U. Schnyder (Eds.), *Evidence-based treatments for trauma related disorders in children and adolescents* (pp. 273–299). Cham, Switzerland: Springer International.

Sharkansky, E., King, D. W., King, I. A., Wolfe, J., Erickson, K. D., & Stokes, L. (2000). Coping with combat war stress: Mediating and moderating effects. *Journal of Abnormal Psychology, 109,* 188–197.

Sheehan, K., DiCara, J., LeBally, S., & Christoffel, K. (1997). Children's exposure to violence in an urban setting. *Archives of Pediatric and Adolescent Medicine, 151,* 502–504.

Sherman, M. D., Blevins, D., Kirchner, J., Ridenere, L., & Jackson, T. (2008). Key factors involved in engaging significant others in the treatment of Vietnam veterans with PTSD. *Professional Psychology: Research and Practice, 29,* 443–450.

Shvil, E., van der Hoorn, K., Papini, S., Sullivan, G. M., Neria, A., & Neria, Y. (2016). Functional magnetic resonance imaging (fMRI) of PTSD: Current status and future directions. In E. J. Bromet (Ed.), *Long-term outcomes in psychopathology research: Rethinking the scientific agenda* (pp. 293–312). New York, NY: Oxford University Press.

Skinner, L., & McLean, L. (2017). The conversational model and child and family counselling: Treating chronic complex trauma in a systemic framework. *Australian and New Zealand Journal of Family Therapy, 38*(2), 211–220.

Snyder, H. N., & Sickmund, M. (2006). Juvenile offenders and victims: 2006 national report. *Department of Justice, Office of Justice Programs, Office of Juvenile Justice and Delinquency Prevention.* Retrieved from http://www.ojjdp.gov/ojstatbb/nr2006/downloads/NR2006.pdt

Solomon, B., Davis, L., & Luckham, B. (2012). Delinquent decision-making and behaviors among adolescent females: The relationship between trauma and delinquent decision making among adolescent female offenders; mediating effects. *Journal of Child and Adolescent Trauma, 5,* 161–172.

Spates, C. R., & Rubin, S. (2012). Empirically supported psychological treatments: EMDR. In J. G. Beck & D. M. Sloan (Eds.), *The Oxford handbook of traumatic stress disorder* (pp. 449–462). New York, NY: Oxford University Press.

Stamm, B. H., & Friedman, M. J. (2000). Cultural diversity in the appraisal and expression of trauma. In A. Y. Shalev, R. Yehuda, & A. C. McFarlane (Eds.), *International handbook of human response to trauma* (pp. 69–85). New York, NY: Kluwer Academic/Plenum.

Stanton, D., & Todd, T. (1982). *The family therapy of drug abuse and addiction*. New York, NY: Guilford Press.

Steele, W., & Malchiodi, C. A. (2012). *Trauma-informed practices with children and adolescents.* New York, NY: Routledge.

Stein, M. B., & Paulus, M. P. (2009). Imbalance of approach and avoidance: The yin and yang of anxiety disorders. *Biological Psychiatry, 66,* 1072–1074.

Strang, H., (2002). *Repair or revenge: Victims and restorative justice.* Oxford, England: Clarendon Press.

Stroud, C., Durbin, C., Wilson, S., & Mendelsohn, K. (2011). Spillover to triadic and dyadic systems in families with young children. *Journal of Family Psychology, 25,* 919–930.

Stubbs, J., (2002). Domestic violence and women's safety: Feminist challenges to restorative justice. In H. Strang & J. Braithwaite (Eds.), *Restorative justice and family violence* (pp. 42–61) Cambridge, England: Cambridge University Press.

Suchman, N. E., DeCoste, C. L., McMahon, T. J., Dalton, R., Mayes, L. C., & Borelli, J. (2017). Mothering from the inside out: Results of a second randomized clinical trial testing a mentalization-based intervention for mothers in addiction treatment. *Developmental Psychopathology, 29,* 617–636.

Summerfield, D. (1999). A critique of seven assumptions behind psychological trauma programmes in war-affected areas. *Social Science and Medicine, 48,* 1449–1462.

Sun, J., Patel, F., Rose-Jacobs, R., Frank, D. A., Black, M. M., & Chilton, M. (2017). Mothers' adverse childhood experiences and their young children's development. *American Journal of Preventive Medicine, 53,* 882–891.

Swift, J. K., & Greenberg, R. P. (2015). Incorporate preferences into the treatment decision-making process. In J. K. Swift & R. P. Greenberg, *Premature termination in psychotherapy: Strategies for engaging clients and improving outcomes* (pp. 79–92). Washington, DC: American Psychological Association.

Taylor, A. J. W. (2000). Tragedy and trauma in Tuvalu. *Australian Journal of Disaster and Trauma Studies, 4*(2).

Taylor, R. (1996). Adolescents' perceptions of kinship support and management practices: Association with adolescent adjustment in African American families. *Developmental Psychology, 32*(4), 687–695.

Taylor, S. (2017). *Clinician's guide to PTSD: A cognitive-behavioral approach* (2nd ed.). New York, NY: Guilford Press.

Tcheremissine, O. V., Rossman, W. E., Castro, M. A., & Gardner, D. R. (2014). Conducting clinical research in community mental health settings: Opportunities and challenges. *World Journal of Psychiatry, 4*(3), 49–55.

Terr, L. (1991). Childhood traumas: An outline and overview. *American Journal of Psychiatry, 148,* 10–20.

Thabet, A. A., Ibraheem, A. N., Shivram, R., Winter, E. A., & Vostanis, P. (2009). Parenting support and PTSD in children of a war zone. *International Journal of Social Psychiatry, 55,* 226–237.

Tolliday, D., Spangaro, J., & Laing, L. (2018). *Therapy with harming fathers, victimized children and their mothers after parental child sexual assault: Forging enduring safety.* London, England: Routledge.

Tran, U. S., & Gregor, B. (2016). The relative efficacy of bona fide psychotherapies for post-traumatic stress disorder: A meta-analytical evaluation of randomized controlled trials. *BMC Psychiatry, 16,* 266.

Travis, W. J., & Combs-Orme, T. (2007). Resilient parenting: Overcoming poor parental bonding. *Social Work Research, 31,* 135–149.

Trepper, T., & Barrett, M. (1989). *Systemic treatment of incest: A therapeutic handbook.* New York, NY: Brunner Mazel.

Tucci, J., Weller, A., & Mitchell, J. (2018). Realizing "deep" safety for children who have experienced abuse: Application of polyvagal theory in therapeutic work with traumatized children and young people. In S. W. Porges & D. Dana (Eds.), *Clinical applications of the polyvagal theory: The emergence of polyvagal-informed therapies* (pp. 89–105). New York, NY: W. W. Norton.

Tucker, J. (2007, August 26). Children who survive urban warfare suffer from PTSD, too. *SFGATE.* Retrieved from https://www.sfgate.com/education/article/Children-who-survive-urban-warfare-suffer-from-2524472.php

Tutkun, H., Yargic, L. I., & Sar, V. (1995). Dissociative identity disorder: A clinical investigation of 20 cases in Turkey. *Dissociation: Progress in the Dissociative Disorders, 8,* 3–9.

Ullman, S. (2003). Social reactions to child sexual abuse disclosures: A critical review. *Journal of Child Sexual Abuse, 12,* 89–121.

Ullman, S. (2007). Relationship to perpetrator, disclosure, social reactions and PTSD symptoms in child sexual abuse survivors. *Journal of Child Sexual Abuse, 16,* 19–35.

Uskul, A., & Oyserman, D., (2010). When message-frame fits salient cultural-frames, messages feel more persuasive, *Psychology and Heath, 25,* 321–337.

Van Boemel, G. B., & Rozee, P. D. (1992). Treatment for psychosomatic blindness among Cambodian refugee women. *Women & Therapy, 13,* 239–266.

van Rooj, S., Kennis, M., Sjouwerman, R., van den Heuvel, M., Kahn, R., & Geuze, E. (2015). Smaller hippocampal volume as a vulnerability factor for the persistence of post-traumatic stress disorder. *Psychological Medicine, 45,* 2737–2746.

van Rooj, S. J. H., Kennis, M., Vink, M., & Geuze, E. (2016). Predicting treatment outcome in PTSD: A longitudinal functional MRI study on trauma-unrelated emotional processing. *Neuropsychopharmacology, 41,* 1156–1165.

Veer, I. M., Oei, N. Y. L., van Buchen, M. A., Spinhoven, P., Elzinga, B. M., & Rombouts, S. A. R. B. (2015). Evidence for smaller right amygdala volumes in posttraumatic stress disorder follow childhood trauma. *Psychiatric Research: Neuroimaging, 233,* 436–442.

Vogt, D. S., King, D. W., & King, L. A. (2014). Risk pathways for PTSD: Making sense of the literature. *Handbook of PTSD: Science and practice* (2nd ed., pp. 146–165). New York, NY: Guilford Press.

Wallach, L. (1993). Helping children cope with violence. *Young Children, 48,* 4–11.

Walsh, F. (2007). Traumatic loss and major disasters: Strengthening family and community resilience. *Family Process, 46,* 207–224.

Walsh, F. (2016). *Strengthening family resilience* (3rd ed.). New York, NY: Guilford Press.

Wampold, B. (2010). *The basics of psychotherapy: An introduction to theory and practice.* Washington, DC: American Psychological Association.

Wampold, B., & Imel, Z. (2015). *The great psychotherapy debate: The evidence for what makes psychotherapy work.* New York, NY: Routledge.

Wampold, B., & Imel, Z. E. (2019). *The basics of psychotherapy: An introduction to theory and practice* (2nd ed.). Washington, DC: American Psychological Association.

Wampold, B. E., Imel, Z. E., Laska, K. M., Benish, S., Miller, S. D., Fluckiger, C., . . . Budge, S. (2010). Determining what works in the treatment of PTSD. *Clinical Psychology Review, 30,* 923–933.

Wamser-Nanney, R., & Steinzor C. (2016). Characteristics of attrition among children receiving trauma-focused treatment, *Psychological Trauma: Theory, Research, Practice, and Policy, 8,* 745–754.

Watters, E. (2011). *Crazy like us: The globalization of the American psyche.* New York, NY: Free Press.

Watzlawick, P., Bavelas, J., & Jackson, D. (1967). *Pragmatics of human communication.* New York, NY: W. W. Norton.

Watzlawick, P., Weakland, J., & Fisch, R. (1974). *Change: Principles of problem formation and problem resolution.* New York, NY: W. W. Norton.

Webster, D., Barth, R., & Needlle, B. (2000). Placement stability for children in out-of-home care: A longitudinal study. *Child Welfare, 79*(5), 614–632.

White, M., & Epston, D. (1990). *Narrative means to therapeutic ends.* New York, NY: W. W. Norton.

Wierzbicki, M., & Pekarik, G. (1993). A meta-analysis of psychotherapy dropout. *Professional Psychology, 24,* 190–195.

Williams, J. R., Herrick, M., Pecora, P. J., & O'Brien, K. (2009). Placement history and foster care experience. *Casey Family Programs.* Working paper no. 4. Retrieved from http://www.casey.org/research

Williamson, V., Creswell, C., Fearon, P. Hiller, R. M., Walker, J., & Halligan, S. L. (2017). The role of parenting behaviors in childhood post-traumatic stress disorder: A meta-analytic review. *Clinical Psychology Review, 53,* 1–13.

Wolff, K., Cuevas, C., Intravia, J., Baglivio, M., & Epps, N. (2018). The effects of neighborhood context on exposure to adverse childhood experiences among adolescents involved in the juvenile justice system: Latent classes and contextual effects. *Journal of Youth and Adolescence, 47,* 2279–2300.

Wolitzky-Taylor, K., Bobova, L., Zinbarg, R., Mineka, S., & Craske, M. (2012). Longitudinal investigation of the impact of anxiety and mood disorders in adolescence on subsequent substance use disorder onset and vice versa. *Addictive Behavior, 37,* 982–985.

Wolpaw, J., & Ford, J. (2004). Assessing exposure to psychological trauma and post-traumatic stress in the juvenile justice population. *National Child Traumatic Stress Network.* Retrieved from https://www.nctsn.org/resources/assessing-exposure-psychological-trauma-and-post-traumatic-stress-juvenile-justice

Yu, N., & Shen, F. (2013). Benefits for me or risks for others: A cross-culture investigation of the effects of message frames and cultural appeals. *Health Communication, 28,* 133–145.

Zuk, G. (1981). *Family therapy: A triadic-based approach.* New York, NY: Human Sciences Press.

INDEX

Tables and figures are indicated by *t* and *f* following the page number

For the benefit of digital users, indexed terms that span two pages (e.g., 52–53) may, on occasion, appear on only one of those pages.

www.ingramcontent.com/pod-product-compliance
Lightning Source LLC
Chambersburg PA
CBHW050811120925
32461CB00027B/403